# Modern Irish Autobiography

*Also by Liam Harte*

CONTEMPORARY IRISH FICTION: Themes, Tropes, Theories (*co-edited with Michael Parker*)

IRELAND: Space, Text, Time (*co-edited with Yvonne Whelan and Patrick Crotty*)

IRELAND BEYOND BOUNDARIES: Mapping Irish Studies in the Twenty-First Century (*co-edited with Yvonne Whelan*)

# Modern Irish Autobiography

## Self, Nation and Society

Edited by

Liam Harte

First published 2007 by
PALGRAVE MACMILLAN
Houndmills, Basingstoke, Hampshire RG21 6XS and
175 Fifth Avenue, New York, N.Y. 10010
Companies and representatives throughout the world

PALGRAVE MACMILLAN is the global academic imprint of the Palgrave
Macmillan division of St. Martin's Press, LLC and of Palgrave Macmillan Ltd.
Macmillan® is a registered trademark in the United States, United Kingdom
and other countries. Palgrave is a registered trademark in the European
Union and other countries.

ISBN-13: 978–1–4039–1268–8 hardback
ISBN-10: 1–4039–1268–8 hardback

A catalogue record for this book is available from the British Library.

Library of Congress Cataloging-in-Publication Data
    Modern Irish autobiography:self, nation, and society/edited by Liam
    Harte.
        p.  cm.
    Includes bibliographical references and index.
    ISBN-13: 978–1–4039–1268–8 (cloth)
    ISBN-10: 1–4039–1268–8 (cloth)
    1. Autobiography.   2. Biography as a literary form.   3. Ireland—
    Biography—History and criticism.   4. Self in literature.   I. Harte, Liam.
    CT25.M565 2007
    941.7082092—dc22                                        2006052971

10    9    8    7    6    5    4    3    2    1
16   15   14   13   12   11   10   09   08   07

Printed and bound in Great Britain by
Antony Rowe Ltd, Chippenham and Eastbourne

# Contents

# Acknowledgements

I would like to thank all of the contributors to this book for their patience, cooperation and commitment during its long gestation. Thanks are also due to Paula Kennedy and Christabel Scaife at Palgrave Macmillan for their editorial support and to the two anonymous Palgrave readers for their helpful critical interventions. I would like to acknowledge the financial support of both the Academy for Irish Cultural Heritages at the University of Ulster and the School of Arts, Histories and Cultures at the University of Manchester. I am gladly indebted to Brian Maguire for granting permission to reproduce his painting, *Children and Self (Remembering)*, on the cover. Finally, I would like to pay special thanks to Yvonne Whelan for her encouragement, inspiration and practical help throughout the writing and editing process.

# Notes on Contributors

**Breda Gray** is Senior Lecturer in Women's Studies at the University of Limerick. She is the author of *Women and the Irish Diaspora* (2004) and has published widely on aspects of Irish gender, migration, citizenship and belonging.

**Liam Harte** is Lecturer in Irish and Modern Literature at the University of Manchester. He is the editor, with Michael Parker, of *Contemporary Irish Fiction: Themes, Tropes, Theories* (2000), and of *Ireland Beyond Boundaries: Mapping Irish Studies in the Twenty-First Century* (2007), with Yvonne Whelan.

**Stephen Hopkins** is Lecturer in Politics at the University of Leicester, where his current research focuses on Northern Irish politics and the French Communist party. His publications include *Passing Rhythms: Liverpool FC and the Transformation of Football* (2001), edited with John Williams and Cathy Long.

**Taura S. Napier** is Associate Professor of English at Wingate University, North Carolina, where she specialises in women's autobiography and Irish and postcolonial literatures. She is the author of *Seeking a Country: Literary Autobiographies of Twentieth-Century Irishwomen* (2001).

**Máirín Nic Eoin** is Lecturer in Irish at St Patrick's College, Dublin. She has published extensively on modern and contemporary literature in Irish, and her *B'ait Leo Bean: Gnéithe den Idé-Eolaíocht Inscne i dTraidisiún na Gaeilge* (1998) won the Irish Times Prize for Literature in the Irish Language. Her most recent book is *Trén bhFearann Breac: An Díláithriú Cultúir agus Nualitríocht na Gaeilge* (2005).

**George O'Brien** is Professor of English at Georgetown University, Washington D.C. Among his numerous publications are three volumes of memoirs, *The Village of Longing* (1987), *Dancehall Days* (1988) and *Out of Our Minds* (1994), and two books on the playwright Brian Friel.

**Eve Patten** is a Lecturer in English at Trinity College Dublin. She has co-written *Irish Studies: The Essential Glossary* (2003) with John Goodby, Alex Davis and Andrew Hadfield, and is the author of *Samuel Ferguson and the Culture of Nineteenth-Century Ireland* (2004).

**Sean Ryder** is Senior Lecturer in English at the National University of Ireland, Galway. He has published widely on various aspects of Irish nationalism and culture and is the editor of *James Clarence Mangan: Selected Writings* (2004). He co-edited *Gender and Colonialism* (1995) with Tadhg Foley, Lionel Pilkington and Elizabeth Tilley, and *Ideology and Ireland in the Nineteenth Century* (1998) with Tadhg Foley.

**Denis Sampson** has taught at Vanier College, Montreal, Université de Caen and Université de Montréal. He is the author of *Outstaring Nature's Eye: The Fiction of John McGahern* (1993), *Brian Moore: The Chameleon Novelist* (1998), and many articles on twentieth-century Irish fiction and autobiography.

**Bernice Schrank** is Professor of English at Memorial University of Newfoundland. She is the author of *Sean O'Casey: A Research and Production Sourcebook* (1996) and editor, with William Demastes, of *Irish Playwrights, 1880–1995: A Research and Production Sourcebook* (1997).

**Barry Sloan** is Lecturer in English at the University of Southampton. His principal research interests are in post-1800 Irish writing, with a particular focus on the interactions between literature, history and religion. He is the author of *The Pioneers of Anglo-Irish Fiction 1800–1850* (1986) and *Writing and Protestantism in the North of Ireland: Heirs to Adamnation?* (2000).

# Introduction: Autobiography and the Irish Cultural Moment

*Liam Harte*

> The myth of autobiography is
> that the story is singularly formative,
> that the gesture is coherent and monologic,
> that the subject is articulate and the story articulable, and
> that the narrative lies there waiting to be spoken.
>
> (Smith and Watson, 1996: 9)

If, in these days of voluminous literary criticism, Irish literature can be said to have a Cinderella genre, then surely it is autobiography. When weighed against the welter of scholarship on Irish poetry, drama and fiction, the critical literature on life writing seems remarkably slight, in quantity if not quality. To date, there has been no systematic book-length survey of an autobiographical tradition persisting across four centuries and, with a few notable exceptions, critical studies of the place of life writing in the oeuvre of individual authors remain unwritten.[1] None of the leading Irish Studies journals has seen fit to devote a special issue to the topic, conferences on Irish autobiography are rare and the subject seldom merits more than a cursory mention in literary companions and encyclopedias.[2] This critical neglect seems all the more curious when one considers the preponderance of life writing in contemporary Irish culture, spectacularly spearheaded by Frank McCourt's *Angela's Ashes* (1996), a book which 'transcended bestsellerdom to become a publishing phenomenon – a million-seller, a prize-gatherer, a cult-former' (Foster, 2001: 165). By the time its sequel, *'Tis*, appeared in 1999, booksellers' shelves were sagging under the weight of copycat texts, proof that the autobiographical gesture was becoming endemic in 'Celtic Tiger Ireland' a.k.a. 'Tribunal Ireland'. The commensurate commercial and affective impact of Nuala O'Faolain's *Are You Somebody?* (1996), which became 'an emotional episode, somehow, in public life in Ireland' (O'Faolain, 1998: 215), suggested that in an era of burgeoning narcissism and affluent secular individualism, personal stories

1

that were once admitted only to partner or priest were now more likely to be committed to the page. In a culture of diminished faith and discredited clergy, the cathartic appeal of the confessional memoir would appear to have thoroughly eclipsed that of the confessional box.

Commentators were quick to bemoan the baneful influence of many such autobiographies on the perception of Ireland in the international popular imagination. 'The miserable Irish childhood memoir is to the 1990s what the label-conscious sex and shopping novel was to the 1980s', opined Kathryn Holmquist. 'The word "Gucci" has been replaced by "Christian Brother" and the Jackie Collins sex scene by the odd priestly hand down the pants' (1996: 4). Parody followed, predictably. Arthur Mathews's *Well-Remembered Days* (2001), the fictional memoir of one Eoin O'Ceallaigh, mocked multiple targets: the unrelenting dreariness of McCourt's portrayal of 1930s Limerick, the angry objections to his doom-laden depictions, the revisionist derivatives the book inspired: 'My own memory of Ireland in those years is that everyone in the country was blissfully happy all the time. The poverty that McCourt harps on about was confined to a handful of malcontents (probably no more than ten or twelve), who, if pressed, would probably admit that their lot was not so bad after all' (2001: 6).[3] At the other end of the literary spectrum, however, the generic subtlety, emotional profundity and authenticating lyrical power of works such as Seamus Deane's *Reading in the Dark* and Dermot Healy's *The Bend for Home*, both of which appeared within months of *Angela's Ashes*, suggested that sensationalism and sales were not the only factors underpinning the new confessionalism in Irish culture. Such highly patterned, self-reflexive meditations on memory, history and storytelling prompted critics to hypothesise that this profusion of autobiography – not all of which can be categorised as autobiographical in the traditional, generic sense – was symptomatic of 'a desire to relate a range of previously unspoken (or only whispered) stories from the margins, or more accurately the interstices, of official island culture' (Smyth, 2001: 134), a desire fanned by convulsive socio-economic change. Others linked what was happening in Irish literary culture to a wider 'memoir boom', the key to which lay in

> the crisis of historical confidence that the last century wreaked on us. We no longer believe in objectivity; we don't trust the history books to tell the story of ourselves, whether because it is too disturbing or merely too mundane. But we are desperate for that story to be told, so we look for lives that intersect with the bits of history that affect us. The great power of the memoir is that, when it works, it [ . . . ] touches a common humanity we sometimes fear no longer exists. (Armitstead, 2001: 10)

This book aims to situate the recent outpouring of Irish autobiography in its many forms, and the various analyses of it, in a longer historical perspective, with a view to offering readers an entrée into what is a large and richly varied literary corpus. As an inaugural attempt to provide a critical atlas of a sprawling and relatively unexcavated terrain, the book's ambitions are necessarily modest and its coverage inevitably partial. Conceived as an exploratory rather than an exhaustive survey of the pervasive themes, modes and self-representational strategies of Irish autobiographers, the book explores some of the disparate ways in which autobiographical identities have been narratively shaped over time and probes the personal, rhetorical and ideological functions that life writing has served in Irish culture from the mid-nineteenth century to the present day. Given the sheer diversity and proliferation of the material under review, the contributors to the book were granted considerable latitude to stake out their own critical ground and choose the subjects they wished to discuss: it is for each reader to decide whether the acts of inclusion ameliorate the sins of omission. Among the questions the essayists address are: what distinguishes Irish autobiographers' engagements with the expressive problems and possibilities that the act of self-writing entails?; what narrative tropes, rhetorical aims and stylistic strategies do they have in common?; how have autobiographers from different eras and backgrounds negotiated the serpentine knot that binds memory, experience, invention and self-portraiture?; how has the expression of private experience been distilled through the sieve of social and cultural change?; how does autobiographical reflection mesh with cultural critique? and what role do voice, form and style play in the reconstitution of life as text?

The book's overarching critical engagement is with the expressive and formal problematics that issue from what, historically, has been the master trope of the Irish autobiographical tradition: the symbolic refraction of the life of the individual through the lens of nation and society. As Michael Kenneally points out: 'the tendency to explore and define oneself in terms of patriotic values and national goals, to equate one's development with national destiny provides the central structural metaphor of twentieth-century Irish literary autobiographies' (1988: 123). This figurative stratagem has a much longer literary lineage, of course, being rooted in bourgeois nationalism's mobilisation of personal narratives for the project of nation-building. The rhetorical fusion of individual identity and collective destiny assumed strategic significance under the aegis of nineteenth-century cultural nationalism, such that much early Irish autobiography effectively became a 'promissory note for a yet-to-be-implemented nation' (Kiberd, 1995: 119). As David Lloyd explains:

> The biography of the national hero is, in the first instance, a repetition of the history of the nation. Through conscious identification with the nation the individual transcends in himself the actual disintegration of the nation by coming to prefigure the nation's destiny: the total

identification of the individual with the spirit of the nation is a figuration
of the total unity of the political nation that is the goal of the nationalist's
labors. (1987: 160)

Examples of such idealised autobiography abound, from the memoirs of
Fenian activists such as Jeremiah O'Donovan Rossa and Tom Clarke to
those of republican revolutionaries Tom Barry, Ernie O'Malley and Maud
Gonne. As George O'Brien pithily observes: 'The tone of these narratives is
extrovert, and their focus is on action, organization and the discovery that
public events possess a permeable structure. The narrators speak as embodiments of a collective aspiration rather than as instances of individuation'
(1999: 46).

The lacunae and aporias that cohere around this mutual articulation
of subject and nation are recurring points of reference and interrogation
for many of the contributors to this book. In the opening chapter Sean
Ryder examines a central problematic of this critical project: the tensions
between the subject's assertion of individual uniqueness and the demands
of the collective discourse for exemplary self-narratives. He examines the
play of these tensions in texts by two highly self-reflexive nineteenth-
century autobiographers, John Mitchel and James Clarence Mangan, neither
of whom is able to resolve the discrepancies of subjective experience
into a narrative of heroic, autonomous individuality. Instead, their texts
raise troubling questions about the reliability of autobiographical representation and the integrity and coherence of personal and national identities. Mangan's impressionistic narrative deviates sharply from the political
demands of national subjectivity, not least in the author's refusal to be
singularly identified, thereby rendering it an ineffective medium for reader
empathy. Similarly, Mitchel's *Jail Journal* (1854) suggests that subjectivity is
always constituted provisionally through multiple contextualities, making
the assumption of a single, coherent narrative of identity a chimera. In each
case, the narrative voices oscillate between particularity and collectivity,
between the cultural and historical scripts that shape them and those they
seek to fashion for themselves.

In highlighting the narrative struggles of early nationalist autobiographers
to make the disharmonies of individual life stories comply with the homo-
genising demands of a national subjectivity, Ryder strikes one of the
keynotes of the collection. What emerges as a pervasive thematic in his
and other chapters is Irish autobiographers' sensitivity to the unstable,
idiosyncratic, illusory nature of self-narration. Although often intended to
offer a template of paradigmatic national collectivity, the textualised selves
that are brought into being by the act of autobiography testify instead
to the plurality of experiences and lay bare the constitutive differences
that comprise the nation. Thus, Bernice Schrank in her chapter underlines
the extent to which the multi-volume autobiographies of George Moore,

W. B. Yeats, Sean O'Casey and Brendan Behan produce a heterogeneously articulated national subject that contests the definitional power of imperial and nationalist discourses alike. In the process, she argues, they 'enable and contribute to the emergence of a multi-vocal, counter-hegemonic post-independence Irish discourse'. These works also create a powerful impression of the passions and energies that were expended in the creation of a discrete Irish cultural identity in an era of social and political tumult. Indeed, there is a strong interlocutory element in revivalist autobiography that underpins its performative and prescriptive dimensions. Not only were Moore, Yeats and O'Casey engaging in finely crafted public displays of identity in their self-narratives, they were also taking part in intertextual dialogues and disputes about the value and purpose of their collective cultural endeavours, thereby demonstrating that there is no singular text of self, no autobiography that does not imbricate other narratives in its own.

As Ryder, Schrank and other contributors here acknowledge, the complex relationship between language and identity lies at the heart of this discursive problematic. What shadows many of the texts under discussion here is the unsettling suspicion that the putative nation may be no more than a rhetorical fiction, as insubstantial and unstable as the (de)composing self, may in fact be no more than an effect of the process of writing. John Mitchel's misgivings about the capacity of language to refer to anything but itself is powerfully borne in upon him as he suffers the depredations of transportation, to the point where his attempt to maintain self-coherence through self-writing is already undone by his awareness of the fictive quality of the autobiographical 'I': 'This book will help to remind me of what I was, and how I came down hither, and so preserve the continuity of my thoughts, or *personal identity*, which, there is sometimes reason to fear, might slip away from me' (1996: 72, original emphasis). Yet such intimations of fracture and insufficiency can also become sources of creativity; the story of the self is narrated, despite the treacheries of language. In one journal entry Mitchel actively indulges his self-division, thus exemplifying one of the recurring tropes of the tradition: the vacillating self, poised between definition and dispersal, enunciation and erasure, affirmation and dissolution. Repeatedly, we come upon acts of self-portraiture that show subjects taking a paradoxical delight in doubleness and ambivalence, even as they strive for self-completion, suggesting that the Irish autobiographical self is most itself in the very process of becoming.

The Wildean and Yeatsian concepts of subjectivity are paradigmatic in this regard, both being largely founded upon ideas of self-division and reinvention. In 'The Death of Synge' Yeats wrote:

> I think that all happiness depends on the energy to assume the mask of
> some other self; that all joyous or creative life is a rebirth as something

not oneself, something which has no memory and is created in a moment and perpetually renewed. We put on a grotesque or solemn painted face to hide us from the terrors of judgment, invent an imaginative Saturnalia where one forgets reality, a game like that of a child, where one loses the infinite pain of self-realization. (1980: 503–4)

Thus, the Yeatsian 'I' that wrote: 'Whatever happens I must go on that there may be a man behind the lines already written; I cast the die long ago and must be true to the cast' (1980: 485), is engaged in a sustained process that melds self-discovery with self-creation. This performative mode resonates strongly through twentieth-century Irish autobiography. Think, for instance, of the creative and potentially interminable proliferation of personae inscribed by the autobiographical writings of Louis MacNeice, whose early self-interrogation: 'I am 33 years old and what can I have been doing that I still am in a muddle?' (1965: 35), reads as an oblique retort to Yeats's admission: 'It is so many years before one can believe enough in what one feels to know what the feeling is' (1980: 103). MacNeice's self-analysis culminates in an apprehension of endless self-deferral (divulged, appropriately, in his book on Yeats) that could stand as an epigraph to much modern Irish literary autobiography, in which the self emerges as a series of productive masks and doubles rather than a singular essence:

If you know what my whole self and my only self is, you know a lot more than I do. As far as I can make out, I not only have many different selves but I am often, as they say, not myself at all. Maybe it is just when I am not myself – when I am thrown out of gear by circumstances or emotion – that I feel like writing poetry. (1941: 146)

Further support for this thesis that modern Irish autobiographical subjectivities are marked by doubleness and deferral rather than singularity and closure is provided by Eve Patten and Taura Napier in their respective chapters. Patten's analysis of the nexus of history and aesthetics in Irish autobiographical fiction begins with a consideration of *A Portrait of the Artist as a Young Man* (1916), the prototypical thematisation of the fraught dialectic between artist and society, in which the hero emerges 'not as a formed biographical entity but as a subject-in-process, struggling in the course of his development to maturity with a series of conflicting languages'. In a reading that is critically alert to *Portrait*'s evolving interpretive history, Patten foregrounds the novel's ambivalent relation to its biographical and historical referents and traces its complex arbitration of the divergent discourses of modernism and nationalism. As both appropriator and artful saboteur of the self/nation paradigm, Joyce bequeathed a cracked template to subsequent practitioners of the *Künstlerroman* genre, so that the fractured fictionalised self-portraits of Francis Stuart and Aidan Higgins further magnify the incipient disjunctions between the personal and the political. Turning to post-war Irish *Bildungsromane*, Patten examines the effects of the gravitational pull of a national communalism on the autobiographical fiction of Anthony C. West, Edna O'Brien, Brian Moore, John McGahern and Seamus Deane, each of whom deploys the trope of family dysfunction as a means of critiquing the social and cultural impediments to self-realisation.

If the discursive association of self, nation and society proved increasingly problematic for twentieth-century Irish male autobiographers, then women writers found the dominant paradigm even more inimical to the expression of an authentic subjectivity. Alienated by the traditional fusion of the feminine with the national, and lacking the guidance of exemplary literary foremothers, their autobiographical narratives frequently enact a struggle for self-articulation in opposition to the idealised, emblematic configurations of the male imagination. According to Taura Napier, one of the ways in which women writers do this is by employing a 'deflected' autobiographical method that allows the writer's narrative persona to be refracted through the prism of significant others. So rather than enlist a protean female muse – Ireland as mother, maiden, mistress, whore – writers such as Katharine Tynan, Elizabeth Bowen and Kate O'Brien typically engage actual subjects in their autobiographical texts, whose perspectives and personalities complement their own. As Napier sees it, this relational, multi-perspectival aesthetic represents a self-legitimising response to patriarchy and colonialism, one that enables the Irish female autobiographer to give expression to her 'often paradoxical identities as private citizen, public artist, professional writer and representative chronicler of her socio-cultural milieu'.

The autobiographical writings of contemporary Irish feminists suggest that this self-abnegatory mode is giving way to a more authoritative form of life writing, even as they thematise the struggles this shift entails. The most compelling articulation of this transition is found in O'Faolain's *Are You Somebody?* and its sequel, *Almost There* (2003), which offers an insightful commentary on the composition and reception of its critically acclaimed predecessor. These works perform the dual task of narrating the author's loneliness and longing as 'an unmarried, childless, agnostic woman in late middle age' (O'Faolain, 2003: 235), while critiquing the cultural sanctions she had to overcome in order to claim authorial possession of her story. In acknowledging the timeliness of her autobiographical acts – 'Ireland, at the end of the twentieth-century, was beginning to allow self-knowledge' – O'Faolain details her private battles with the 'inner voices that mocked my self-importance' (2003: 59, 33). Even though her 'male' job as a journalist afforded her the opportunity to speak about her private life, autobiographical authorisation did not come easily. The inhibiting effects of family and nation on female self-revelation far outweighed any speaking rights she could lay claim to as 'an honorary man':

> I couldn't take possession of the first-person voice. I couldn't manage an 'I' if it was going to be real, as opposed to the 'I' in my opinion columns which was cheerfully fake-authoritative. I had all kinds of theories why this was so – for example, that it was because I was Irish and female and had had the message drummed into me all my life that female isn't nearly as interesting and important as male. (2003: 22, 31–32)

It is only later that she realises the extent of her narrative self-creation: 'Writing has brought me up from underground. I've been my own Orpheus' (2003: 168).

It would be a mistake, however, to conclude that the narrative of patri- archal nationness has lost its definitional power completely for twenty-first- century Irish women autobiographers. Máire Cruise O'Brien's *The Same Age as the State* (2003), for example, reads at times like a roll-call of legendary Irish patriarchs, and O'Faolain's own memoirs are full of dialogues with the dead, specifically dead parents, both actual and symbolic. Her vexed relation- ship with her alcoholic mother, 'the she-within-me' (O'Faolain, 2003: 25), is painfully recapitulated in *Are You Somebody?* and the oppressive maternal imaginary reappears to threaten the narrator's hard-won self-possession in *Almost There*: 'My own self goes threadbare as her powerful self takes over' (2003: 234). The latter work also interrogates O'Faolain's interpellation by the Oedipal jurisdiction of the father. In one particularly telling chapter she anatomises her Freudian relationship with a married lover whom she transforms into an emblem of eroticised paternalism:

> Because he intimidated me, I made him stand for my grandfather and father and the priests and judges and presidents and other old men who had always run Ireland and the world. [ ... ] And when he trembled because I was in the room, wasn't I subverting the structure of power that had always pressed down on me? Wasn't it like having the patriarchy tremble? (2003: 77–78)

Two earlier, very different, feminist self-narratives – Edna O'Brien's *Mother Ireland* (1976) and Eavan Boland's *Object Lessons* (1995) – are similarly concerned with the problem of writing the female self up from under the latticed layers of patriarchal Irishness. In these cases, however, the exper- ience of emigration to England is figured as an important catalyst in the articulation of gendered selfhood, O'Brien's cool detachment – 'Leaving Ireland was no wrench at all' (1978: 87) – contrasting sharply with Boland's sense of radical severance: 'an ordinary displacement made an extraordinary distance between the word *place* and the word *mine*' (1996: 36, original emphasis). Such works help to refute the claim that 'At the heart of the Irish migrant experience there is a caution, a refusal to speak, a fear of the word' (O'Connor, 1993: 16). There is in fact a significant body of autobiographical writing by first- and second-generation migrants in Britain dating back to the early 1700s which contains a rich array of subjective insights into their diverse social and private realities. For many such migrants, self-writing provided a means of comprehending their complex positioning between a typically antipathetic British culture, in which they have traditionally existed as marginalised others, and an apparently sympathetic Irish culture which exerts a powerful but problematic hold over them. As my own chapter seeks to demonstrate, the self-representational practices of second-generation Irish autobiographers offer particularly instructive insights into the changing processes of identity configuration, not least in their conceptualisation of diasporic Irishness as a continuum of multiple identifications rather than as a monolithic cultural category.

In an analysis that both counterpoints and complements my own, Breda Gray in her chapter explores the role of emigration and gender in the making of cultural memory in post-war Ireland. Focusing on two oral life narratives that were recorded as part of the *Breaking the Silence* project at University College Cork, she examines the forms of gendered subjectivity produced by decisions to stay put or emigrate in the 1950s and their relation to modes of remembering and self-narration in the present. Her discussion shows how the subjectivities narrated by her female subjects are shaped as much by their discriminatory othering of emigrant and non-emigrant women as by prevailing discourses of Irish femininity centred on notions of duty and family reproduction. Gray also attends to the shaping power of the contexts of oral narration, noting how her subjects' testimony encodes a view of identity as social and collective, the narrators implicitly seeing themselves as ordinary witnesses rather than exceptional individuals. Máirín Nic Eoin identifies a similar narrative impulse at work in Gaeltacht autobiography, much of which she categorises as autoethnography on the grounds that the narrating 'I' is known through and embedded within the communal practices and affiliations of a cultural group. Nic Eoin foregrounds the role of critical intermediaries in determining the form and content of many Gaeltacht autobiographies and traces writers' preference for social documentation over self-revelation to the collaborative mode of literary production. Non-Gaeltacht autobiographers, by contrast, are more likely to eschew documentary modes in favour of self-mythologising strategies which accentuate the processes of identity configuration and call into question one of the key preconditions of autobiography, memory.

Memory's prodigious powers and their relation to the process of self-writing are also central to Barry Sloan's analysis of Irish Protestant life writing in chapter 8. Sloan's emphasis on the provisionality of the memory acts that shape the self-representations of Forrest Reid, Robert Harbinson,

Edith Newman Devlin, Richard Murphy, Annabel Davis-Goff and Hugh Maxton foregrounds Irish autobiographers' profound fascination for what Walter Benjamin called 'the mysterious work of remembrance – which is really the capacity for endless interpolations into what has been' (1979: 305). It is not merely the apprehension that memory 'is always acting upon us, making us what we are, acting both backwards and forwards, creating our sense of identity beneath the stream of time' (Devlin, 2000: 40) that compels, or even the realisation that 'as times change *tempus* fudges' (Marcus, 2001: 264). The acts of recollection and forgetting themselves form part of the narrative strategies of much recent Irish autobiography, so that writers' meditations on memory become metaphors of the process itself. Several of these meditations, moreover, form a kind of intertextual web, such that Hugh Maxton's observation: 'Nothing is remembered as it was. The process of memory corrodes or it enhances; operates like rust, oozes outwards in grotesque relief, reacting between the immediate climate of feeling and the iron assumptions of the past' (1997: 21), resonates with Dermot Healy's intimation: 'What happened is a wonder, though memory is always incomplete, like a map with places missing. But it's all right, it's entered the imagination and nothing is ever the same' (1996: 33), which in turn obliquely glosses Ciaran Carson's suggestion that

> Over and over, though we flit incessantly into the moment, our pasts catch up with us, and apprehend us at the endless intersections, where fingerposts are unreliable, and mileages are tilted. I realize, now, that I've travelled back from secondary to primary school by the arbitrary short-cut of a synapse, down one worm-hole of the riddled memory, which stores everything we've ever known, and more, if we could only find the portals to its vast, inconsequential realms, where the laws of time and space work in reverse. (1997: 208)

Benjamin's own attempts to penetrate the enigmas of memory led him to imagine it as a labyrinthine metropolis and evolve a topographical-spatial concept of life writing that refused the name 'autobiography': 'For autobiography has to do with time, with sequence and what makes up the continuous flow of life. Here, I am talking of a space, of moments and discontinuities' (1979: 316). It is certainly possible to detect Benjaminian echoes in contemporary autobiographers' attentiveness to the formative role of space in the narrative constitution of the self. Works such as Carson's *The Star Factory* (1997), Michael Cronin's *Time Tracks: Scene from the Irish Everyday* (2003) and Chris Arthur's *Irish Nocturnes* (1999) and *Irish Willow* (2002) – each of which represents a different mode of autobiographical socio-cultural analysis – write the self as the performative subject of space, showing how identities and social relations are defined not only by the palimpsestic accretions of time, but also by a spatialised landscape of mundane objects and activities. Each of these texts traces the local habitations of memory, reading its sinuous character analogically in so many edifices and artefacts that the narrators emerge as versions of Lévi-Strauss's *bricoleur*, who ' "speaks" not only *with* things [...], but also through the medium of things: giving an account of his personality and life by the choices he makes between the limited possibilities' (1972: 21, original emphasis). Carson pores over the minutiae of Belfast's *lieux de mémoire*, imagining the city as a giant 'memory theatre' teeming with narratives: 'For every stick and bit implies a narrative, and we ascribe their provenances' (1997: 67, 12). *Time Tracks*, too, thematises the ways in which the commodity-filled domestic and public spaces of Dublin are constitutive of narratives of the self, while Arthur exhibits a psychometric sensitivity to the ways in which 'Things play their part invisibly in a thousand human dramas, whether ordinary or extraordinary; the fabric of circumstance is woven into all manner of shapes without our cognizance' (1999: 51).

Yet for all their hyper-vivid materiality and sensuously imagined specificity, these works also strive towards typicality in the way that they continually collapse personal biography into collective history. While on the one hand, Carson, Cronin and Arthur artfully arrange fragments of memory to create 'Bildung-stories' (Cronin, 2003: 60) located in specific points in space and time, on the other, they consistently elide the gap between individual and social memory, translating their private recollections into emblems of a shared past. Cronin's collectivising 'you' is perhaps the clearest stylistic marker of this; the word 'I' never once appears in *Time Tracks*. Instead, the second-person point of view invites Irish readers of a certain age and class to submerge their memories in a narrative of common belonging, one that pre-dates the social realignments brought about by globalisation, immigration and multiculturalism. There is a sense, therefore, in which the 'autobiographer' is effectively remembering a whole generation's past on its behalf, writing an obituary for a bygone era by giving voice and shape to the ineffable personal narratives that lie buried in the forgotten details of daily lives.

Other autobiographical acts of collective remembering are more overtly political in nature, the record of personal experience being made to serve as a means of validating a particular ideology or bearing witness to shared privations and aspirations. This communal ethic is especially strong in the memoirs of Northern Irish politicians and paramilitaries, who typically speak on behalf of certain groups and organisations. Stephen Hopkins argues in his chapter that many of the autobiographies published since the Belfast Agreement exemplify the use of memoir as a proxy weapon in the ongoing political struggle in the North, a fact which compromises their truth-telling claims without necessarily detracting from their capacity to captivate and inform. In an analysis that is deftly attuned to memoirists' capacity for retrospective self-justification, Hopkins highlights the tensions between telling and silence that are exposed by narrative lacunae and examines the issues raised by the involvement of journalistic interlocutors in the composition of autobiographies by ex-paramilitaries. He also notes the parochial nature of many such works, especially those written by former republican activists, whose tendency to concentrate on local paramilitary activities to the exclusion of wider political considerations, Hopkins argues, limits the historical usefulness of their memoirs.

The circumspection with which contemporary historians treat politically motivated forms of autobiographical remembrance from the North of Ireland contrasts sharply with the high degree of credulity elicited by the many abuse-survival memoirs that have recently emanated from the Republic. This sub-genre, which includes the personal testimony of orphans, adoptees, single mothers and former residents of Ireland's vast network of industrial and reformatory schools, has been valued for exposing a hidden social history of Irish childhood and challenging authorised accounts of the past (Ferriter, 2002). Viewed collectively, these works demonstrate the radical uses of autobiography by marginalised subjects whose assertion of a personal narrative voice, which also speaks beyond itself, is a compelling means of cultural inscription. It is not just a matter of giving voice to grievance or setting the record straight. By situating personal accounts of pain and suffering within wider social and institutional contexts, these confessions critique larger cultural and political forces and so reconfigure the relations between self, nation and society in counter-hegemonic ways. Works such as Mannix Flynn's *Nothing to Say* (1983), Paddy Doyle's *The God Squad* (1988) and Bernadette Fahy's *Freedom of Angels* (1999) represent the very antithesis of the nationalist autobiographical paradigm discussed above. That which was once the object of heroic self-identification is now figured as a pathological entity capable of sanctioning violence, victimisation and exploitation. Certainly, such memoirs represent a damning critique of Ireland's 'architecture of containment', which functioned 'to confine and render invisible segments of the population whose very existence threatened Ireland's national imaginary' (Smith, 2001: 112). Yet, as George O'Brien observes here, they also 'rehearse the possibility of recuperating the subject's abjection and advance the desire for social structures willing to integrate rather than segregate, to cherish rather than punish, to acknowledge individuality rather than dismiss it'.

Not all Irish childhoods were miserable, of course, as Denis Sampson reminds us in his chapter on the loss and recuperation of Irish boyhoods. Nor were they always as meticulously anatomised as they have been in recent Irish memoir. Sampson notes the virtual invisibility of childhood in the work of the first generation of post-independence autobiographers, before proceeding to examine the ways in which childhood functions as 'a site of an elaborate mythology of both personal and cultural significance' in the work of Maurice O'Sullivan, Frank O'Connor, Patrick Kavanagh, John McGahern and George O'Brien. All but one of these autobiographers affirm, to varying degrees, the emblematic role of mothers and fathers in the moral and aesthetic development of the aspirant writer. The exception is O'Brien, whose *The Village of Longing* (1987) recovers his unconventional childhood, shaped as it was by exuberant talk and expressive silences, in order to underline the empowerment of 'voice itself' (O'Brien, 1987: 25). O'Brien himself reprises this theme in his clear-eyed analysis of his own autobiographical 'troubles' in the final chapter, which reviews many of the cultural and aesthetic challenges discussed elsewhere in this collection from the perspective of a distinguished practising autobiographer. In analysing the obstacles that attended his own assertions of selfhood, he endorses autobiography's valuable capacity to reconjugate the collective 'we' as so many distinctive 'I's, each of which productively modifies the myth of homogeneity in 'a culture where confession carries a variety of complicated hidden detonators'. Considering O'Brien's claims for the form's productive powers of provocation and dissonance, it seems more surprising than ever that the myriad functions, complex effects and continuing mystique of autobiography in Irish culture have not been subject to fuller, more sustained critical scrutiny. If the diverse perspectives offered by this book help to inaugurate such scrutiny, its goal will have been accomplished.

## Notes

1. For short but critically perceptive overviews of the Irish autobiographical tradition, see Brown, 1985; Deane, 1991; O'Brien, 1999 and Hughes, 2001. Napier (2001) and Grubgeld (2004) have written book-length studies of Irish women's literary autobiography and Anglo-Irish autobiography, respectively. W. B. Yeats's autobiographical writings are analysed at length in Neuman (1982) and Wright (1987). Sean O'Casey has been well served by Kenneally (1988), as has George Moore by Grubgeld (1994). Olney (1998) is particularly insightful on the place of autobiography in the work of Samuel Beckett.
2. The excellent two-volume *Encyclopedia of Life Writing* (Jolly, 2001) is a notable exception. In addition to a survey essay on Ireland, it contains entries on the autobiographical writings of Brendan Behan, George O'Brien, Sean O'Casey, Peig Sayers, Wolfe Tone and W. B. Yeats.
3. The parodic relation of Mathews's book to *Angela's Ashes* resembles that of Flann O'Brien's *An Béal Bocht/The Poor Mouth* (1941) to Tomás O'Crohan's *An tOileánach/The Islandman* (1929).

# 1

# 'With a Heroic Life and a Governing Mind': Nineteenth-Century Irish Nationalist Autobiography

*Sean Ryder*

## I

Irish nationalist autobiographies of the nineteenth century were shaped by two cultural imperatives in particular. One was the demand from nationalism for tales of representative men and women; the other was the wider Victorian demand for self-defining narratives, a symptom of what Thomas Carlyle called these 'Autobiographical times' (1896b: 75). In fact, autobiography emerged as a privileged genre in nationalist culture at the same time as it became a favoured form of self-definition in bourgeois culture generally (Gay, 1996: 103ff). In nineteenth-century nationalist Ireland the most influential and well-known autobiographies were those of Wolfe Tone, John Mitchel and Jeremiah O'Donovan Rossa, but many of the leading figures of the Young Ireland and Fenian movements also published popular memoirs, including Charles Gavan Duffy, Michael Doheny, John O'Leary, John Devoy and Joseph Denieffe. Lady Morgan, James Clarence Mangan and William Carleton, literary figures on the fringes of the nationalist movement, also wrote autobiographies, though all were published posthumously. Anne Devlin, who played a crucial role in the Emmet rebellion, dictated an account of her experiences before her death, though the manuscript remained unpublished until 1960. Several autobiographical accounts of the United Irish rebellion were also published in the nineteenth century. The idea of making private self-examination and self-knowledge a matter of public scrutiny was not a nineteenth-century invention, however; indeed, the Western autobiographical tradition may be said to have begun with Augustine's *Confessions* in the fifth century. That said, autobiographical publication reached a level of unprecedented growth in the eighteenth and nineteenth centuries that corresponds with other developments in the realm of social and political life: the increased secularisation of society,

14

the rapid growth of print culture and middle-class literacy and the ideological privileging of individual experience as the focus of knowledge. These events coincide also with the rise of bourgeois nationalism in Europe and North America, which itself gave new urgency to questions about the relations between private self and public duty, between individual and national identity and between individual agency and the determining power of history and culture.

Peter Gay has argued that 'the nineteenth century was intensely preoccupied with self, to the point of neurosis' (1996: 3). This preoccupation was itself partly a symptom of the apparent waning credibility of external sources of knowledge such as God, Scripture and medieval cosmology. In the post-medieval and post-theocentric world, with its rapid social change and ideological ferment, the search for stable foundations for moral and psychological knowledge turned inward, towards the self, rather than outward towards the divine, as formerly. In taking this turn, however, one risked opening up the troubling vista of moral and epistemological relativism, and the difficulty of authenticating any objective, impersonal, unchanging truth beyond the realm of subjective impressions. In these epistemological conditions, as William Spengemann argues, writers and thinkers of the early nineteenth century sought to locate a centre of reality 'in a place that was at once sufficiently mobile to keep pace with the changing shape of reality and sufficiently stable to provide some assurance that a principle of continuity and purpose underlies all change' (1980: 77). This 'place' was the personal self, the location of truths that were guaranteed by the laws of 'human nature'. As part of this shift, autobiography – the authentic representation of the self – became 'the prime instrument of Romantic knowledge' (Spengemann, 1980: 77). Autobiographies implied that the self was a fixed identity (the author's fixity is represented by a 'real name', an unchanging personality, or an apparently solid accumulation of experiences), while simultaneously acknowledging that selfhood is also a 'process' subject to contingency, historical accident and the forces of social and political life. To make a life into a narrative, as autobiography does, is to bring the apparently incoherent fragments of experience under the controlling structure of a story that has a beginning, a middle and an end. The anxiety produced by the sense that life may be essentially fragmentary, a disconnected flux of experience, is dissipated by the presence of a reflective autobiographical narrative voice. This voice has a comforting confidence in its ability to tell the truth and to discern the essential pattern or meaning of a life.

In addition to such changes in the perceived value of selfhood, the Romantic and Victorian periods also saw changes in the nature of historiography which encouraged the writing and reading of biography and autobiography. The nineteenth-century approach to history gave special attention to the question of how much the individual self is an agent of historical change. Opinions on the question swung from the determinism of Marx and

Engels, which stressed the subjection of the individual to larger historical forces, to the 'great man' theory of Carlyle, which stressed the power of the strong individual to shape the course of history. Carlyle's theory of history allotted great importance to biographical narratives by arguing that 'History is the essence of innumerable Biographies' (1896a: 86) and, even more reductively, that 'The History of the world is but the Biography of great men' (1993: 26). To study such biographies was not merely to become acquainted with the historical record; it had an even greater, ultimately ethical function: 'We cannot look, however imperfectly, upon a great man, without gaining something by him' (Carlyle, 1993: 3). On the other hand, European nationalists like Giuseppe Mazzini argued strongly against Carlyle's privileging of the mighty few on the basis that 'The shadow thrown by these gigantic men appears to eclipse [. . .] every trace of national thought of which these men were only the interpreters and prophets, and of the people, who alone are its depository' (Mazzini, 1887: 125). So where Carlyle sees individual will, Mazzini sees 'national thought' and 'the people' as the ultimate driving forces of history, a view in which the individual will is subordinated to the power of ideology and collective agency.

One of the central questions for Irish nationalism in the nineteenth century was precisely the one addressed by Carlyle and Mazzini: how to define and represent the relation of the individual to the movement of history and to collective forms of identity such as 'the nation' or 'the race'. David Lloyd has theorised more specifically the ways in which the genre of autobiography was used to answer these questions:

> Biography, generically including autobiography, is intimately linked to the aesthetic politics of Romantic nationalism. The biography of the national hero is, in the first instance, a repetition of the history of the nation. [ . . . ] [T]he total identification of the individual with the spirit of the nation is a figuration of the total unity of the political nation that is the goal of the nationalist's labors. The nationalist hero is thus doubly productive: in the mundane sense, his political labors further the cause of national unification and liberation; in a secondary, but generally more significant, sense, his life story serves as an 'inspiration,' enjoining and mediating the identification of each individual with the nation to which all ideally belong and without which they are incomplete and inauthentic. (1987: 160)

The nationalist autobiography thus serves multiple functions. In place of the discontinuities and fissures of actual history, it offers reassuring stories of order, continuity and completion. As historiography, it gives a first-hand and attractively vivid account of the nation's history. As a narrative, it also provides a structure for understanding national history as a whole. The story of the individual hero becomes a synecdoche for the history of the nation itself; for instance, a story of an honourable struggle against externally imposed injustice. Furthermore, in a more pragmatic way, the act of reading an autobiography allows the reader to make empathetic connections between his or her own life and the life of the hero, through the usual mechanisms by which narratives encourage identification and sympathy with characters and events outside one's own self. Autobiography is, in fact, precisely one of the ways by which the 'imagined communities' we call nations are constructed. It enables the national subject to participate in a communal identity and to imagine that participation as a fulfilling thing.

There is nevertheless a tension between autobiography's revelation of the individual's uniqueness and its assertion of the same person's typicality. This central tension in the autobiographical form takes on a special significance in nationalist autobiography, where the individual's uniqueness or eccentricity can pose a threat to the qualities that make the writer 'national' (and the autobiography valuable). Rousseau was able to justify the relentless exposure of what he believed to be his uniqueness – 'I am not made like any that I have seen; I venture to believe that I was not made like any that exist' (2000: 5) – by arguing that awareness of the *difference* between his unique life and the reader's uniqueness might actually be ethically useful: 'I should like each person, in order that he might learn to judge himself correctly, to have at least one other point of comparison; that he should know himself and one other person, and that other person will be me' (2000: 643). The politics of nationalist autobiography, however, require that the egocentric emphasis on uniqueness be subordinated to an emphasis on what makes the autobiographer's life paradigmatic or representative. In nationalist discourse uniqueness is a value displaced from the individual onto the idea of the nation itself. Every nation must be unique, but each authentic subject within that nation must be stereotypical. The sense of being simultaneously unique (compared to the world abroad) and stereotypical (compared to other Irish people) is a particular feature of nationalist consciousness. For Rousseau and other bourgeois autobiographers, what is common among people is common by the basic virtue of their being human. The complication of nationalism, however, is that what is held to be 'common' by nationalist discourse is normally defined as that which is shared only by a subset of humanity – the members of a particular nation. Thus the function of identification in nationalist autobiography is more limited than it is for bourgeois autobiography in general. An English reader, for example, may sympathise with, but is hardly expected to *identify* with, the struggles of the Irish nationalist hero. Of course, the non-Irish reader is not entirely excluded as an addressee of the text: as we shall see, it is a frequent self-justification in nationalist self-narratives that what they offer are corrective, objective truths about Irish history that have been obscured to Irish and non-Irish readers alike, all of whom will benefit from being told the facts.

## II

How did nineteenth-century Irish nationalists themselves define the role of autobiography? Thomas Davis laid out a template for nationalist cultural work that applied to autobiography as much as to any other form of activity: 'we must [ . . . ] try, by teaching and example, to lift up the souls of all our family and neighbours to that pitch of industry, courage, information, and wisdom necessary to enable an enslaved, dark, and starving people to become free, and rich, and rational' (1910: 83). In Davis's mission for liberty, solidarity, enlightenment and productivity, autobiography had a multiple role. In the first place, the very writing of it is a political act; thus the Young Irelander Michael Doheny was able to describe his autobiographical effort as 'my latest labour in [Ireland's] cause' (1920: vi). Secondly, as a text, it teaches and exemplifies what the nationalist subject is obliged to perform. Davis, for instance, recommends the reading of Wolfe Tone's 'glorious memoirs' as an important part of nationalist consciousness-raising, seeing them as both a primary source of historical information and a record of an exemplary life (1910: 222). Echoing Carlyle, Davis asserts the value of recognising 'the pressure of a great mind on his times, and on after-times' (1910: 90) – the value, that is, of the heroic model. Two generations later, Pádraic Pearse was to define the inspirational importance of Tone's memoirs in a more intensely charged manner by arguing that they were effectively the 'gospel of the New Testament of Irish Nationality' (1962: 168), as if to confirm Benedict Anderson's insight that nationalist discourse operates in ways analogous to religion (1991: 12). In fact, Davis himself took on something of the role of the exemplary reader of just such a gospel or inspirational tale. In a striking sentence from the manuscript of his own unfinished biography of Tone, held in the National Library of Ireland (MS 1791/2), Davis imagines a scene for the projected frontispiece of the book in which 'Liberty takes down the sword suspended from the ivied wall over Tone's grave and hands it to *me*!' Here the desired interrelation of national destiny, personal identity, attentive reading and patrilinear inheritance come together in a remarkable way.

One of the cherished practical projects of the Irish nationalism associated with Davis and the *Nation* newspaper in the 1840s was the publication of cheap, popular texts in a series known as the 'Library of Ireland', intended as a series of shilling volumes of biography, poetry and criticism which would, in the words of Charles Gavan Duffy, 'feed the national spirit or discipline the national morals' (1895: 230). Among the biographies written or projected for the series were Davis's life of Tone (never completed because of his early death); a life of Hugh O'Neill by John Mitchel; an account of the earls of Desmond by C. P. Meehan; and Thomas D'Arcy McGee's life of Art McMurrough, the fourteenth-century antagonist of Richard II. Less politicised biographies and autobiographies were considered useful too. The Young Irelander Thomas MacNevin, for example, suggested the organisa- tion of a nationwide program of public readings stressing the 'biography of self-sustaining energetic men' like Benjamin Franklin, whose autobiography MacNevin had been reading in public with great success (quoted in Lloyd, 1987: 159). Franklin's memoir is in fact an exemplary narrative of bourgeois autobiography. As the very model of a 'self-sustaining, energetic' man, he explains his life as one in which, through providence, individual integrity, discipline and ingenuity, he has 'emerg'd from the Poverty & Obscurity in which I was born & bred, to a State of Affluence & some Degree of Reputation in the World' (Franklin, 1986: 3). He describes the reason for publicising his successes in autobiographical form as not merely one of personal vanity, but as an educational one not dissimilar to that of the nationalist project: 'my Posterity may like to know, as they may find some of them suitable to their own Situations, & therefore fit to be imitated' (Franklin, 1986: 3). This basic structure of Franklin's story is one in which the narrator remembers the chief turning points of his life, progressing from a state of immaturity and lack of knowledge through a series of problematic encounters and obstacles that must be overcome, in the process establishing his credentials as an ethical being. He finally arrives at a plateau of maturity, integrity and success from which the relationship between self and world appears resolved, stable and secure.

What nationalism did was to adapt the structure of such bourgeois narratives to the story of the nation. The writer's initial environment is shown to be national as well as familial; the story's turning points in terms of action and maturation have to do with political events or education; and the concluding vantage-point from which the life is surveyed is one in which the individual's commitment to the national cause has been proven and personally vindicated, even if the ultimate political goal of national independence has not yet been achieved. He or she has also emerged as a fully realised ethical subject, not just by remaining true to the dictates of reason and human nature, but through sustained personal commitment to the nation. This pilgrimage through life mirrors the story of Ireland itself, which can be imagined as a story of a nation which, like a person, has an honourable pedigree (an ancient civilisation); is faced with a series vicissitudes and injustices (invasion and colonial rule); awakens to a mature realisation of its innate dignity and capacity for action (the nationalist movement); and arrives at a moral, if not political, triumph in the present. Unlike earlier forms of chronicle, nationalist history imagines historical movement as an organic narrative; in nationalist discourse a nation, like an individual, has uniqueness, a linear history, a soul, a mind and a physical reality with geographic and political boundaries analogous to the limitations of the human body. Like many before them, Davis and his colleagues frequently described Ireland anthropomorphically:

> [Ireland] is still a serf [ . . . ], but she is struggling wisely and patiently, and is ready to struggle, with all the energy her advisers think politic, for

liberty. She has ceased to wail – she is beginning to make up a record of English crime and Irish suffering, in order to explain the past, justify the present, and caution the future. She begins to study the past – not to acquire a beggar's eloquence in petition, but a hero's wrath in strife. (Davis, 1910: 83)

From here it is not difficult to imagine the coincidence of the destiny of the nation and the destiny of the individual national hero.

Of course, nationalism was not the only form of political movement that deployed autobiography to such effect. Radical and working-class movements in England also produced such narratives, both as a way of bearing witness to oppression and as instruments for defining communities on a class basis. Even more influentially, Frederick Douglass's autobiography (the first version of which was published in 1845, not long before his visit to Ireland) told the tale of an individual's struggle against slavery that was structurally almost exactly like the tale Irish nationalism wished to tell. One nineteenth-century critic, George Ruffin, summarised Douglass's autobiography in rhetoric very similar to that of early-nineteenth-century Irish nationalism: 'Frederick Douglass was born a slave, he won his liberty; he is of negro extraction, and consequently was despised and outraged; he has by his own energy and force of character commanded the respect of the Nation' (Douglass, 1996: 467). It is interesting, too, that the opening of Douglass's final version of his life story describes the landscape and culture of his birthplace in terms of desolation and aridity that are strikingly similar to nineteenth-century nationalist accounts of post-Union Ireland:

[My birthplace was] a small district of country, thinly populated, and remarkable for nothing that I know of more than for the worn-out, sandy, desert-like appearance of its soil, the general dilapidation of its farms and fences, the indigent and spiritless character of its inhabitants, and the prevalence of ague and fever. It was in this dull, flat, and unthrifty district or neighborhood, bordered by the Choptank river, among the laziest and muddiest of streams, surrounded by a white population of the lowest order, indolent and drunken to a proverb, and among slaves who, in point of ignorance and indolence, were fully in accord with their surroundings, that I, without any fault of my own, was born, and spent the first years of my childhood. (1996: 475)

Compare this to Thomas Davis's biography of a representative Irish peasant of the 1840s, which similarly describes how the degradation of the environment and the individual are mutually reinforced by oppression:

In a climate soft as a mother's smile, on a soil fruitful as God's love, the Irish peasant mourns. [ . . . ] Consider his griefs! They begin in the cradle – they end in the grave. Suckled by a breast that is supplied from unwholesome or insufficient food, and that is fevered with anxiety – reeking with the smoke of an almost chimneyless cabin – assailed by wind and rain when the weather rages – breathing, when it is calm, the exhalations of a rotten roof, of clay walls, and of manure, which gives his only chance of food – he is apt to perish in his infancy. [ ... ] Advancing youth brings him labour, and manhood increases it; but youth and manhood leave his roof rotten, his chimney one hole, his window another, his clothes rags (at best muffled by a holiday *cotamore*) – his furniture, a pot, a table, a few hay chairs and rickety stools – his food, lumpers and water – his bedding, straw and a coverlet – his enemies, the landlord, the tax-gatherer, and the law – his consolation, the priest and his wife – his hope on earth, agitation – his hope hereafter, the Lord God! (1910: 194–95)

Such accounts throw into relief the scale of the task facing the nationalist hero who must overcome and transform these conditions. The potential reward, however, is great: the hero's personal redemption will coincide with the redemption of the nation.

Yet Irish nationalism also had to grapple with the inescapable tension produced by the uncertain relationship between individual agency and the effects of historical and ideological environment. How much of human motivation and action is self-generated and how much determined by forces beyond individual control? Even Charles Gavan Duffy, who played a major role in Irish nationalism over an unusually long life and who might well be entitled to narrate his life in terms of heroic personal achievement, urges in one of his autobiographical narratives that the reader recognise, in the spirit of Mazzini rather than Carlyle, that ideas more than individuals drive historical change:

The thoughtful reader will not fail to note that the narrative at bottom is not the history of certain men, but essentially the history of certain principles. Controversy, rather than meditation, is the nursing-mother of popular opinion; and to the controversies and conflict which I have undertaken to record may be traced back, for the most part, the opinions which influence the public mind of Ireland at present, or promise to influence it, in any considerable degree among the generation now entering on public life. (1884: viii)

At an ideological level, too, contradictions are visible. Bourgeois ideology assumes that individual uniqueness is necessary for one to exercise self-determination and agency, thereby achieving the status of a mature and ethical being. At the same time, too much individual autonomy threatens one's proper integration into the collective needs and responsibilities of the nation. It is the deep-seated ideological privileging of the ideas of liberty and autonomy that produces this paradox, since the exercise of autonomy by the individual may not always serve the interests of the nation, especially in the latter's attempt to exercise its own supposed autonomy in relation to geopolitics. Thus, it cannot be always possible to reconcile the values of the autonomous individual with the demands of national subjectivity. With this complication in mind, it nevertheless remains true that bourgeois Irish nationalism ultimately found the narrative features of the individual life story to be powerful instruments for imagining and analysing the Irish past and present. Irish culture became an exemplary site for what Benedict Anderson identified as a widespread 'structural alignment of post-1820s nationalist "memory" with the inner premises and conventions of modern biography and autobiography' (1991: xiv).

## III

Most of the nineteenth-century Irish nationalist autobiographies share a recognisable set of formal characteristics. Two such features to examine here relate to the purpose of the typical autobiography ('truth-telling') and to its narrative structure (the journey motif). Within these conventions there are interesting variations that allow us to glimpse the play of tensions described above. The first point to recognise is that all of the nationalist autobiographers agree that the prime function of their narrative is that of truth-telling. This purpose is used both to justify the writing of the memoir in the first place and to explain the narrative's concentration on public events. The precise task that the publication of the truth is required to perform sometimes differs, however. Some argue that they are writing to correct the misinformation about Irish history put about by English or politically biased writers. John Mitchel's *Jail Journal* (1854), for instance, is partly intended as a form of insurance against future attempts to distort the record of his imprisonment: 'I set down all these trifling particulars relating to my usage here because I foresee the worthy "Government" will have occasion to tell official falsehoods on the subject before all is over; otherwise, they are of no importance to me at all' (1996: 32). But not all truth-telling is aimed only at the pernicious stratagems of government and its propagandists. The truth-telling of Young Irelander Michael Doheny and the Fenian Jeremiah O'Donovan Rossa is primarily directed at dissenting groups within the nationalist movement itself. Doheny's *The Felon's Track* (1849) was written in the immediate aftermath of the failed 1848 rising, in response to the 'fierce contest agitating, dividing and enfeebling the Irish-American population' (Doheny, 1920: xxviii) over the causes for the rebellion's failure. Doheny attempts to explain that the failure of the rising was not due to cowardice, stupidity or hubris – accusations that were being made against the rebellion's leaders. O'Donovan Rossa prefaces his *Recollections* (1898) with a promise to deliver certain truths that previous nationalist accounts had failed to record: 'No true or correct history of the movements of my day was yet written, and though my book was to be a historical one, the story of my life-time is, if I can tell it properly, such a story as will tend to set right many things that many writers have set wrong' (1972: vi). To the plethora of second-hand accounts purporting to tell the story of Fenianism, O'Donovan Rossa adds his personal and therefore definitive witness.

Sometimes, too, truth-telling is not merely a matter of correcting erroneous historical information, but of responding to personal slander. Lady Morgan, in the spirit of Rousseau, explains that having been so often

> abused, calumniated, misrepresented, flattered, eulogized, persecuted; supported as party dictated or prejudice permitted; the pet of the Liberals of one nation, the *bête-noire* of the ultra set of another; the poor butt that reviewers, editors and critics have set up – [I] may, perhaps, be pardoned for wishing to speak a few true and final words of [myself]. (1862: 1)

Gavan Duffy similarly used his *My Life in Two Hemispheres* (1898) to rebut the 'mis-statements and slanders' (1898: 67) of one-time friend and ally John Mitchel, whose *Jail Journal* had charged Duffy with cowardice in the aftermath of the 1848 rebellion. Nor is the purpose of truth-telling confined to autobiographers of the nationalist movement: Irish liberal unionists or political agnostics like W. Steuart Trench, Joseph Le Fanu and William Carleton also claimed that they wrote in order to give, as Trench puts it, 'a clear and truthful account of occurrences which virulent party spirit or local prejudices have [ ... ] distorted through a false medium' (1868: vii). Trench, in his *Realities of Irish Life* (1868), imagines his audience as English, not Irish, readers, who need to be divested of prejudice before the Union between the two countries (of which he approves) can be made successful.

The rationale of truth-telling depends, of course, on the assumption that the author is a reliable witness and that the language and literary forms being used are adequate vehicles for the transmission of such truth as they possess. These assumptions were by no means unproblematic in nineteenth-century Ireland. The memoirists themselves frequently draw attention to the way events are constructed differently by the writings of others, and especially by the 'official' discourse of the government. Apart from *bona fide* errors of memory, there are dangers of bias, relativity and partiality of perspective, especially in a culture which so visibly fractured into competing sects, factions, classes and interest groups. The difficulty of achieving an objective or transcendent perspective on Irish life haunted Irish fiction in the same period and made writers themselves self-conscious about their search for forms adequate to the representation of the 'truth' of Irish experience. Maria Edgeworth recorded the frustration of trying to fit the truth of Irish life into the form of the novel – 'the truth is too strong for the fiction, and on all sides pulls it asunder' (1820: 350) – and Terry Eagleton has noted the prevailing sense that nineteenth-century Ireland 'gives the slip to realist representation' (1995: 183). Thus the attempt to impose any written form on experience raises the possibility of distortion. Yet these anxieties are generally left unexamined by nationalist autobiographers. For that reason, two exceptions to the general rule are particularly interesting: Mitchel's *Jail Journal* and the poet James Clarence Mangan's *Autobiography* (written in 1848 and first published in 1882).

Mitchel's book is the most complex and self-reflective of nationalist auto-biographies. In one remarkable passage, written on a prison hulk in Bermuda one month after his transportation, he explains his motive for writing as partly the preservation of a coherent sense of self under the pressure of disorientation and trauma:

> Nothing ever happens to me. What have I to write? Or, if I write my nothings, who will ever read? May not the 'chief-mate' come in any morning and take away my log for his own private reading – or, if he think it worth while, deliver it to the superintendent, who may deliver it to the governor, who may deliver it to the prime minister? So it may even come to do me harm another day: for I am in their power.
>
> Yet, notwithstanding all these considerations, I feel much inclined to jot down a page or two now and then, though it were but to take note of the atmospheric phenomena; or to praise or abuse some book that I may have been reading; or, in short, to put on record anything, whether good or bad, that may have occurred in my mind – if one may use so strong an expression as *mind* in this seaweed state. After all, in so very long a voyage, one might well forget from whence he set sail, and the way back, unless he have some sort of memoranda to refer to. This book will help to remind me of what I was, and how I came down hither, and so preserve the continuity of my thoughts, or *personal identity*, which, there is sometimes reason to fear, might slip away from me. These scrawls then will be in some sort as the crumbs which the prince (I forget his name) scattered on his way as he journeyed through the pathless enchanted wood. (1996: 71–72, original emphasis)

These problems of identity loss and the need for self-definition are recurring issues in Mitchel's autobiography and one of the ways in which they mani-fest themselves is in his preoccupation with the relation between language and identity, especially as registered by the act of naming. *Jail Journal* opens with a bold statement of Mitchel's 'proper' name, followed by the first of his new criminal names, a gift of the British legal system: 'On this day, about four o'clock in the afternoon, I, John Mitchel, was kidnapped, and carried off from Dublin, in chains, as a convicted "Felon" ' (1996: 19). As the *Journal* continues over the course of many months, Mitchel is alternately amused and perturbed by the power and truth-value of naming, and draws attention to the ways in which individual identity is continually redefined by both the self and the external agencies. Although they purport to identify one single individual, the various names and epithets applied to Mitchel himself do not necessarily add up to a coherent persona; rather, they show the individual as a spectrum of roles and characters. The spectrum ranges from the respectable 'gentleman' 'John Mitchel, sometime of Upper Leeson Street', to the felonious 'convict Mitchel', prisoner 2014 and a fugitive 'man of five feet ten, with dark hair' (1996: 65, 133, 51, 300). He records the various ways in which he is interpellated by the discourse of others: through a court verdict, through newspaper articles and parliamentary speeches, through police posters, through personal encounter. On board the hulks, he overhears a fellow convict identify him with a curse (' "Blast his bloody eyes! What is he but a convict, like the rest of us – a damnation, bloody convict?" – *Meaning me*'), and at one stage is reduced to nothing more than an objectified 'body', for ownership of which the ship's captain takes a receipt (1996: 77, 52).

Furthermore, the hostile press treatment of Mitchel's close and mild-mannered friend John Martin, a fellow exile, leads Mitchel to recognise the degree to which identities are constructed in strategic ways to fit conventional narratives and stereotypes:

> Who and what is this John Martin? A political adventurer seeking to embroil the state, in hope of somehow rising to the surface of its tossing waves? or a needy agitator, speculating on a general plunder? or a vain young man courting puffs, paragraphs and notoriety? or a wild Jacobin, born foe of order, who takes it for his mission to overthrow whatever he finds established, and brings all things sacred into contempt? (1996: 78)

In fact, Mitchel argues, the 'real' Martin is none of these. His argument in the *Journal* is that like the artificial versions of Martin found in the conservative press, his own criminal identities are actually false and superficial ones, based on a perversion of natural justice. Yet the *Journal* as a whole seems to acknowledge that the fluidity of identity, while deeply unsettling, is also inescapable, often pleasurable and sometimes necessary for survival. In one journal entry he makes a virtue of personal incoherence, gleefully splitting himself into two antagonists – a pompous 'Ego' and a cynical 'Doppleganger' – who conduct a half-serious, half-comic dialogue about the apparent inconsistency of his politics. In exile in Van Diemen's Land, he playfully imposes nicknames on his companions John Martin ('John Knox') and Kevin O'Doherty ('St Kevin'). Where false names have previously been a sign of persecution, here they are tokens of friendship and intimacy. Most importantly, his deliberate adoption of false names after revoking his parole ('Mr Wright' and then 'Mr Warren') proves necessary to his escape from the penal colony.

James Clarence Mangan's autobiography raises questions about the 'truth' of autobiographical representation in a more troubling way. As with his poetry, Mangan's memoir shifts frequently between realist description and dreamlike fantasy, and draws attention to the role of the subjective mind in the interpretation of 'reality'. On the basis of poems like 'Dark Rosaleen' (1846), Mangan was adopted by Young Ireland as a 'national' poet whose work embodied the spirit of the nation in a pure and authentic way. Mitchel, indeed, though he would not have read Mangan's manuscript autobiography, famously identified him as a 'type and shadow of the land he loved so well', on the basis that his biography offered a direct and accurate representation of the history of the nation itself; like Ireland, Mangan's light had flickered briefly and brilliantly, but was snuffed out as a consequence of oppressive colonial rule (Mangan died of the effects of malnutrition and cholera at the end of the Famine) (Mitchel, 1860: 15). Yet Mangan's life and work, as Lloyd has argued, are actually profoundly unsettling to nationalist aesthetics. His continual use of translation, his many pseudonyms, and his refusal to adhere to a single coherent vision, national or otherwise, make his work as a whole an ineffective mechanism for the reader's identification with the nation, unless the nation be defined as radically eclectic and contradictory. Similarly, as a record of the objective 'facts' of Mangan's life, the poet's autobiography is blatantly unreliable. When C. P. Meehan, who described the autobiography as 'the merest *Reve d'une Vie*, with here and there some filaments of reality' (Mangan, 1909: xxiv), confronted him about the autobiography's exaggerated description of the wretchedness of the Mangan family home, the poet readily acknowledged its fantastical nature, remarking airily that he had 'dreamt it' (Mangan, 1909: xli). Mangan gives us no dates, little external detail and few material anchors to reassure us of the validity of the account. Instead, the narrative is largely impressionistic.

The autobiography's representation of the poet's father, for example, stresses his symbolic meaning rather than his activities in real time and space: 'If any one can imagine such an idea as a human boa-constrictor *without his alimentive propensities*, he will be able to form some notion of the character of my father' (Mangan, 2004: 418, original emphasis), and Mangan's description of the office conditions in which he was employed as a scrivener seems to reflect a terrifying inner psychological reality more than an external and verifiable one:

my office-companions affected me in a manner difficult to conceive [ . . . ] I seemed to myself to be shut up in a cavern with serpents and scorpions and all hideous and monstrous things, which writhed and hissed around me, and discharged their slime and venom over my person. These hallucinations were considerably aided and aggravated by the pestiferous atmosphere of the office, the chimney of which smoked continually, and for some hours before the close of the day emitted a sulphurous exhalation that at times literally caused me to gasp for breath. (2004: 425–26)

The awkwardness for the nationalist project here is that the protagonist's experience veers sharply away from the common or the communal. Experiences of this nature cannot easily be shared in a collective sense because they are so mediated by private, creative reconstruction. It is also significant that Mangan's autobiography exists in two different forms: first as a short 'biographical sketch' published posthumously in 1850 under the pseudonym 'E. W.', though written by Mangan himself, and secondly as an incomplete manuscript published in 1882. These two versions share some elements, but are different in tone and occasionally in detail. Their very existence confirms again the provisionality of Mangan's writing and reminds us that autobiographical writing is as much a product of the time of its composition as it is a reflection on that time.

A second formal convention that effectively displays the tensions of the autobiographical project is a structural one. The story of the nationalist hero conventionally draws upon the motif of pilgrimage or journey, especially, in the case of Irish nationalism, the journey of exile. The pilgrimage narrative is common to autobiographies in general: it gives meaning to the flux of experience in the form of a physical, emotional or psychological journey towards a redemptive goal. Conversion narratives, *Bildungsromane*, indeed all narratives of individual development, can be read as somehow structured around a journey through time and space, during which a profound change or maturation takes place. In nationalist autobiography the journey is often one from the country to the city, or an educational journey from the province to the metropolis and back, or sometimes a journey through the country itself by which the hero is forced to transcend his or her own class or regional limitations and become truly national in perspective. The impetus for the journey may be external to the hero – an arrest, a flight from the authorities, an enforced exile – or, more rarely, it may be a moment of epiphany or enlightenment like that described by the Fenian John O'Leary:

> Sometime in the year 1846, while recovering from a fever, I came across the poems and essays of Thomas Davis, then recently dead. [ ... ] Perhaps it may give some notion of the effect produced on me to say that I then went through a process analogous to what certain classes of Christians call 'conversion.' I can but vaguely remember my unregenerate state. Doubtless (from my surroundings) I was not anti-Irish or West-British: but then I am confident I was not strongly Irish. [ ... ] Now, however, everything was changed. The world was an altered world to me. I felt in quite a new sense that I was an Irishman, and that for weal or woe my fate must be linked with that of my country. (1969: 2–3)

But whatever its impetus, exile is the definitive form of journey in Irish nationalist autobiography. In the opening pages of O'Donovan Rossa's

*Recollections*, a stark picture of the exiled and diasporic nature of his own family is generalised to the point where it seems constituent of Irish identity itself:

> And that is the story of many another Irishman of the old stock. Families scattered in death as well as in life; a father buried in Ireland, a mother buried in Carolina, America; a brother buried in New York, a brother buried in Pennsylvania, a sister buried in Staten Island. The curse that scattered the Jews is not more destructive than this English curse that scatters the Irish race, living and dead. (1972: 6)

Such narratives of exile allow the nationalist autobiography to carry considerable emotional and moral power. Wolfe Tone's memoirs illustrate this particularly well. The emotional register of his diaries fluctuate between the pain of separation – 'There is one thing which I have had occasion to remark tonight, and a thousand times before, since my arrival in France, *viz. "That it is not good for man to be alone"* ' – and his stoic determination to carry through his political project of raising French support for an invasion of Ireland: 'Nothing on earth could sustain me now but the consciousness that I am engaged in a just and righteous cause. For my family, I have, by a desperate effort, surmounted my natural feelings so far, that I do not think of them at this moment' (Tone, 1998: 735, 668). Each emotional pain and strategic setback that he suffers as a result of his exile provides the reader with proof of his supreme unselfishness and dedication to principle, without losing sight of his endearing qualities as an ordinary, human, caring individual. This ability to integrate opposing qualities is conventional for the nationalist hero, representing as it does the ideal unifying power of the nation itself. Tone's case in particular appealed to Thomas Davis, who eulogised his capacity to unite 'feminine' heart and 'masculine' intellect: 'For in him the heart of a woman combined/With a heroic life and a governing mind' (Davis, 1910: 333). *Jail Journal* contains similar passages that record the pains of exile, though where Tone's exile is self-imposed Mitchel's is forced upon him. Initially he can even feel some excitement at the prospect of the journey, as if it were a freely chosen adventure:

> But for the thought of those children and their mother, and what temporary inconveniences they may suffer before arrangements can be made for their leaving Ireland – but for that I should feel absolutely jolly to-day. There is something independent in setting forth on a voyage of three thousand miles, with an old brown coat on my back, and a few shillings in my *tricolor* purse. (Mitchel, 1996: 33)

As the narrative progresses, however, Mitchel records an incident of uncontrollable weeping, feelings of loneliness, thoughts of suicide and the agonies of chronic asthma. In Van Diemen's Land, exhausted by the struggle and despairing of the future, he almost decides to relinquish his political struggle and settle down to the life of a Tasmanian farmer. In the end, however, he rouses himself to continue his journey. Where Tone's journey (though not his autobiography) had ended with his return to Ireland and death, Mitchel's *Journal* ends with something less final: his arrival in New York, which is figured as a kind of surrogate homecoming, as he is greeted by his mother, brother and former Young Ireland companions. He has achieved his freedom, though his exile remains unfinished.

Michael Doheny's journey, as recorded in *The Felon's Track*, is a somewhat different one to Tone's and Mitchel's. Doheny's book records an internal exile and is almost an ironic response to Davis's earlier call for Irish people to visit the nation's spectacular scenic spots as a matter of pleasure, education and patriotic economics (Davis, 1910: 200–204). With a reward on his head for taking part in an attack on a police barracks in 1848, Doheny goes on the run with James Stephens, travelling from Tipperary through Cork and into west Kerry, sleeping rough, sheltered and fed by peasants and farmers, noting local customs, plotting to kidnap the British prime minister and visiting famous beauty spots, including Carrantuohill, Ireland's highest peak, and the romantic lake at Gougane Barra. The resulting text is an unexpected mixture of political argument, social commentary and travelogue, all framed by the suspense of being pursued by the armed forces of the state. Finding themselves in west Kerry, Doheny decides to add the role of tourist to his roles as lawyer, patriotic journalist and insurgent:

> In either alternative which our fate presented, there was no hope of ever beholding these scenes again, and we could not omit this last opportunity of minutely examining and enjoying what was grandest and loveliest in our native land. We resolved, therefore, to leave no glorious spot unvisited, whatever toil it cost, or risk it exposed us to. (1920: 247)

Climbing up to view the lakes of Killarney, his rhapsody is brought to an abrupt and somewhat amusing halt by the intrusion of political reality into his tourist's gaze: 'Standing on that green hill, it is impossible to divest the mind of the idea, that the scene is one of pure enchantment. But we were destined not to realise it. There was a police-station immediately on our way' (1920: 248). Doheny's journey, like Mitchel's, is completed by escape to the 'new Ireland' of the United States.

Each of these journeys of exile, for all their differences of detail, serve the same structural and ideological function: they prove the degree to which the nationalist hero has integrated his personal desires and responsibilities with those of the nation itself. This is all the more clear when we consider those autobiographies that do not quite fit the pattern. The autobiography of Anne Devlin, Robert Emmet's assistant and housekeeper, articulates her perspective on the events of 1803. Her nationalist credentials are established early in the framing narrative provided by a Brother Luke Cullen, who took down Devlin's oral account in the late 1840s. The Devlins were important United Irishmen in Wicklow and Anne's involvement in nationalism is thus seen to be rooted and natural. Her achievement as representative national heroine is proven by her devotion to Emmet and her refusal under torture and grief to betray the names of the other conspirators. Her particular heroic qualities also draw upon established conventions of politicised femininity: deferential personal loyalty, passive resistance, quiet courage (Ryder, 1992/93). Yet considered in terms of the nationalist journey motif, Devlin's life story is much more problematic. Cullen's account tells the reader that he discovered Devlin living in dire poverty, grieving for her dead children and husband, forgotten by the nationalist movement she had helped create, and grown bitter. For Anne Devlin, there was no public moral triumph, no martyr's death, no heroic exile, only a decline into obscure and impoverished old age (Devlin, 1968).

Mangan's autobiography, though unfinished, also charts a journey that defies nationalist convention. Its hysteric misery, paranoia and self-pity belie the narratives of personal growth and forward progress that characterise the life journeys of Tone, Mitchel, Doheny and others. Mangan imagines his autobiography not as an instruction manual for how to link one's destiny with that of the nation, but rather as a cautionary tale in the tradition of De Quincey's *Confessions of an English Opium-Eater* (1821), with the stated aim of demonstrating human frailty and acting as a moral 'warning to the uneducated votary of Vice' (Mangan, 2004: 417). His story does not progress beyond the passive endurance of personal and familial disaster and therefore cannot move forward into self-directed recuperation or restorative relation with either family or nation. It is only in a negative and cautionary sense, as Mitchel's 'type and shadow' comment suggested, that Mangan's life and Irish national history can be made analogous. Furthermore, the analogy can only be useful to nationalism insofar as Mangan's trauma is seen to represent the Irish past rather than the national present or future.

It is also interesting to note the effect of the diary form in autobiographical accounts. The immediacy of the diary entry, as found in parts of Tone's *Memoirs* and in Mitchel's *Jail Journal*, allows the reader to perceive the hero's journey as more contingent, accidental and vulnerable than is the case in retrospective autobiographies. The narrator of a diary entry has not yet formulated the overall pattern of his or her life and thus appears more spontaneous in judgement and expression. Varieties of tone, mood and style become possible, accentuating all the more the tension between the uniqueness of individual experience and the political requirement that the individual's life be aligned with national destiny. The ways in which these two aspects of the life are to be reconciled appear less certain in diaries than in autobiographies proper, and perhaps because of this unpredictability diaries can be all the more engaging for readers. The retrospective voice of conventional autobiography does not, of course, guarantee a tight narrative structure. O'Donovan Rossa's *Recollections*, though written in 1898, wanders randomly across time and intersperses personal memories with poems and lengthy quotations from letters, the narrative coherence being maintained only by the eccentric movement of the narrator's mind. Seán Ó Lúing rightly compares Rossa's method to that of a *seanachie*, concerned to tell an entertaining story rather than lead the reader on a linear path from past to present (O'Donovan Rossa, 1972: viii).

For the present-day reader, conditioned to expect intimate self-revelation from memoir, the autobiographies of nineteenth-century Irish nationalists may seem excessively political, convention-bound and emotionally reserved. Many would doubtless echo Virginia Woolf's complaint about memoirs in general: 'They leave out the person to whom things happened. [ . . . ] [T]hey say: "This is what happened"; but they do not say what the person was like to whom it happened' (1985: 65). Yet in many ways this twentieth-century critique misses the point of nineteenth-century nationalist autobiography. It may be true that for the most part these works do fail to probe the inner consciousness of the subject, as indeed did many other bourgeois autobiographies of the time, but what they do instead is image in quite pragmatic ways the relationships between self and society, between personal identity and national history. In the process they illustrate the problems as well as the possibilities of those relationships at a politically charged moment in Irish history when such questions had a pressing urgency.

# 2
# Creating the Self, Recreating the Nation: The Politics of Irish Literary Autobiography from Moore to Behan

*Bernice Schrank*

## Introduction

In a recent essay in the *Irish University Review*, Eamonn Hughes observed that '[a]utobiographies of the Revival period can be productively read as a series of meditations on and arguments about Ireland and Irishness' (2003: 28). Hughes's position is a refinement of Declan Kiberd's contention that 'autobiography in Ireland becomes, in effect, the autobiography of Ireland' (1995: 119). Clearly, Kiberd and Hughes agree that Irish autobiographical writing merges personal and national identities but not, in Hughes's view, without a struggle. His phrase 'arguments about' indicates that, in his reading of revivalist autobiography, 'Ireland' and 'Irishness' are contested terms. Drawing on the autobiographical work of George Moore, Sean O'Casey, Brendan Behan and, to a lesser extent, W. B. Yeats, I would like to take Hughes's observation a step further by arguing that, in telling their stories, these writers assert their Irishness by opposing both colonial and nationalist versions of Irish identity. The Ireland they critique is too repressive, too Catholic, too indifferent to its poor. In its place they seek a pluralistic and tolerant society, hospitable to artistic achievement and to social idealism. In essence, then, these writers define their 'Irishness' as a political act to enable a cultural, religious and social transformation of Ireland. Premised on a view of Irish autobiography as both cultural narrative and personal document, the first section of this chapter describes the discourses of colonialism and nationalism against which these autobiographies are written. The following sections discuss the ways by which Moore, Yeats, O'Casey and Behan each construct their lives so as to authenticate their Irishness, while undercutting the restrictions and deformations of both colonial and nationalist ideologies. The final section suggests the political uses to which the current interest in Irish autobiography may be put.

Because autobiography is the literary form most closely associated with revelations of the self, the autobiographical writings of Moore, Yeats,

O'Casey and Behan invite consideration as embodiments of the writers' autonomous lives, so it is not surprising that these autobiographies have, as independent works, attracted considerable critical attention.[1] Critics who have examined these writings individually argue that the lives portrayed are not precisely the unmediated authentic selves the reader undoubtedly expects, but literary constructions of those selves. Certainly, each author transposes events, muddles chronology, invents episodes (O'Casey, for example, witnesses his mother's labour bringing him into the world) and adds and subtracts characters so as to present a particular view of his growth and development, a literary strategy not too different from that used in the creation of nineteenth-century *Bildungsromane*. Treated as individual literary works, then, these autobiographies reveal many elements of novelistic fiction. The emphasis on such matters as form and theme, however, diverts attention away from the historical forces that shape the lives and the writings of the authors discussed. These autobiographical works are deeply embedded in, and so reflect on, the economic, political and cultural realities of Ireland from the late colonial period to the second half of the twentieth century. Indeed, read in the sequence of their publication, they provide a historical overview of Ireland from the agitation over Home Rule in the late nineteenth century to independence and its aftershocks, including most especially the long blight of successive de Valera governments.

What the autobiographical writings of Moore, Yeats, O'Casey and Behan do, then, is create multiple layers of perception in which the intricacies and improvisations of individual consciousness become inseparable from the political realities of power, oppression and the long dream of Irish independence. In other words, they function simultaneously as individual life stories and as cultural narratives. That said, there is yet another, more general and political way of viewing these autobiographical works. Beyond the immediacy of their personal and historical detail, these texts collectively respond to – and nearly always subvert – the discourses of colonial domination and nationalist exclusivity that, from the second half of the nineteenth century to the middle of the twentieth, held sway in Ireland. In this way, they enable and contribute to the emergence of a multi-vocal, counter-hegemonic post-independence Irish discourse. The next section lays out the discursive contexts against which I propose to read the autobiographical works of my chosen writers.

## Celticism, Orientalism and nationalism

In *Writing Ireland* David Cairns and Shaun Richards characterise Irish literature in terms of the troubled relationship between the colonising English and the colonised Irish, arguing that colonialism brought into being a variety of discourses, first to entrench and later to undermine that relationship. As the dominance of the colonising English continued to rely on force, 'a succession of Anglo-Irish intellectuals sought to produce forms of sentimental connection which would make it possible for the Ascendancy to assume the leadership' (Cairns and Richards, 1988: 21) of the Irish population, predominantly Gaelic and Catholic though they were, without the need for military intervention, thus conveniently leaving the power relationship of colonised and coloniser unchanged. At its most effective, such domination creates and maintains the comforting perception that the coloniser is engaged, not in exploitation or oppression, but in a civilising mission of uplifting backward natives by bringing to them the benefits of the coloniser's superior law and literature and language. When domination achieves its fullest power, it reaches beyond the coloniser and implicates the colonised in a network of barely perceptible acquiescence that leaves the power imbalance intact. Writing about colonisation in the Near and Far East, Edward Said gave the name 'Orientalism' to these hegemonic practices. Despite its encapsulation of a different geography, Orientalism as a description of colonial power relationships has great relevance to the Irish situation; as Cairns and Richards note, Celticism is the Irish version of Orientalism (1988: 47–48).

The Celt created by Celticism was not always overtly regarded as a racial inferior. In the influential work of Matthew Arnold the Celt was, in fact, a far more complimentary construct. In the Arnoldian formation, the Celt was a deeply emotional figure; his feelings were profoundly engaged by whimsy, beauty, rhetorical display, sentimental excess and spiritual essences. Unfortunately, however, these positive qualities were undermined by an often charming and childlike wilfulness and ineffectuality. Certainly, the people constituted in Arnold's Celtic mode could not be trusted to make policies, run governments, control their own destinies. Thus, Arnold's Celticism left the power relationship between England and Ireland fundamentally unchanged (Cairns and Richards, 1988: 42–57; Deane, 1985: 17–27). Even so, Celticism lent itself to nationalist adaptation. Instead of using Arnold's essentialism to justify the colonial relationship, Irish nationalists used his formulation to validate their own claims to self-government. It was reasonable and appropriate for Ireland to seek independence, they argued, because it was inherently different from (and better than) Britain. A crucially important agency for the dissemination of this nationalist variant of Celticism was the Irish Literary Revival, a diffuse body of cultural activities that ranged from the teaching of Irish through the Gaelic League to the gathering, recording and publication of Irish myths, legends and folktales. The political importance of cultural nationalism is implicit in its advocacy of deanglicisation and its pursuit of a pre-colonial Gaelic past, both of which affiliated revivalism with broader forces opposed to British domination. Revivalist discourse confirmed nationalist claims by providing abundant evidence of Irish cultural difference from Britain, which was then used to justify demands for political separation (Eagleton, 1995: 226–72; Kiberd, 1995: 136–54).

Within the broad scope of mutually reinforcing nationalist and revivalist discourses, certain strains appeared. The Anglo-Irish Ascendancy nationalists and the native Irish nationalists developed different attitudes towards what exactly was to be revived, based on the post-independence positions they hoped to occupy.[2] The minority Ascendancy class, descendants of various colonising efforts from the time of Elizabeth I onwards and inhabitants of many of the Great Houses, were a hybrid creation. By virtue of their Irish birth, they were no longer considered, nor did they consider themselves to be, English, but by virtue of their religion (Protestant) and class (landholding aristocracy and gentry) they were not unproblematically Irish either. From their ranks came, among others, Tone, Parnell, Wilde, Shaw, Lady Gregory, Synge and of course Yeats, one of the chief architects of revivalism. In Yeats's seductive formulation, the Ascendancy class sought affiliation with a pre-conquest pagan and peasant world. As he imagined it, upper-class Anglo-Irish and pagan peasantry were natural allies against the materialism and the philistinism of the British and the native Irish middle-classes alike (Deane, 1985: 28–37). From the perspective of Ascendancy nationalists, this formulation had at least two closely related virtues. First, it marginalised the majority of the Irish, who were primarily Catholic and increasingly middle-class, if not in fact then in aspiration. Second, it maintained the power of the Ascendancy. However, by the time of its fullest flowering in Yeats's middle and late poetry, this construction of Ireland's past had no political future, mainly because it was contested by the native Irish, who did not welcome their marginalisation by a privileged garrison (Eagleton, 1995: 27–103; Foster, 1988: 167–94). United by their Catholicism and a common history of famine, eviction, emigration and penal legislation, the native Irish nevertheless shared with the Ascendancy a desire to be rid of the British. Like the Ascendancy, the past to which they wanted to return in the future was rural and Gaelic; where they differed, however, was in their insistence that the nativist past/future was Catholic (Cairns and Richards, 1988: 58–64; Foster, 1988: 195–225). In post-independence Ireland, it was this nativist view that prevailed. From the early 1930s to the late 1950s – the period most closely identified with the leadership of Éamon de Valera – postcolonial Ireland fashioned repressive domestic policies in support of rural life, patriarchal domestic arrangements, small shopkeepers and farmers, artistic censorship and Catholicism. But even before the establishment of the Irish Free State (the precursor to the Republic), nationalist discourse began to show the strains of its own suppressions, displacements and omissions.

Independence, Frantz Fanon insists, does not necessarily bring with it genuine emancipation; it has to be struggled for even in the post-independence phase. An Ireland that did not take into account the needs of women, socialists, communists, workers, trade unionists, free-thinkers, Protestants, artists and other non-conformists inevitably invited resistance and reformulation (Schrank, 1993). As the American sociologist Craig Calhoun notes: 'every collective identity is open to both internal subdivision and calls for its incorporation into some larger category of primary identity.

This is not only an issue for alternative collective identities, but for individuals who are commonly treated in this discourse as though they were unitary and internally homogenous' (1994: 27). Late colonial and postcolonial Irish cultural and political experience conforms to this trajectory of redefinition by subdivision and revision by enlargement. Those excluded from the dominant nationalist discourse sought to recreate nationality so that, collectively and individually, they might have a stake in the action, whether by hyphenation of individual identity or by affiliation with a larger, often internationalist, collectivity. Just as the formation and consolidation of Irish nationalist discourse depended on cultural intervention as well as political action, so too did the project of resisting and revising that discourse. To quote Calhoun again: 'as lived, identity is always project, not settled accomplishment; though various external ascriptions or recognitions may be fixed and timeless' (1994: 27). Calhoun here takes the position that identity is historical and performative, an analysis that provides a useful framework within which to read the autobiographical writings of Moore, Yeats, O'Casey and Behan. These works undermine the discourse of colonialism by asserting an independent Irish voice and identity that has nothing to do with the fey fabrications of Arnoldian Celtic consciousness. Perhaps more importantly, these writings also contest and subvert Ireland's 'official history' by providing a more complex, variegated and pluralistic view of what it means to be Irish than is found in the sectarianism of nationalist ideology. Seen in this way, Irish literary autobiography is a means by which national identity can be simultaneously asserted and challenged. Each writer insists on his Irishness, yet each rejects crucial aspects of the nationalist *gestalt*, in particular the role of Catholicism and the restrictions placed upon artistic expression. In the following sections, therefore, I propose to analyse in greater detail the critique of British colonialism and Irish nationalism embodied in the autobiographical writings of these four influential writers, beginning with Moore.

## George Moore: A portrait of the autobiographer as middle-aged aesthete

When George Moore was 17, his family moved from Ireland, where he was born, to England. In 1873, aged 21, Moore relocated to Paris. He enrolled in art classes and became acquainted with Monet, Manet, Degas, Pissaro and other late-nineteenth-century impressionist painters. In 1880 Moore returned to England and began writing fiction. Twenty-one years later he returned to his native land where he resided for 10 years, before leaving in 1911 to return to London. Moore tells the story of his time in Ireland in *Hail and Farewell* (1911–1914), first published in three separate volumes: *Ave* (1911), *Salve* (1912) and *Vale* (1914). His record of his complex interactions with his younger brother, Maurice, his friends, including Yeats, George Russell, Lady Gregory and John Eglinton, and, most especially, Edward Martyn, not only illuminates Moore's literary and personal preoccupations at midlife, but also provides a history of Ireland between the fall of Parnell in 1891 and the 1916 Easter Rising, during which deanglicisation advanced by peaceful means. The story Moore tells, however, is not of revivalism triumphant, but of revivalism failed. Whatever his initial enthusiasm, *Hail and Farewell* demolishes revivalist goals and values. It does not take Moore long to realise that Gaelic cannot replace English either as a demotic or as a literary language, and he is sufficiently irritated by the efforts of the clergy to control sexual behaviour and censor artistic expression that he first denounces and later renounces Catholicism. A cosmopolitan aesthete, Moore happily leaves his brother to look after his estate, seeing rural Irish life as barren and the peasantry as shrewd, uneducated and unworthy of adulation. With unmistakable irony, he is driven to conclude that he can best express his Irishness by returning to England. Moore's method reinforces his meaning. Casting his expansive autobiography in the first person, he treats his Irish years as an epic journey undertaken to redeem the country from colonial oppression as well as cultural backwardness. Interspersed with high-toned descriptions of and meditations on his lofty task are pointless debates, boring conversations, pedestrian gossip, bitchy asides and petty arguments, all of which are deflationary indicators of the ultimate absurdity and futility of the author's epic effort.

Yet for all this, Moore's experience with revivalism begins positively. Even before he commits to taking up residence in Dublin, he embraces the efforts to restore Gaelic and create a distinctly Irish literature. His enthusiasm, which is the main subject of the first volume of *Hail and Farewell*, is made more intense by his disgust at the unrestrained exercise of British imperial power against the Afrikaners in the Boer War and the implications of Britain's aggression for Ireland. Moore affiliates with revivalist organisations in the belief that, by so doing, he will facilitate the restoration of Ireland to her past glory and independence and participate in the creation of a cosmopolitan cultural elite to maintain and perpetuate the revivalist achievements. His association with the Revival is clearly a political act, intended to signal his desire to curtail British influence in Ireland. Over the course of his 10-year stay in Ireland, however, Moore grows increasingly disillusioned with both nationalism and revivalism. To be sure, it is his nature to subject to critical scrutiny whatever he passionately embraces. Early in *Ave*, during a tedious dinner at the Shelbourne Hotel in which speaker after speaker extols the virtues of a revitalised Ireland, a cynical guest assures Moore that he will 'get used to hearing people talk about working for Ireland, helping Ireland, selling boots for Ireland, and bullocks too' (Moore, 1985: 136). These words amuse rather than offend him. After all, Moore has experienced the sophistication of Paris and London; it stands to reason that, like the nameless guest, he will, even at this early stage in his Irish sojourn, find the unceasing and unqualified praise of the as yet unrevived Ireland unpersuasive.

It is not only revivalist rhetoric that gives Moore pause. As the offspring of a long line of Catholics, Protestants and converts, he disputes the revivalist idea of a pure Gaelic race professing Catholicism. Indeed, throughout *Hail and Farewell* he examines his genealogy in an effort to discover more evidence of the family habit of intermarriage and conversion in either direction. Such practices, he learns, have occurred with some regularity in alternating generations, a clear indication that the nationalist insistence on the link between Gaelic identity and Catholicism lacks credibility. Even worse from a nationalist perspective is his discovery that these intermarriages and conversions had little to do with religious conviction and more with personal convenience and business advantage. So, far from being a pure race with a devout religious faith, Gaelic families like the Moores – and Moore treats his family as a prototype of the Catholic landed gentry – reveal a long history of religious hybridisation and opportunism. Moore also disputes nationalist claims for Gaelic racial purity. As a large landowner, he did not share in the revivalist glorification of the Irish peasant. Growing up in Mayo, he had close contacts with the tenants on his father's estate, which subsequently passed to him, and views them as rough, uneducated and occasionally threatening. Given his class interests, therefore, it is not surprising that he harbours reservations about assigning too great a role in the renewed Ireland to an illiterate peasantry, whether Gaelic-speaking or not.

Consistent with his hard-nosed assessment of the peasant is his unease regarding nationalist agitation for land reform and agricultural development. His most caustic satire in *Hail and Farewell* is directed at the newly formed Department of Agriculture and Art, an agency established primarily to modernise agricultural practice and to ameliorate the condition of the peasantry. In Moore's view, Horace Plunkett and T. P. Gill, the director and secretary of the new organisation, are grossly incompetent. He presents their various schemes to improve life in rural communities as if they were the deranged projects of Book Three of *Gulliver's Travels*. Plunkett and Gill fund plans to turn peat into coal; to develop a Galway oyster fishery using the wrong oysters; to diversify the egg and poultry industry by introducing capons without providing the information necessary for their care; to grow melons which no one will eat, and to send out cooking instructors to teach the peasants how to use unfamiliar food. The apex of these 'mad' projects is a scheme to improve the breed of asses in Ireland, which Moore clearly believes is beyond improvement. All these ventures fail; rural Ireland is not transformed. What is most interesting is how little sympathy Moore has for the principles of land improvement and rural development that underlie Plunkett and Gill's misguided efforts. The imagined Ireland to which Moore devotes his creative energies keeps the peasant at the margins of power.

Moore's most serious disagreements with prevailing nationalist and revivalist orthodoxies centre around his efforts to create an indigenous Irish literature in Gaelic and his anger at the ways by which the dominant religion frustrates those efforts. As a believer in the right of the individual to artistic self-expression, he was outraged that Catholic clerics with no claim to refined artistic judgement attempted to censor free thought and expression. It did not take him long to feel the power the church exerts over Irish creative life. As co-director of the Irish Literary Theatre, Moore was involved with the staging of Yeats's *The Countess Cathleen* in 1899. A pamphlet written by a cleric denouncing the play as heretical provoked unruly outbursts in the audience sufficient to require the presence of police in the theatre. Yeats and Moore ignored the uproar, but Edward Martyn, a devout Catholic, was willing to stop the play if it were deemed to be heretical. In the end, the play was cleared of the charge, but the episode revealed the sensitivity of Irish cultural life to the opinions of the church. Moore's clerical hostility was further fuelled by his frustration at the failure of the Gaelic language to take hold amongst ordinary men and women, and by the non-emergence of a world-class Irish literature, both of which he blamed on Catholicism.

Moore's representation of the Gaelic League and the Irish Literary Theatre exemplifies his method of supporting and deconstructing the organisational framework of cultural nationalism. Throughout *Ave* his devotion to the restoration of the Gaelic language is unwavering, yet he suggests that Catholic repressiveness impedes the popular use of the language. Moreover, he concludes that English is an exhausted tongue, partly in reaction to British propaganda during the Boer War and partly in response to the playing out of the possibilities of the naturalistic style he used in *Esther Waters* (1894) and other early novels. In the Gaelic League's efforts to reclaim Irish, therefore, Moore perceives a freshness and a vitality that may well serve as a means of renewing national life and recharging his own artistic abilities. Gaelic, for Moore, is 'A new language to enwomb new thoughts' (Moore, 1985: 55), yet despite this infatuation he does not actually learn it nor, for that matter, does Yeats. Before long, moreover, Moore crosses swords with League bureaucrats who resent his self-assurance and refuse to allow him the unfettered access to its newsletter that he believes he deserves by virtue of his literary prominence. His relationship with the League further deteriorates when he suggests that there is no literature worth reading in the language. His plan to have popular works such as *The Arabian Nights* translated into Gaelic meets with a swift and ferocious rejection from the League; Moore quotes one columnist as saying: 'Mr George Moore has selected *The Arabian Nights* because he wishes an indecent book to be put into the hands of every Irish peasant. We do not take our ideas of love from Mohammedan countries; we are a pure race' (1985: 337). At this point Moore's efforts to advance Irish through an affiliation with the Gaelic League collapse.[3]

Moore's collaboration with Yeats and Martyn in creating an indigenous Irish theatre brought with it its own set of frustrations, the three men being frequently at loggerheads.[4] Martyn's *The Heather Field* (1899), for which Moore wrote an introduction, was a great success which he was unable to repeat with his next play, *The Tale of a Town* (1902), a work Moore and Yeats dismissed as wooden. After many unsuccessful efforts at revision, the aggrieved Martyn handed the play over to Moore, who rewrote it as *The Bending of the Bough* (1900), an episode that diminished Martyn's appetite for further collaborative projects. Moore's work with Yeats reveals similar strains and a sense that Moore's contributions are not worthy of his talent. Yeats and Moore worked together on *Diarmuid and Grania* (1901), having by now resolved to forge an Irish theatre in English rather than pursue an all-Gaelic theatre. To that end, Yeats proposed that Moore should write *Diarmuid and Grania* in French, explaining: 'Lady Gregory will translate your text into English. Taidgh O'Donoghue will translate the English text into Irish, and Lady Gregory will translate the Irish text back into English' (1985: 248). Yeats offers to add style to what emerges from this convoluted process, but Moore is naturally irritated by the poet's assumption of literary infallibility: 'Yeats was a sort of monk of literature, an Inquisitor of Journalism who would burn a man for writing that education was progressing by leaps and bounds. Opinions make people cruel – literary as well as theological' (1985: 210).

Whatever the achievement of the Irish Literary Theatre, Moore is haunted by the fact that most of plays it produces are second-rate at best. Thus, while Yeats continues to write for the theatre, Moore abandons drama and returns to English-only prose. In time, he begins to wonder what it is about Ireland that has thus far hindered the creation of a corpus of great literature and concludes that the fault lies with Irish Catholicism. He and Martyn heatedly debate this matter in the central sections of *Salve*. When Moore asserts: 'The decline of art was coincident with the union of the Irish Church with Rome; till then Ireland was a Protestant country', Martyn, a practising Catholic, is predictably incredulous: 'A Protestant country! St. Patrick a Protestant!' (1985: 352). Enjoying himself, Moore insists that St Patrick was indeed Protestant, 'in the sense that he merely preached Christianity, and the Irish Church was Protestant up to the eleventh or twelfth century' (1985: 210). He then decides to write an article arguing that 'ninety and five percent of the world's literature was written by Protestants and Agnostics' (1985: 363), since Catholic dogma, for him, imprisons the intelligence and the imagination. Moore's fear of the negative impact of Catholicism on creativity is so deeply rooted that he, like some of his ancestors, converts to Protestantism, a decision he makes public in a letter to the *Irish Times*.

Having rejected all the assumptions of nationalism and revivalism, Moore has no further role to play in Ireland. *Vale*, the concluding volume of *Hail and Farewell*, describes his leave-taking, his departure being accelerated by an epiphany in which he casts himself as a Messiah sent 'to redeem Ireland from Catholicism', a task he cannot accomplish at home due to the stifling forces of nationalism, revivalism and Catholicism (Moore, 1985: 608). Such redemption, he discovers, can only be achieved by returning to England to write his autobiography, a realisation that prompts him to visit Moore Hall for the last time. The tasteless transformation of the estate confirms for him that the world it represents is irretrievably lost. Once a finely proportioned dwelling, the eighteenth-century house has been 'spoilt by the new roof and by the plate-glass that my father had put into the windows of the hall and dining-room and drawing-room' (Moore, 1985: 616). Moore's brother has exacerbated matters by making their father's dressing room into a bathroom. Moore's sadness, however, is tempered by his recognition of the inevitability of change in the Irish countryside: 'But we cannot rebuild ancient Ireland, and it is clear to me that as soon as I am gone Moore Hall will be pulled down to build cottages in Derrinanny and Ballyholly, or the house will become a monkery or a nunnery' (1985: 627). The old order, the world of the Great Houses, Catholic and Protestant alike, is definitively over. The Catholic landed gentry to which Moore belongs, like their Anglo-Irish counterparts, have no future in the new Ireland and, for all his zeal to liberate Ireland from Catholicism, he is a sufficient realist to recognise that the church will flourish in the ruins of the estate. In this context, Moore's leave-taking, like that of Joyce and O'Casey, is experienced as a liberation.

Although he rejected exile as an option, W. B. Yeats's autobiographical writings echo Moore's critique of the role of Catholicism in Irish culture. Like *Hail and Farewell, Autobiographies* (1955) is written in the first person, but whereas Moore's style appears formless and endlessly variegated, Yeats's is more disciplined. His prose mirrors his emotional and intellectual growth, beginning with his earliest memories and ending with his public oration delivered to the Royal Academy of Sweden on the occasion of his receiving the Nobel Prize for Literature in 1923. Whereas Moore forged a highly icono-clastic autobiographical identity, highlighted by an ostentatious conversion and a messianic calling, Yeats's version of Irishness is consistent with the values of the Ascendancy class that he admired and emulated. His auto-biographical prose articulates his social and aesthetic ideals in terms of a Protestant aristocracy of taste and breeding, a class that benevolently exer-cises power, supported by artists of distinction and a native peasantry whose links to Ireland were forged in pre-Christian times. Although he eliminates from this hierarchical social vision the middle-class Catholics whose vulgar materialism offends him, he recognises that these are the very people to whom power has passed in the new Free State. However, Yeats's disappoint-ment with the outcome of the nationalist project intensifies rather than diminishes his efforts to discover a just and cultivated society in which politics, religion and artistic expression are harmoniously integrated. His autobiographical writings may thus be read as a quest for a prose version of his poetic Byzantium, a quest that culminates in a powerful apprehension of unity of being and culture that occurs not in Catholic Ireland but in Protestant Sweden.

The first five segments of *Autobiographies* deal almost exclusively with Yeats's life in Ireland, in particular his role in the creation of an indigenous Irish theatre, thus establishing the 'authenticity' of his identity. Towards the end of *Estrangement*, however, he complains bitterly: 'The soul of Ireland has become a vapour and her body a stone' (Yeats, 1980: 488), the despairing tone of which prepares the way for the openly elegiac qualities of 'The Death of Synge', in which Yeats laments that his social vision of Ireland is no longer viable. It is in this context of disillusionment that the final section, 'The Bounty of Sweden', must be read. Yeats has come to understand that wholeness of being requires wholeness of culture, by which he means a tolerance for the diversity of its constituent elements. But Ireland, still haunted by sectarian and social divisions, is far from whole. Sweden, on the other hand, strikes the poet as a place which has a long history of democratic government by which a merito-cracy of intellect has been empowered and artistic endeavour supported. Thus Yeats finds in the great Town Hall in Stockholm, a space created by and for the people, the embodiment of a cultural sensibility that values both social coherence and artistic expression. It is indigenous art, yet it recalls the achieve-ments of all the great civilisations of the past and so 'carries the mind backward to Byzantium' (Yeats, 1980: 554). In short, this 'master-work of the Romantic movement' (1980: 554) expresses a habit of mind and feeling, as well as a social outlook, that is completely at odds with the Irish, who have marginalised Yeats and his kind. What Yeats says about Sweden in the *Autobiographies* is, then, an implicit critique of the exclusionary policies of the Free State, and a none-too-subtle call for a politics and culture of inclusivity.

## Sean O'Casey: The Irish autobiographer as socialist

The Stockholm Town Hall in which Yeats invests his social and aesthetic idealism speaks to the power of collective effort and taste, but it does not address the issue of class that fuels Sean O'Casey's critique of Irish nation-alism. During his long English exile, O'Casey recreated his life story in six volumes: *I Knock at the Door* (1939), *Pictures in the Hallway* (1942), *Drums Under the Windows* (1946), *Inishfallen, Fare Thee Well* (1949), *Rose and Crown* (1952) and *Sunset and Evening Star* (1954).[5] O'Casey's autobiographical writ-ings are a passionate restatement of his claim to an Irish identity at precisely that moment in his life when, at least on the surface, it is being undermined by his political and emotional alienation from Ireland, as well as by his phys-ical separation. His narrative strategy differs from that of Moore and Yeats in that instead of using first-person narration, O'Casey chooses to tell his story in the third person and creates an autobiographical persona, Johnny Cassidy, who later Gaelicises his name to Sean O'Casey, thereby reaffirming his Irishness. While there are many similarities between the author and his persona, they are not identical; from time to time the author introduces and reorders events in the life of his persona for artistic or polemical effect.

O'Casey's style, like Moore's, is characterised by abundance. Realistic description and mock-heroic inflation are mixed with prose and poetry throughout, creating a stylistic diversity that allows him to capture the ambiguities of his social position. O'Casey did not fit into the dominant class and religious divisions of early-twentieth-century Ireland. Although poor, he was not Catholic, unlike most of his Dublin neighbours. Although Protestant, his family was poor; O'Casey earned his living as a manual labourer until middle age, when his plays provided him with sufficient income to live on. It is hardly surprising, therefore, that he wrote his autobiography as a direct challenge and flat contradiction to those versions of Irishness advanced by Ascendancy figures like Yeats on the one hand and nationalist writers such as Daniel Corkery on the other. Both versions define Irish nationality in exclusivist terms that, in effect, marginalise and disempower a comprehensive segment of the Irish population, including workers, women, socialists, trade-unionists, Protestants (in Corkery's view) and heterodox writers and artists.

The first three volumes of O'Casey's autobiography record his growing political engagement. He was, from the start, deeply committed to the anti-colonial struggle in Ireland, but he was also a devoted trade-unionist for whom the defining event of his early manhood was the Dublin General Strike and Lockout of 1913. In the years between 1913 and 1916, however, O'Casey came to believe that the groups dominating the movement for Irish independence (both Ascendancy and nativist) did not necessarily express or protect the interests of the Irish working class to which he, despite his nominal Protestant affiliation, belonged. So, in the aftermath of the General Strike, O'Casey abandoned Irish nationalism for the cause of international socialism and, as a consequence, did not join the Rising. In *Drums Under the Windows*, which ends with the Rising, O'Casey represents the activity of the nationalist factions as self-indulgent and absurd posturing. He envisions a disparate group of ideologues rushing about under 'the sulky green tent that Dublin called the sky', each purveying his own version of Irish nationality:

> There goes Bulmer Hobson with a gigantic volume of Mazzini's sermons strapped between his shoulders like a nobsack; and Yeats [ . . . ] as he murmured longingly, I will arise, and go to Inisfree; and George Russell rushing around, booming, *Come, acushla, with me to the mountains old, There the bright ones call us waving to and fro – Come, my children, with me to the ancient go.* (O'Casey, 1963a: 625)

He also imagines the writer and politician Count Plunkett dressed ostentatiously in his papal uniform playing to the crowd, a sure sign to O'Casey of the unhealthy influence of the Catholic church on Irish nationalism. Arthur Griffith is present also, momentarily distracted from his Hungarian monarchy project, working to obstruct the socialist influence of James Connolly. O'Casey's portrayal of the multiplicity and impracticality of nationalist thought subverts any notion that these men are capable of bringing into being a new nation with a progressive social agenda. Moreover, through his unflattering cameo portraits he suggests that nationalist self-absorption and solipsism may well explain why the ordinary people of Dublin failed to rally to the cause during the Easter Rising.

O'Casey does not spare his younger self from this sweeping defla-tion. However idiosyncratic his perspective, his mature judgement remains sound. He understands, albeit retrospectively, that the nationalist movement embodied the dominant energies of the moment and that his internationalist perspective, whatever its theoretical merits, was irrelevant to the unfolding political spectacle. He presents the youthful Sean as being alienated from the nationalist struggle, self-absorbed and isolated, sitting on 'a pediment of a column keeping up the facade of the Post Office, reading, reading the new catechism of the *Communist Manifesto* with its great commandment of Workers of all lands, unite!' (1963a: 626). O'Casey does not fault young Sean's analysis: he believes a Marxist critique has much to offer the nation-alist project. But just as Yeats is driven by circumstances to realise that his political views will not prevail in Ireland, so too is O'Casey. As he had anti-cipated in the first three volumes of his autobiography and in his other writings, the achievement of Irish independence brought little alteration in the country's internal social and economic arrangements.

*Inishfallen, Fare Thee Well* effectively captures O'Casey's frustration and disappointment that a political revolution was occurring without a corres-ponding social revolution from the period after the Rising to the establish-ment of the Irish Free State in 1922. He begins with a variation on one of Yeats's most famous lines (from 'Easter 1916'), but immediately distances himself from the poet's majestic commemoration of the Rising. For O'Casey, Yeats's words, appropriately modified, are a fitting epitaph not only for the pointless blood sacrifice of Easter Week, but for the political mess that was to follow: 'Things had changed, but not utterly; and no terrible beauty was to be born' (1963b: 3). Worse still is his realisation, which he registers with an irritation similar to Yeats's, that the chief beneficiaries of political change were not the workers, in whom O'Casey had invested so much of his polit-ical idealism, but the Catholic middle class. Recalling the hopes embodied in the Proclamation read by Patrick Pearse on Easter Monday, O'Casey contrasts the heady political ideals of the Rising with the tired, conservative Catholic realities of the Free State. Parodying Pearse, he enumerates the 'rights' that constitute 'freedom' in the new political dispensation, which include:

> The right to give the catholic clergy the first word, the last word and all the words in between, whatsoever they may be on any and every question, whatsoever, without any reservation whatsoever either.
>     The right to consider such men (once referred to as Irishmen) as Tone, Emmet, Mitchel, Parnell, Synge, Yeats, and Joyce; and all such women

(once referred to as Irishwomen) as Betsy Gray, Sarah Curran, Fanny Parnell, Lady Gregory, Eva of the Nation and Speranza as non-gaels, non-Irish and so *non est perpetua*. (1963b: 134)

As Sean sees it, the Free State has defined him and his political and cultural interests out of existence. 'Irish' has become synonymous with the most repressive elements of the Catholic middle class and Sean, a working-class Protestant Irishman, no longer has a political role to play in Ireland. Moreover, the country is just as inhospitable to his dramatic efforts to deconstruct the history of the newly independent nation as it is to his internationalist political vision. *Inishfallen Fare Thee Well* records his early success at the Abbey and the rejection that followed. Not only had the nationalists hooted down *The Plough and the Stars* in 1926, but far more hurtful is the fact that the directors of the Abbey, Yeats chief among them, rejected Sean's new play *The Silver Tassie*. O'Casey recounts Sean's bitterness most fully in *Rose and Crown*: 'Yeats's denunciation of *The Silver Tassie* had done Sean's name a lot of violence. The Nobel Prize winner, the Leader of English literature, was a judge against whom there was no appeal for the time being' (1963b: 302).

Unacceptable to the custodians of official nationalist history, Sean now understands that he is also unacceptable to the patrician Anglo-Irish guardians of culture. The only solution for O'Casey's younger self, and it is a painful one, is to turn his back 'on the green and gold, on the old hag that once had the walk of a queen!' (1963b: 125), a plan of action he follows in *Rose and Crown* by emigrating. England, ironically, proves to be a convenient refuge from the inhospitable artistic and political climate of Ireland, close enough to home for O'Casey's persona to realise with relief that 'the same blue sky tented London as once had tented Dublin; and now, the same moon, so beloved of him in Ireland, shone silently and grand in the English night-sky' (1963b: 310). Not only is a London production of *The Plough and the Stars* successful, but Sean has no trouble getting *The Silver Tassie* staged. And while the England of Sean's early exile is politically Conservative, a Labour government led by Ramsay MacDonald soon takes office. Despite serious reservations about MacDonald, Sean finds the Labour agenda far more compatible with his socialist views than either the policies of the Dublin government or the Conservatives' programme. In England Sean is artistically and politically acceptable. After such an overwhelming experience of rejection in Dublin, it is not surprising that he makes Devon, that corner of England closest to Ireland, his new home. As his autobiographies make clear, however, geographical separation does not lead to a severing of emotional attachment, yet an Ireland sufficiently tolerant to provide O'Casey with the scope his art and his politics required would not come into being until after his death.

## Brendan Behan: Ironies of freedom, ambiguities of imprisonment

Brendan Behan, like O'Casey, was born into a working-class Dublin family with strong ties to the labour and nationalist movements. Growing up during the early days of Irish independence, he was drawn into republican activism and soon found himself in involuntary exile in a series of English penal institutions following his arrest in Liverpool in 1939 for taking part in an IRA bombing campaign. However, his imprisonment turns out to be a surprisingly liberating experience as he details it in his neglected autobiographical work, *Borstal Boy* (1958). Although Behan tells his story in the first person, he nevertheless creates a critical distance between his older and younger selves by exploiting a full range of ironic effects to undermine his younger self's grandiose and thoroughly unrealistic sentiments. In prison his republican loyalties weaken, his addiction to the rhetoric of nationalist discourse passes, his Catholicism falters, and his appreciation of the complexities and contradictions that underpin national affiliations grows. In essence, *Borstal Boy* is a study of Behan's disengagement from the confines of a narrow and stultifying Catholic nationalism whose contours fail to conform to the demands of a complex social reality.

Behan begins his journey of liberation as a teenage patriot on a bombing mission in England on the eve of the Second World War. A complete innocent, he is arrested almost immediately on his arrival in England and makes a cocky statement to the police in which he defines his role as a would-be bomber in the language of Irish martyrology: ' "My name is Brendan Behan. I came over here to fight for the Irish Workers' and Small Farmers' Republic, for a full and free life, for my countrymen, North and South, and for the removal of the baneful influence of British Imperialism from Irish affairs. God save Ireland" ' (Behan, 1990: 4). Nonplussed by this bravura rhetoric, the arresting officer seeks to introduce a less histrionic note into the statement: ' "Here, what's this about small farmers? It's your statement, Paddy, and you can put what you bloody well like in it, but I never seen a small farmer, Irish or English; they're all bloody big fellows with bulls' 'eads on 'em, from eating bloody great feeds and drinking cider" ' (1990: 5). Although Behan is in no condition to appreciate the common sense and good humour in the policeman's remarks, he comes to realise just how untenable his heroic posturing is during the two months he spends at Walton Prison, which set the stage for his 'conversion'. Here he learns, among other things, that the only information one can deduce from the fact that a person is Irish is putative nationality. From Larry, who speaks with a Munster-English accent and who, Behan suspects, 'had helped to murder people with the Black and Tans', to Liverpool-Irish Dale who 'didn't like Irish people', the Irish Behan encounters at Walton range from the merely unpleasant to the utterly treacherous (1990: 9, 75). His sense of betrayal by these people is intensified by the contrast between their hostility and the support and protection offered by some of the English boys who are linked by the commonalities of working-class life. Most particularly, Behan is drawn to Charlie, with whom he forms an immediate friendship that renders matters of nationality irrelevant. The fact that Behan adopts Charlie's term 'china' (Cockney slang for 'friend') to define their friendship signifies the weakening of his nationalist commitment. While he does not abandon his Irish speech patterns, he happily expands his vocabulary to include Cockney English, and in so doing implicitly rejects the exclusivist claims of those nationalists who insist on Gaelic as the appropriate language of the Irish people.

Charlie, for his part, is apolitical. Rather than being outraged by Behan's insurrectionary activities, he is impressed, believing them to have more class than his own petty thievery. Indeed, Charlie encourages Brendan to sing Irish patriotic songs, which provide light relief from the drabness of prison routine, despite the anti-British sentiments of the lyrics. Clearly, national loyalties are less important to Brendan and Charlie than personal friendship, and despite the overt antagonism of many of the guards and prisoners towards Behan, Charlie remains loyal. Their relationship is passionate, apolitical and crucial to Behan's physical and emotional survival in prison. The friendship of English Charlie, particularly when set against the hostility of the Irish prisoners and guards, persuades Behan that he would 'sooner be with Charlie and Ginger and Browny in Borstal than with my own comrades and countrymen any place else' (1990: 121). That commitment is tested when Behan is called upon by an Irish political prisoner, Callan, to participate in what he recognises to be a futile protest against the execution of several Irish prisoners held in other English jails. Behan displays an unexpected degree of self-protecting unpatriotic cynicism as he attempts to appear to meet the demands of Callan while avoiding any real participation:

There was an unmerciful roar from a cell beneath me: 'U-u-u-u-up the Rep-u-u-u-u-ub-lic!' roared Callan.

That the devil may choke you and the Republic, I snarled to myself, and why the fughing hell isn't he satisfied with his own exclusive martyrdom without dragging me into it. [ . . . ]

'Breeeeeeeeeeeennnnnn – daaaaaaaaaannnn Beeeeeeeee – hann! Get up and give a shout! – a sh–oooooouuuuuuut!'

A kick up the ballocks is what I'd like to give you, said I, resentfully. [ . . . ]

I gave a discreet shout down the ventilator of 'Up the Republic'.

'I caaaaaaaa–n't heeeeeeeer youuuuuu riiiiiightly,' answered Callan.

'I'm shouting,' I said in a low tone down the ventilator, 'but the walls here are three feet thick.' (1990: 133–34)

As this passage indicates, Behan's enthusiasm for the old nationalist histrionics wanes with his dwindling devotion to the cause. Indeed, one of the most significant indicators of Behan's attitudinal change is his growing reliance on a less rhetorical, more intimate and eclectic language composed of Anglo-Saxon obscenities, prison argot and, as discussed above, Cockney slang.

Behan's religious beliefs also alter as a result of his imprisonment. At Walton, before his sentencing, Behan is excommunicated because of his IRA affiliation. It is a terrible moment for him; alone and afraid, he is denied his only emotional prop. The rest of *Borstal Boy* depicts his recovery from this bleak state. Excluded from the consolations of Catholicism, he begins a spiritual journey that culminates in his discovery of a new ecumenical faith, unfettered by the orthodoxies of conventional religion. Based on the intensities of his prison friendships, the unexpected kindnesses and deep loyalties amongst the inmates, the acts and attitudes that transcend national and sectarian differences, Behan comes to a profound acceptance of the God in mankind, a theology that ties him to no specific dogma or church. Even more, he comes to believe that the rituals of humiliation, the diminutions of life, the solitary confinement, the acute loneliness, the intimidation, deprivation and abuse routinely endured by the outcast prisoners bestow on them a special sanctity. At Hollesley Bay, the borstal of the title, with its country setting, agrarian pursuits and overtones of homosexual love, imprisonment becomes a kind of ironic pastoral. In this congenial rural atmosphere, Behan records his readiness to abandon completely the stifling categories of nationality and religion and share his mystical sense of oneness not only with the prisoners, but also with the guards.

All of the individual moments of intuitive understanding and private sympathy in Behan's borstal experience flow into the love-in at the beach at the denouement of the autobiography. Led by 538 Jones, who knows how to avoid the land mines, Charlie and several other of Behan's prison mates go surreptitiously to the beach for a swim. The sight of so much sun glittering on the water creates a sense of peace, wonder and awe so intense that the boys replace their usual verbal crudities with bursts of lyrical poetry. In this heightened mood, they spend the day in joyous celebration of their comradeship. The importance of this finely wrought scene is that it is a shared mystical moment of secular transcendence and love, the harmony of which contrasts starkly with the violence of society. After Charlie's death at sea, killed when his ship is sunk off Gibraltar by the Germans, casually noted details of social disintegration, such as the presence of Jewish refugee children at Walton or the mining of Hollesley Bay, become, in hindsight, sinister indications of the fragility of the boys' transcendent experience. Having already established the exemplary nature of the borstal community, Behan suggests in the final pages of his autobiography that the real criminals are not these boys but the outside world that tolerates the large-scale destruction of war. By the time his expulsion order arrives, Behan's paradise has already been lost, overwhelmed by the catastrophe of the Second World War.

The concluding segment of *Borstal Boy* is unmistakably elegiac. Welcoming Behan on his return to Ireland, the immigration officer asserts: ' "It must be wonderful to be free"', to which Behan sardonically responds: '"It must" (1990: 372). While the officer interprets this statement as an endorsement of his own sentiments, Behan's response carries with it the weight of his borstal experience. It is subject to the ironic implication that it was within the English penal system that he was able to free himself from the demands of Irish nationalism and the commands of Catholicism, systems of belief and affiliation that, by their exclusions and restrictions, diminished and oppressed him. Also implicit in his response is a recognition that, whatever the pleasures of homecoming, returning to Ireland after he has outgrown its political and religious preoccupations is unlikely to be an unqualifiedly wonderful experience. Behan's 'freedom' in Ireland is at least as problematic as his 'imprisonment' in England.

## Conclusion

The changes in Irish society that the autobiographical writings of Moore, Yeats, O'Casey and Behan call for have in large measure been realised in recent decades. The Ireland of today is a more heterogeneous and less repressive place than at any time in the recent past. While the achievement of such pluralism cannot be directly attributed to the works discussed here, its preservation may well depend on them. The Europeanisation of Irish society has not occurred without its critics. Social and political change frequently brings with it a nostalgia for some invented past when national identity and cultural values appeared to be stable and secure. Declan Kiberd's critical treatment of O'Casey's *The Plough and the Stars* in his highly regarded *Inventing Ireland* exemplifies this tendency at its most elegant and plausible (1995: 229). Kiberd's point – in essence a throwback to the arguments made by the Abbey rioters at the time of the play's opening in 1926 – is that O'Casey disrespects the sacrifices made by the heroes of Easter Week. The resurgence of this type of criticism reflects, I believe, an underlying unease about the waning of nationalist feeling and the transformations that Irish identity is currently undergoing. In response to Kiberd and others who share his views, R. F. Foster insists on the pluralism of Irish history and argues that there are many versions of the past, including the one embodied in Yeats's *Autobiographies*. For Foster, Yeats's autobiographical writings provide one important component in the excavation of a usable past, a means of illustrating the multiplicity of Irish experience long before the changes of recent times (Foster, 2001). It seems to me that it is not only Yeats's writing but also the literary autobiographies of Moore, O'Casey and Behan that enable the articulation of usable pasts. Certainly, with their depictions of Irish heterogeneity and their critique of hegemonic notions of Irish identity, these writers lend considerable weight to Foster's view of a complex and multifaceted 'Irish story'.

## Notes

1. On Moore, see, for example, Shumaker, 1971; Farrow, 1978. On Yeats, see Ronsley, 1968; Neuman, 1982; Wright, 1987. On O'Casey, see Lowery, 1981; Kenneally, 1988. On Behan, see Kearney, 1979; Phelps, 1979; Schrank, 1992.
2. Although it may seem from my discussion that the phrase 'Anglo-Irish Ascendancy' refers to a monolithic class with a homogenous set of beliefs, readers should be aware that there were different shades of political opinion within Ascendancy culture, from staunch unionists to liberal nationalists.
3. Moore has already had his say about racial purity in a conversation with Yeats at the dinner at the Shelbourne Hotel. When one of the speakers at that dinner proclaims the genius of the Irish race, Moore turns to Yeats and remarks that the man 'is talking nonsense. All races are the same; none much better or worse than another' (Moore, 1985: 138). The remarks of the Gaelic Leaguer needs to be read in this context. Moore's interest in his family genealogy is, as I note, tied to this recurrent theme of racial purity.
4. The programme of the Irish Literary Theatre, the precursor of the Abbey, was to foster Irish drama about Ireland. It also wished to produce plays in Irish, though this proved difficult since few of those writing for the Theatre were fluent in the language. The linguistic problem was resolved when Yeats and Synge came to appreciate the possibilities of using Irish idioms in English.
5. These first appeared individually but were later collected in the two-volume *Mirror in My House* (1956), reissued as *Autobiographies I* and *Autobiographies II* in 1963.

# 3
# 'Life Purified and Reprojected': Autobiography and the Modern Irish Novel

*Eve Patten*

## Introduction

Discussions of the autobiographical novel frequently begin with the difficulty presented by the genre's characteristic blurring of fact and fiction. For theorists who argue, somewhat wearily, that all autobiography is essentially fiction and all fiction, to some extent, autobiographical, this approach is artificial and pointless, merely leading the reader into what Paul de Man, citing Proust, describes as a *'tourniquet'* or 'whirligig' of speculation. The more significant questions, de Man claims, deal with the horizon beyond the personal: 'Since the concept of genre designates an aesthetic as well as a historical function, what is at stake is not only the distance that shelters the author of autobiography from his experience but the possible convergence of aesthetics and history' (1984: 70). De Man's assertion has a particular bearing on autobiographical fiction, which foregrounds exactly this convergence. 'Although autobiographical novelists freely plunder episodes from their past', suggests Michael Kenneally, 'their concern is with wider, suprapersonal goals which have more to do with society than individual history, with aesthetics than the self, with literature than biography' (1989: 114). To a greater extent perhaps than memoir or autobiography 'proper', therefore, the autobiographical novel negotiates the historical through its symbolic extension of the self into the social, or the personal experience into some larger political narrative. But if the resultant transcendence of an individual's real life alleviates some of the pressures on the 'truth claim' of the form, it also brings into play another 'whirligig', in the complex intersection between the process of aesthetic self-reconstruction and the shaping determinants of history.

Debates within the human sciences have repeatedly queried the nature of the relationship between autobiography and historical consciousness.[1] That relationship takes on added weight in an Irish context, given the tendency in Irish cultural and critical tradition to rely on the auto/biographical as a legitimate historical resource, a product of the close intersection between the individual and the major political events of the modern nation's evolution. Irish texts exist under constant pressure to represent at some level an evolutionary national dynamic through the lens of personal aspiration. Arguably, Irish autobiographical fiction has often had most popular appeal when deliberately constructed along these lines, as in Michael Farrell's hugely successful semi-autobiographical saga of the century, *Thy Tears Might Cease* (1963), or, more recently, Seamus Deane's masterful politicised self-portrait, *Reading in the Dark* (1996). But even if no such structure is explicit, it will invariably be read as implicit, and the individual consciousness schematised in terms of a political unconscious. The roots of this symbiosis have been traced to the close identification of self with nation at key points of historical development in Ireland. During the Irish Literary Revival and immediate post-Revival period, for example, the distinction between fact and fiction was frequently blurred as the novel was drawn into the shaping culture of a new nation conceived in deeply personal terms. At this time, James H. Murphy suggests, 'the novel was perceived to be an only semi-fictional locus both for autobiographies of the struggle with Catholic Ireland and also for testing whether various new Irelands could be brought to birth out of the expected decay of *petit bourgeois* society' (1995: 225). Autobiographical fiction joined memoir, therefore, as an instrumental medium of a developing political sensibility and mode of expression. Prior to this point, however, the fusion of self and nation had already been channelled through the discourse of nineteenth-century cultural nationalism. Taking John Mitchel's autobiographical *Jail Journal* (1854) as the cornerstone of his argument, David Lloyd has illustrated the process of conscription through which the individual came consciously to inhabit a national identity, symbolically obliterating the fissures in an existing political context and signifying the nation's imagined and holistic destiny. In these terms, he suggests, 'the total identification of the individual with the spirit of the nation is a figuration of the total unity of the political nation that is the goal of the nationalist's labors', and the nation's actual disintegration or degradation is effectively bypassed (Lloyd, 1987: 160).

While Lloyd's thesis as a whole relates to a nineteenth-century dynamic, aspects of his argument are also useful in a survey of twentieth-century Irish autobiographical writing. Of particular relevance is his adaptation of a Freudian framework to posit that a determining tension with a progenitor – real or desired – shapes the development of all autobiographical forms, fictional and non-fictional. Metaphorically, the autobiographical relationship between son and father becomes the basis for a re-construction of nationhood according to the dynamics of the Freudian 'family romance': the individual seeks to overcome an existing paternity, which is corrupted or contaminated, and to identify instead with a transcendent 'metafather', an idealised inheritance signifying continuity and self-possession. In this way, the individual subject becomes 'representative of the race itself, partaking of and reproducing both its lineage and its destiny' (Lloyd, 1987: 162–63). This pattern, Lloyd suggests, governs an autobiographical lineage extending from Wordsworth's *Prelude* (1805) to the apotheosis of the genre, James Joyce's *A Portrait of the Artist as a Young Man* (1916), a novel which foregrounds, through a contest with paternities, the difficult integration between individual imagination and the 'uncreated conscience' of the Irish race. *Portrait* fails to resolve that critical integration, and its protagonist's *'non serviam'* merely heightens, ironically, the tension in the antithesis between artist-hero and an Irish social order. At the same time, this defining text in the development of a twentieth-century Irish autobiographical aesthetic has forced its readers towards a series of generic, compositional and interpretative questions quite distinct from the issue of its 'national' profile. How does the novel, which is, after all, closer to D. H. Lawrence's *Sons and Lovers* (1913) than to *Jail Journal* and explicit about its own aesthetic methodology, engage with European literary transitions towards modernism? What is the relationship between *Portrait* and its earlier incarnation, *Stephen Hero*, written during 1904–1907? And to what extent does Joyce's chosen form of the *Künstlerroman* – the novel of the development of an artist – limit the biographical basis of the fictionalised Stephen Dedalus?

This chapter will begin by following up these questions in relation to Joyce's seminal text. It will demonstrate how the complexity surrounding the translation of the novel's autobiographical basis into fiction, and its simultaneous rupture and confirmation of a biographical referent, underlines the fact that Joyce, instead of securing a viable Irish template for the aesthetic 'autoportrait', merely queered the pitch for his successors in the *Künstlerroman* tradition. The segregation of an artistic consciousness from its social and political context remained problematic for subsequent Irish writers who struggled against the pull of a national narrative to formulate a valid artistic *apologia*. In his novel *Black List, Section H* (1971) Francis Stuart makes direct allusion to Joyce as an overture to his own strategically fractured self-depiction, a triumph of transparent and wilful self-making awkwardly imposed on the authentic material of history. Aidan Higgins, meanwhile, contrives in a succession of quasi-autobiographical novels published between 1972 and 1983 to undermine completely the deracinated Irish artist as a viable and credible textual referent. But if Joyce's artist offered a difficult model, the 'young man' of his portrait provided more security as a reference point for writers working within the tradition of the European *Bildungsroman*, the form originating in German philosophy's preoccupation with modernity and adapted from the prototype of Goethe's *Wilhelm Meister*.[2] In the context of the developing Republic, Irish *Bildungsromane* tend to parallel the adolescence of the individual with the adolescence, as it were, of the political nation as a whole. Emphasising social rather than philosophical or spiritual rites of passage, these novels frequently subvert their protagonists' route to mature social integration and chart instead their alienation from the ethical and moral foundations of the community. Personal liberation from the debilitating conditions of modern Ireland takes precedence over aesthetic self-realisation and artistic distinction. For this trajectory of Irish fiction, writes Thomas Kilroy, 'freedom [ . . . ] has a pronounced sociological stress; the emphatic burden of Irishness, and it is not just simply of the Catholic variety, is so strong that the novels tend to submerge; little space is left for exploring human development in its essence' (1985: 70).

In foregrounding youth as a symbolic state, epitomised by 'mobility and interiority' (Moretti, 1987: 4–5), the *Bildungsroman* provided an apposite means to convey the fragmentation and transition of Irish society in the middle decades of the twentieth century. While Irish autobiographical novels in this category range from the comic picaresque to the embittered and grotesque, they tend to share a dominant trope of family dysfunction which acts as a metaphor of the failure of the nation and is frequently represented in terms of a father/son struggle which updates the nineteenth-century Freudian model described by Lloyd (Grubgeld, 1997). This might suggest that the traumatic evolution of the nation is predominantly read in masculine terms, but critics have also noted the significant lineage of female *Bildungsromane* produced in the same period, which further complicates the representation of a parent culture and its dissenting offspring (St Peter, 2000: 45). In a pattern typifying the female version of the form, these novels effectively reverse the European *Bildungsroman's* momentum of integration and socialisation: the female protagonist ends up isolated from her community, insecure in her identity and alienated from her culture.

Following my discussion of Joyce's *Portrait* and the Irish *Künstlerroman*, I will survey a number of Irish *Bildungsromane* as the novels most often identified with an Irish socio-political dynamic. The 1960s emerge as a key decade of national self-analysis here, during which time the fiction of writers such as John McGahern, Edna O'Brien, Anthony C. West and Brian Moore was preoccupied with obstacles to self-realisation. At the same time, the strength of autobiographical narrative in this period sustained the register of the Irish 'self' as sign of the nation, thereby laying the basis for the strategic and post-structuralist deployment of the *Bildungsroman* in more recent writing. For the contemporary autobiographical novel, finally, the political function of self-representation is seen to have come full circle from Mitchel's *Jail Journal*, by way of Stephen Dedalus, to culminate in Seamus Deane's strategic combination of personal history and fiction, *Reading in the Dark*.

## Portraits of artists

When it first appeared in serial form in *The Egoist* in 1914, *A Portrait of the Artist as a Young Man* was considered by many readers to be a straightforward fictionalised account of its creator's own experiences from childhood to adolescence and, finally, exile. The novel's early critics, led by Harry Levin, whose *James Joyce: A Critical Introduction* was published in 1941, were largely content to treat the novel as a recognisable if unconventional *Bildungsroman*, while the substantial amount of biographical and compositional information made available by Richard Ellmann in his 1959 biography of Joyce, and by Robert Scholes and Richard Kain in *The Workshop of Dedalus* (1965), subsequently helped to confirm a close biographical identification of writer and subject. Since its initial publication, however, the interpretative density of Joyce's text has generated a different critical agenda, and theoretical approaches from post-structuralism to feminism have forced a distance between author and protagonist, rupturing the autobiographical surface of the novel with their emphasis on its discrepancies, contrivance and irony (Beja, 1973; Wollaeger, 2003). Obviously, Joyce's novel calls attention to itself as an aesthetic construction. Its titular echoes of Henry James's *Portrait of a Lady* (1881) and Oscar Wilde's *The Picture of Dorian Gray* (1891) combine with its less overt allusions to Edmund Gosse's *Father and Son* (1907) and silent if deprecating nod to George Moore's *Confessions of A Young Man* (1888) to signal its literary community. More significant is its development of the early-twentieth-century *Künstlerroman*. Commenting on autobiographical fiction of the modernist era, Susan Nalbantian explains that the *Künstlerroman* typically supplants an Augustinian narrative of religious conversion with one of conversion to art, displacing any naturalistic 'plot' of its protagonist's linear development and charting instead significant moments of interior vision or 'psychic intensity' (Nalbantian, 1997; Diment, 1994). For Joyce, such moments were characterised by the 'epiphanies' he had been collecting since 1902 – episodes or images drawn from ordinary life but manifesting some aspect of the quintessential and universal. By the time *Portrait* appeared, the Joycean epiphany had evolved into the transfiguring moments of insight or revelation Stephen experiences on his journey towards a heightened artistic consciousness. In its rendering of the commonplace into the spiritual, the epiphany paralleled the de-personalisation of the biographical subject into the disengaged and comprehensive artist.

Teasing out the actual historical referents of Joyce's *Portrait* goes against the grain of its formal architecture, therefore, and undermines the novel's distance from its autobiographical foundations. Internally, too, the text emphasises, as a guiding aesthetic, the necessary transformational processes which distinguish the material of art from the material of life. In chapter 5 Stephen memorably outlines his thesis on the hierarchical progression of artistic form, from the immediacy of lyric expression, via the brooding extensions of epic, to the distancing effects of the dramatic, in which 'the personality of the artist, at first a cry or a cadence or a mood and then a fluid and lambent narrative, finally refines itself out of existence, depersonalises itself, so to speak'. Through its protagonist's pronouncements on aesthetic theory, the work heralds its own transfigurative project: for Stephen, 'The aesthetic image in the dramatic form is life purified and reprojected from the human imagination' (Joyce, 1978: 219). In this manner, *Portrait* not only employs the techniques of transformation in its thematic reshaping of the author's background; it is in effect *about* such transformation. The description of the book's origins provided by Stanislaus Joyce, the author's brother, confirms this. Despite its closeness to life, he claims that *Portrait* 'is not an autobiography; it is an artistic creation' which emerged from Joyce's idea of how 'a man's character, like his body, develops from an embryo with constant traits'. According to Stanislaus, the accentuation and modulation of those traits in response to hereditary and environmental forces provided the core of Joyce's systematic psychological outline, while the character of Stephen supplied a model to be configured and reconfigured by the shaping consciousness of his adult self (Joyce, 1958: 39–40). Rather than claim any 'truth to life', therefore, the book highlights the gaining of an interval from the biographical self through the plasticity of art and through the filtering processes of time, reflection and maturity.

As is often noted, this aspect of *Portrait* anticipates the 'Scylla and Charibdys' chapter of *Ulysses* (1922) and the discussion that takes place between Stephen and John Eglinton in the National Library in Dublin. Here, Stephen's counter-attack on George Russell's opinion that the artist's private life – 'the poet's drinking, the poet's debts' – be kept separate from his art consists of an extended *jeu d'esprit* on the life of Shakespeare, not as historically conceived but as speculatively identified in the thematic concerns of the sonnets and plays. The exercise is ludic but the ideas expressed bear closely on Joyce's aesthetic reshaping of his own being through both text and time:

> As we, or mother Dana, weave and unweave our bodies, Stephen said, from day to day, their molecules shuttled to and fro, so does the artist weave and unweave his image. And as the mole on my right breast is where it was when I was born, though all my body has been woven of new stuff time after time, so through the ghost of the unquiet father the image of the unloving son looks forth. In the intense instant of imagination, when the mind, Shelley says, is a fading coal, that which I was is that which I am and that which in possibility I may come to be. So in the future, the sister of the past, I may see myself as I sit here now but by reflection from that which then I shall be. (Joyce, 1992: 249)

Rejecting the concept of the self as a discrete and finished entity, Stephen contemplates the artist's identity as fluid and evolutionary, capable of transfer from the physical corpus into the imaginative body of the text. This aspect of *Portrait*, picked up by *Ulysses* and the shift of emphasis from Stephen to Leopold Bloom, reinforces its proximity to a modernist enterprise and the prioritising of art over life. The old stable ego of character – even when that character is a version of the author himself – slips finally towards the vatic personality of the universal artist-martyr.

But a reading of *Portrait* as the work of a writer who was, in his brother's words, 'unhampered by the shackles of autobiography' is obviously incomplete. While the reader may be compelled by Stephen's aesthetic transformation of the material world, it is the very materiality of that world and the materiality of Stephen as a Joyce-like figure which give the book its impetus. It is also relevant, of course, that the final text is itself a filtering of previous narrative drafts. In 1904 Joyce wrote an autobiographical story entitled 'A portrait of the artist'. In 1905 he started work on a novel, *Stephen Hero*, which was significantly revised, after 1908, into the final text of *Portrait*. These revisions illuminate the particular process of evolution and transformation involved in the releasing of the artist from his real-life trappings, the two versions differing chiefly in their incorporation and exclusion, respectively, of autobiographical material. In *Stephen Hero* the Daedalus (*sic*) family is much more fully realised and the domestic set-up more clearly depicted than in *Portrait*. The earlier work also contains two elements that might have been deemed inextricable: the shocking scenes of the death and burial of Stephen's invalid sister Isabel, and the close relationship between Stephen and his brother Maurice, the character based on Stanislaus. Yet both Maurice and Isabel are effectively excised from the final version. So too are the dramatised conversations between Stephen and his mother, which, like many of the earlier text's dialogues, are pointedly replaced in *Portrait* with extensive interior monologue and Stephen's drama of interiority. As in the later novel, the protagonist of *Stephen Hero* is engaged on an aesthetic mission which overrides every other impulse: 'Stephen did not attach himself to art in any spirit of youthful dilettantism but strove to pierce to the significant heart of everything' (Joyce, 1969: 37). Yet the sense of his world is acutely real, fleshed out with details of his educational environment, the political scene and the legacy of the cultural revival, as well as his infatuation with the character named Emily Cranly, referred to more enigmatically in *Portrait* as 'E C'.

During the period of the novel's composition, Joyce's letters to Stanislaus repeatedly request information and verification, indicating the extent to which he was committed to an authentic recreation of events. Though much of this material was eventually discarded, it remains an invisible presence in the final, elliptical text, with *Stephen Hero* providing a securely autobiographical underlay to the conceptual and patterned study it predated. The allusion to the complete time span of Joyce's autobiographical compositions retained in the dateline at the end of *Portrait* – 'Dublin, 1904 Trieste, 1914' – suggests, too, that the earlier and distinctly more material drafts of his life can be understood to exist in a creative tension with the published and strategically distanced end product, just as the Joycean artist was seen to manoeuvre in a dialogical or adversarial relation to the social world itself.

*A Portrait of the Artist as a Young Man* remains in this respect an undeniably autobiographical work, while simultaneously proclaiming its own distance from autobiography. A preoccupation with real and constructed individuality, however, fails to address the question of the social and political 'self' constructed in the novel. This focus has been very much to the fore in Bakhtinian readings of the text, in which the language of the novel is marked as a dynamic *heteroglossia*, a multi-stranded weave of the popular cultural and political discourses of Edwardian Dublin (Kershner, 1989; Booker, 1995). Located within these discourses Stephen Dedalus is reduced in agency: language itself 'precedes the individual and supplies a context within which identity can be created' (Seed, 1992: 29–42). From this perspective, the 'portrait' shifts from its individual moorings and comes to represent a plurivocal society and its diverse cultural currency. Despite his aspirations towards freedom, Stephen is a public personality, a filter for communal interests and an integral, contingent figure. The effects of such critique are in some ways ambiguous, but provide the basis for a reading of Stephen as the embodiment of a social – and by extension *national* – personality. Joyce's novel is thus returned to an overarching cultural and metaphoric alliance between self and nation. Taking her lead from Bakhtin and citing Lloyd's model of the centrality of autobiographical form to cultural nationalist discourse, discussed above, Emer Nolan reads Stephen's life story as perversely mimetic of an evolving Irish national consciousness:

> While the content of his quest is in complete contrast to the aspirations of contemporary cultural nationalism – a project which was effectively dominant in the cultural milieu of Joyce's youth – none the less the aestheticist self-creation pursued by Dedalus offers a structural homology to the artistic mission to which it is ostensibly opposed. In his resolutely individualistic self-fashioning, Dedalus ironically re-enacts the self-making and self-discovery of the nationalist cultural project (1995: 38).

The dialogic quality of the text reinforces this interpretation. Stephen emerges not as a formed biographical entity but as a subject-in-process, struggling in the course of his development to maturity with a series of conflicting languages. And in his attempt to subdue or to combat these alien discourses, he effectively and ironically demonstrates 'a kinship with cultural nationalism' (1995: 46), a likeness, in effect, to the contemporaneous project of nation-forming. Stephen's biographical referent is not James Joyce, but the conflicted and evolutionary Irish nation itself.

If the complexity of readings surrounding *A Portrait of the Artist as a Young Man* highlights the pliability of this text within the competing critical contexts of modernism and literary nationalism, it also affirms the slipperiness of stylised Irish autobiographical fiction in general. The creative tensions hinted at in *Portrait* are magnified several times over, meanwhile, in the work of subsequent writers such as Francis Stuart, who similarly attempted to resolve through pattern or mythology the strained dialectic between the Irish artist and society. Stuart's *Black List, Section H* covers the turbulent first decades of the twentieth century in Ireland and describes the major events in the author's life through the persona of Luke Ruark, referred to by the narrator as 'H'. The novel includes reconstructions of Stuart's contact with Yeats and the Irish literary scene, his troubled marriage to Maud Gonne's daughter Iseult, his involvement with republican forces and subsequent internment during the Irish Civil War, and his acceptance, finally, of a university position in wartime Berlin, where he undertook anti-British propaganda broadcasts on behalf of the German authorities. Though historically specific, *Black List, Section H* is primarily intended as a portrait of an aspirant writer, tracing H's creative development and his initial forays into publication and the literary world. The frame of reference is self-consciously bookish, with descriptions of H's response to reading Tolstoy or Dostoevsky and his opinions on Lawrence or Hemingway. Joyce is a significant presence; only a few pages into the novel, the protagonist is intrigued on seeing a copy of *Portrait*, and subsequently comments on the need for Irish writers to look to Joyce's 'smoky torch' (Stuart, 1996: 177) as a beacon in the prevailing gloom of conservative Irish realism. The relationship is not straightforward, however, as H is both fascinated and repelled by his mentor: 'He felt that at the heart of Joyce was a pool of acidity in which certain fragile treasures, prized by H for their insubstantiality, were completely destroyed' (1996: 151). But Joyce, 'although too much of a meticulous little filing-clerk' (1996: 224), is nonetheless the most appropriate model available for the kind of writer H himself wishes to become, a writer who goes beyond the familiar and mundane, taking risks with the imagination and prioritising aesthetic self-creation over the demands of any social community.

Like Joyce with *Stephen Hero*, Stuart had previously drafted some of his autobiographical material in a different form. *Things to Live For* (1934), his memoir of childhood and adolescence commissioned by the publisher Jonathan Cape, gives certain leads towards an understanding of how the writer ultimately framed his own life. Predictably, there are Wordsworthian sequences dominated by the child's sensory celebration of a natural environment, followed by sections on the writer's schooldays and his passion for horse racing and gambling. But as Stuart's focus shifts to the traumatic experiences of an adult world, specifically his internment and hunger-strike during the Civil War, he expresses his need to shape events according to what he identifies as the fundamental terms of all narrative: battle, quest, romance and sacrifice. Again, like Joyce, who read Renan's *Life of Christ* while composing *Portrait*, Stuart turns for inspiration to the spiritual lives of the devotional martyrs of Catholicism – Saint Therese of Liseux, Saint Bernadette of Lourdes and Saint Catherine of Sienna – figures who provided paradigms not only of spiritual development but of alienation and self-sacrifice. These were the models mapped onto his quest for artistic fulfilment, and in *Black List, Section H* Stuart adds to them H's discovery of the Christian mystics who were celebrated for their antithetical states of mind in which 'intense emotion was joined to a daring imagination that seemed natural to him, though it was rare in contemporary literature' (1996: 127).[3]

Stuart needed some kind of fictional structure – the 'shape' his autobiographical memoir lacked – in which to review his own life. 'The worst of writing a book like this', he said of *Things to Live For*, 'is that so much has to be left unfinished. There is so little "rounding off" that I can do; it is so little like a novel' (1934: 86). But *as* a novel, *Black List, Section H* itself is structurally and stylistically idiosyncratic, the untidiness of Stuart's biographical life competing with and frequently swamping his containing narrative of artistic self-validation. Doubtless, the intrinsic historical interest of H's engagement with real people – W. B. Yeats, Liam O'Flaherty, Éamon de Valera, Michael Collins – is a factor in the way the book fails to subsume everything into its governing pattern. Beyond this, however, there are strains in Stuart's attempts to translate actual political and social events into the terms of his personal artistic agenda. The Civil War becomes an opportunity to herald H's – and his own – path of revolution, 'a private war which he hoped might cause a few cracks in the walls erected by generations of pious and patriotic Irishmen around the national consciousness' (Stuart, 1996: 80). His numerous acts of political betrayal, including an occasion on which he provides an enemy soldier with petrol for his car, are, similarly, manifestations of his artistic non-conformism, his deliberate refusal of moral and political beliefs, his purposeful self-alienation. But the superimposition of this dissenting apologia is tortured and uneasy, a contrivance which highlights the fissured nature of the book as a whole and gestures towards the implausibility of its protagonist. Where Joyce achieved a fluid transition from Stephen's outer to inner life, Stuart problematises H, drawing attention to the gap between his thoughts and actions and, indeed, to the chronological distance between protagonist and author. This heightens the reader's difficulty in distinguishing a valid narrative of artistic development from a strategic retrospective project of self-exoneration. Castigated for what were perceived as his pro-Nazi sympathies during the Second World War, Stuart uses his autobiographical novel as a first line of defence, subjecting his own recuperation of domestic, national and international events from the 1920s and 1930s to a rationale of artistic martyrdom. Hence, the reconstruction of a conversation between the young H and Yeats on the subject of Ireland's draconian censorship laws suggests the smug self-justification of Stuart as mature writer rather than the naivety of H as literary apprentice:

Yeats had lifted his head and was regarding H intently.
    'You believe that the artist is bound to be rejected? You equate him with the prophet?'
    It was costing H a lot of nervous energy to formulate concepts for Yeats to take hold of. And, apart from that, he mustn't forget he was a nobody in the literary world addressing a Nobel Prizewinner.

'A poet may escape persecution because his vision is veiled from the literary arbiters, but the novelist who speaks more plainly is bound to scandalize them.' (1996: 137–38)

Several critics have sanctioned Stuart's artistic evangelicalism and strident ratification of the writer as existential outcast (Deane, 1986: 215–17). The detail in which the novel is embedded, however, makes it difficult to release its protagonist from the implications of the author's own life. The later chapters, which deal with H's time in wartime Berlin, continue an extravagant commentary of self-validation and the result is a dramatic splicing of history and ego. Thus, autobiography fuses with rearguard tactics and the integrity of the true artist is pushed repeatedly as a cover for the failings, errors or political misalliances of the man. Stuart made no attempt to disguise this strategy, which he had initiated less explicitly in earlier works such as his 1949 novel, *Redemption*. Indeed, the autobiographical character of much of his fiction suggests that his creative oeuvre is, as a whole, a crucial means of self-management. Furthermore, *Black List, Section H* advertises its own manipulative practices through its internal narrative structure. During the course of the novel H himself is seen composing an autobiographical fiction in which the main character, 'X', must similarly bear the weight of his author's pragmatic moral and aesthetic idealism. The resultant web of fabrication is, like Stuart's stylistic awkwardness, strangely apt in a novel of hesitant sexual engagement, desultory relationships, half-hearted political activism and a wayward, itinerant personality. Overall, *Black List, Section H* might be seen to function as a form of Irish anti-narrative in which a lack of coherence and a failure of credibility undermine any possibility of reading the autobiographical subject as a representative of fluid national development. Straining at the leash of realism, Stuart's novel thwarts the autobiographical process; its fragmented and at times fabular nature project H – like Stephen Dedalus – as a confabulation and not a reflection.

A writer who similarly announces his Joycean affiliations, and whose literary territory negotiates a distinctly Joycean intersection between Ireland and continental Europe, is Aidan Higgins. Over the course of several related texts, Higgins plays with the artifice of the 'writerly' autobiographical novel. His *Scenes from a Receding Past* (1977) begins with deliberate echoes of *Portrait* in its representation of an infant's perceptions of his world, and recreates through the persona of Dan Ruttle the experiences of the author's schooldays and adolescence in Co. Sligo, up to the point of his first departure for Europe. This novel provides a prequel to Higgins's earlier, quasi-autobiographical fiction, *Balcony of Europe* (1972), which describes the death of Ruttle's mother and his subsequent love affair while living as a painter in Andalusia. The autobiographical subject is then carried over into a later epistolary novel, *Bornholm Night Ferry* (1983), a highly self-referential text in which novelist Finn Fitzgerald – yet again, a tenuous version of Higgins himself – contemplates his life and writing in an exchange of letters with his mistress. She, in turn, is reading Fitzgerald's previously published '*Bildung*' and responding to it in her replies. The allusion made at one point in the novel to the letters between 'Jams Joys and Norah Barnacle' is both calculated and predictable.

In these disparate and convoluted excursions into self-portraiture Higgins artfully frustrates not only any sense of linear autobiographical development, but also any possibility of accepting without question the fluid passage of life into literature. Again, as with Stuart, the fractured profile of his subject is compounded by a seemingly deliberate stylistic recalcitrance: the prose is impressionistic, fragmentary and frequently overblown. In Higgins's portrait of the artist, a mannered literary intensity never amounts to a credible aesthetic agenda; rather, in the words of one of his critics, 'copulation simply alternates with cogitation', and the autobiographical project is consciously sabotaged (Garfitt, 1975: 231). More to the point, the possibility of the author providing any kind of historical or social cipher is blown. The self-conscious assault on generic boundaries, meanwhile, is continued in the publication of Higgins's actual autobiography, *Donkey's Years: Memories of a Life as Story Told* (1995), which, together with its two sequels, *Dog Days* (1998) and *The Whole Hog* (2000), perversely and extravagantly presents his life story as fiction.

## The autobiographical *Bildungsroman*

In post-independence Irish fiction the aesthetic 'autoportrait' was closely tied to Joyce's model, with its links to modernism and a European literary tradition. In many ways this form sat uneasily alongside an emerging Irish society and its domestic preoccupations. Even in Joyce's own lifetime, Stephen Dedalus and his ilk had become an occasion for parody, lampooned in the priggish and bogus 'biographical reminiscences' of Flann O'Brien's undergraduate narrator in *At Swim-Two-Birds* (1939). But in a companion strand of autobiographical fiction, conventional realism was offering an alternative to Joycean modernism and Stuart's grafted experimentalism. Autobiography would have a legitimate role to play in charting the development of the modern nation, and the autobiographical novel began to project the 'self' as a recognisable social constituent. As the century unfolded, the hero of the Irish *Bildungsroman* became increasingly characterised by ordinariness not artistry, and motivated by a struggle with the social, demographic, cultural and sexual conditions of an evolving nation. Not surprisingly, the mid-twentieth-century Irish *Bildungsroman* tended to focus on the swiftly passing, emblematic world of the rural farm and the pressures of an agrarian ideology. From the early years of the new state, fiction had begun to document the transition from rural to urban community, or to express the individual's aspirations to an intellectual or political life outside the boundaries of provincial Catholic experience. Patrick Kavanagh's *The Green Fool* (1938) and his more autobiographical *Tarry Flynn* (1948), described as the 'soft' and the 'harsh' versions of a rural upbringing and adolescence, are already tinged with nostalgia for a lost idyll and framed by a metropolitan consciousness (Deane, 1986: 219). From the same period, Michael MacLaverty's eloquent *Call My Brother Back* (1939) exposes the proximity of traditional island life to the sectarianism of Belfast, while in Ben Kiely's early novel, *Land Without Stars* (1946), the protagonist abandons the religious and economic backwater of rural Tyrone for the cultural vibrancy of Dublin.

The classic Irish *Bildungsroman* was to flourish in the 1960s, however. This was a decisive period of ideological change in Ireland, when the promise of economic modernisation heralded the demise of traditionalism, together with a series of rigorous self-analyses on the failings of the existing social and educational infrastructure. Public attention turned to the question of the Irish child and the impoverished conditions of childhood in what was, theoretically, a developed nation. Welfare and legislative bodies highlighted the harsh restrictions of Irish marriage laws and the difficult living conditions experienced by the typical Irish family. At the same time, the decade provided a staging post for a cultural process of self-exposure and a stage from which Irish novelists could review, through the lens of personal experience, the problematic adolescence of the new nation. A classic example of Irish *Bildungsromane* of this period is Anthony C. West's *The Ferret Fancier* (1963). Set during the early years of the Irish Free State, the novel is often dismissed as a titillating romp through a pastoral world, filtered through the sexually charged mind of an adolescent boy. In fact, it is a precise and self-conscious novel of socialisation which focuses on its protagonist's attempts to reconcile his 'two reasonable lives', the private, imaginative one and the 'so-called social one, secular and religious, that most times contradicted if not entirely denied the warm hereditaments of the natural human heart' (West, 1983: 32). Alongside its scenes of sexual voyeurism and masturbatory games in the school privy, its autobiographical account of a boy's loss of innocence offers a series of insights into the complex world of Irish adulthood. The sexual awakening of Simon Green is shadowed by his awakening to the divisions of sect and class lying close beneath the surface of his farming community. Shocked by the impoverished circumstances of a local Catholic family, Simon recognises himself as part of a generation that would reckon with the inadequacies of the new government and its ideology. Through his metaphoric identification with his hunting ferret, meanwhile, the rural idyll which he inhabits exposes its elemental forces of sex, plunder, competition and death, and in a Lawrentian subtext the supposed sanctuary of pastoral Ireland is undermined.

Like so many autobiographical fictions of the period, *The Ferret Fancier* stresses the process of sexual initiation as both a real and a symbolic marker of transition from childhood innocence to adult responsibility. Beyond the boundaries of the immediate community, sex is posited as the ethical and social pressure point of the changing nation. This fact is dealt with more explicitly in a female version of the same process, Edna O'Brien's *The Country Girls* (1960). Written in first-person narrative, O'Brien's novel details the troubled passage to adulthood of her heroine, Cait, tracing the dissolution of her damaged family through the drowning of her mother and the accelerating drunkenness of her father, and dramatising her expulsion from the local convent with her friend Baba. The climax of the novel, however, is the departure of the two country girls for the city of Dublin, where they are exposed to a lapsed world of loose living and sexual transaction. Here, Cait's attempt to sustain her personal faith in the formulae of romantic love, invested in her fledgling affair with a manipulative married man, Mr Gentleman, is tested to breaking point and eventually shattered. With a reputation for frank sexual detail it never really deserved, even by the more conservative standards of the 1960s, O'Brien's novel has been upheld as the classic autobiographically based narrative of Irish female experience. James Cahalan remarks that 'as an Irish *Bildungsroman*, *The Country Girls* reveals secrets found nowhere in *Portrait* or other such novels' (1988: 287). In fact, the novel is more conventional than is often supposed, tracing the same transition from rural to urban life as that presented in male-authored *Bildungsromane* of the period. For Cait and Baba, Dublin turns out to be full of country*men*, who return home each summer to cut the turf. The loss of rural Ireland, meanwhile, is felt keenly even under Cait's excitement at 'the neon fairyland of Dublin', and the jaunty tone of the girls' escape is countered by their apprehensiveness about the city itself, punctuated by lyrical reminiscences of home:

> Outside in the avenue it was evening. The children were gone. The street was lonesome. A child's handkerchief blew on one of the spears of our railing. There were houses stretching across the plain of city, houses separated by church spires, or blocks of flats, ten and twenty storeys high. In the distance the mountains were a brown blur with clouds resting on them. They were not mountains really but hills. Gentle, memorable hills.
> (O'Brien, 1963: 141, 139)

*The Country Girls* splices realism and symbolism, and indeed, it is Cait's symbolic value in representing *national* as much as *sexual* innocence which it highlights. The full cultural allusiveness of her name is drawn out when Mr Gentleman looks at her 'for a long time. That look of his which was half sexual, half mystic; and then he said my name very gently. ("Caithleen") I could hear the bulrushes sighing when he said my name that way and I could hear the curlew too and all the lonesome sounds of Ireland' (1963: 174). Cait remains a potent symbol of Irish youth – male and female – in her difficult route to adulthood and freedom. In the novel's sequel, *The Lonely Girl* (1962), she leaves Ireland behind to pursue a passionate but doomed affair with an older man, and sails with Baba for Liverpool on the appropriately named *Hibernia*, a detail that obliquely signals the fact that O'Brien's autobiographical fiction pays sustained homage to Joyce, a figure frequently referred to throughout her writing.[4] Like him, O'Brien wrote from a position of exile, reflecting on an Irish upbringing after her move to London and composing *The Country Girls* from a perspective of metropolitan hindsight. The positioning is significant in terms of the trajectory of her fiction from innocence to experience. The third in the trilogy, ironically titled *Girls in Their Married Bliss* (1963) and covering the London afterlives of her heroines, shifts the narrative focus from the vulnerable Cait to the pragmatic Baba, thereby signalling the eclipse of a particular kind of idealistic Irish youth and its replacement with a soured, deracinated maturity. The comedy of the early material wanes towards bitter realism and a suicidal culmination which departs, ultimately, from autobiography into fiction proper. With this strong narrative arc, *The Country Girls* trilogy dominates a configuration of female *Bildung* novels through which the cultural and sexual ethics of the Irish nation have been systematically critiqued.

Predominantly, however, the terms of young Ireland's confrontation with its older self have been masculine, developed emblematically in autobiographical fiction through father–son conflict. According to Moretti's analysis of the *Bildungsroman*, this represents a manifestation of the defining tension in the form between self-determination and socialisation (1987: 15–17). Such tension is central to what is perhaps the most perfectly constructed Irish *Bildungsroman* of the 1960s, Brian Moore's *The Emperor of Ice-Cream* (1965), a closely autobiographical novel about a young man who comes of age in Belfast at the outbreak of the Second World War. The story outlines Gavin Clarke's alienation from the institutions of an adult world, in which his place at university, his success with his girlfriend and, crucially, his relationship with his demanding and disappointed father are each threatened by his inability to accept their terms and conditions and almost totally sabotaged by his increasing recourse to alcohol. But Gavin's route to mature adulthood is suddenly and dramatically accelerated when his job as an Air Raid Patrol warden brings him into contact with the vivid reality of human history. Following the bombing of the city by the *Luftwaffe*, he volunteers to deal with the gruesome mountain of bodies in the hospital morgue. This sobering experience becomes a determining rite of passage, giving Gavin the confidence to deal with the adult world and the insight, crucially, to meet his father on equal terms and in mutual understanding.

With its emphasis on the clash of cultural values and, frequently, the black comedy of adolescence, Moore's novel shows how the Irish *Bildungsroman* of the 1960s echoes, in many respects, the British 'Angry Young Man' genre of the same era. In Ireland, however, the pressures on the individual are undoubtedly more intense. The restrictions of a post-war class hierarchy which motivated Britain's 'angries' are compacted in the Irish novel with the dogmatism of church and state, and the forceful energies of Catholicism and nationalism emerge through the metaphoric father-figures of religious and political leadership who, within the new national order, replicate and endorse the authoritarian family patriarch. In John McGahern's *The Dark* (1965) paternal authority thus represents an overwhelming ideological compound and the vulnerability of the adolescent protagonist to sexual and physical abuse at the hands of his widower father parallels his susceptibility to the indoctrination of the priest, Father Gerald. As with Stephen Dedalus, the boy's key to liberation is his own intelligence, and his securing of a university scholarship holds out the promise of escape from the misery of his background and culture. But his self-esteem has been systematically eroded and university proves a leap too far. Having internalised the ideology passed down to him, he ends by taking the submissive route – a safe civil service position in a state company. In place of reconciliation there is the capitulation of youth, in symbolic compliance with the authoritarian structures of the nation itself.

*The Dark* is undoubtedly the most resonant Irish *Bildungsroman* for a generation caught in the ideological grip of twentieth-century Irish nation-building. While McGahern's material is essentially autobiographical, it gestures towards collective experience. This is reinforced by the novel's formal devices: the protagonist is never named and the episodic plot is alternately presented in first-, second- and third-person narrative, cutting through the limits of the autobiographical and implying a fluid, representative self. Additionally, and with great precision, McGahern embeds the individual in a broader context of social uncertainty and hesitant transition. At one stage in the novel Father Gerald, who takes on the boy as his *protégé*, attempts to convey to him his place within Irish societal development and the gradual shifts of economics and culture accompanying 40 years of freedom:

> 'Did you ever hear of the word *bourgeoisie*?'
> 'Yes, father. I did.'
> 'It comes out of French strangely enough. Most of us in Ireland will soon be that, fear of the poor-house is gone, even the life your father brought you up on won't last hardly twenty years more. A priest who ministers to the *bourgeoisie* becomes more a builder of churches, bigger and more comfortable churches, and schools, than a preacher of the Word of God.'
> (McGahern, 1977: 73–74)

This conversation is casual but deeply relevant; the exchange between boy and priest can be seen to replay – and replace – the discussion on language which takes place in *Portrait* between Stephen and the Dean of Studies. Where *Portrait* reconnoitred the warping effects of a colonial legacy on Irish culture, *The Dark* registers the ramifications of Ireland's class structure – less visible perhaps than its British counterpart but no less restrictive – and confirms its silent endorsement by a religious and cultural traditionalism against which the individual has little resistance.

So ingrained in Irish autobiographical fiction is the symbiosis of self and nation, or indeed the antithesis of self and nation, that the structures of the *Bildungsroman* are frequently carried over into fiction proper, in novels which aspire to comment in some way on the national condition. If Laurence Sterne's *Tristram Shandy* (1760–1767) initiated the conceit, Flann O'Brien's *The Hard Life* (1961) extended it into the twentieth century in a biting comic satire on Irish adolescence. In recent years, Patrick McCabe's *The Butcher Boy* (1992), set in 1950s Ireland, is an artful first-person extravaganza of individual and national psychosis, while Roddy Doyle's *A Star Called Henry* (1999) attempts a kind of 'faux' *Bildungsroman* in its historical pastiche of the events of early-twentieth-century Ireland and their intersection with the formative years of an unlikely nationalist hero, Henry Smart. Just as the demands of autobiography led to its conscription of the novel form, so has Irish fiction, in its turn, strategically and artfully appropriated the structures of biography and autobiography as pertinent narrative machinery. Any stable distinction between fiction and autobiography collapses completely, however, in Seamus Deane's 1996 novel *Reading in the Dark*. Composed in sections over ten years, the narrative covers the period of the author's childhood and adolescence in Derry, but consciously situates these in the wider time frame of Northern Ireland's post-war fragmentation and descent into violent civic disorder. While the basis for the narrative is autobiographical, it assumes a general voice, and Deane has claimed it to be the kind of story common to several families from his Derry childhood (Harte, 2000: 150). The book gains further purchase as a self-conscious literary fiction through its allusions to an Irish *Bildungsroman* tradition: the school episodes are haunted by Stephen Dedalus, the dramatic rat-catching chapter rewrites an almost identical episode from *The Ferret Fancier*, and Deane's protagonist, like the boy in *The Dark*, remains nameless throughout.

Writing on the subject of Irish autobiography in the *Field Day Anthology of Irish Writing* (1991), Deane suggested that in Ireland autobiographical events can be read as 'radical revelations of the ceaseless discovery and loss of identity and freedom, which is one of the obsessive markers of cultures that have been compelled to inquire into the legitimacy of their own existence by the presence of another culture that is forever foreign and forever intimate' (1991: 380).[5] For this author, then, autobiography is implicitly political and the writing of the self a means of forcefully confronting the other which has shaped that self and brought about its losses. The novel's protagonist – nameless, fragmented, subordinated – is thus translated into a paradigm of a colonised community and his childhood and adolescence located within the context of a constitutional deficit or fracture. Liam Harte has shown how Deane's novel is shaped as a mystery story of repression, silence and interrogation, in which the central character confronts the conflicting languages of his environment, struggling for self-articulation and determining to 'read through' the obscurities of his political and historical reality (2000: 152–62).[6]

Like Stephen Dedalus, Deane's autobiographical subject evolves as a result of his contest with competing discourses, ultimately moving towards the goal of a secure and independent self-articulation. In the shift from Joyce's Dublin to Deane's Derry, finally, the postcolonial *and* national subtexts shadowing the representation of the Irish self in the twentieth century are brought, geographically and politically, to their most prominent point of visibility.

Are we so certain, asks Paul de Man, that autobiography depends on reference?:

> We assume that life produces the autobiography as an act produces its consequences, but can we not suggest, with equal justice, that the autobiographical project may itself produce and determine the life and that whatever the writer does is in fact governed by the technical demands of self-portraiture and thus determined, in all in aspects, by the resources of his medium? (de Man, 1984: 69)

As a fictional text which purposefully assumes the tropes of autobiography, *Reading in the Dark* answers this question in a most dramatic and convincing form. The events of an individual life are made fully compliant with the demands of a political narrative and the structure of the autobiographical *Bildungsroman* provides the terms in which that narrative finds imaginative expression. Deane's novel simply exaggerates, however, the tendency of autobiographical fiction generally to determine the life through the structure of the novel and the tendency of Irish autobiographical fiction in particular to refer, through the self, to a national or political metanarrative. Twentieth-century Irish writers have not failed to recognise the extent to which the autobiographical novel re-presents individuality in communal and symbolic terms. The Joycean *Künstlerroman* may foreground the artist's willed detachment from society, but it ultimately underscores, even if by default, the strong pull of social discourse. The Irish *Bildungsroman* has capitalised, meanwhile, on its implicit symbolic trajectory, from dysfunctional family via dysfunctional community towards dysfunctional nationhood. The result is a tradition which reinforces a cultural identification of self and nation. Beyond the personal horizon, aesthetics and history do converge, as Paul de Man suggests, and the Irish autobiographical novel operates strategically and self-consciously at the point of their intersection.

## Notes

1. Laura Marcus (1994) traces philosophical discussions of the intersection of auto-biography and history from William Dilthey to Christopher Lasch. See also the introduction to Olney, 1980.
2. Franco Moretti (1987) documents the development of the European *Bildungsroman*, tracing the form as a synthesis of *Entwicklungsroman* (novel of individual develop-ment) and *Erziehungsroman* (novel of education).

3. Stuart visited Lourdes several times and published a book, *Mystics and Mysticism*, on this subject in 1929.
4. O'Brien has produced a 1999 critical study entitled *James Joyce*. In *The Country Girls* Baba advises Cait: 'Will you for Chrisake stop asking fellas if they read James Joyce's *Dubliners*? They're not interested. They're out for a night. Eat and drink all you can and leave James Joyce to blow his own trumpet' (1963: 159).
5. Deane continues with some illuminating comments on Louis MacNeice: 'He understood the personal in terms provided by the culture and then reconverted the cultural back into the personal' (1991: 383).
6. See also Gerry Smyth's (2001) discussion of autobiography and Deane's novel.

# 4
## Pilgrimage to the Self: Autobiographies of Twentieth-Century Irish Women

*Taura S. Napier*

## I

For millennia, well-known and uniquely talented women have negotiated linguistic paths through the social constructs of gender which surround them. It has been the female writer's conundrum to determine the manner in which she speaks of her own life in a world where all 'dignified' available narrative methods are based on male experience. Her enterprise has been to write as an artist, philosopher, politician or religious without apologising for being female, obscuring her gender to the detriment of an authentic self-narrative, or absorbing male language and narrative strategies to the point that her voice becomes either male or androgynous. The Irish female autobiographers examined in this chapter had in most cases achieved public literary status before they engaged in life writing. So having approached the 'master narrative' of the *littérateur* early in their careers, they were already experienced negotiators of dominant narrative paradigms when they became autobiographers. Their writings form a continuum of Irish women's literature from the late nineteenth to the late twentieth century, and their critical reception shows how theories of autobiography have progressed with the development of the genre. Autobiography, indeed, seems particularly susceptible to the influence of criticism, as theoretical texts influence autobiographers and critics alike. Examples of this influence pervade the life narratives of women; in the very act of self-writing, they tend to deny that autobiography is their objective, since for women the genre is often associated with exposés, 'true confessions' and other 'non-literary' forms.

A useful theoretical model that has particular resonance for the self-narratives of Irish women is the deflected autobiography, a narrative mode in which the protagonist is ever present yet not apparently central, where the author resists being identified as the heroine of her own work. The autobiographical 'I' of Irish women characteristically pre-empts accusations of arrogance and self-centredness by privileging the journeys of others in articulating the self. In the deflected self-narrative, the written life is expressed both in the texts themselves and in what they obscure or exclude. If the auto-biographer is not immediately present in her work, her narrative persona appears in the space created by her absence and in the prismatic versions of self that are her envisioned others. Through this method, essential aspects of the self are dispersed among the *dramatis personae* whom the author encoun-ters. By doing this she avoids the censure that may result from imputations of self-aggrandisement, while nevertheless displaying those aspects of her personality that separate her from other figures in her narrative. She herself remains off to one side, never far from those qualities that she has ascribed to others, and which are in fact her own, yet never openly admitting that she is the *doppelgänger* of her most prominent others. Many of these altern-ative personae serve as negative qualifiers for the female autobiographer; she employs descriptions of them to show either what she is not and why this is fortunate, or what she is through a larger-than-life portrayal of a char-acter emotionally proximal to her. In the deflected autobiographies discussed here, strong and positively portrayed characters neither strive against nor stand in for the narrator; rather, their portrayal underscores what the writer herself wants the reader to witness as a feature of her own life.

In a 1981 article on Irish literary autobiography Kevin Reilly claimed: 'The reasons for writing autobiography manifest the human impulse to under-stand the self and to have the self accepted by otherness' (1981: 80). Because his primary concern is the Irish male autobiographical tradition, Reilly's other is the Irish goddess figure, who serves as both muse and intimate observer of the autobiographical act. However, when Irish women autobio-graphers employ the other, it is usually in the form of actual persons. The female muse, long the province of male writers, is rejected as a catalyst, as are the legendary female figures of Cathleen ní Houlihan, Dark Rosaleen and the various incarnations of the Poor Old Woman. Consequently, there is no supernormal, aestheticised female object to legitimate writing, not even a mother, as is the case with many Irish male autobiographers. Instead, the narrative is populated with actual subjects equal in power and limitation of viewpoint to the autobiographer herself. The community of voices that results from this pluralising infuses the autobiographer's single subjectivity with alternative, often opposing, possibilities. Ten years after O'Reilly, Seamus Deane also identified the other as a narrative device common to Irish autobiographers, but argued that the idea of otherness arises not from the autobiographer's dispossession within his own culture, but as a result of an outside, colonial force:

> Events such as the Easter Rising, the Civil War, the Northern crisis, are read [ . . . ] as bright moments of liberation that have within them the darker moments of oppression, radical revelations of the ceaseless discovery and loss of identity and freedom, which is one of the obsessive marks of

cultures that have been compelled to inquire into the legitimacy of their own existence by the presence of another culture that is forever foreign and forever intimate (1991: 380).

This is demonstrably *not* the case with Irish women autobiographers. In connecting their lives with those of other persons, they show that the colonial culture is not the only one that must be surmounted in order for them to speak. Their practice of interweaving the stories of others within their own narratives suggests their awareness that they are outside the realm of the Irish literary establishment, and so must engender a network by which they are legitimised as individual women, rather than retreat into a solipsistic sphere, away from either 'hostile' or 'liberating' forces.

Irish women autobiographers typically use the trope of the other in two ways. The first, as already suggested, entails deflecting the narrative focus away from themselves onto another person or persons in order to present their lives without censure and with a greater degree of self-honesty than might otherwise be possible. The second – which, incidentally, is also a feature of Irish male autobiography – involves the creation of an imaginary other, a serviceable double through which aspects of experience that are born of fear and desire, and are usually sequestered in the imagination, may be expressed.[1] Historically, significantly fewer women than men have employed this device, a fact that may be due to their 'double bind' of living under a colonial power and within a patriarchal society. In what follows, I examine how five prominent writers – Lady Augusta Gregory, Katharine Tynan, Elizabeth Bowen, Kate O'Brien and Eavan Boland – demonstrate the usefulness of the deflected autobiographical self in articulating the creative impetus alongside the traditional obligations of the female autobiographer. In each case, narratives of family, social class and community are interspersed with assessments of the Irish nation and the individual woman's place within it, so that the female autobiographer's life is refracted through her often paradoxical identities as private citizen, public artist, professional writer and representative chronicler of her socio-cultural milieu. In *The Tradition of Women's Autobiography* Estelle Jelinek depicts female life writing as embodying 'disjunctive narratives, replete with anecdotes, digressions, flashbacks, and inserted material such as letters and literary samples' (1986: 188). All such discursive elements are present in the work of the women writers discussed here and, taken together, suggest a unified purpose: to harmonise the artistic vision with the autobiographical voice, blending candour and integrity with good storytelling, while disarming critics of the female writer's significance with engaging literary narratives.

## II

Lady Augusta Gregory (1852–1932) was an artist of intriguing and rather startling paradoxes. She devoutly adhered to her Protestant upbringing yet despised the clergy, causing W. B. Yeats to complain in a letter to Olivia Shakespear: 'she hates all clergy though she never misses church and is a great reader of her bible and, as she believes, very orthodox' (quoted in Kohfeldt, 1984: 278). She modestly maintained that she began writing plays to provide an alternative to Yeats's material, yet heroically announced to reporters who asked how she had become identified with the theatre movement: 'I didn't become identified. Mr. Yeats and I started it. We *were* the movement' (quoted in Kohfeldt, 1984: 234). In *Our Irish Theatre: A Chapter of Autobiography* (1913), the self-narrative in which her position as subject and narrator is most exclusively central, she begins three chapters (1, 2 and 5) with addresses to her grandson, Richard Gregory, explaining how the theatre often kept her away from him as he was growing up, and asking his forgiveness and approval as the male representative of the family. Yet at a time when moralism and the control of sexuality, especially that of women, were at their apex, Lady Gregory had two affairs. One occurred early in her marriage with a neighbouring landlord, Wilfrid Scawen Blunt, who was later jailed for taking part in a tenants' insurrection; the other was with John Quinn, a self-made American businessman and art collector, when she was a 60-year-old widow. In the midst of these seeming paradoxes, she faced the challenge of writing about them, and about herself, with coherence, historical accuracy (a particular obsession of hers), self-honesty and discretion. The way that she negotiated these extremes constitutes one of the centrally defining features of her autobiographical persona.

Lady Gregory's use of different voices in *Our Irish Theatre* provides an example of her conventional autobiographical style. Here the autobiographical 'I' is sometimes deferential and motherly, particularly in passages addressed to her grandson. But when she begins speaking of her creative development as a playwright, her narrative voice begins to exhibit the authority she represented within the Abbey. Recalling her shift from comedies to historical drama, she explains:

> Perhaps I ought to have written nothing but these short plays, but desire for experiment is like fire in the blood, and I had had from the beginning a vision of historical plays being sent by us through all the counties of Ireland. [ . . . ] I began with the daring and light-heartedness of a schoolboy to write a tragedy in three acts upon a great personality, Brian the High King. I made many bad beginnings, and if I had listened to Mr. Yeats's advice I should have given it up, but I began again and again till it [*Kincora*] was at last moulded in at least a possible shape. It went well with our audience. There was enthusiasm for it, being the first history play we had produced. (Gregory, 1972: 57–58)

Similarly, in *Coole* (1931) her voice, although somewhat muted, remains that of heroine and artistic champion. She begins the autobiography with

Yeats's 'Coole Park, 1929' and goes on to interweave her personal biography with the history of the estate on which she spent her adult life. Like the Abbey Theatre in which she continued to ground her identity, she employs her house and garden as others upon which to deflect her self-narrative. Elizabeth Grubgeld describes this volume as 'an interaction between her body and the body of her house [...]. The close identity between her being and that of the house presses her own story into the apocalyptic mode in which her friend W. B. Yeats openly cast it' (1997: 138). Gregory ends the work with a catalogue of the company she now keeps: the 'woodpigeons assembling in the trees that overtop the grey wall', the 'nectarine-thieving rats', the weasels, wild ducks and pheasants:

> And as I sit here in the winter time or rough autumn weather I sometimes hear the call of wild geese and see them flying high in the air, towards the sea [...]. I have gone far out in the world, east and west in my time, and so the peace within these enclosing walls is fitting for the evening of my days. (1931: 50)

Because of her multiple roles within the Irish cultural revival – playwright, poet, translator, folklore collector, theatre director – Gregory could speak securely from the standpoint of a mythmaker, producing a narrative that reflects her diversity of artistic energy and vision. But while this aspect of her style is important, it is not the sole component of her autobiographical voice, nor is it intrinsic to its origins. Sometime between her marriage to Sir William Gregory in 1880 and his departure for Ceylon in 1883 to take up the post of governor, Gregory began writing what she cryptically titled 'An Emigrant's Notebook'.[2] She was at the time in her late twenties, a young enough age to turn to autobiography. Yet what she produced is an exemplary work of memory, portraiture and life made poetic, while remaining rooted in self-honesty and the desire for truth. Although it remains unpublished and has received little critical attention, this, the earliest of her literary autobiographies, provided the foundation for much of the later work for which she is best known. The 'Notebook' includes no letters or biographical material as do Gregory's other autobiographies and some of her journal entries, but instead presents a series of portraits of acquaintances and places where she has lived. Like her other self-narratives, it eschews an extravagantly egotistical style, yet it is arguably the most purely autobiographical work she produced. However, the seemingly descriptive title – the second section records her stays in Italy, France and Egypt before her marriage – may also be read metaphorically, suggesting a permanent emigration of the self from the place and time that figure in the narrative. James Pethica makes the additional argument that the 'Notebook' was begun almost immediately after her affair with Blunt and that its title connotes a psychological and sexual departure from her former self (1987: 72). Elizabeth Coxhead maintains that the presence of an alternative ending in the third and last volume indicates that it was written with a view to publication, an idea that is borne out by the second volume of her diaries in the New York Public Library's Berg Collection, which seems to be a precursory version of the work.[3] She wrote this volume, she explains, 'trusting that there will be some few who will be glad to hear of an Ireland neither all rollicking nor all bloodstained – to hear of some Irish people possessing feelings like ourselves I give these leaves to the publishers'.[4] As Coxhead affirms, the characters evoked in the 'Notebook' prefigure those in her subsequent plays: 'When she does become a professional writer, this is the writer she will be, this is the material she will use. She has found it before her meeting with Yeats and Hyde' (1961: 32).

Whereas in *Our Irish Theatre* Gregory's story is so inextricably woven with that of the Abbey that her history of it effectively embodies her own self-narrative during this period, 'An Emigrant's Notebook' is intended solely as an elucidation of her personal history. Near the end of the first volume she explains: 'It was [...] in consequence of finding all so changed within the last year or two that I wrote down these recollections [...] of the time when we loved our people and they loved us.' Here she writes for the sake of the narrative itself, not for relatives or descendants, as she does in *Our Irish Theatre* and, to a lesser extent, in *Seventy Years* (1974), her final autobiography. In general, she voices her opinions of family members obliquely in the 'Notebook'. Her mother is referred to as 'the Mistress', her father as 'the Master', and her older brother Richard, with whose care she was entrusted in her mid-twenties, as 'my invalid'. While the descriptions register no overt resentment, they do express a profound sense of distance and alienation from her family. There are few overt references to the proselytising activities of her mother and sisters and more humorous anecdotes focusing on members of the community. Conversely, she speaks more openly of her younger self and includes more stories of her mother in *Seventy Years*.[5] The fact that Gregory ultimately returns to the more discreet style employed in the 'Notebook' to deal with family members in *Seventy Years* attests to her intention to publish her earlier self-narrative, an important consideration in the light of her unwillingness to publish *Seventy Years* during her lifetime. Indeed, it is arguable that the latter, which was discovered among family papers some 40 years after her death, is no more or less a component of her published literary autobiographies than 'An Emigrant's Notebook', as she intended to have both published but never did.

Of the five autobiographers considered in this chapter, Lady Gregory is perhaps the most compelling negotiator of prevailing social and cultural *mores*. By interweaving the personal, the public and the philosophical dimensions of her experience, she moulds her autobiographical narratives to capture the subtle contours of diverse spheres: her family's character; the iconic living space of her estate; her administrative and creative contribution to the Abbey Theatre; her roles as sister, mother, friend and daughter of Anglo-Ireland. Although wholly different in outlook and beliefs, Katharine Tynan (1861–1931) shared with Gregory and with Yeats, her childhood friend, a desire to produce literature for an Ireland undergoing far-reaching change, and to further effect this change through her writings. But whereas Yeats responded with art that deepened the fears of those opposed to artistic revolution, ambushing bourgeois sensibilities and denigrating the 'Paudeen and Bridget' Irish merchant classes, Tynan's works assuaged those fears, catering to her audience with great effectiveness and winning popular and critical praise. She received particularly strong approval from religious magazines such as the *Catholic Monthly* for her devotional pieces, until her support for Parnell became widely known. During the scandal over the Irish leader's relations with Katherine O'Shea, Tynan refused to renounce her loyalty either to Parnell or to the Catholic church, much as she resolved not to relinquish her love of England or Ireland in spite of their political animosities. These divided loyalties seem to have strengthened Tynan's readership, and because she 'measured only the golden hours' (Tynan, 1922: 27), she was favoured by politically neutral readers as well as by those with strong allegiances.

In her self-writings Tynan evokes certain ordinary moments with powerful realistic precision. In *Twenty-Five Years* (1913), for example, she describes the sitting room that her father furnished for her with such vividness that its atmosphere can be experienced authentically: 'The drawing-room at my old home [ . . . ] was always filled with a dim green light from the creepers about the windows and the little half-glass door which led into the garden under an arch of boughs' (1913: 141). She gives equal attention to Ireland's grief at the death of Parnell and her own despair at the near-death of her young son, weaving together these events by her own unwavering narrative presence. She is also particularly perceptive when writing of her friendships and the personalities of those around her, and in this regard is similar to other Irish female autobiographers. Tynan gives primary narrative space to herself and her father; after these come figures such as Yeats, Christina Rossetti, Lady Wilde and her fellow poets. But of her mother and siblings there is little mention. In *Twenty-Five Years* she writes of her childhood home that 'baby succeeded baby until we were eleven living', and a few pages later recalls her mother for the first and last time: 'My mother was a large, placid, fair woman, who became an invalid at an early age and influenced my life scarcely at all' (1913: 23, 27). After this, Tynan's mother is discarded as an autobiographical subject. She reappears just once, in *Memories* (1924), as part of the portrait of her father, of whom she tellingly writes: 'I can see him taking the place my mother might have taken if he were less dominant and she another type of woman [ . . . ]. She counts for no more in my life than if she had been a person in a book' (1924: 389–90).

Where Tynan differs from other early-twentieth-century Irish women autobiographers is in her inclusion of quotidian details as they bear directly upon her life and work. In this regard she is closer to Jean-Jacques Rousseau and her compatriot Liam O'Flaherty, whose self-absorption defines their autobiographical personae. She frequently incorporates little-known personalities into her work to bring their unrecognised potential to the reader's attention, and illuminates careers interrupted by death or illness, even as she makes it clear that it is only she who can do this, by virtue of her having both the time and the generosity. In *Twenty-Five Years*, for example, Tynan memorialises the obscure figure of Cassie O'Hara, a young poet disfigured by lupus, expressing the wish that through her portrait she may be remembered:

> Everyone fretted to think of how she would face the world terribly disfigured, and she but in her early twenties. God opened a door. There was a tercentenary or some such occasion of St. Teresa. The Spanish Carmelites, among other celebrations, offered a large sum of money for a prize poem on St. Teresa. Cassie O'Hara's poem was adjudged the best. Through this they offered her admission to the Order [ . . . ]. As Sister Teresa of Jesus, Cassie O'Hara disappeared most happily into the life where she need never meet the eyes, the shrinking of her fellow creatures. (1913: 113–14)

Cassie's memorial, a consummate Victorian Gothic *vanitas* melding beauty, disease and piety, not only draws the reader's attention to Tynan's self-advertised compassion, but also shows that for her, such accreditation is inseparable from the genuine desire to immortalise those she admired.

Yet while Tynan's works embody the traditions of women's autobiography discussed above, they also depart from them in significant ways. There are, for example, signs of cyclical and discursive elements in her anecdotes and a perpetual psychological return to her father's doting and indulgence, as well as extensive use of letters and literary fragments. But the autobiographical self is essentially egocentric; the text revolves solely around Tynan. Yeats's letters, for example, are cited only for their approbatory comments on her writing or their friendship. Her autobiographical honesty is nevertheless revelatory and almost confessional, as if by showing the reader her less admirable traits she is creating alternative versions of her personality for comparison and judgement. In *The Middle Years* (1917), for example, she recalls her editorship of the 'Autolycus' column of the *Pall Mall Gazette*. Her pride in securing this prestigious and well-salaried post is offset by her admission that she drew on her neighbours' lives for journalistic copy and then 'lived in dread and terror' of being found out: 'For several days I did not meet anyone of the Family Next Door. As they went to and fro I used to peep at them from behind my window curtain, wondering if they *knew*. I was a sad coward in those days – made so doubtless by the unpleasantness of my Irish friends and neighbours when they were written about' (1917a: 151, original emphasis). Similarly, in *The Years of the Shadow* she candidly admits that she wrote 11 articles on the 1914 Women's Congress in Rome without attending its sessions, yet expects her 'eyewitness' accounts to be taken seriously. Tynan presents such artistic idiosyncrasy obliquely in terms of her nearsightedness, which she rationalises as a function of her aesthetic vision in 'The Purblind Praises the Lord': 'I miss the common and the dull,/The small details of things,/And only keep the beautiful,/The stars, the flowers, the wings' (1917b: 14). Yet in her autobiographies the 'small details of things' are precisely what Tynan does *not* miss, and 'the common and the dull' surface alongside them to produce an extensive but ultimately incomplete characterisation of self.

Karl Weintraub writes of 'the naïve individuality' (1978: 140) of Benvenuto Cellini, whose autobiographical persona shares remarkable similarities with that of Katharine Tynan. Like Cellini, Tynan is not in search of herself in her autobiography and like him, she is also quick to accentuate her successes and bolster them with statements from her admirers, while at the same time ingenuously illuminating her shortcomings. And while she registers changes in others throughout her six volumes of autobiography, she does not present herself as a historically developing self. Thus, the narrative desire to reach understanding by tracing the gradual growth of the self does not function as a key to Tynan's autobiographies. As non-interpretive self-narrators, both she and Cellini forfeit the artistically propitious device of complex personal interpretation, yet because of this they are able to function more clearly as storytellers. Self-obscurity is impossible in the unexamined life; the full complement of the lived life is ascertainable in the written one, and the story grows richer through the teller's unselfconsciousness.

Unlike Lady Gregory and Katharine Tynan, Elizabeth Bowen's (1899–1973) life experiences cannot be apprehended solely through her declared works of autobiography, which are made up of the companion-pieces *Bowen's Court* (1942) and *Seven Winters* (1943), *A Time in Rome* (1960) and the posthumously published *Pictures and Conversations* (1975). Taken together, these volumes provide an account of her life as writer and 'enjoyer', as she described herself. But because she was first and foremost a fiction writer, her novels and short stories also comprise varieties of autobiographical revelation. Indeed, as befits a writer who was an avid enthusiast of detective stories, Bowen leaves subtle clues to the placement of her autobiographical self throughout her fictional narratives.[6] *The Last September* (1929), her acclaimed novel about the demise of the Ascendancy class in Ireland, is perhaps the best known example of this. Bowen said that the work had 'a deep, clouded, spontaneous source' in that Lois, the protagonist, 'derives from' her 19-year-old self (1962: 99–100). Certain of her attributes and mannerisms reflect those Bowen saw in herself at this age, such as displays of 'unfathomable silliness' and a feeling of 'distinct pride at having grown up at all, which seemed an achievement like marriage or fame' (1950: 188). The correlation between heroine and author is further underlined by comments she made regarding the fictional Danielstown House and its relation to Bowen's Court, her ancestral Cork home: 'I *was* the child of the house from which Daniel-stown derives. Bowen's Court survived – nevertheless, so often in my mind's eye did I see it burning that the terrible last event in *The Last September* is more real than anything I have lived through' (1962: 100, original emphasis).[7]

Throughout her life, Bowen's Court remained her haven, a quiet 'green retreat' much like the literary salon Tynan's father provided for her, a space conducive to creation which embodied a vision of 'peace at its most ecstatic': 'I suppose that everyone, fighting or just enduring, carried within him one private image, one peaceful scene. Mine was Bowen's Court. War made me that image out of a house built of anxious history' (1999: 457). In addition to providing her with an image of idealised history, the house also gave her a framework around which to recreate the lives of her ancestors. In her fiction Bowen was most fond of the male cad, whom she juxtaposed with male characters who are either 'cold fish' or 'born uncles', and women who are either innocent to the point of oblivion or irretrievably depraved. As her biographer points out, the cad figure was clearly an extension of Bowen's own character; his outlandish bad behaviour was only permissible because he was a gentleman, reflecting the author's own aristocratic ideals (Glendinning, 1977: 126). The description of her first ancestor in Ireland demonstrates this. In tracing her Welsh ancestry, Bowen fixes on the figure of Colonel Henry Bowen, a member of Cromwell's army and founder of the Bowen's Court family in Ireland. The Colonel, who scorned Cromwellian abstemiousness and military camaraderie, is compared to 'a bad boy at a "good" school', thereby identifying him as her preferred hero, the noble cad (Bowen, 1999: 67). Her fascination for this distant colonial ancestor also brought her mythopoeic autobiographical tendencies to the fore. Colonel Bowen evidently loved the sport of hawking, so much so that on coming into possession of his Cork lands he took a hawk as his crest, a story which, despite its unverifiability, beguiled Elizabeth:

> The tale – it is more than a legend – of the Bowen Hawk [...] gathers force in the telling, and though I cannot find it written down anywhere it is the last story I would ever doubt – it has a psychological, if not a strictly historical, likeliness. Like all stories retold with gusto, it has its variations: every Bowen tells it as seems to him or her best. I will give the version that most appeals to me. (1999: 67)

As the writer herself was the first to admit, she did not deliberately try to infuse her writings with critical commentary, except in retrospect. It is therefore all the more interesting that in recalling her family's history she also articulates a description of her autobiographical method – 'the version that most appeals to me' – that entails moulding history and legend into a more pleasing pattern. Thus, she seizes upon the more vivid of the two versions of the story of how the Colonel came by his Cromwellian bequest, preferring to believe that, having first incurred the Protector's wrath by his 'ungodly and frivolous' interest in hawks, he was later pardoned and granted as much land as his hawk could fly over. While acknowledging that the story 'has been a little upset' by what she later learned about hawks' propensity for vertical rather than linear flight, she refuses to allow this to interfere with her novelistic exploitation of the narrative possibilities of the tale:

> I can only suggest that *his* hawk was a mythological bird, made free of every power and property; or else, that his hawk was his familiar [...] and that he murmured something close to its sleek head; upon which the released hawk, loyal, broke with its usual motion and made off in a long cross-country flight with the humdrum, unflagging patience of a carrier pigeon. (1999: 68, original emphasis)

Given the opportunity, Bowen clearly felt at her interpretive leisure to contribute her own brand of historiography to *Bowen's Court*. This included fiction as well as intimations of the mystical and supernatural which later informed her ghost stories, but which in this work are manifested in a purely speculative form that connects historiography, mythology and storytelling. John Dorst, in a study of autoethnography in the late twentieth century, characterises the ethnographic, culturally preservationist impulse as the will 'to concretize, to specify, to go and look, to record and gather, to mark the Site' (1989: 206). Read in these terms, *Bowen's Court* is more than just an account of a family home or a peaceful retreat. It is also an ethnographic site replete with quaint 'souvenirs': the family, their stories and the myriad *accoutrements* of the Big House tradition in Ireland. As a souvenir of her own cultural history, Bowen is simultaneously inclined to restore and deconstruct 'a conservative idealization of the past' (Dorst, 1989: 208) through the book's numerous photographs: of the kitchen, with Bowen in a tweed suit chatting with the cook and a housemaid; of the parties, literary and otherwise, that she gave; of the annual hunt; of the grand ballrooms. Like Lady Gregory's Coole Park, the house is crucially positioned within its owner's narrative; its destruction in 1959 has hardly lessened its power as a permanent feature of the Irish cultural imagination. Tourists still frequent it as an ethnographic site, just as they do the Coole demesne and Lissadell House in Sligo, former home of Constance and Eva Gore-Booth, and its moment is made permanent as much by Bowen's honesty regarding the Anglo-Irish Ascendancy as by the vision of her home as a 'picture of peace' (1999: 457).

Whereas the autobiographical nature of *Bowen's Court* must be extrapolated from the genealogical and historiographical material, *Seven Winters* is a more conventional memoir in which Bowen evokes her early Dublin childhood. But this short work is also a family history, the continuing story of the Bowens as they leave their ancestral estate and begin to move into a world in which they are not solely extensions of their demesne. Bowen illustrates this by paying particular attention to her Dublin surroundings, which is both in keeping with her professed adherence to places rather than people and an indication that she has become a child not merely of the Ascendancy but of urban Ireland: 'I find myself writing now of visual rather than social memories. On the whole, it is things and places rather than people that detach themselves from the stuff of my dream' (1999: 470). The book embodies a dialogue between self and city, filtered through a child's consciousness, and informed by Bowen's incipient sense of the limitations imposed by her social class and cultural identity. Throughout, streets and buildings are ascribed human traits and personalities, sometimes leading to a blurring of the narrator's subjective and objective realities: 'The neighbourhood seemed infused with a temper or temperament of its own, and my spirits, on morning or afternoon walks, corresponded with this in their rise and fall' (1999: 492). Stylistically, Bowen employs a *métissage* of history, documentary and creative prose to express her status as both outsider and native.[8] Though full comprehension of her cultural ambivalence was still some years away, she effectively evokes her early awareness of Catholics as ' "the others", whose world lay alongside ours but never touched', and whom she regarded with 'an almost sexual shyness' (1999: 508). In addition to the permanence of place that Bowen finds in Dublin, there is the conviction that the city is a model, a whole that is unassailable, 'of which there were imitations scattered over the world' (1999: 474). This view also informs her childhood perception of her native country: though raised Protestant and Unionist, Bowen found in Ireland a sovereign, universal model for other island nations. Indeed, her early misunderstanding of the phonetic differences between 'Ireland' and 'island' led her to believe that they were synonymous, and therefore to consider her country a prototype from which all other lands surrounded by water derived their generic name:

> It seemed fine to live in a country that was a prototype. England, for instance, was 'an ireland' (or, a sub-Ireland) – an imitation. Then I learned that England was not even 'an ireland,' having failed to detach herself from the flanks of Scotland and Wales. Vaguely, as a Unionist child, I conceived that our politeness to England must be a form of pity. (1999: 474, original emphasis)

*Pictures and Conversations*, Bowen's final autobiographical work, contains observations of herself as a developing and as a mature writer, while also placing people and events within the framework of her literary career. The autobiographical 'I', while present, is not teleological; rather, her imaginative growth is presented as a continuing process that occurs independently of any conscious desire for fame. As Howard Moss wrote in the *New York Times Book Review* shortly after her death: 'She was more generous than can be imagined and had no sense of the "strategy" of literary careers or the dark scrimmage of "reputations." She had so much intrinsic power that I don't think the idea of acquiring any ever crossed her mind' (quoted in Bowen, 1975: xiii). Her death occurred before she could properly speculate on how being a writer may have influenced her technique as an autobiographer, consigning to the unknown her theories on her own self-writing. Yet in 'People', the final completed section of the work, Bowen wonders if her tendency to fictionalise real people may have impeded her potential as an autobiographer:

> But I ask myself, could those early dodges of mine queer the pitch for me as an autobiographer? What *was*, as opposed to what I chose to imagine, is what I want to unearth [ . . . ]. To the fraction of the past that is in my keeping, I should like to give the sobriety of history: facts, events, circumstances demand to be accurately recorded: that is my aim. But, people? – the denizens of those times and places? With people, the impossibility of 'accuracy' begins. Those I have lived among and therefore know to have lived, after all and by the end of it all, what were they? [ . . . ] Gone they remain – elusive as ever. (1975: 59, original emphasis)

Certainly, Bowen can be identified through her novels and short stories, as well as through her critical articles. But without self-articulation her own thoughts on the variety of her identities would be unavailable and interpretation would be left entirely to others. In writing her autobiographical essays, travelogues, family histories and childhood impressions, she sought a means of self-identification, in order that her vicarious fictive and nonfiction selves would coalesce into an immortal identity that would satisfy both her and her readers. As a self-created landmark, she positions herself permanently within the literary moment that defines and is defined by her.

Throughout her life, the chief focus of Kate O'Brien's (1897–1974) writing was Ireland, specifically Limerick, which was less than friendly to its native daughter. Three years after her death, John Liddy recalled 'the refusal of certain Limerick bookshops to handle her books and the ungenerous (if unimportant) refusal of our City Fathers to confer the freedom of the city' on her (1977: 3). He went on to recount a story told to him by O'Brien's friend, Mary Hanley, in which the writer overheard two elderly men discussing her outside a bookshop. Pointing to a book in the window, one said: 'Doesn't that one write dirty stories', to which the other replied: 'Not at all, sure isn't she Tom O'Brien the horse breeder's daughter.' O'Brien laughed all the way up the street (Liddy, 1977: 4). The anecdote illustrates the complexities of O'Brien's literary identity. On one hand, she appears as a *persona non grata*, a stigmatised purveyor of 'dirty stories'; on the other, she is recognised as an established member of Limerick's Catholic gentry. Like Bowen, O'Brien harkens to her caste and class (although neither survived into the era in which she wrote), while also harbouring an ambivalence towards her background: though removed from it by her own choice, she remained fascinated by it in a way that transcends both cold analysis and sentimental nostalgia.

The self-writings in which O'Brien's autobiographical 'I' is consistently present are *Farewell Spain* (1937), *My Ireland* (1962), *Presentation Parlour* (1963) and a collection of autobiographical fragments that would have become her *Memoirs* had she lived to complete them. But even in writing these she was suspicious of the confessional mode. In introducing *My Ireland*, for example, she deflects attention away from herself and onto her implied readers:

> The intention is to recall, revisit and recreate scenes, places, moods and manners of Ireland that have been a part of my experience, and to share these, for their possible entertainment, but anyhow for their judgement, with readers who may know Ireland better than I do, or in a manner different from mine; but also with those who come in from outside, to whom we are foreign, but who hope that, moving amongst us in holiday or study, they may be entertained, refreshed, surprised – or even reassured. (1962: 16)

Although little of O'Brien's unfinished *Memoirs* made it into print, she refused to label the book an autobiography. In a 1966 radio interview she said: 'I'm writing another book which is a bit difficult to describe – sort of memories of people who influenced me, or people I was interested in [...]; not autobiography, but impressions, external impressions of life.'[9] The paradoxical nature of this statement reveals an essential element of O'Brien's autobiographical style: every personal aspect is deflected onto another person, thing or experience. Bullfights in Spain, the Irish landscape and its archetypes, teachers, parents, aunts and other family members all become filters through which she projects her psychological inner self.

*Farewell Spain*, published when O'Brien was 40 years old, is both a witty travel memoir and a self-analytical cultural study. Throughout the book she wryly observes the activities of '13-day trippers' on summer vacations from Britain and Ireland, who move in querulous, sunburned packs searching for their bilingual consul. Alongside this, we have O'Brien's own journey towards remembering her adopted country and coming to terms with the changes it was undergoing in the mid-1930s. The book's cast of characters are celebrated and criticised in equal measure, as they form the substance of O'Brien's textualised life. A year earlier, in *Mary Lavelle* (1936), O'Brien had introduced the idea of 'the real Spain' as perceived by foreigners, structuring the novel around the different ways in which the country is experienced by various visitors, including – where her own voice is most audible – the seasoned foreign traveller who is intimately familiar with Spain yet still culturally removed from it. But in *Farewell Spain* O'Brien is speaking of herself not as an omniscient narrator but as a highly self-aware artist dedicated to literary composition. As such, the travel autobiography attests to her life as a writer and, like Gregory's 'An Emigrant's Notebook', appears to be a sketch-pad for chronicling thoughts, impressions and emotions. In one chapter, 'Blondes and Fountains', O'Brien objectifies and comments upon the nature of female beauty. The 'unfortunate seriousness' of Spanish women's attitudes towards twentieth-century beauty culture is, she believes, the reason that such women 'on the whole, are not beautiful – because they try so damn hard. Let them alone, let them grow up and grow old away from cosmetic shops and movies and women's pages, away in their lost mountains – and they are beautiful. I have seen them' (1985: 182). Such passages illuminate ideas of female beauty that are usually expressed only in O'Brien's fiction; scholars researching her lesbian identity might learn from them that the aesthetics of the female form were at least as important to her artist's eye as whatever physical desires she might have. As a woman who was ambivalent about the received identity and role of her gender in the early twentieth century, O'Brien sought to challenge and disrupt the sovereignty of this aspect of patriarchal tradition. As an artist who was sexually oriented towards women, she represents them scopically, as objects of desire seen from the point of view of both a creator of the fictional and a connoisseur of the actual. So when Agatha Conlon says to Mary Lavelle: 'I like you the way a man would' (1984: 285), this is to be taken literally, with all its voyeuristic implications. O'Brien's 'I' in *Farewell Spain* is the possessive, ardent voice of a lover who falls at the feet of her *femme fatale*, defending and desiring even as she distinguishes imperfections.

In *My Ireland*, composed 25 years after *Farewell Spain*, O'Brien writes from the standpoint of the 'accidental national', commenting on the place that engendered and later rejected her. But in spite of this rejection and her implicit references to it throughout the text, there is a distinct air of loyalty to her homeland. Although she had not dedicated a book in nearly thirty years, she made an exception for Limerick, which she maternalistically calls 'my dear native place' in the inscription. The most extensive and moving stories in the book are those concerning women whose lives became intertwined with her own during her travels. One such woman is Mrs Stone, a 90-year-old Antrim shopkeeper with whom she struck up a conversation about literature that became a friendship. O'Brien's account of their meeting dominates her chapter on Antrim, and her description of their last evening together is particularly poignant, expressing a connection between the two women as mutually supportive creators and thinkers:

> I talked over Mrs Stone's fire until half-past one in the morning. And then she insisted on walking the length of the street with me to my hotel. It was a clear, cold night, very still; we could hear the gentle voice of the sea off to the left. [ . . . ] At the hotel door she thrust a great roll of paper into my hands. 'It's foolscap,' she said, 'hard to get now. Do you write on

it?' I told her that indeed I did, but that I could not take that great roll from her. 'You must,' she said. 'It's a present. Cover it with good words.' (1962: 92)

Perhaps it was passages such as this that led Eavan Boland (b.1945) to *My Ireland*, through which she contemplated the occlusion of women in the Irish literary tradition in an essay published two decades after the novelist's death. Boland acknowledges the aesthetic differences between herself and her predecessor – 'For me womanhood and the body gave access to the visionary adventure; for her they were the source of those conflicts which define the spirit' – while also noting their shared membership of a literary milieu that flourished in spite of cultural antipathy:

For a poet like myself who began to write in a culture inflected at every turn by male assumptions, the absence of a writer like Kate O'Brien was an important mystery. For a woman poet or novelist, wishing through her particular statement to avail of a psycho-sexual as well as an historic identity, this was a crucial barrier; the more oppressive for being unadmitted. (1993: 19–20)

Boland herself belongs to a generation of Irish women who have been far more willing to employ themselves as autobiographical subjects. As pilgrim natives, their voices have become louder during recent decades, thereby confirming Sidonie Smith's claim that during periods of cultural ferment women autobiographers 'have been able to promote their own vision of empowering selfhood' more effectively (1986: 174). The inner 'I', with its triumphs and preoccupations, has begun to converge with the subject of the text; the self-consciously crafted narrative has become sovereign. For this to happen, however, the complex weave of womanhood and nationhood has had to be carefully negotiated. Many of the essential differences between the autobiographies of Irish women and Irish men, while subtle in terms of style and tone, are often magnified when it comes to their treatment of the nation. For women autobiographers, the concept of nation tends to limit severely, rather than complete, their apprehension of a full identity. The received artistic and poetic dicta of woman-as-nation (and vice versa) is so entrenched in modern Irish literature that female literary autobiographers take particular care to separate the ideas of nation and self. Eschewing association with their country of origin, they identify themselves as autobiographical subjects through the viewpoint of a literal and figurative self-exile. Even nationalist writers such as Lady Gregory and Katharine Tynan present themselves as advocates and interpreters of their nation, rather than its embodiment. Gregory's 'An Emigrant's Notebook', for example, is replete with close, nostalgic descriptions of her family home and the surrounding landscape, the political intent of which is unmistakeable. But in writing of 'the time in which we lived in peace and charity with all men and loved our people and they loved us', she is careful to articulate her role as a member of the Irish 'family', cast as 'a group of stepbrothers and sisters', whose characteristics are so diverse 'as to always prevent full accord and harmony'.

Boland is the autobiographer who most forcefully interrogates the disjunctions produced by 'the nationalization of the feminine, the feminization of the national' in Irish culture (1996: 196). In *Object Lessons* (1995), a book which gives fresh impetus to literary autobiography by contemporary Irish women, she decodes this dialectic and shows that for the Irish woman writer neither element can be wholly embraced or ignored. In depolarising these long-standing oppositions, she usurps the symbolism of a defeated and impoverished Ireland as female and an independent Ireland as male. Moreover, she provides other women writers with what she lacked: stories about the contradictions and constraints she faced as a woman poet in Ireland:

> I know now that I began writing in a country where the word *woman* and the word *poet* were almost magnetically opposed. One word was used to invoke collective nurture, the other to sketch out self-reflective individualism. Both states were necessary – that much the culture conceded – but they were oil and water and could not be mixed. It became part of my working life, part of my discourse, to see these lives evade and simplify each other. I became used to the flawed space between them. In a certain sense, I found my poetic voice by shouting across the distance. (1996: xi)

Boland's dual emphasis on the woman poet's need for expressive freedom and the importance of her own experience prompts her to provide a series of object lessons for other women poets, grounded in her own subjectivity. What emerges most strikingly from these is her stubborn specificity, her persistence in using actual and imagined events to represent a larger whole. This objective is announced in the preface, where she introduces a leitmotif that resurfaces throughout: the room in which she wrote her first poems: 'That room appears often in this book. I can see it now, and I have wanted the reader to see it. It was not large. [ . . . ] And yet for me, as for so many other writers in so many other rooms, this particular one remains a place of origin' (1996: xv–xvi). What the narrative discovers, however, is that for the Irish woman writer, origins are fraught with all kinds of obscurities, absences and elisions. In 'Lava Cameo', the opening chapter of *Object Lessons*, Boland elegantly interweaves her account of her search for her grandmother's life story with her narrative quest for her own poetic identity. Her astonishment at how much she feels the 'small, abstract wound' of not being able to find her grandmother's grave in a Co. Louth graveyard becomes 'a sign for a wider loss' of voice, memory and identity:

The way to the past is never smooth. For a woman poet it can be especially tortuous. Every step towards an origin is also an advance towards a silence. The past in which our grandmothers lived and where their lives burned through detail and daily incidence to become icons for our future is also a place where women and poetry remain far apart. What troubles me is not how difficult and deceptive my relation to this past – and to this figure within it – may be but that it might not have existed at all. (1996: 23–24)

Like Alice Walker, whose search for the unmarked grave of the novelist Zora Neale Hurston forms the basis of her meditation on the fate of black women writers, Boland records her search for her grandmother's obscured memorial in order to signify the loss and exclusion of which her own literary journey is largely composed. Moreover, her imaginative journey into this mysterious past is effected and deflected through the journeys of others, from dead precursors such as Sylvia Plath to living contemporaries Medbh McGuckian and Eiléan Ní Chuilleanáin, each of whom has had to confront the absence of artistic authorisation for a woman's life, 'its sexuality, its ritual, its history' (1996: x–xi). In imagining the truncated journeys taken by Plath on the one hand and her own grandmother on the other, Boland deflects her own evolution as woman, mother and poet, while also reconfiguring their journeys as parallel voyages into the unknown. During her undergraduate years, she began to face the difficulties of bridging the distance between the life of a poet and the life of a woman. In a 1965 letter to Michael Longley she expressed a youthful desire for 'the people' as both subject and audience:

All that I want to be as a poet is in those lines from *King Lear* when he's on the edge of the cliff and speaks of all the 'shivering wretches' in the storm, and perceiving his brotherhood with them, throws away his kingship in the marvellous line 'O I have ta'en too little thought of this.' [ . . . ] I believe that the poet redeems, [ . . . ] catches things before they can become nonsense, and shows their meaning – and God the same.[10]

Such sentiments are often expressed by writers, but Boland's somewhat patronising wish to be a 'poet of the people' seems to have been problematised, and therefore made honest, by living among them in 'the so-called ordinary world' (1996: x). Instead of creating mere emblems, as Irish poetic convention had done by relegating women to the realms of the *spéirbhean* and the *seanbhean*, she eventually learned to write out of her experiences as a suburban housewife and mother, whose multiple, evolving identities were both inextricable and perpetually unresolved.

In her exploration of her complicated inheritance as an Irish woman poet, Boland addresses prevalent postcolonial themes: the search for a name, the discovery of dispossession, the retrieval of narrative forms and the power of the margins to challenge the discourse of the centre. Indeed, she is a writer who has searched for new areas of aesthetic meaning throughout her career. She found in the Dublin suburb of Dundrum, to which she moved in 1970, uncharted poetic territory, 'a country of the mind' in which to work towards the resolution of her dilemmas: a poet whose gender was invisible, a woman whose material, bodily existence was absent from poetic tradition, eclipsed by 'Custom, convention, language, inherited image' (1996: 27–28). Gradually, she discovered in everyday suburban activities 'a sequence and repetition which allowed the deeper meanings to emerge: a sense of belonging, of sustenance, of a life revealed, and not restrained, by ritual and patterning' (1996: 170). But this did not mean that her contradictions were neatly resolved: 'The dilemma persists; the crosscurrents continue. What I wished most ardently for myself at a certain stage of my work was that I might find my voice where I had found my vision. I still think this is what matters most and is threatened most for the woman poet' (1996: 253–54).

Throughout her autobiographical and critical writings, Boland is adamant about the enabling potential of poetry to challenge received notions of the 'inviolate' literary past. At the end of her 1996 address to the Modern Language Association, she considers the implications of a future for which the present will become history:

> I have a great curiosity to sit in some room, [ . . . ] with no recognitions to aid me, and talk to a poet from a world that has not yet occurred. A world fifty or a hundred years from now and a poet constructed by the aims and assumptions of our moment. Everything we do and say about poetry, however casual and contentious, may become part of that poet's world [ . . . ]. We have a duty to ensure that our present can become the sort of past that future poets can enter, can love, can quarrel with, and, above all, can change. (1997: 17)

As these words suggest, Boland's reclamation of self is a continuing process of reconfiguring female destiny and artistic responsibility within the context of poetic form. The affirmation echoed throughout *Object Lessons* exhorts the future writer to interrogate history and the 'national tradition', but likewise to acknowledge their totality: 'If a poet does not tell the truth about time, his or her work will not survive it. [ . . . ] Our present will become the past of other men and women. We depend on them to remember it with the complexity with which it was suffered. As others, once, depended on us' (1996: 153).

## III

Throughout the twentieth century, patriarchal constructs of nationhood and womanhood disrupted the Irish female artist's idea of self as an individually legitimate part of her nation. As the next millennium unfolds, the literal and figurative lost ground of that identity continues to be recovered. Irish women's literary autobiography can therefore be characterised as a corrective to the ways in which women have been perceived, particularly as artists; it reacts by creating a more authentic world which the female writer can occupy only as autobiographer. But the conflict between Irish women's artistic and social identities has created a tension that separates their self-narratives from the larger body of women's autobiography in English. As outsiders, citizens and critics, they share a tripartite identity; as women, they endow it with a diversity of narrative options. Yet even though they perceive themselves as being alienated from Ireland to varying degrees, their autobiographical personae are nevertheless profoundly inscribed by their experiences of their originary place and culture. It is here that they find their most potent others, through which they seek to give the self definition. 'A relation to the other', observes Northern Irish novelist and critic Linda Anderson, 'does not prevent mobility, rather it becomes a way of engendering it' (1997: 126). Only when the self is fully apprehended is the recognition of others possible; only when these others can be brought to life in narrative form is autobiography possible. Although each of the autobiographers discussed in this chapter embarked upon various forms of exile, all returned to write autobiographies that speak out of the desolations and consolations of exile, so that they may again locate themselves within their place of origin.

The deflected autobiography of Irish women writers is infused with qualities at once cyclical and prophetic; like the spokes of a wheel, the others radiate from the autobiographical 'I'. As alternative versions of the subject, these others are given unique characterisations through their individual personalities and their specific relationships to the autobiographer. Elizabeth Bowen evokes something of this narrative method in her essay, 'Autobiography as an Art', when she writes: 'The "I" in the narrative stands for something more than consistent viewpoint or continuity; it provides the visionary element, in whose light all things told appear momentous and fresh – though they may not be new, though they may have happened before' (1951: 9). Irish women's literary autobiography may be identified with Heraclitus' moving stream in terms of its disregard for linear time and its multilayered present. But in consideration of its history and the provisions it has made for its future, it may be better compared with the Farset, a Belfast river, which poet Ciaran Carson describes in terms of its innovative potential: 'The river remembers spindles, arms, the songs of mill girls. It remembers nothing: no one steps in the same river twice. Or, as some wag has it, no one steps in the same river once' (1990: 49).

## Notes

1. Patricia Horton considers the use of the *doppelgänger* to be particularly prevalent among male writers in contemporary Northern Ireland, and manifested in such

ways as the Jekyll-and-Hyde trope and the loss of identity that is retrieved by the double (personal communication).

2. I. A. Gregory, 'An Emigrant's Notebook', Gregory Family Collection, item 624, box 46, Special Collections, Robert W. Woodruff Library, Emory University, Atlanta, Georgia. The work fills three small handwritten notebooks, all of which are unpaginated. Elizabeth Coxhead tentatively dates the 'Notebook' to 1884 based on evidence in the second volume of Lady Gregory's diaries in the New York Public Library's Berg Collection. However, Ann Saddlemeyer hypothesised in a conversation with the author that the 'Notebook' was produced closer to the time of Lady Gregory's marriage. James Pethica, on the other hand, argues that 'the winter of 1883–84 is a certainty for Augusta Gregory's work on [the 'Notebook'] as a complete literary entity. She may have written some parts sooner after marrying, but winter 1883 is the moment she returns to Ireland and more particularly Roxborough for the first time as an "emigrant"' (letter to the author, 4 July 1995). The inner cover of the first volume of the 'Notebook' is signed with Lady Gregory's early signature, 'IA Gregory, Coole' so it is certain that the work was produced at Coole.

3. The Berg diaries include more explicit critiques of her parents and more details of her home life. In the first volume of the 'Notebook' only stories relating to the Irish countryside and its inhabitants remain, indicating that Lady Gregory intended the 'Notebook' specifically as a work of Irish literature.

4. I. A. Gregory's diary, 3 June 1882 through 7 June 1910, Lady Gregory Archives of the Henry W. and Albert A. Berg Collection, The New York Public Library.

5. Gregory's emotional responses to events outside the family are more freely expressed in the 'Notebook'. For example, in the opening pages she writes of Land League activities near Roxborough with a sense of grief and outrage that is rarely audible in *Seventy Years* or in her other published autobiographies.

6. Victoria Glendinning explains: 'The only above-board children's stories for grown-ups, Bowen thought, were detective stories, and those she read for pure pleasure all her life' (1977: 32–33).

7. The event in question is the burning of Danielstown House by the IRA.

8. Françoise Lionnet (1989) uses the term *métissage* to describe the braiding of diverse cultural forms which autobiographers from colonial societies use to express their cultural dislocations dialogically.

9. Kate O'Brien, 'Personal Choice', Radio Telefís Éireann radio interview with Francis Russell, 3 May 1966 (RTÉ sound archives, tape A-3329). The most substantial portion of her unfinished memoirs can be found in *The Stony Thursday Book 7*, which contains a three-page fragment of the work.

10. Eavan Boland, letter to Michael Longley, 30 January 1965 in Michael Longley Papers, coll. 744, box 1, folder 3. Robert W. Woodruff Library Special Collections.

# 5
# 'Loss, Return, and Restitution': Autobiography and Irish Diasporic Subjectivity

*Liam Harte*

## I

The tradition of autobiographical writing by Irish migrants in Britain is amorphous, diverse, fragmentary and difficult to trace.[1] Although distinct Irish enclaves existed in British towns and cities since Elizabethan times, first-person narratives of the migrant experience were slow to emerge, for the obvious reason that few such individuals had the means, the opportunity or the inclination to record their lives in print. Indeed, it is highly likely that the vast majority of poor, rootless seventeenth- and eighteenth-century migrants were incapable of writing their names, let alone their autobiographies, and even if they did they would not have identified them as such. It is almost impossible, therefore, to point with any confidence to a foundational text of Irish migrant autobiography in the way that, for example, the 1791 memoirs of James Lackington have been identified as the earliest manifestation of 'the individualist self' in English autobiography (Mascuch, 1997). Instead, we must listen for the incidental confessional voices that penetrate the fog of anonymity that envelops the mass of Irish men and women in Britain until the late nineteenth and early twentieth centuries, when a greater number of individuated autobiographical voices began to assert themselves.

Of course, when one delves back beyond the 1800s, problems of nomenclature immediately arise. Since the word 'autobiography' was not coined until the 1790s, eighteenth-century self-narratives are properly described as 'proto-autobiographical' (Marcus, 1994: 12). This term is certainly applicable to a corpus of texts that registers some of the very earliest Irish migrant voices: the confessions and dying speeches of condemned criminals held in London's Newgate prison. From the 1680s until the 1760s, these confessions were published several times a year, on the morning following an execution, by the prison ordinary or chaplain under the title *The Ordinary of Newgate, His Account of the Behaviour, Confession and Dying Words of the Malefactors who were Executed at Tyburn*. As Michael Mascuch points out, this body of penny folio broadsheets 'constitutes the immediate forerunner of the modern auto-biographical tradition', despite the didactic, formulaic and condensed nature of the narratives (1997: 175). In her analysis of a sample of the *Accounts* of Irish female felons, Barbara White observes that they 'are invaluable [...] in lifting the mass of poor Irish immigrants out of the anonymity that is normally assigned to them', containing as they do 'a rich store of information about the lives, aspirations and crimes of an otherwise voiceless under-class of labouring poor amongst the London Irish' (1996: 16, 12). This is certainly true, though her claim that 'the individuality and personality of the condemned remained intact' fails to take adequate account of the medi-ated nature of these auricular confessions, which inevitably compromised the speakers' power to authorise an autonomous, individualised 'I'.

Issues of subjectivity, authority and agency must be central to any reading of first-person accounts by members of dispossessed or subordinate groups, as they must be to readings of proletarian autobiography in general, into which category many Irish migrant memoirs fall. The process of seizing what Edward Said calls 'the power to narrate' (1993: xiii) is an inherently political act which transforms the subject from an anonymous object of speculation into a known narrator of specific personal histories. Sidonie Smith and Julia Watson contend that the 'assertion of agency is particularly compelling for those whose personal histories include stories that have been culturally unspeakable' (1996: 14), as accounts of much Irish migration have been historically. By giving voice to 'unrecited' cultural narratives, therefore, migrant autobiographers may be said to be participating in 'the cultural work of reframing the meanings of the speakable, of voicing the speakable differently' (1996: 15). This kind of life writing, Mary F. Brewer argues, typically provides

> the 'other' side to histories either previously untold, or already told but misrepresented and distorted [...]. Consequently, the genre of auto/biography for subcultural writers is often used counter-hegemonically – that is, as part of an attempt to render their own account of the lived experience of their particular social groups more convin-cingly than those versions put forward by representatives of the dominant cultural group. (2001: 722)

This process of claiming narrative agency – translating oneself into a char-acter in one's own story – is far from straightforward, however. The very process of writing an autobiography is an atypical activity for a member of any class, let alone an unlettered economic migrant. Indeed, there is an ironic appropriateness in being reminded of this fact by one of the most powerful dramatic representations of the type, Harry Carney, the embodi-ment of boorish alienation in Tom Murphy's *A Whistle in the Dark* (1961), who dismisses the very idea of the migrant memoirist with brusque sarcasm:

'None of us goin' writing books of memories later' (Murphy, 1997: 49). This barbed remark speaks volumes about attitudes to authorship, storytelling and self-revelation among Irish migrants from a certain class and culture, whose modes of expression were predominantly oral and collective. It also calls to mind Regenia Gagnier's observation that 'subjectivity – being a significant agent worthy of the regard of others, a human subject, as well as an individuated "ego" for oneself – was not a given' (1991: 141) for working-class autobiographers historically, a point vividly exemplified by Mayo-born Bill Naughton's recollection of the powerfully inhibiting effects of a deeply ingrained class deference on his literary aspirations:

> there was an almost inborn impression of belonging to the ignorant, the poor, and the uneducated – the ones who had nothing to give to the world but the labour of their two hands, and the best thing to do was not to expose yourself to ridicule by writing, but to conceal yourself and your thoughts – keep your mouth shut, stick to your job, and leave writing and the running of the world to your superiors and those in authority above you. So forcibly was this concept thrust upon one that it became a fact of life, against which it seemed pointless to struggle. (1987: 5)[2]

For those who persevered in the face of such formidable cultural impediments, the blank page held its own expressive challenges, not least of which were the canonical conventions of self-portraiture. Autobiographical identities are always narrated, at least in part, according to the cultural scripts available to people in specific historical and economic contexts, and the dominant norms of literary autobiography weighed heavily on many nineteenth- and twentieth-century working-class migrants, forcing them to adapt their experiences to existing models of self-narration in order to speak autobiographically. Such processes of adaptation are often fraught with tensions, leading to productive deviations from the established paradigms of subjectivity and schematic modes of self-narration, as exemplified by such diverse works as Patrick MacGill's *Children of the Dead End* (1914), Tom Barclay's *Memoirs and Medleys: The Autobiography of a Bottle Washer* (1934) and Patrick Gallagher's *My Story* (1939). In each of these texts there is an audible, dynamic interplay of stylistic modes and rhetorical strategies as the authors struggle to control the stories they tell about themselves – stories of deprivation, exploitation, self-justification and social indictment – within inherited autobiographical templates. What results may be characterised as a series of autobiographical acts where, to borrow Smith and Watson's terms, 'discourses intersect, contradict, and displace one another, where narrators are pulled and tugged into complex and contradictory self-positionings through a performative dialogism' (2001: 109).

This critical description provides an apposite point of departure for a discussion of the self-representational practices of Irish migrant autobiographers in Britain. For centuries, Irish people have been (made) acutely conscious of their racial and cultural alterity in a society which constructs Irishness as other to its core values and ideologies. And even though the proximity of Ireland to Britain has enabled varying degrees of cultural exchange over time, generations of migrants have nevertheless been forced to confront, through their own experiences, the implications of being seen as both different and inferior in a culture that is at once foreign and intimate. As Marella Buckley states:

> The tensions and belligerence in Anglo-Irish political relations make emigration to Britain a challenge with which most other destinations cannot compare. Just being an Irish person in Britain plunges Irish people there into a dramatisation of their identity because Britain has been so thoroughly and problematically involved in the construction of what we now know as Irishness and the Irish. Whenever an Irish person enters England, or when an English person enters Ireland, a hurricane of history is blowing on them. (1997: 119)[3]

The richly textured body of autobiographical writings by migrants depicts the multiple performances of identity figuratively invoked by Buckley, and in the process registers that which she tends to overlook: the importance of differentiating when, where, why and to whom the act of migration happened. All migrants did not feel the force of this putative hurricane equally or uniformly; indeed, for the privileged few, changing countries occasioned little more than a gentle breeze. In deterring us from seeing emigration as a generalised condition, therefore, the historically situated self-narratives of migrants give voice to what Homi Bhabha terms 'borderline or borderland identifications' in that they display 'that very peculiar weave of elements of lives lived iteratively, lives lived interstitially' (1994: 198). The performative quality of such identifications constitutes an important part of my reading of these texts in so far as performativity suggests 'a form of contingent positioning rather than any claim to authenticity' (Anderson, 2001: 125), a point further elaborated by Smith and Watson:

> A *performative* view of life narrative theorizes autobiographical occasions as dynamic sites for the performance of identities constitutive of subjectivity. In this view, identities are not fixed or essentialized attributes of autobiographical subjects; rather they are produced and reiterated through cultural norms, and thus remain provisional and unstable. (2001: 143, original emphasis)

With this in mind, I wish to examine the extent to which Irish migrant self-narratives, particularly those written by second-generation autobiographers, can be read as sites for the staging of transgressive subjectivities that not only complicate preconceived notions of nationality, but also invite us to think about hyphenated identities in more nuanced terms. The most self-reflexive of these autobiographers highlight the heterogeneity of affiliation *within* second-generation identities by variously configuring the different components of their identities in sequential, hierarchic and dialogic terms. As such, they support a conceptualisation of second-generation Irishness as a continuum of multiple and partial identifications rather than as a monolithic cultural category. Further, these texts, when viewed collectively, offer revealing historical perspectives on some of the vexed questions that define migrant or diasporic identities, questions to do with 'belonging and distance, insider spaces and outsider spaces, identity as invention and identity as natural, location-subject positionality and the politics of representation, rootedness and rootlessness' (Radhakrishnan, 1996: 213). But before looking in more detail at this literary sub-genre, I want to consider, by way of an oblique prologue, an eighteenth-century first-person narrative that features the beguiling voice of an Irish female migrant who, on arrival in England, is drawn into an elaborate identity performance in order to withstand the force of the ideologically charged hurricane that bears down upon her.

## II

Mary Davys (1674–1732) was arguably the first Irish woman writer to dramatise the potent cultural encounter between Irish immigrant and English native. Davys is one of those enigmatic literary precursors about whom nothing is known, not even her maiden name, prior to her marriage to Peter Davys, a Dublin clergyman and schoolmaster who was an acquaintance of Jonathan Swift. Widowed in 1698, she emigrated to England and settled in York, where she began her writing career. The commercial success of her play, *The Northern Heiress; Or, The Humours of York* (1715), enabled her to open a coffee house in Cambridge, where she spent the rest of her life. As Siobhán Kilfeather notes, Davys's historical importance lies in her being part of the first generation of women to have had their work published and 'the first known Irish woman writing in English to explore national and sexual identities' (1986: 14–15).[4] The work that most effectively thematises these issues is *The Fugitive; Or, The Country Ramble* (1705), revised and reissued as *The Merry Wanderer* in 1725, in which she records her migrant travels through provincial England and Wales. One of the most compelling passages in *The Merry Wanderer* occurs at the start of the narrative when, 'after sixty very bad Miles riding' from Holyhead, Davys and her companions stop for supper at an English inn. Here they encounter an Englishman named Hodge who is curious to see some of the 'wild Irish' in the flesh. His request sets the scene for a witty canard in which Davys plays upon hostile English stereotypes of the Irish by gulling her credulous inquisitor:

Come Friend, *said I*, you have, I hear, a mind to see some of the wild *Irish*. Yes, Forsooth, *said he*, an yo pleasen, but pray yo where are they? Why, *said I*, I am one of them. Noa, noa, *said he*, yo looken laik one of us; but those Foke, that I mean, are Foke wi' long Tails, that have no Clothes on, but are cover'd laik my brown Caw a whom with their own Hair. Come, *said I*, sit you down, and I'll tell you all; when I was three Years old I was just such a thing as you speak of, and going one day a little farther than I should have done, I was catch'd in a Net with some other Vermin, which the *English* had set on purpose for us; and when they had me, they cut off my Tail, and scalded me like a Pig, till all my Hair came off; and ever since I have been such another as you. Well, Forsooth, *said he*, yo tellen me Wonders, but pray yo, cou'd yo speak? Speak, *said I*, no I could only make a gaping inarticulate Noise, as the rest of my Fellow-Beasts did, and went upon my hands as well as Feet, in imitation of them; but for any other Knowledge, I had it not till I got into *English* hands. Well, *said poor Hodge*, yo may bless the Day that ever yo met with that same Net: By'r Lady, I have often head of the waild *Irish*, but never saw any of 'em before. One Word more, Forsooth, and I have done: Could you not let a Body see the Mark of that same Tail of yours, where it was cutten off? No, Friend, *said I*, that may not be so very decent; I find you are a Man of much Curiosity, but must beg you must take my Word for once without ocular Demonstration. Mercy on me, *said the Fellow*, what's that? Why that, *return'd I*, is, without staying any longer, to make haste home, and tell your Wife and Neighbours what you have heard and seen. (Davys, 1725: 162–63)

There is much that could be said about this complex act of gendered subversion. Most obviously, Davys's lampoon comprises a caustic riposte to the discursive tradition of Irish barbarism perpetuated by Edmund Spenser and his contemporaries. Her satiric representation of her transformation from mere bestiality into enlightened self-possession at the coercive hands of the English deftly ironises the colonial antitheses. The docking of her 'tail' symbolises her civil regulation, the taming of her disorderly Irishness and femininity being the prerequisite for her entry into language. It also represents the attempt to negate her dangerous libidinal attraction to the coloniser, who must master both his own truant desires and the disruptive energies in the Irish body politic. Hodge's desire to see the mark of her sexual and racial taming, however, suggests that the coloniser's voyeuristic and libidinal fascination for the other is itself untameable. Further, her teasing remark that 'ever since I have been just such another as you' does more than merely mock his gullibility; it also serves to highlight the similarity of the English and the Irish, the subliminal awareness of which so distressed the colonial mind (Kiberd, 1995: 11).[5] Davys's anecdote thus encodes an unsettling countertruth: the same process that allows for the recuperation of the barbarous native also admits the possibility of the settler's lapse into degeneracy.

Davys's deft marshalling of the discourses of race, sexuality and national identity relies on sophisticated but problematic acts of narrative ventriloquism and improvisation. Not only does she fix her English interlocutor in a position of inferiority through her use of provincial dialect, she herself poses as a risen savage exacting linguistic revenge on the coloniser through her eloquent mastery of English. There is more to her mimicry than this, however. Davys's mockery of colonialist stereotypes is complicated by the dualities emerging from her status as a Protestant Anglo-Irish female migrant. English colonial discourse was, after all, primarily directed at the native Catholic Irish, so in order to challenge it Davys must pretend to be one of them, must falsely present herself as an exemplar of newly converted Irish civility. In so doing she effectively colludes in colonial condescension, as when she characterises the Irish language as 'a gaping inarticulate Noise'. As Kilfeather puts it: 'She identifies with them [the native Irish] only long enough to create a stereotype, from under which she then slides out' (1986: 25).[6] This act of cultural double cross is made all the more treacherous by Davys's recent crossing of geo-political boundaries. Fresh from the borderlands of the Tudor state – the English Pale in Ireland – this already mediated subject finds the troubling incongruities of her composite identity shifting beneath her parodic performance of colonialist prejudice. Thus, the migrant trickster is ironically undone, unable to control within her own terms the destabilising forces unleashed by her movement from the colonised periphery to the imperial metropole.

Mary Davys's knowing representation of her struggle to counter her English hosts' construction of her as an exotic other constitutes a piquant inscription of the sinuous complexities of the identity performance produced by the act of migration. This pithy anti-imperial anecdote, which discloses subversion and collusion, anticipates some of the recurring themes and preoccupations of Irish migrant autobiography: the performative negotiation of prejudice and racism; the fragmentation and transformation of identity under the pressures of migration; the crisis of individuation engendered by the clash of cultures, attitudes and ideologies. Davys's sudden sense of being radically unhoused, of shuttling between two shores of separation, is amplified in the memoirs of later first-generation immigrants and subtly recast in the writings of second-generation autobiographers, each of which inscribes and is inscribed by a particular history of migration, as well as by specificities of gender, class and other markers of difference. It is to the latter category of writers that I now wish to turn in order to examine the multiple self-positionings they embrace through their autobiographical practices. The writers under discussion flourished in disparate times and places, ranging from post-Famine Liverpool to contemporary London, and as such are products of vastly different socio-historical and cultural landscapes to the one inhabited by Mary Davys. Clearly, I do not have space here to rehearse these radical contextual differences, which relate not only to transformations in the pattern, volume and character of Irish immigration during the nineteenth century, but also to the development of autobiography as a literary form and to changing conceptions of selfhood and its determinants. Instead, I propose to proceed by way of a detour, routing my analysis through that point in *The Merry Wanderer* which affords an oblique perspective on the contrasting forms of ethnic visibility that frame first- and second-generation identities in a migrant context.

As I have suggested above, the discourses of seeing and surveillance – 'ocular Demonstration' – are central to Davys's representation of the encounter between migrant and native. Indeed, the whole satirical thrust of her consummate baiting of Hodge hinges on his failure to read the distinguishing signs of her ethnic otherness, blinded as he is by stereo-typical thinking: 'Noa, noa, *said he*, yo looken laik one of us'. Herein lies a suggestive springboard to a consideration of the submerged ethnicity of the second-generation Irish population in modern Britain, whose public invisibility is a key factor in their incorporation into the hegemonic category of white Britishness. Recent research has shed much light on the articulation of second-generation Irish identities within the public domain of contemporary Britain and their inflection by factors such as gender and geographical location (Campbell, 2002; Hickman *et al.*, 2005). Rather less attention has been paid to historical constructions of second-generation identity, especially those configured in first-person narratives, of which there is a small but important corpus. This is not to say that such works have been wholly ignored; the aforementioned autobiography of Tom Barclay, for example, has been scrutinised by scholars from different disciplines for its insights into the shifting cultural loyalties of a Leicester-born 'would-be Irishman' (Barclay, 1995: 102) in Victorian England (Campbell, 2000; Harte, 2003). What is missing, it seems to me, is a fuller historical appreciation of the differentiated nature of second-generation autobiographical identities and the multiple, potentially conflictual, allegiances they enact. Barclay's depiction of the sequential development of his cultural identity, which evolved from a childhood rejection of his Irish heritage to an essentialist adult desire to 'become' unambiguously Irish, is but one narrative model of second-generation belonging, albeit a particularly vivid and engaging one. It is, I suggest, properly read alongside other texts in a variegated literary sub-strand which collectively inscribe a continuum of second-generation self-representation. In the remainder of this chapter, therefore, I will explore particular configurations of autobiographical identity that illuminate the heterogeneous ways in which second-generation writers compose and perform multivalent subjectivities along the axes of memory and history, migrancy and belonging.

## III

The first migrant memoirist to raise the issue of second-generation cultural affiliation was the Home Rule activist and historian John Denvir (1834–1916) who, in *The Life Story of an Old Rebel* (1910), entered a brief but heartfelt endorsement of the nationalist credentials of people of Irish descent in Britain. Denvir, who was born in Antrim and brought to England as an infant, spent most of his life in Liverpool, a city he described as 'a "stony hearted stepmother" to its Irish colony' (1910: 9). It was there that he established a successful building firm and carried on his 'outpost work' (1910: 1) for the Irish nationalist cause as journalist, publisher and political organiser. In 1873 he became a founder member and first secretary of the Home Rule Confederation of Great Britain and later served as its national agent and organiser. Through this work he gained an intimate knowledge of Irish nationalist networks and personalities in late Victorian Britain, which he chronicles at length in his autobiography. Denvir's desire to bear accurate historical witness to the growth and development of emigrant nationalism, and so assert its moral authority, means that his private self is effectively subsumed into the political narrative throughout. This classically nationalist autobiographical strategy is indicative of his deeper desire to validate his own claim, and that of the migrant community to which he belonged, to be considered a full part of the nascent Irish nation, a claim underwritten by his unremitting work for the Home Rule cause. His life story thus becomes a paradigm of diasporic patriotism in which selfless devotion to the aspirations of the motherland not only betokens the emigrant's rightful membership of the 'imagined' political community but also serves as a compensatory substitute for effective revolutionary action.

Denvir's promotion of the claims of the British-born Irish to full membership of the Irish nation was hotly contested by many cultural nationalists who posited a 'purer' conception of Irish nationality that pre-dated English influence and was equated with physical rootedness in the actual soil of Ireland. To such ideologues, emigration represented a form of national betrayal, notwithstanding the fact that expatriate Irish communities worldwide provided nationalist Ireland with a crucial reservoir of political, financial and military support. The literary corollary of this viewpoint was later expressed by Daniel Corkery who, in one of the most influential texts of postcolonial Irish criticism, *Synge and Anglo-Irish Literature* (1931), sets out a version of the Irish literary canon from which migrant writers, along with those from an Anglo-Irish background, were excluded. As Roy Foster explains: 'Careerist expatriates like Shaw and Goldsmith were turned back at the border. Echt-Irish people like Colum and O'Flaherty voluntarily ruled themselves out by emigration' (2001: 108). Second-generation writers, of course, did not even register on Corkery's literary Richter scale and it is this brand of narrow-gauge nationalism that Denvir implicitly challenges in the opening chapter of his autobiography when he asserts:

Anyone who has mixed much among our fellow-countrymen in England, Scotland and Wales knows that, generally, the children and grandchildren of Irish-born parents consider themselves just as much Irish as those born on 'the old sod' itself. No part of our race has shown more determination and enthusiasm in the cause of Irish nationality. (1910: 2)

What is notable about Denvir's attempt to introduce such migrant affiliations into monological conceptions of Irishness is his portrayal of the second- and third-generation as hyper-nationalist, untainted by traces of partial or ambivalent identification. While manifestly sincere, this characterisation effectively reinforces the Manichean model of identity it seeks to displace, leaving no room for bi-cultural affiliations. It fell to second-generation writers themselves, therefore, to articulate more nuanced versions of their sense of cultural hyphenation, one of the subtlest of which is expressed in *My Struggle for Life* (1916), the autobiography of Joseph Keating (1871–1934). Born to Irish parents in the mining village of Mountain Ash in South Wales, Keating worked at a variety of jobs before turning to writing in the late 1890s and went on to achieve success as a popular novelist and playwright. His autobiography is in the *Künstlerroman* mould of literary memoir, chronicling his 'zig-zag course' from the obscurity of a Rhondda coalmine to 'Grub Street, the coal-mine of literature', in rich social and psychological detail (Keating, 1916: viii–ix). The narrative is infused throughout with a muted didacticism that stems from the author's belief that 'a child of the workers might be born with as much intellectuality, spirituality, and manhood as the child of any other sort of people' (1916: 250). This leads him to present his literary success as a triumph of working-class aspiration over social disadvantage, which he offers as an exemplum to 'young men who see the golden flower of their ambition on the mountain-top, but can find no way up to it' (1916: v).

As a historical account of Irish migration, Keating's intimate portrait of the cultural mores and attitudes of 'a little colony of Irish emigrants' (1916: 4) in late-nineteenth-century Wales provides a useful corrective to negative representations of the immigrant Irish as a socially malign influence. As Paul O'Leary notes, the 'emphasis on community solidarity, shared cultural values and moral rectitude is at odds with the prevailing views of contemporary social commentary which had become fixed during the crisis decades in mid-century' (2000: 132). Read from a literary-cultural perspective, Keating's conception of nationality is equally revisionary insofar as it uncouples the Irish revivalist equation of authentic belonging with birth and residency in Ireland. Towards the end of the book he interrogates the meaning of home in terms of the lack of congruity between his immediate and his ancestral origins, explaining that whereas he regards Ireland as his country, Mountain Ash is his home:

The place where a man spends the first twenty years of his life remains for ever in the centre of his heart, and is, for him, the centre of the world. That was how I had always felt about Mountain Ash. A curious element was in that fact. I was entirely Irish in every way – in blood, traditions, sympathies, training, and temperament. I regarded Ireland as my country; and not only as mine, but as God's; and its people as a race chosen, above all other nationalities, by the Almighty, to establish the ideals of spiritual perfection, moral perfection, and intellectual perfection, 'the triple tiara of the Gael,' as an enthusiast phrased it.

Now Mountain Ash was Welsh. Yet this bit of Wales, where I was born and had spent my first twenty years, was so rooted in my Irish heart that I neither would nor could think of any other place on earth as my home. It seemed to me that the feeling of nationality had nothing to do with the land of birth, but was inherited in the blood. Irish children, scattered to the ends of the earth, loved the lands in which they were born, yet still regarded Ireland as their country, though they had never seen it. (1916: 268–69)

Keating's succinct disaggregation of home and nationality is quintessentially diasporic in that it 'opens up a historical and experiential rift between the place of residence and that of belonging' (Gilroy, 1997: 329). As such, it prefigures by several decades Avtar Brah's contention that '[t]he *concept* of diaspora places the discourse of "home" and "dispersion" in creative tension, *inscribing a homing desire while simultaneously critiquing discourses of fixed origins*' (1996: 192–93, original emphasis). His claim to Irish rather than Welsh nationality also contains a strong anticipatory echo of Vincent Buckley's notion of Ireland as a 'source-country' for people of Irish descent, outlined in his 1979 essay 'Imagination's Home'. For Buckley, a third-generation Irish-Australian writer, Ireland was 'a source in the sense that the psyche grows from and in it, and remains profoundly attuned to it'; it is 'a knowledge which goes very deep into the psyche, and it has an almost superstitious integrity' (1979: 24). So although he was born and raised in Melbourne, he claimed that 'for feelings of source, Ireland is primary, and Australia secondary' (1979: 24). Keating's relationship to the Irish and Welsh aspects of his identity is remarkably similar in its hierarchical configuration, generational and geographical differences notwithstanding.

A comparable hierarchised ordering of ethnic allegiance is evident in *The Autobiography of a Liverpool Irish Slummy* (1934), the picaresque memoir of Pat O'Mara (1901–1983). Born in a Liverpool slum tenement to a first-generation Irish mother and a third-generation Irish father, O'Mara grew up in a multiethnic 'diaspora space',[7] surrounded by 'Negroes, Chinese, Mulattoes, Filipinos, almost every nationality under the sun, most of them boasting white wives and large half-caste families' (O'Mara, 1934: 11). His vivid recollection of his abjectly poor childhood reads like an Edwardian version of *Angela's Ashes*, complete with pious mother, alcoholic father, doomed infants and serial evictions, though without McCourt's self-pitying sentimentality. O'Mara escaped this brutalised environment by signing up as an ordinary seaman on the eve of the First World War. Six years later he emigrated to America and settled in Baltimore, where he was working as a taxi driver at the time his autobiography appeared. As a self-styled 'paradoxical' Irishman (1934: 193), O'Mara is notably more willing than Keating or Barclay to acknowledge the entangled, indeterminate nature of his cultural identity, which he presents as having fractured under the twin pressures of an imperialist English Catholic education and an Irish nationalist upbringing, rendering him unable to identify unequivocally with either nation. What we find articulated in the text, therefore, is a hybridised version of belonging in which Irishness is mutually constituted with Britishness; yet Ireland remains the primary focus of ethnic identification:

> The best I can say is that what I derived from my elementary English-Irish schooling was an intense love for the British Empire and an equally intense hatred for England as opposed to Ireland.
>
> Our mothers and fathers, of course, were unequivocal in their attitude – destroy England, no less! But we children at school, despite the intense religious atmosphere of the Catholic school, were rather patriotized and Britishized – until we got back to our shacks, where we were sternly Irishized [ . . . ]. The paradox has remained in my make-up for years – the sound of a patriotic Irish air will make me want to get out my shillalah for the old wrongs of Ireland; but the moment the music is over, common sense will warn me to put it back. My mental prejudices, today as an adult, work something like this; ferocious, sacrificial Irish-Catholic (die for Ireland's freedom) first; ferocious sacrificial Britisher second; and patient, wondering dreamer third. [ . . . ] And what is true of me is true certainly of most slummy Irish-Catholic 'Britishers'. (O'Mara, 1934: 74–75)

O'Mara's emphasis here on the influential role of the English Catholic primary education system in denationalising children of Irish ancestry is echoed by later second- and third-generation Irish autobiographers, and lends historical weight to the argument that 'whereas education has been a prime way in which the public mask of Catholicism has rendered Irishness invisible in Britain, the family has provided a counterpoint to the school and its incorporating strategies' (Hickman *et al.*, 2005: 163). Equally striking are those moments in the text that register the disparity between the narrator's carefully calibrated ordering of his 'paradoxical' cultural loyalties and the blunt essentialist prejudice of others. Even in the diaspora space of cosmopolitan New York, where he worked for a time in a restaurant, O'Mara found himself being harangued by a Hungarian Jew for his perceived lack of 'authentic' Irishness: ' "Liverpool Irish – that's not *real* Irish" ' (1934: 249, original emphasis).

This spectre of inauthenticity continues to haunt the contemporary second-generation autobiographical imagination; indeed, one of the most intriguing aspects of the increased recognition of Irish ethnic difference in contemporary Britain is the phenomenon of authors of Irish descent using their own biographies and family histories as touchstones to trace the transgenerational ramifications of diasporic identities. Recent years have seen the publication of a small corpus of works in which autobiographic and biographic modes, or a hybridised form of them, have been mobilised to explore the implications of Irish identity loss and continuity both within and beyond the migrant generation. Although thematically linked, these works differ ideologically and formally, ranging from unconventional memoirs to scholarly theses. Chief among the latter is Bronwen Walter's *Outsiders Inside: Whiteness, place and Irish women* (2001), a study that serves as a prism through which to view other texts in this loose affiliation. It is also the most anomalous insofar as Walter admits to having no Irish ancestry. Yet by fruitfully utilising Brah's concept of Britain as a 'diaspora space' she identifies points in her family background where her ' "Englishness" is mutually constituted with "Irishness", but in ways which are so deeply embedded they have to be teased out of very mundane situations' (Walter, 2001: 27). In this way, she begins to deconstruct the myth of a homogeneous white British identity by revealing 'the myriad ways in which outsides and insides have always constituted each other' (2001: 27). Walter then moves beyond her own biography to examine Irish migrant women's negotiations of identity outside and inside the societies in which they live, with particular reference to the specificities of their spatial and socio-economic positioning.

Published more than a year after *Outsiders Inside*, Blake Morrison's *Things My Mother Never Told Me* (2002) reads like a literary analogue to it, so closely does the life story of the author's mother, Killorglin-born Agnes O'Shea, corroborate key aspects of Walter's thesis. Part memoir, part biography, the book explores the embeddedness of an Irish presence in an English social landscape by tracing the appropriation of one Catholic woman's identity by a particular brand of xenophobic Protestant Englishness. Determined to make a medical career for herself in post-war England, Agnes reinvented herself as 'Kim' on meeting and marrying Arthur Morrison, and subsequently performed a range of accommodation strategies to negotiate the deeply ingrained anti-Irish and anti-Catholic prejudices of the provincial middle classes. Rather than assert her ethnicity she neutralised it, becoming 'taciturn, chameleon-like, self-erasing' (Morrison, 2002: 24). Having silently relinquished her name, accent, origins and religion, she eventually became as English as the English themselves: 'Effacement wasn't her only way of coping. She also told jokes against her tribe. The Irish as stupid, feckless, drunk, poverty-stricken – the thing was to get in first, before the English did' (2002: 290). In fact, Morrison's mother 'reinvented herself [ . . . ] so thoroughly that she failed to set the record straight with her own children'

(2002: 24). Her son's account of his search to uncover the truth of her elided past is the anatomy of an absence, therefore, a contemplative circling of the aporetic space at the heart of the family: 'To be invisible was her objective, and she succeeded with a vengeance [ . . . ]. What began as a secretion of her otherness became a talent for self-occlusion. After the erasure, in life, of Agnes, the oblivion, in death, of Kim' (2002: 293–94).

Morrison's quasi-memoir contains a striking set of contrasts and comparisons with Richard White's *Remembering Ahanagran* (1998), which is based on the life stories of the author's mother, Sara Walsh. Born in Kerry in 1919, Sara's narrative of migration is both analogous and antithetical to that of Agnes, from whom she was separated by a mere two years in time and 40 miles in distance. Whereas Agnes went east to England and reinvented herself there, Sara west to Chicago and quickly began to Americanise herself by dropping the 'h' from her baptismal name, Sarah. 'The *h* is a small thing', White reflects, 'but it marked a direction, a trajectory into America and away from Ireland. From necessity, she left little parts of herself behind as she moved forward' (White, 1999: 159). Her self-amputations stopped short of self-erasure, however. Unlike Morrison's mother, for whom migration meant the renunciation of origins, Sara Walsh continually recapitulated her Kerry past in the stories she told her children. *Remembering Ahanagran* is the product of her son's fascination with these stories as sites 'where history and memory meet' (1999: 6). His 'anti-memoir' records the tense dialogue between 'crafted memory' and 'recovered history', the mother obstinately insisting on the primacy of memory, the son cleaving to the complicating power of history: 'The part of the past she claims most fiercely is the part she wants forgotten. Against her memory, my history rummages and pries and guesses' (1999: 264, 222). The fact that Sara is an active collaborator in the creation of her son's book rather than a dead interlocutor intensifies this contest to narrate the past; Morrison's struggle, conversely, is with the 'still, small voice of conscience' (2002: 95). Yet just as Morrison is troubled by his becoming a belated voyeur of histories he would otherwise not have known, White worries about 'the cruelty of recovering what memory seeks to bury or disguise' (1999: 5). By making the private public, he realises that he risks hurting people, 'telling what they do not wish widely known, in the service of a dead thing – history' (1999: 86). Although the tensions between history and memory sometime 'seem so strong that the book itself must die', White continues to pursue this 'dangerous conversation' in the belief that mutual subversion can also bring mutual enrichment (1999: 86, 272).

In bodying forth migrant lives from fragmentary written and oral remains, *Things My Mother Never Told Me* and *Remembering Ahanagran* participate in several genres: biography, autobiography, history, sociology, even fiction. Morrison, indeed, explicitly alludes to his protean status: 'Archivist, editor, biographer, novelist – I'm a little of all of these' (2002: 246). Other recent meditations on the fate of transgenerational Irish identities share this generic transgressiveness, even as they make more extensive use of the autobio-graphic mode than either White or Morrison. Hilary Mantel's 'No Passes or Documents are Needed' (2002) is a case in point. Published in a volume of essays on modern British fiction, it is ostensibly an examination of how, as an English-born novelist, she can lay claim to 'the collective life of the European imagination' (Mantel, 2002: 93). A good part of the essay, however, is given over to a consideration of the personal consequences of the author's loss of a sense of Irishness during her Derbyshire childhood. Mantel recalls: 'As a small child I grew up in what was essentially an Irish family, surrounded by Irish people who were old. By the time I was 10 almost all of them were dead. My consciousness of being Irish seemed to die with them' (2002: 95). But this did not mean that she could easily subscribe to dominant forms of Englishness, which discursively constructed her as an inferior other on the multiple grounds of gender, religion, class and ethnicity:

> As I grew up I came to see that Englishness was white, male, southern, Protestant, and middle class. I was a woman, a Catholic, a northerner, of Irish descent [ . . . ]. All these markers – descent, religion, region, accent – are quickly perceived and decoded by those who possess Englishness, and to this day are used to *exclude* [ . . . ]. If you want to belong to Englishness, you must sell off aspects of your identity. (2002: 96, original emphasis)

Surveying the possibilities of self-definition, Mantel explains that she chose to define herself as a European writer until she was led back to Ireland in the course of writing her novel *The Giant, O'Brien* (1998). Her visit, she says, inspired her to 'confabulate' a sense of Irish-European identity, which was symbolised for her by a copy of a Viking armlet purchased in Dublin's National Museum: 'And now I hardly ever go out without this symbol on my wrist, because at the beginning of the twenty-first century I am a primitive person, and not so secure as to leave my current place of residence without a marker to lead me "home" ' (2002: 102).

Mantel's account of the loss and reinvention of a sense of Irish iden-tity resonates strongly with Walter's claim that 'Because of strong pres-sures in British society to incorporate Irish people and render their cultural specificity invisible, particularly after a single generation, the personal rami-fications of Irish connections in Britain are rarely acknowledged' (2001: 27). This is a point also borne out by Terry Eagleton's *The Gatekeeper* (2001), which robustly amplifies Mantel's cogent critique of bourgeois Englishness, though emphatically not her feel-good fetishisation of a synthetic Irish-ness. *The Gatekeeper* also underscores Walter's notion of the diasporic Irish as 'outsiders inside'. 'To be Catholic was not really to be English', claims Eagleton, but rather to be attuned to an alternative culture of 'secrecy and doubleness' (2001: 33, 40); hence his characterisation of his childhood self as a mediator between polar realities. And while it is not in the nature of his 'anti-autobiography' to disclose too much about the writer's inner life, it is tempting to see some element of truth in his assertion of a link between his religious upbringing and his intellectual formation: 'Catholicism was a world which combined rigorous thought with sensuous symbolism, the analytic with the aesthetic, so it was probably no accident that I became a literary theorist' (2001: 33). Tempting, because another leading English-born academic of Irish descent posits just such a link, without any of Eagleton's drollery.

In a reflective essay entitled 'More Secondary Modern Than Postmodern' (2001) Patrick Joyce elucidates the shaping impact of the twin experiences of second-generation Irishness and working-class Catholicism on his historical imagination. Recalling his north London childhood of the 1940s and 1950s, he explicitly identifies himself as 'An outsider who was also an insider', one whose cultural duality combined with his religious upbringing to engender a unique awareness of 'the interconnectedness of things' (Joyce, 2001: 369, 375). This double perspective – what Salman Rushdie calls 'stereoscopic vision' (1992: 19) – stimulated in turn his scholarly interest in the way power operates within history and society:

> My experience of Catholicism [ . . . ] gave me a sense of what it was like to live in a structure of meaning which embraced almost everything, and then moving beyond this embrace I could see quite clearly the inter-connectedness of faith and life. Similarly, moving within the British social system, together with the displacements of being English-born Irish, enhanced this interest in how social integration worked, and in what the social was. (2001: 375)

Joyce goes on to conceptualise his diasporic Irish identity as 'a kind of master stratagem for inciting the past into being', since it is 'in its nature about separation but also about the possibility of return, and often the possibility of restitution' (2001: 377, 378–80). His articulation of the deeper workings of this stratagem is allusive, informed by a perceptive understanding of the relationship between a scholar and his sources: 'the tidal swell of separation and return seems to mimic the actions of the historian in the archive, forever separated from and returned to the past' (2001: 377).

Joyce's account of the intellectual legacies of a second-generation Catholic upbringing is highly suggestive in its metaphorical and analytical subtlety. For example, his evocation of the cultural versatility of second-generation Irish urbanites – 'versed in the ways of London and moving in the city like fish through water' (2001: 369) – obliquely inflects James Clifford's concept of diaspora as 'dwelling-in-displacement' (1994: 310). In the same way, his conception of diasporic identity as a cadence of 'loss, return, and restitution' (Joyce, 2001: 380) recasts the paradigm of migrant identification put forward by Aidan Arrowsmith in his analysis of recent 'Irish-English' writing.

Arrowsmith argues that the indeterminacy of second-generation affiliation gives rise to a tripartite negotiation of identity in contemporary fictional and dramatic narratives. Initially, there is a rejection of parental heritage, accompanied by a desire to conform to hegemonic English norms. This gives way to a reassessment of cultural 'roots' that typically engenders a nostalgic essentialism for 'authentic' Irishness. Such nostalgia then mutates into 'a more productive third position', whereby the migrant subject interrogates 'the very possibility of accessing any "authentic" memory, history or identity' (Arrowsmith, 2000: 38–39). Arrowsmith points to the drama of Martin McDonagh as the most sophisticated expression of this emancipatory third phase, in that it evokes 'a sense of second-generation diasporic identity which is truly, genuinely, inauthentic' (2000: 42).

Arrowsmith's argument is a persuasive one, though his thesis seems to me to be weakened somewhat by his failure to consider the representation of lived experience in the autobiographical narratives of contemporary second- and third-generation writers. As I have indicated above, such writers' constitution of themselves as anomalous 'outsiders inside', possessors of both/and identities, modifies linear, progressive models of identity negotiation by figurative characters. Perhaps the most exemplary recent example of this is John Walsh's *The Falling Angels: An Irish Romance* (1999), a middle-class memoir that plots new co-ordinates by which to map a version of 'genuinely inauthentic' diasporic identity onto the symbolic terrain of 'authentic' Irishness. In contrast to McDonagh's caustic deconstruction of rural migrant desire, Walsh's self-reflexive memoir embodies an affectionate critique of second-generation nostalgic essentialism that is grounded in a lived awareness of the seductive appeal of the romantic myth of authenticity. This critique insists that for the second-generation subject there is no one, true self to be accessed in the parental homeland but rather a range of different identities to be improvised and performed. Yet the narrative also testifies to a persistent longing for some form of redemptive rootedness in the ancestral culture long after the desire for authentication has been renounced. In Walsh's text this dialectic expresses itself as an imaginative desire to authorise a form of identity that, while rooted in the reality of living 'between' his immediate and his ancestral origins, seeks to go 'beyond' the 'essences' of both. This is a version of belonging that, to cite Brah again, 'places the discourse of "home" and "dispersion" in creative tension, *inscribing a homing desire while simultaneously critiquing discourses of fixed origins*'. Although this conception of 'home' ultimately exists only as an effect of autobiographical narrative itself, it too is susceptible to romantic mythicisation, as Walsh's rhapsodic ending attests.

Anxieties engendered by a perceived lack of authenticity are also at the heart of the work with which I wish to conclude this discussion, John Boyle's *Galloway Street: Growing Up Irish in Scotland* (2001), a vividly realised evocation of the author's childhood in a Paisley tenement, centred on the years 1945 to 1951. Just as Walsh highlights the centrality of voice to his 'neither-one-thing-nor-the-otherness', presenting it as a matter of 'having the wrong voice with which to speak' (Walsh, 2000: 70, 67), Boyle traces his identity crisis – and therefore the origins of his memoir – to a decisive moment of vocal uncertainty which occurred during his visit to Achill Island for the funeral of his aunt in 1993. Boyle had spent several months with his relatives on the island as a child and his return stirred deeply charged memories which disrupted his adult composure and sparked a desire 'to rediscover – truthfully, without embroidery – the boy I had been' (2001: x). This need for some form of spiritual reconnection with his boyhood self was heightened by feelings of spiritual ennui brought on by impending crises in his personal life and 'years of expatriate drift', which he presents as having dismembered him from both his community of origin and his 'essential' self. This self-alienation is figured as a vocal ambivalence which was dramatically crystallised when he stood at the lectern to read from Scripture at his aunt's funeral service:

> I had made up my mind to do this in my own voice, and not in the actorly tones I adopt for commercial voiceovers, only to falter when I started reading: I was no longer sure what my true voice was. Whatever doubts had surfaced to unsettle me, I came to believe that my reading had been sabotaged, and for good reason, by that ten year old boy. (2001: x)

Calling forth the voice of his childhood self is, therefore, central to the book's autobiographical – and performative – impulse. It prompts Boyle to abandon his attempt to write a memoir in two distinct voices in favour of a style which ventriloquises his long-vanished Paisley accent and idiom. *Galloway Street* is thus a text which foregrounds the process of its own narration and its role in reconstituting an autobiographical identity. The narrative is more than an attempt to recreate a childhood past; it is also an attempt to *re*-member a lost self through reinstating the erased voice of childhood, a voice which continually mocks 'the middle-aged raconteur' (2001: x) the author has become. Boyle's self-injunction to 'Let the boy tell his own story' (2001: xi) is the signal for the restorative first-person narrative to begin, as if his former self is waiting to be rediscovered whole, his childhood voice and vision retrieved in their 'pure' state. A stream of impressionistic memories are thus recollected and reordered as the basis for an alternative, more authentic subjectivity enabled by, but in tension with, the author's fake adult persona, which is beset by confusion 'about who I was or where I belonged' (2001: ix).

What unfolds, of course, is a narrative reconstruction of the past rather than the recovery of any 'true voice' or authentic identity. The remembering subject finds that he has no access to a preserved past, but rather encounters only a spectral likeness, the 'ghost' of a former self who is figured as a taunting *doppelgänger*: 'He stands on the sidelines of my life, in the shadows, watchful, reproachful. He knows all my anecdotes; he beats me to the punch-lines; he is not impressed. *Cummoan*, he says, *ye know fine there wis mair tae it than that'* (2001: xi). So in contrast to the hierarchised ordering of identities fashioned by Keating and O'Mara, Boyle, like Walsh, frames his second-generation subjectivity in dialogical and contrapuntal terms, presenting it as an ongoing conversation between warring selves. In the process, he appears to relinquish the 'ghost' of authentic belonging. The book ends with Boyle preparing to leave Achill and deciding to take with him a photograph of his younger self, seeing it as 'the only inheritance that mattered' (2001: 223). In figuring this photograph as a potent synecdoche for his lost, inno-cent self, the author tacitly acknowledges that this visual supplement is as close as he can get to the past 'as it really was'. The framing of this moment within a memoir further underlines the impossibility of restoring an original identity, since autobiography can never be more than a substitute, a textual supplement to lived experience. Yet, as each of the works discussed in this chapter illustrates, autobiography, by virtue of its protean adapt-ability, can offer those with multiple or partial identities a vital narrative means through which to compose, proclaim and perform their multi-faceted senses of belonging. Attending to the contrasting models of identification these autobiographers authorise helps us to understand better the continual making and unmaking of second-generation identities at different times and places, thereby undoing any notion of second-generation homogeneity, both historically and at the present time.

## Notes

Portions of this chapter appeared in *Irish Studies Review*, 11:3, 2003 and *Irish Studies Review*, 14:2, 2006. See http://www.tandf.co.uk/journals. I am grateful to the editors for permission to reprint them here.

1. The term 'the Irish in Britain' is not unproblematic. Although it is usually used inclusively to refer to all migrants born on the island of Ireland, it nevertheless homogenises a significant number of people, notably those from a Protestant unionist background, who would not consider themselves to be Irish, or at least not only Irish.
2. Although Naughton eventually realised his literary ambition, he confessed to harbouring a lifelong unease with 'the mantle of "author"', regarding himself as 'a retired coalbagger, on to a good thing with the profitable recreation of writing, and the pleasurable one of reading' (1987: 51–52).
3. The silent slippage from 'Britain' to 'England' here is a familiar, if problematic, feature of much Irish cultural criticism.
4. Despite her article's subtitle, Kilfeather reads both *The Fugitive* and *The Merry Wanderer* as autobiographical texts. She confirms this reading in the headnote to her extract from latter work in the fifth volume of the Field Day anthology (Kilfeather, 2002: 777).

5. Eudoxus's remark to Irenius in Spenser's *A View of the Present State of Ireland* – 'Lord, how quickly doth that country alter men's natures!' – encapsulates the coloniser's anxieties about Ireland's potential to corrupt.
6. This strategic identification with the Gaelic Irish can itself be read as teasingly ironic, since as a woman Davys would have known something of their social and political disenfranchisement.
7. Brah argues that the 'diaspora space is the site where *the native is as much a diasporian as the diasporian is the native*' (1996: 209, original emphasis).

# 6
# Breaking the Silence: Emigration, Gender and the Making of Irish Cultural Memory

*Breda Gray*

In the second half of the twentieth century the relatively new practice of telling, listening to and recording life narratives – variously described as oral history, oral testimony and oral life narrative – gained recognition as a useful mode of historical and experiential reconstruction. In Ireland, the development of an oral history approach to research led to the establishment of new sound archives and opened up fresh ways of narrating and engaging with lives lived in a variety of contexts (Beiner and Bryson, 2003). However, oral historical studies of Irish migration have tended to focus primarily on emigration, arrival and settlement, with little serious attention being devoted to experiences of staying 'at home' and the relationships between migration and gendered subjectivity. Taking a sociological rather than an oral historical approach, this chapter attends to staying-put as part of the dynamic of migration. More specifically, it examines the kinds of subjectivities produced in the life narratives of one woman who emigrated and another who remained in Ireland in the 1950s, during which time nearly half a million people left, with about two-thirds of these emigrating to Britain.[1] The two narratives in question were recorded as part of *Breaking the Silence: Staying 'at home' in an emigrant society*, an oral archive project carried out by the Irish Centre for Migration Studies at University College Cork.[2] The project's aim was to document and archive individual experiences of staying in Ireland in the 1950s, while they were still available in living memory. Following extensive media publicity in early 2000, 117 people in the 65–74 age bracket indicated an interest in contributing to the project.[3] A small team of researchers was trained to conduct and digitally record the interviews, and by the end of the project 78 life narratives were archived in sound and a further 12 in text.[4] All of the interviewers used a guide which loosely directed each interviewee through his or her life-course, focusing on their negotiations of staying or emigrating, and ending with questions relating to their circumstances at the time of the interview. Although this guide influenced the narrative, it was primarily used as a checklist to ensure that certain topics were covered, rather than as a rigidly administered interviewing tool. The enthusiastic response from potential and actual contributors points to the continuing significance of mid-twentieth-century decisions to emigrate or stay-put in structuring subjectivity in Ireland at the beginning of the twenty-first century. The project's focus on memories of the 1950s, moreover, struck a chord with many of those over 65 years of age who articulated a desire to challenge what they saw as a collective amnesia with regard to Ireland in the middle decades of the last century.

Life narratives, as Sally Alexander argues, tell us 'something of what has been forgotten in cultural memory' because they 'always describe or rehearse a history full of affective subjectivity' (1994: 234). They also give us access to what Foucault calls 'subjectification', which includes evidence for the ways in which human beings actively initiate their own formation into 'meaning-giving selves' (Rabinow, 1984: 11–12). In addition, they provide clues to the nature of remembering and how it binds individuals into subjectivities and collectivities. However, in order to remember, it is necessary to locate the flux of memories within 'meaningful narrative sequences' (Connerton, 1989: 26) which make events '*memorable* over time' and produce a '*shareable world*' (Kearney, 2002: 3, original emphasis). Narrative is, therefore, central to memory, subjectivity and community. However, only some narratives are permissible or 'tellable' at specific moments in time (Plummer, 2001: 186). The narratives discussed in this chapter are narrated by Mary, who emigrated to the US from County Clare and returned after 12 years, and by Cavan-born Annie, who stayed in Ireland despite her desire to emigrate. I have chosen these women's accounts because they both come from counties that experienced high out-migration in the 1950s, and because as narratives of staying-put, emigration and return, they offer important points of contrast and comparison. Also, as narratives of women's lives they help to address the relative absence of female experiences of emigration and staying-put in popular and academic literature. My aim here is not to assume the coherence of the category 'women', or the homogeneity of women's experience, but rather to consider the conditions of narration and the kinds of Irish female narratives rendered 'tellable' at the turn of the twenty-first century. Before considering the narratives themselves, however, I want to discuss the recent cultural turn to memory and its relationship to changing notions of the self.

## Memory, narrative and subjectivity in the twenty-first century

Memory and remembering as collective and individual practices took on new significance in the West in the latter decades of the twentieth century, prompting a considerable amount of critical and theoretical attention, much of which locates this renewal of interest within specific theorisations of social change. My aim in this part of the chapter is to address briefly three approaches to the theorisation of memory, biography and the self. The first is the view of sociologists such as Anthony Giddens and Ulrich Beck who regard 'biographical autonomy' as a central characteristic of the late modern self, though the former's analysis of individualisation and identity is much more optimistic than the latter's (Giddens, 1990, 1991; Beck, 1992; Lash and Friedman, 1992: 1–30). The second is the argument posited by Andreas Huyssen and others that fragmented narratives of the self are produced by globalising technologies and amnesiac consumer culture (Huyssen, 1995). Thirdly and finally, I wish to examine the assertion that contemporary concerns with memoir and testimony represent a kind of superficial feminised culture.

If in modernity 'we are fated to be free', then in Weberian terms we become responsible for the consequences of our actions and our life-course has to 'be ordered by ourselves' (Lash and Friedman, 1992: 5). Late modernity is characterised by increased individualisation and a fragmentation of traditional categories of belonging. Individualisation – understood as the compulsion to create and manage one's own biography at a time when most aspects of life have become options amongst numerous possibilities – is identified by some sociologists as a central feature of contemporary social change. The individual is seen as taking primacy over community with the effect that 'biographical autonomy' becomes the central attribute of the late modern subject. Thus, Giddens argues that the self is a reflexive project in so far as 'we are not what we are but what we make of ourselves', and goes on to claim that because the late modern individual is confronted by rapid social change, personal meaninglessness becomes a problem, to which tradition and memory are posited as potential solutions (1991: 9, 75). According to this view, the individual is engaged in a constant process of self-monitoring and an integrated sense of the self is produced through narrative. As Giddens explains: 'A reflexively ordered narrative of self-identity provides the means of giving coherence to the finite lifespan, given changing external circumstances' (1991: 76, 215). Furthermore, the perceived decline in the significance of categories of identity such as class, gender, nation and religion is understood as progressively releasing the individual from external forms of authority which are being replaced by the authority of the individual, so that, in the context of late modernity, 'the standard biography becomes a chosen biography' (Adkins, 2002: 16). And as globalisation, consumer culture and individualisation become more characteristic of Irish society in the early 2000s, similar analyses are being applied to 'Celtic Tiger' subjectivities (Coulter and Coleman, 2003). My discussion of the two life narratives below both supports and challenges this sociological characterisation of biography and the late modern self. In line with this characterisation, a 'traditional' Catholic morality is invoked in one of the narratives, not as emanating from a church- or family-based authority, but as a reflexively chosen mode of Irish femininity. Yet both narratives also point to the continuing operation of 'traditional' categories of gender and class in regulating available feminine selves.

Theorists of postmodernity posit the fragmented, dispersed self as its exemplary subject. This is often linked to new modes of remembering.

Huyssen argues that in a postmodern world, memory works in fragmentary and chaotic ways in contrast to the consistent mode of memory associated with nation-state modernity. In the Irish context, Foster (2001) argues that the memory frame of the national liberation narrative is being replaced by the 'presentism' of memoir, heritage and commemoration culture, practices of remembering which, he argues, involve new modes of memory regulation, including the celebration of only certain forms of memoir and a selective approach to the past. The presentism of public culture in early twenty-first-century Ireland is also associated with the amnesia of televisual instant entertainment and the spread of consumer culture. In his discussion of stories and changing modalities of memory, Kearney suggests that in the 'cyber world of the third millennium' we are encountering the end of the story, which is displaced by depthless simulation, chat shows, parody and pastiche (2002: 10). This culture is seen as surrendering the individual to an eternal presentness marked by moments of transience and the instantaneous, so that notions of a unified self and narrativised self-identity have to be revised. Kearney argues that a 'vulgarisation' of intimacy and privacy via television chat shows and radio phone-ins means that the human need 'to say something meaningful in a narratively structured way' is being continually undermined (2002: 10). Yet Kearney is optimistic that new technologies and fragmented modes of remembering will produce new relationships between memory and narrative, and with them 'alternative possibilities of narration' (2002: 12). George Marcus implies a similar synergy between new technologies and autobiographical genres. He argues that in 'the electronic information age' individual autobiography and personal testimony have gained new significance because they communicate historical experiences in personalised and accessible ways. Collective representations, he argues, are 'most effectively filtered through personal representations' at a time when 'the long-term memory function of orality and story-telling' is being displaced (Marcus, 1992: 317). So while postmodern theorists of memory and selfhood suggest fragmentation, inconsistency and presentism, thinkers such as Kearney and Marcus see technologically mediated postmodern societies as having the potential to facilitate new modes of memory, narration and the self.

The proliferation of memoirs and media programmes based on personal testimony is also identified in different ways with feminine modes of telling and with forms of feminist politics (Summerfield, 2000: 106). Nancy K. Miller draws attention to the 'ambiguous back and forth between lives and stories, between experience and history' that has been central to the development of feminism, but which has also, perhaps in less positive ways, fed into 'the evolution of confessional culture in the nineties more generally' (2002: xiv). The project of making the private public has, she suggests, contributed to transformations in women's lives since the 1960s, though it is easily denigrated as part of what has developed into a 'climate of over-the-top self-revelation' at the turn of the century (2002: 1). Miller argues that auto-biography, memoir, confession and life-telling are all important genres of contemporary culture, but that we need to be able to distinguish between the different sites and practices of these genres and their disparate effects. In an attempt to recover some of the potential for what she calls the 'memoir boom', Miller suggests that this should not be understood 'as a proliferation of self-serving representations of individualistic memory but as an aid or a spur to keep cultural memory alive [ . . . ]. Indeed, the point of memoir [ . . . ] is to keep alive the notion that experience can take the form of art and that remembering is a guide to living' (2002: 14).

In the first of the three approaches to memory and autobiographical narration outlined above, the late modern self is recognised by biograph-ical autonomy and an ability to create and re-create narratives of the self. The second, postmodern perspective suggests that we live in an amnesiac, 'infotainment' culture in which narratives of the self are fragmented, super-ficial and transient. This view posits contemporary subjectivity in terms of psychic discontinuity and incoherence, but also opens up new practices of memory and self-narration. The third position identifies a turn to memory and memoir as both features of confessional culture and modes of polit-ical claims-making that often centre on keeping cultural memory alive. But what is central to all three of these perspectives is the complex and chan-ging relationship between memory and subjectivity, as indeed it is to the *Breaking the Silence* project. Not only can the project be seen as sympto-matic of a confessional culture, it can also be said to be simultaneously reinforcing the 'biographical autonomy' that Giddens identifies with late modernity, and producing an accessible mode of memory in response to the amnesiac culture discussed by Huyssen.[5] More importantly, perhaps, the project offers the opportunity to scrutinise the presentation and uses of memory and self-narration in early twenty-first-century Ireland. If histor-ians make 'the memory of the past "as it was" [ . . . ] the watchword of their vocation' (Samuel, 1994: 15), this project represents a *fin-de-siècle* paradigm shift towards the workings of memory and practices of remembering and forgetting in the present.

In the discussion of the two life narratives that follows, I consider the relationships between modes of remembering, narration and the female self and examine how, in the early 2000s, my chosen subjects 'step into the landscape' and see themselves as women who, in the 1950s, stayed or emig-rated and returned (Steedman, 1986: 24). Like Nancy Miller, I believe that the contemporary memoir boom has some potential for making narrated remembered experience a guide to present-day living (2002: 14). I am also of the view that life narratives give us access to an understanding of how our relationships to ourselves are governed by prevailing discursive norms, while simultaneously opening up spaces that allow us to contest the limits that regulate what can and cannot be told. Chief among the questions I ask, therefore, are: what kinds of femininity were enabled or prohibited for women coming to maturity in the 1950s, at a time when migration was an accepted route to adulthood as well as a necessary means of individual, familial and national survival?; what devices are used to narrate memories of staying and going in the 1950s?; and in what ways are Irish feminine selves constituted and reconstituted over time in these narratives?

## Cultural imperatives of femininity and the migrant/returned self

Mary was born in 1934 and grew up in a village in County Clare, the eldest of 13 children, one of whom died as a child.[6] She explains: 'By the time that I went to America in '53, I was 19 and my baby brother was only six months, that would give you an idea.' When she left primary school at 15, having stayed on until eighth class, she went to work in the local box factory, where her earnings of 'seventeen and sixpence a week' made a significant contribution to the family income. The early parts of her narrative are marked by a profound sense of kinship between the US and Ireland. Her mother's stories of an aunt who returned from the US to rear her and her siblings after her own mother died, and of another emigrant aunt who 'used to send them home barrels of food [ . . . ], barrels of American Beauty apples [ . . . ], barrels of bacon', render America an outpost of family and home in Mary's childhood imagination. And while she herself did not articulate a desire to go to America, emigration eventually became an option for her three years after she began work at the factory. Around this time, a letter arrived from her mother's cousins in New York 'stating that they would like to bring the oldest member of the family to America, which turned out to be me'. In response to a question about her reaction, Mary said: 'I always thought about America because my mother had it instilled in us [ . . . ]. It was always felt in our house that there was a great safety by going to America, there was no worry [ . . . ] no matter how far away it was.' As the eldest of the family, Mary was identified as the one to go, a decision made by others on her behalf. This proposal was normalised by her mother's stories of family in America and the generalised sense that the US was a part of their lives. Moreover, when compared with staying on at the factory, the opportunity of going to America made emigration virtually inevitable, even though Mary had never been any further than Ballybunion in Kerry. It took six months to organise her papers, for which she had to go to the US Embassy in Dublin, which, she recalls, was 'like another world'. The date of her departure and travel arrangements were also decided by Mary's American relatives: they 'had booked me to travel on [ . . . ] the *SS Georgic*, and that was going off from Cobh on the 7th of August [1953]'.

Mary's narrative of leaving has the quality of a film script, in which she plays the role of the emigrant in an extended familial plot. She remembers that she left Cobh on a Friday, because meat was not allowed, and that her mother bought her a tin of salmon for the trip, thus ensuring that this smell would forever evoke the day when her status changed from that of an embodied and recognised member of a family and community to that of another anonymous emigrant: 'All you've to do to me is mention salmon, and I can describe one day in my life from early morning, until that night – just the smell of salmon.' The initial sense of depersonalisation that resulted from her being identified as the one to leave was compounded by the insensitive nature of her departure. Mary's account of leaving Cobh holds little of the romance of a stereotypical scene of emigrant departure. There are no farewells or defining moments of sorrow or excitement, only a sense of a young woman surrendering in stages to the deterministic imperatives of emigration:

> The tender was going out at a certain time [...]. There was a kind of galvanised shed, and once you went inside that door, that was closed, and that was good-bye then to your family, they were gone. And you were there amongst the crowd waiting to go on this tender [...]. They opened up a hatch, a door, and they put a ramp from the *Georgic* to the tender and we went up on that [...]. They hustle you in, they don't care, they were English; it was an English boat [....] and we were given a cup of tea, and it was my first time in my life seeing a roll [...]. A white roll was put on a plate and we all got a cup of tea, a roll and a piece of butter.

Mary here explains her sense of loss and depersonalisation in terms of the nationality of the (English) ship rather than the (Irish) socio-political conditions that produced mass emigration. Food again assumes symbolic value, as the white roll, like many of her experiences of emigration, becomes both a source of pleasure and a reminder of her disconnection from all that is familiar. But whereas the scene of departure is evacuated of romance, the moment of arrival is saturated with stereotypical images of the American Dream and the anticipation of a new life in the 'promised land'.

Mary's arrival in New York harbour coincided with her attending Mass on the ship:

> We were docking on Saturday morning [...]. We had Mass [...] because it was a holy day, the 15th of August [...]. I can remember well standing up for the gospel inside at Mass and looking out the window, and I can never forget the sun as long as I live. It was huge, and the colour of it. I never saw a sun like that here [...]. And right behind the sun as we came up along into New York harbour, we passed the Statue of Liberty. You know, you don't forget the likes of that, you just don't [...]. We had no interest in Mass at that time I can tell you, it was just looking up at this beautiful symbol of liberty and freedom and welcoming, it was beautiful.

Breda: And what did you think it would bring you?
Mary: Fulfilment I suppose. A nice way of life. But that is there, there is no denying that, there is a nice way of life in America. Their standard of living is superior to the rest of the world I think.

Symbols of the American Dream here vie with the Mass for Mary's attention, but it is a most uneven contest. The morning sun and the Statue of Liberty are described in heavenly terms as emblems of beauty, liberty, freedom and the prospect of a fulfilling life. At this narrative moment, Mary's identification with America and the American Dream seems virtually complete. Almost immediately, however, this harmony is threatened by the question about what she thought America would bring her. To answer it, she has to overlook her own difficulties in settling there (articulated elsewhere in the narrative) in order to maintain the notion of America as a land of opportunity which offers 'a nice way of life'.

The physical discomfort of wearing the heavy suit sent to her by her relatives introduces a further note of uncertainty and ambivalence:

So here I landed on the 15th of August in a heatwave with a woollen suit on. And if I was naked I'd have been warm, you know. But to have the nervousness of meeting them [her relatives], that clammy feeling in my body, and I couldn't wait to get home to get off these clothes [ . . . ]. One of my aunts, I can remember her saying to me, 'Now Mary, it is the month of August, and don't think for one minute that you won't need a winter coat'. So she said, 'You'd better buy your winter coat now while the sales are on'. I didn't know what a sale was.

This uncomfortable scene of arrival is another defining moment of depersonalisation for Mary because her relatives are not expecting to recognise her personally, but rather the suit she is wearing. Dress here functions less as 'a gesture of independence' (Alexander, 1994: 219) and self-definition, as in many women's autobiographical narratives, and more as a sign that she had followed her relatives' emigration plan and successfully negotiated her passage. Thus, her aunt's advice to buy a winter coat is a reminder that the New York to which she has come never stays the same, and that clothes have a functional purpose.

The America of Mary's mother's stories and of her childhood imagination was not the America of her migrant experiences. Her first job was in an insurance company in Newark, New Jersey. She later moved to New York to be near friends and got a job with Blue Cross health insurance, where there were other Irish workers. However, she found it hard to settle down and notes that after a few years, when none of her siblings had followed her to the US, she resolved to return to Ireland. Just after she bought her return ticket, however, she met her future husband who was also from Clare.

They were married in New York and had two children there before finally returning to Ireland for good in 1965, by which time three of Mary's siblings had emigrated to the US. In response to my question about what changes she found on her first return visit in 1960, Mary described her shock at the lack of acknowledgement of the money and parcels she had sent home in the intervening seven years:

> Instead of buying a winter coat, I sent home packages. I wasn't in America two months when they had a package at home. And at that time you had to go to the store, and you had to get a cardboard box, you had to buy brown paper, you had to buy twine. You had to go to the post office and get the tags that you'd put on the packages [ . . . ]. And the maximum weight was 22 lbs to send to Ireland, and many a time I had to bring them back again, open them up and take out some of the clothes [ . . . ]. But then I landed home in 1960 and I find that every single one of my younger [family] members, I expected them to say 'thanks Mary'. Never. This is the one thing I noticed in 1960, they had too much compared to what we had, they didn't appreciate what we had sent from America. They really didn't.

This account suggests that in the course of her seven-year absence, Mary's Irish family had effectively become 'other'. 'They' had 'too much', otherwise they would have been appreciative of her efforts to support them from abroad. Her detailed description of the work involved in sending parcels home is a reminder of the assumed purpose of her emigration in the first place, which was so 'naturalised' that it did not require recognition. It also points to how quickly a complex cultural 'time-warp' emerges between emigrant and non-emigrant experiences.

Mary finally realised her desire to return to Ireland to live when she refused to go back to the US after a holiday with her husband in 1965. She notes: 'I suppose we had a silent pact that we'd love to go home for good', and describes arriving back in Ireland as follows:

> The day I landed, I found myself, I could be myself. I suppose I am so Irish to the core, you know.
> Breda: What does that mean?
> Mary: It was like as if when you live in a foreign country, you are conscious of being different, and you mix with so many different nationalities that you have to have a certain level of pretence, or to live up to their expectations, you know [ . . . ]. By going to America I became very broadminded [ . . . ]. I know if I had stayed in Ireland I would have been very narrow-minded. I always knew that, because people were held down [ . . . ], from your parents to what they expected you not to do, to the parish priest who was the ruler of the parish [ . . . ]. Emigration showed

both of us what we were capable of and it proved that we were capable of anything.

If Mary's narrative of emigration is characterised by inevitability, depersonalisation and non-recognition, her narrative of return is marked by her coming into her own – becoming herself. The 'homeland' is here constructed as a place of familiarity and authenticity, and she articulates a sense of unity between her sense of self and the larger abstraction, Ireland, which connotes cultural recognition, belonging and security. Her encounter with difference in America is seen as opening up horizons and revealing her personal potential, so that she comes 'home' a changed woman to a known Ireland that reinforces her sense of herself as 'Irish to the core'. Thus, her emigrant experience enables her to inhabit Ireland with new potential. At the same time, however, the narrow confines of Irish belonging policed by family and church during the 1950s represent 'unhomely' aspects of Irish society that are projected onto those who stayed. So in order to construct her native place as a site of 'origin' and 'homeland' where she does not have to work at fitting in, as she did in America, cultural difference and change have to be evacuated from the national space in order to make it congenially inhabitable.

In nearly all of the life narratives archived by this project, the concluding sections are marked by an attempt to bridge the gap between the narrated events and the storytelling event, between the then and the now. In Mary's case, her final reflections on her life invoke a moral discourse of Irish femininity which reveals the kinds of self-monitoring practices that she uses in order to produce herself as a 'good' woman:

> Our parents, they loved us, they took good care of us, but I think myself they were a bit over-protective. When I think of how innocent I was at 19, going to America [ . . . ]. I was let go out into the wild, wild world so innocent, you know. [ . . . ] Speaking now as a girl, I was never told the facts of life. Never. But I had the instinct not to do wrong, and that was all I needed. I didn't have to be told anything. But once you know that you don't do wrong, you are protected right there. And all of my friends were the very same, [ . . . ] we'd go to dances and we always knew who to avoid [ . . . ]. And the different life we have today. Okay, it's a different society, but I still don't think it's right. I honestly think a girl is demeaning herself, the fellas will take advantage at any time of a girl. I don't care who he is.

Young Irish femininity in the 1950s is constructed here through discourses of innocence and sexual self-regulation. Innocence, as Gráinne O'Flynn argues, was the 'leading female characteristic and mode of action' associated with ideal Irish womanhood in the mid-twentieth century (1987: 79). Furthermore, the instinct 'not to do wrong' was produced at the time by educational messages and other public discourses which framed the female body as dangerous (O'Flynn, 1987: 92–93). Young women's practices of self-surveillance included knowing 'who to avoid' and how to 'stand firm' while remaining ignorant/innocent of matters of sex and sexuality – practices which are represented as 'second nature' in Mary's narrative. However, the moral authority of these discourses depended on the everyday rituals, statements and rules of church, school and family which produced in some young women what appeared to be a 'natural' sense of self-monitoring and sexual restraint. At the time, the apparent 'naturalness' of these gendered imperatives was underpinned by the social concealment of women who became pregnant outside of marriage, either via emigration or institutionalisation in Mother and Baby homes (Milotte, 1997; Garrett, 2000).

The repression of female sexuality by constructing it as a threat, therefore, becomes a naturalised disposition that is learned, embodied and internalised through socially prescriptive discourses. Yet while Mary's narrative identifies church and family as perpetuating censorious and narrow-minded attitudes, this interpretation does not extend to their roles in reproducing Irish femininity as pure, asexual and maternal. It is Irish women's sexual practices that come to mark both social change and continuity of the self in Mary's story. Ireland is recognised as 'a different society' now because of young women's sexually active lifestyles. Thus, the idea of women's bodies and sexuality as vulnerable to exploitation and in need of regulation by women themselves represents a 'truism' that links her past and present selves. As in many of the other archived narratives, women are implicitly assumed here to be the guardians of society's morals, both in the past and in the present. And despite her invocation of the sexual 'order of things' as a marker of continuity, it is notable that Mary's relationship to sexuality is portrayed as a reflexive one, framed by a discourse of 'choice' between the different possibilities of Irish femininity and sexuality available to women at the time of her narration.

## Narrating 'home', femininity and staying-put

Annie was born the second of six children in 1931 in rural County Cavan.[7] At the time she narrated her life story, she described herself as a retired farmer and widowed mother of six children, and her parents as 'small farmers up on the mountain'. One of her sons was killed in a tractor accident when he was eight years old; his death haunts the narrative, especially when she reflects on her present circumstances. Besides her account of this tragedy, the most poignant narrative moments are those in which she describes her adoption at the age of six by a childless aunt and uncle. One day in December 1937, Annie and her older brother John returned from school to find that their mother and three younger siblings were missing. When her father failed to answer her questions, a neighbour revealed that her mother had gone away for a while and that her siblings were with a neighbour. She heard later in her life that her mother had been admitted to hospital with post-natal depression. Annie's aunt and uncle had offered to adopt her younger brother Joe, but because he refused, Annie offered to go instead. She recalls:

> And I went, sad though, wasn't it? And I never went back [ . . . ]. She said, 'Will you go?', and I said, 'I will'. But I had no shoes and John said, 'I will give you my boots'. [ . . . ] I remember I put on the boots and couldn't get away quick enough in case he changed his mind and took them back. That is the truth, and I can remember that so well, it was a very trying thing, it was very sad. So I went there, and stayed there. Then I used to hear the people saying, 'Mrs McGarry [the pseudonymous name of Annie's aunt] you have a big child'. She had no family of her own, they were the same as my mum and dad to me [ . . . ]. I always said if I had twenty children I wouldn't let one of them go, but they were so good to me.

This recollection conveys the confusion of feelings that Annie associates with her six-year-old self: sadness about the circumstances of her leaving, indebtedness to her aunt and uncle, and anger at her parents for letting her go. Her brother's generosity in giving his boots to her adds to the poignancy of her departure, and deepens her guilt about taking his boots when her aunt and uncle gave her so much. Like Mary's narrative, Annie's is deeply marked by the workings of obligation and loss. The obligation to be the adopted one not only meant the loss of her family and 'home', but also of her personal identity when she found herself 'standing in' for her aunt's child. This experience in turn produced a longing to be reunited with her family and a simultaneous indebtedness to her aunt and uncle.

Later in the narrative Annie describes leaving school at 14 because her aunt was ill, and her subsequent attempts to emigrate:

Breda: So you were thinking of going to England as well?
Annie: I would have loved to be a nurse, a maternity nurse, and still to this day, if I could have, that was a job I would have loved to do [ . . . ]. I would get forms and the letters would come and my aunt would give out to me about it, and not to go, so it ended up I stayed [ . . . ]. I was half afraid that when I went to England I wouldn't be able to do it. Fear. I left home when I was six and that loneliness – it is hateful being on your own [ . . . ]. She didn't want me to go and if things went sour, how would I get back?
Breda: The next option was America, and what happened about that?
Annie: My aunt said not to go and to stay on, and whatever they had, they'd give it to me. She asked what would happen to her, and put her arms around me and I stayed. If I promised something I would never go back on it. I could never understand promising things and going back on it. All the years I said to myself I wished I had gone to America.

If one of the promises of modernity is that it is possible to transcend everyday life to find something special, then this promise is located in the US and England at this point in Annie's narrative. Emigration is constructed here as a desirable route to personal and professional fulfilment, part of the impetus for which, interestingly, comes from Annie's mother. By contrast, staying is constructed as a matter of obligation, entrapment and missed opportunities. But staying also represents security and belonging, while the prospect of emigration produces a fear of the unfamiliar. Having lost her first home at six, Annie's desire to emigrate is tempered by a fear of losing another home if her plans go awry. 'Home' is therefore an unstable phenomenon in Annie's narrative, one which is continually subject to re-negotiation. Furthermore, the fact that her narrative is structured around the opposition between familial duty and individual desire, with the former taking precedence over the latter, means that her obligation as an adopted daughter is invoked as the moral justification for giving up opportunities to emigrate and to train as a nurse. Instead she takes on the burden of being 'a good daughter' (Steedman, 1986: 105) who will remain loyal to her adoptive parents and repay them for bringing her up. Staying, therefore, becomes a matter of keeping a promise and keeping a 'home' for herself, though it continues to be inflected by a lingering desire to emigrate.

The dominance of family survival and 'home' as cultural markers that give meaning to staying-put means that personal longings and desires, although available as modes of articulating the self, are ultimately relegated to a subordinate position in Annie's narrative:

Breda: Do you still wish you'd gone to America?
Annie: No not one bit, I love the children, and if I'd have gone to America, I'd have had no children, no husband. For 41 years I was happy as Larry and [there were] times when I hadn't a shilling [ . . . ]. I never knew what it was to be unhappy.

Whereas emigration had the potential to lift Annie's life out of the drudgery of hard work and poverty earlier in her narrative, hardship, staying-put and family here become the resources upon which she draws to narrate a sense of contented selfhood in the year 2000. Emigration to England or America might fulfil desires for excitement and career opportunities, but it is seen as offering little potential for marriage and family. Indeed, Annie's emigrant peers are invoked as evidence that, in the end, she made the better choice by staying:

They'd talk about the great time they had away. I'd be surprised then at the men they ended up with. I would then think to myself, 'Did I miss much?'[ . . . ]. They would say, 'I am married, I am separated, but I don't mind'. I'd hate that. I'm glad I did that [stayed] [ . . . ]. I made her [her aunt] happy, and didn't build up her hopes that when she was dead and gone that no one could care for her. I never regret that. I have good health myself, the children were good, and I got what I wanted from life.

Annie's loyalty to her aunt extends beyond her aunt's lifetime because, by inheriting and running the farm, she sees herself as memorialising her. Moreover, the tensions around the decision to stay are reconciled by taking up the subject positions of 'good daughter' and 'good wife and mother', and by constructing emigrant women as failing in the domains of marriage and family. Her childhood loss of home and family is counterbalanced by her successful creation of her own home and family in adulthood. Similarly, her desires to be a maternity nurse and to go to America are repressed at the moment that family in Ireland is embraced as evidence that staying was the best decision. Indeed, staying can only be articulated as the better option by portraying her emigrant peers as losing out in the areas of marriage and family. As she sees it, the 'great time they had away' came at the cost of losing 'Irish' family values. This othering of the emigrant may be adopted as a strategic means of allowing the non-migrant self to be positively narrated, and as such is common to many of the narratives of staying-put in the archive.[8]

A reflective meta-narration takes place towards the end of Annie's story, in which she positions the storytelling event in relation to the events narrated (Bauman, 1986: 100). Reflecting on emigration as a significant aspect of both her own life and that of the community, she states:

I miss all the people I knew that are gone and there is no one to listen, they [the young generation] can't understand you. I think they are ashamed to think the people were poor [ . . . ]. To a certain extent, the people who never had to emigrate, they are lucky. You hear people say, 'I didn't go'. I'd have loved to go. Yet I am happy with what I did do, I had no worry in the world. You've no regrets and don't know much about the modern life in foreign countries either.

A notable feature of Annie's desire to tell her story was her sense that in 'Celtic Tiger' Ireland nobody wanted to hear about 'old times', an impression that she registers in the above excerpt. The storytelling event thus offers her an opportunity to bring her memories of times past into the present, and to reconcile her original desire to emigrate in the 1950s with the lingering remnants of that desire in the present. Tensions remain, however, and emerge in the shift from the first person to the second person to articulate the absence of regrets about staying in Ireland. The risks that emigration represented in young adulthood were avoided by staying within the known and familiar. Indeed, Annie's decision to stay is couched in terms of knowing her 'place' in the world, which she locates in the familiar environs of Cavan rather than the 'modern' milieux of 'foreign countries'. At this point in her narrative she takes control of the past and becomes reconciled with it, so that the past becomes grounds for the present truth of the self (Probyn, 1996: 116). Yet despite this attempt at narrative continuity and closure, the present truth of the self remains ambiguous.

In both of the oral life histories discussed here, particular versions of 1950s Irish femininity are narrated, the most obvious being the 'good daughter' who knew her place in relation to family duty, sexuality and personal desire. Indeed, the figure of the 'good daughter' emerges as a central device in accounting for both the migrant and the non-migrant self. In each case, individual desire and agency bend to the moral demands of family obligation and the apparent inevitability of staying or emigrating. By the 2000s, however, both women's self-articulation has more to do with the notion of a chosen self and an emphasis on family as an important marker of a successful life as a woman in Ireland. This shift from 'good daughter' to 'good wife and mother' enables a continuity of the self, despite the many discontinuities that mark both life narratives. The adoption of morally evaluative relationships to other women – emigrants in Annie's account, young contemporary Irish women in Mary's – further facilitates the narration of a coherent sense of the self. 'Biographical autonomy' is therefore achieved through adherence to the dominant disciplinary practices of Irish femininity and through the discriminatory construction of 'others' in the narration of a chosen self.

It must also be noted that belonging is imagined in these narratives as extending beyond Ireland, taking in America and Britain as possible locations of personal and professional fulfilment. In the process, notions of 'home' emerge as the product of historical and contemporary negotiations of staying-put, migration and return. But despite this transnational imagining of belonging, a division arises between a 'familiar' Ireland and 'foreign' emigrant destinations. Although both narratives suggest that 'home' and belonging have to be worked at, they also embody a desire for attachment based on an uncomplicated familiarity with the native place. In Annie's account in particular, threats to this familiarity are located in the 'foreign' journeys of emigrants and the bodies and practices of emigrants themselves. Both of these women, moreover, step into the landscape of early twenty-first-century Irish femininities and see themselves as self-styled repositories of older, more 'traditional' feminine and family values. In each case, emigration and staying-put authorise these feminine selves in remarkably similar ways, in that these processes are woven into narratives of successful Irish femininity based on duty, obligation and family reproduction.

## The orally narrated self and the autobiographical self

In the final section of this chapter, I wish to consider oral life narrative as a genre that is both similar to and different from written autobiography. My aim is to reflect on the multiple relations that exist between several discursive elements – 'experience' and life narrative, oral history and its representation in transcript form, the orally narrated self and the autobiographical self – in order to distinguish between the different sites, practices and effects of these two genres. As Plummer reminds us, the narrative of a life is not the life itself, and the occasions and conventions of narration shape life stories more than 'the contours of the life as lived' (2001: 186). This is certainly true of the two narratives discussed above. In each case, what is remembered and told is not just a particular experience but a socially prescribed mode of interpreting it, so that it is narrated using prevailing moral norms and accepted causal discourses (Diprose, 1994: 84). It is important, however, to avoid collapsing experience into discourse completely. Shari Stone-Mediatore warns against reading experience as 'a mirror of available discourses [ . . . ] with no excess' (2000: 115), and Avtar Brah insists that discursive categories work through embodied living subjects who experience them as 'realities'. Brah also points out that at any point in time 'the subject-in-process experiences itself as the "I", and both consciously and unconsciously replays and resignifies positions in which it is located and invested' (1996: 125). In the case of Mary and Annie, their narratives force us to engage with the relationships between emigration, the family and disciplinary practices of femininity in modern Ireland. They also revise the accepted relationships between emigration, memory and subjectivity by highlighting the mutual othering of emigrant and non-emigrant women, the silences that imperatives of family loyalty impose, and the operation of gendered modes of remembering in reproducing coherent self-narratives.

Oral life narratives and autobiographies, then, follow the conventions of narration but are not contained by them. And while narrative conventions structure both of these genres, interpretation involves different considerations in each case. Whereas matters of form and style are central to analyses of written autobiographies, the occasion of telling assumes greater significance in oral life narratives (Tonkin, 1992: 53). This is because the latter are staged performances framed by a verbal exchange between a subject and an interlocutor, so that the text is jointly produced. Interpretation begins when the project is conceived and continues during the interview process, whereby the oral narrative is materialised on tape and embedded in wider interpretive contexts by the institutional frameworks and discourses that frame both the narration and the recording. The first person to speak is usually the interviewer who, in the case of the *Breaking the Silence* project, began with the question 'Where were you born?', thereby establishing 'the basis of narrative authority' (Portelli, 1997: 9). In the case of the two narratives discussed above, both women responded to local newspaper articles about the project, each feeling strongly that they had stories to tell. Although emigration and staying-put were the stated themes of the project, the memory frames of the narrators often touched on other, unrelated life events, so that the interviewers had to nudge their subjects continually towards engagement with memories of the 1950s and decisions about emigration.[9] As with conventional autobiography, the anticipated audience affected the content and direction of the oral life narratives to a significant degree. For many of those who took part in the project, the prospect of family members hearing their accounts meant that certain things remained unsaid, thereby undoing any illusion of a complete or transparent life story. Thus, the resultant narratives can be shown to be intimately conditioned by the contexts of telling, which include the interviewer's research frame, the narrator's memory frame, the institutional basis of the research and the immediate and anticipated audience.[10]

It is also important to note that the ideological context of the occasion of narration often differs from that of the actual events being narrated. Mary and Annie, for example, both narrated their experiences of 1950s Ireland in the very different socio-economic and cultural contexts of the early 2000s. At first reading their stories suggest a certain fatalism about their own destinies, in that their 1950s selves, as constructed through their negotiations of staying-put and emigrating, appear inseparable from the general pattern of life in Ireland at that time.[11] Yet there are moments in each text when the self shifts outside this pattern. For example, a lived complexity emerges from Annie's account of how her career and family aspirations were modified by her desire to emigrate, and from Mary's description of how she renegotiated her emigrant status to bring about her return to Ireland. Nonetheless, when the ideological context has changed and 1950s concepts have lost their purchase, it is more difficult to mobilise language to account for earlier experiences. Thus, both narrators tend to invoke explanatory modes that are consonant with 1950s ideology but which conflict with twenty-first-century discourses of individualisation predicated on 'choice'. This dissonance inflects both women's subjectivities and highlights the social and temporal gap between the narrated events and the occasion of narration.

A further disjunction emerges when there is a gap between the agenda of the researcher and the narrator's ability to articulate experiences which are the object of study, or when there is an absence of language to account for specific life events. A central framing agenda for the *Breaking the Silence* project was the question of how *staying* in Ireland during a period of mass emigration was experienced and remembered. The available cultural discourses, however, tend to focus on the act of leaving. The effects of this are evident in Annie's narrative, which is structured around accounts of her attempts to leave and her perceptions of emigrant life and emigrants themselves. That is to say, staying as an object of reflection, or as an event within the life narrative, is constituted in her story through available discourses of emigration and family. Furthermore, staying-put only becomes a legitimate autobiographical discourse at the point when she reflects on her life as daughter, wife and mother and her location in the familiar surroundings of rural Cavan. So the absence of a discourse of staying-put, while in some ways a limitation, nevertheless enables a pushing at the boundaries of prevailing ways of speaking and thinking about emigration and Irish society.

Another feature of the oral life narrative genre relates to the way oral testimony is undermined by its representation in written form. Oral narration is seen as having lost much of its authority as a result of cultural modernisation and the concomitant privileging of literacy and literature (Gugelberger, 1996: 1–22). The impetus to textualise as a means of communication and dissemination is almost unavoidable; even in a technological age where sound recordings are more accessible, the perception remains that narrative meaning is transmitted more quickly via textual representation. Oral life narratives force us, therefore, to confront the ways in which the literary colonises the oral (Gugelberger, 1996: 10–11). While the oral narrative can be seen as 'an extraliterary or even antiliterary form of discourse' (Beverley, 1996: 37), it is rendered textual, if not literary, via transcription. The problem, however, is that the significance of the occasion of telling is undermined by this transcription process, since it is 'necessarily reductionist, a skeleton standing in for a live body' (Tonkin, 1992: 16). Portelli notes that a transcript written in a way that is 'so minutely faithful to sounds that it turns a beautiful speech into an unreadable page can hardly be described as "accurate"' (1997: 15). Moreover, transcription means that the intentions and ideology of the transcriber are imposed on the narrative, thereby creating further ambiguities and absences. Thus, the transcription process produces a form of genre bending, whereby the oral narrative mutates into a kind of hybrid autobiography.[12]

Significant differences between the genres remain, however. In the oral life narrative the researcher is always present as a mediator whose intentions, alongside those of the narrator, shape the telling. Furthermore, the 'relations of production' and the occasions of narration are necessarily more prominent features of oral life narrative than of autobiography, and the transcribed testimony is always haunted by the non-textual and extra-linguistic aspects of its narration.[13] There is also a sense in which oral narratives have more of the 'modest proposal' about them than autobiographies, in so far as they are elicited rather than self-initiated. This aspect is underlined by the fact that an oral narrator usually speaks within the context of a research project and so tends to be seen as an ordinary witness or 'a "real" popular voice', rather than as an exceptional individual or cultural 'hero' (Beverley, 1996: 34). So whereas the conventions of autobiography imply an ideology of individuation based on a unique and coherent selfhood, those of the oral narrative suggest the subject's embeddedness in a set of shared, communal experiences. This means that the oral narrator's testimony tends to be more indicative of a particular group or class situation than is usually the case in a conventional autobiography (Beverley, 1996: 35). Thus it can be seen that both Mary and Annie articulate a desire to bear witness to what they regard as forgotten times and experiences of (non-)migration in the 1950s. In this way, their life narratives become forms of testimony in which their concern is not just to tell, but to take responsibility for social events beyond their personal stories which have 'general (non personal) validity and consequences' (Feldman and Laub, 1992: 204).

In contrast to the individual desire that typically drives the autobiographical self, therefore, the oral narrative is often seen as articulating modest, everyday experiences, frequently negotiated in relation to wider familial and communal concerns, as in the case of both Mary and Annie. This distinction needs to be nuanced, however. There are moments in both women's narratives when the selves they articulate are more individualistic than relational, such as when they talk about the ways in which they triumphed over life's obstacles. Although couched in the feminised terms of familial relationships, at these moments their narratives take on a tone of heroic masculine transcendence and produce the narrator in the mode of cultural 'hero', a mode that can be read as a conservative means of authorising situations of relative privilege and playing down the need for social change (Beverley, 1996: 36). As the past becomes the grounds for the present 'truth' of the self, some of the women's adversities – whether they relate to staying-put or to involuntary emigration – are transcended and reinvoked as resources for an achieved subjectivity anchored in family and national community.

## Conclusion

Personal memories invoke cultural, national and other collectively shared memories that offer insights into the workings of memory in the production of the self. The life narratives collected for the *Breaking the Silence* project tap into a popular memory rich in the stories of family, locality and nation, and offer unique access to the quotidian negotiations of self and identity in a cultural context of high out-migration. They also identify moments of 'social specificity' (Steedman, 1986: 5) that can help with the revisioning of both the Irish past and the Irish present. Because certain languages of description, explanation and judgement come to acquire the value of 'truth', they tend to structure cultural memory and to reproduce particular forms of subjectivity. But memory and subjectivity cannot be understood only as effects of discourses. Although experience is always constructed through available social discourses, it is in the tensions between experience and discourse, and at the junctures of intersecting discourses, that the potential for unsettling accepted 'truths' emerges.

In this chapter I have examined the elusive yet pervasive presence of emigration and gender in the making of Irish cultural memory. In mid-twentieth-century Britain and Ireland, women's lives were identified primarily within the domain of domesticity and with what Alison Light calls 'conservative modernity' (1991: 1–19). However, defining women in this way can be seen as a symptom of the gendered dynamics of modernity, which position working-class women in particularly insecure and circumscribed positions. Furthermore, since women have traditionally been 'denied the authority to define the cultural past', the remembered lives of Mary and Annie represent the 'struggle for a new way of looking back' (Haaken, 1998: 2). And while conservative impulses are produced by this process, so too are feminist moments that can be mined for analyses of how Irish women's subjectivities are narrated by women themselves. In order to contest the naturalisation of Irish femininity as familial, it is necessary to understand how this operates as a discursive structure that constitutes subjective experiences of gender. In the narratives discussed here, the women are both subject to disciplinary discourses of ideal Irish femininity and capable of invoking aspects of this discourse as a compensatory strategy that helps them to resolve their contradictory positioning in relation to continuity and change in modern Ireland.

The subjectivities narrated by Mary and Annie are characterised by two particular contradictory impulses: the desire for a reconciliation of past and present, and the desire to engage with often painful memories of the past that embody the ghosts of other possible selves. Towards the end of each narrative, however, there is a movement towards 'biographical autonomy' and a construction of unchosen life events into a willed self-narrative, whereby past experiences are manipulated to create a coherent present self. Although it can be argued that this mode of narrative memory 'merely reproduces the present as an effect of the past, of past causes' (Probyn, 1996: 117), certain moments are imbued with special, continuing significance. In Annie's case, her adoption juts out of her past into her present as a decisive moment of self-definition, while in Mary's narrative, the non-recognition of her provision for her siblings while she was an emigrant produces a potentially more reflexive relationship to family and obligation. At such moments, prevailing discourses of emigration and the family come under pressure, and the resultant contradictions, tensions and silences open up new possibilities for the reconfiguring of the relationship between past and present subjectivities (Probyn, 1996: 118). This mode of engagement with personal history ultimately means that the past exists not to explain the present, but rather to encourage new forms of becoming, moments that can offer fresh starting points for the self.

## Notes

1. By the end of the decade, emigration stood at a rate of 14.8 per 1000 of population, with those in the 15–29 age group being the most likely to leave (Delaney, 2000: 160–225).
2. The *Breaking the Silence* project was undertaken between 2000 and 2002 and was partly funded by the Higher Education Authority under the PRTLI1 initiative.
3. Of those who contacted us to take part in the project, 73 were men and 43 were women. While conducting the study, we tried to target more women and ensure

a geographical spread. The urban/rural divide and class distribution were not easily quantifiable because of social and geographical mobility. Some individuals who emigrated and returned were included because of their particular interest in questions of staying-put, and in some cases because they identified themselves as the ones who stayed. The interviews usually took place in the interviewee's home and lasted for periods of one to four hours.

4. This archive of 90 contributions (78 in CD-ROM, minidisk and cassette tape formats and 12 textual contributions) is located in the Boole Library, University College Cork. Another outcome of the project was an innovative Internet archive in real audio format of those narratives with appropriate copyright permission. This site can be accessed via http://migration.ucc.ie/.

5. This project coincided with a series of revelations about clerical and institutional child abuse and the establishment of tribunals of inquiry into corruption in Irish planning, politics and business.

6. Mary's narrative exists in CD-ROM, minidisk and cassette tape sound formats, with a textual summary, chronological log and demographic details, in the Irish Centre for Migration Studies (ICMS) *Breaking the Silence* Archive at the Boole Library. I interviewed Mary at her home on 5 July 2002.

7. Annie's narrative exists in CD-ROM, minidisk and cassette tape sound formats, with a textual summary, chronological log, demographic details and correspondence, in the ICMS *Breaking the Silence* Archive at the Boole Library. I interviewed Annie at her home on 23 October 2000.

8. Although those who stayed are othered in Mary's account of her first return visit, this is a temporary othering, as she eventually returns to live in Ireland. The fact that she has to incorporate both migrant and non-migrant selves into one narrative means that this dichotomy cannot work in the same way as in narratives of staying-put.

9. A memory frame emerges from what popular memory theorists refer to as the cultural circuit, which is a feedback loop between personal accounts and pubic discourse (Summerfield, 2000: 95).

10. The interviewer's research frame 'influences the path through the past which the narrator takes, and requires the narrator to remember where they have been' in particular ways and within specific parameters (Summerfield, 2000: 95).

11. In this respect, they accord with Richard Hoggart's observation about the fatalism of working-class people in 1950s Britain (1959: 91).

12. It remains the case that most academic discussions of oral narratives collude with the privileging of the textual form by working from the transcription, as indeed I do in this chapter, though my use of interactive extracts acts as a reminder of the dialogic context of the narration. It is also important to remember that orality and writing have co-existed for centuries. As Portelli points out: 'If many written sources are based on orality, modern orality itself is saturated with writing' (1991: 52).

13. The dilemmas that arise with regard to representing the occasion of telling centre on the problem of weighing the text down with situational details that can render it unreadable.

# 7
# Twentieth-Century Gaelic Autobiography: From *lieux de mémoire* to Narratives of Self-invention

*Máirín Nic Eoin*

Autobiographical writing was a central and defining aspect of twentieth-century Irish-language literary production and is still one of the most prevalent literary genres in the language. The earliest autobiography to be published in book form was *Mo Sgéal Féin* (*My Story*, 1915) by Cork-born novelist, critic and language activist An tAthair Peadar Ua Laoghaire (1839–1920), which records the social background and early life of one of the most active and controversial figures in the Gaelic revival and literary movement. While autobiographical works of different kinds have appeared regularly ever since, the sub-genre to receive the most sustained critical attention to date has undoubtedly been the autobiography of Gaeltacht life, usually the result of a collaborative effort involving an unlettered 'author' and various intermediaries. The bulk of this chapter will focus on the importance of this kind of autobiography, though consideration will also be given to other types of life writing, including the accounts of non-native speakers of Irish and texts dealing with particular social, political or cultural experiences, including travel. While accepting the theoretical usefulness of differentiating various forms of life writing – memoir, travel journal, diary, autobiography, auto-ethnography and so on – it will be argued that the mode of production of much Irish-language autobiography has often resulted in the confusion of such generic categories.[1] The chapter will take the form of a historical overview, identifying key texts and critical approaches, and concluding with a consideration of the relationship between autobiography and Irish-language fiction.

## Gaeltacht lives: autobiography as *lieu de mémoire*

*An tOileánach* (*The Islandman*, 1929) by Tomás Ó Criomhthain (1855–1937) is the most significant work of autobiography to have been written in Irish and was a milestone in the emergence of twentieth-century Gaeltacht literature in general. It was unusual in its time in that it was the work of a fisherman who was literate in Irish, though its production – like that of most Gaeltacht autobiographies – depended on the active encouragement, practical assistance and editorial efforts of certain critical intermediaries. Ó Criomhthain was born on the Great Blasket Island and learned to read Irish as an adult during sojourns in the nearby mainland village of Dunquin. As an exceptional Irish speaker and storyteller, he attracted the attention of a number of distinguished scholars, including the Norwegian linguist Carl Marstrander and the English Celticist Robin Flower, who became a close friend and a regular visitor to the island. Through his contact with Irish scholars, Ó Criomhthain came under the influence of the Gaelic League and wrote regularly for Irish-language periodicals in the period from 1916 to 1934. It was through the encouragement of Brian Ó Ceallaigh from Killarney, however, who introduced him to the work of Pierre Loti and Maxim Gorky, that Ó Criomhthain began to record scenes of island life and then to draft an account of his own experiences on the island. The result was two books: *Allagar na hInise* (*Island Talk*, 1928) and *An tOileánach* (1929), the first editions of which were arranged and edited by Kerry-born scholar and editor Pádraig Ó Siochfhradha ('An Seabhac'). While drawing on similar material, these two works are very different in form and technique. The immediacy of the impressionistic and episodic *Allagar na hInise*, much of which is dialogue presented in diary form, is replaced in *An tOileánach* by a more conscious presentation of socio-economic details in a narrative mode which is decidedly, though at times awkwardly, autobiographical.

Ó Siochfhradha's editorial role in shaping the first edition of *An tOileánach* has been widely commented upon (Ó Siochfhradha, 1992; Ó Coileáin, 1992, 1998). Not only was he responsible for shaping the material into chapters, he also augmented or omitted passages as he saw fit. While this was done in many cases to avoid repetition or tedium, he also edited out words, phrases and passages which were deemed to be lacking in decorum, and requested that Ó Criomhthain supplement his original account with additional descriptions, such as that of an island house, which was published as chapter 3 in the first edition (and again in Pádraig Ua Maoileoin's 1973 edition). It has been argued that the final chapter in particular, which provides the book's rationale, reflects the historical sensibility of its editor rather than the spirit of the author (Ó Coileáin, 1998: 39–42). It features the most famous passage of all, one which articulates a conscious sense of rupture with the past and a need for a more modern form of record-keeping to replace community memories:

Do scríobhas go mion-chruinn ar a lán dár gcúrsaí d'fhonn go mbeadh cuimhne i mball éigin ortha agus thugas iarracht ar mheon na ndaoine bhí im' thimcheall a chur síos chun go mbeadh ár dtuairisc 'ár ndiaidh, mar ná beidh ár leithéidí arís ann [ . . . ]. Beidh an Blascaod lá gan aenne de'n dream atá luaidhte agam sa leabhar so – ná aenne go mbeidh cuimhne aige orainn. Tugaim buidheachas do Dhia a thug cao' dhom gan an méid de'n tsaoghal a chonnac féin agus go rabhas ag bruic leis, a dhul amú, agus go mbeidh 'fhios im' dhiaidh conus mar bhí an saoghal lem' linn, agus na comharsain do bhí suas lem' linn. Ó lasadh an chéad teine insan oileán so níor scríobh aenne a bheatha ná a shaoghal ann. Adhbhar maoidhimh domh-sa mo scéal féin agus scéal mo chomharsan a chur síos. 'Neosaidh an scríbhinn seo conus mar bhí na h-oileánaigh ag déanamh sa tsean-aimsir. (Ó Criomhthain, 1929: 265–66)

I have written minutely of much that we did, for it was my wish that somewhere there should be a memorial of it all, and I have done my best to set down the character of the people about me so that some record of us might live after us, for the like of us will never be again [. . .]. One day there will be none left in the Blasket of all I have mentioned in this book – and none to remember them. I am thankful to God, who has given me the chance to preserve from forgetfulness those days that I have seen with my own eyes and have borne their burden, and that when I am gone men will know what life was like in my time and the neighbours that lived with me. Since the first fire was kindled in this island none has written of his life and his world. I am proud to set down my story and the story of my neighbours. This writing will tell how the Islanders lived in the old days. (O'Crohan, 1951: 244–45)

Such sentiments mirror those of Brian Ó Ceallaigh as expressed in an unpublished essay to which Ó Siochfhradha as editor had access. In referring to life as he witnessed it on the Great Blasket, Ó Ceallaigh clearly states his intentions:

I thought it a pity that this life should die, unrecorded, and I felt that Tomás could make it live on paper for future generations. I tried therefore, to make him realise what interest everyday incidents which were occurring around us would possess for people who were accustomed to a more comfortable and complicated existence. 'Write about what is happening here every day to yourself and to others,' I said. (quoted in Ó Conaire, 1992: 231)

Despite the important roles played by Ó Ceallaigh (as instigator) and Ó Siochfhradha (as editor) in shaping *An tOileánach*, it should be borne in mind that Ó Criomhthain did not respond to all editorial requests, but rather had his own ideas about what was appropriate and communicable. When Ó Siochfhradha suggested that he provide a fuller account of how he came to terms with the termination of his youthful love affair when a more pragmatic match was made for him by his sister, he did so in the hope that Ó Criomhthain would be encouraged to give a more illuminating account of the effect this course of events had on his life. But the request was to no avail, as Ó Siochfhradha explains:

> Á cheapadh bhíos go bhfaighinn caibidlí soilse uaidh a léireodh fealsún-acht agus tuairim fholaithe a aigne ar na nithe is bunúsaí agus is discréidí bhaineann le croí an duine – pé aca tuata nó léannta. Ach ní scríobh-fadh Tomás ach a bhfuil i gcló uaidh. Ar nós na seanmhuintire go léir sa Ghaeltacht – agus i dtuath na hÉireann i gcoitinne – ba neamhfhonn leis nithe discréideacha a anama a nochtadh. Bhí cion ar an dá mhnaoi sin aige agus urraim thar barr aige dhóibh. Ach b'in rud a bhain lena anam folaithe istigh, agus ba thréas in aghaidh a gcuimhne na rúin a bhí idir é is iad a sceitheadh. Ba rud coisricthe é a bhí i gcoimeád discréide ina chroí agus níor rud é chun bheith ag cur síos air le pobal Éireann. (Ó Siochf-hradha, 1992: 203)

> I thought I would get illuminating chapters from him that would clarify his philosophy and his mind's secrets in relation to the most fundamental and sensitive issues of an individual's heart – whether he be learned or not. But Tomás would only write that which is now published. Like all the old generation in the Gaeltacht – and in rural Ireland in general – he was unwilling to bare the secret affairs of his soul. He loved those two women and respected them accordingly. But that was a matter for his inner soul, and it would be a mark of disloyalty to their memory if he were to disclose the secrets he shared with them. It was a sacred thing to be held in the confidence of his heart and it was not something to be recounted to the people of Ireland.[2]

While the interactive process that produced *An tOileánach* may be further illuminated by Seán Ó Coileáin's recent edition, which presents the text as it is in the original manuscript, it is worth bearing in mind that the book was produced in the context of a larger field of cultural influence. Some of Ó Criomhthain's later journalistic writings would lead one to believe that he had a palpable awareness of the vulnerability of his native community and their culture.[3] Even some of his earlier writings, such as the songs published in the periodicals *An Lóchrann* and *Misneach* in 1917 and 1919, would indicate that he saw his own compositions as part of a larger nation-building project.[4] But whatever the origin of the sentiments expressed in the concluding chapter, the original edition of *An tOileánach* – which soon gained the status of a modern Gaelic classic – was to provide a model for later autobiographical depictions of Irish-language communities on the cusp of modernity. By representing a community on the verge of dissolution, Ó Criomhthain's book succeeded in making a *lieu de mémoire* of the Great Blasket Island and of Gaeltacht autobiography itself. In the words of Pierre Nora: 'Our consciousness is shaped by a sense that everything is over and done with, that something long since begun is now complete. Memory is constantly on our lips because it no longer exists' (1996: 1).

While Ó Criomhthain characterises his account as one of pure unmediated memory – 'Níl curtha síos agam ach an fhírinne; níor ghádh dhom aon cheapadóireacht mar bhí an aimsir fada agam agus is mór fós im' cheann' ['I have set down nothing but the truth; I had no need of invention, for I had plenty of time, and have still a good deal in my head' (1951: 242)] – a stylistic analysis of *An tOileánach* reveals the hand of a very conscious literary artist. However, whether the work is best read as a factual depiction of the life of an island community, as Ó Siochfhradha believed it was, or whether it satisfies contemporary notions of autobiography is a matter of ongoing critical debate. Cathal Ó Háinle (1999) – drawing on the most recent theoretical work of Cockshut, Eakin and Olney – has quite rightly foregrounded the tendency of critics to treat Ó Criomhthain's books and Gaeltacht life writing in general as social documents, thus failing to take adequate account of their distinctly autobiographical features. He has also pointed out the limitations of critical analyses which problematise the autobiographical tendency to fictionalise, acknowledging instead that fictionality is as innate a form of autobiographical composition as the assumption of referentiality associated with what Philippe Lejeune terms 'le pacte autobiographique'. Though Ó Háinle has undoubtedly identified a theoretical deficit in contemporary criticism of autobiography in Irish, he fails to take adequate account of the critical dilemma posed by the mode of production of most Gaeltacht autobiographies, which makes them fall more easily into the category of autoethnography than that of modern autobiography.

Autoethnography, as I wish to employ this debated term here, refers to first-person ethnographic accounts by individuals who are themselves natives of, and participants in, the community they are describing (Watson, 2001). While these accounts may be autobiographical, their authors are usually motivated less by a need to present the self and more by a desire to represent accurately the social experience of a cultural group. The development of Gaeltacht autobiography as a form of autoethnographic writing owes much to the archival spirit analysed by Nora, a spirit clearly discernible in the development of the folklore movement in Ireland (Ó Giolláin, 2000: 114–41). The impetus to record traditional lore and accounts of traditional lifestyles led to the direct involvement of folklorists – and scholars whose commemorative consciousness led them to memorialise what they saw as a dying Gaelic culture – in the production of Gaeltacht autobiography. When one considers the effect the collaborative mode of production had on the resultant texts – including editorial involvement in eliciting, recording, organising and presenting the material – it becomes clear why these books came to be analysed more for their sociological content than their literary qualities. It is ironic that such a modern literary form – whose essence, as Ó Háinle quite rightly points out, is 'the revelation of the author's perception of his or her own personality from the standpoint of the time of writing and in the light of remembered experience' (1999: 371) – was superimposed on modes of oral narrative which traditionally eschewed the overtly autobiographical. The result is a variety of hybrid forms, where the tension between the literary and the oral modes of address results in accounts which are episodic rather than thematic, inclusive rather than selective, agonistic rather than analytical, and objective and impersonal rather than subjective or confessional. It is hardly surprising, therefore, that many of these works strike contemporary readers as dull and repetitive, lacking the psychological impact of much modern prose literature, and of interest more for their ethnographic and social content than for the insights they offer into what Paul John Eakin (1985) regards as the central autobiographic processes of self-invention and identity formation.

The exceptionality of *An tOileánach* must be acknowledged, however. Its innate literary qualities, as exemplified by Ó Criomhthain's finely tuned idiom and terse use of language, have been seen to embody the essence of the man's personality, so much so that one critic, Máire Cruise O'Brien, went so far as to state that 'the objective record is so involved with the personality of the author that, on setting down the book, you feel you have come to know the man' (1977: 26–27). And while it has been faulted for its impersonality and lack of psychological depth, recent criticism displays a more nuanced appreciation of Ó Criomhthain's conscious literary style and his ability to present and embellish particular historical incidents (Ó Háinle, 1978, 1985, 1992, 1993). But whatever its merits or shortcomings, there is no doubt but that the publication of *An tOileánach* encouraged other Blasket Islanders to produce their own autobiographical accounts, the most famous of which are those of storyteller Peig Sayers (1873–1958) and the younger islander Muiris Ó Súilleabháin (1904–1950).

Autobiographical works relating the life of Peig offer clear examples of the syncretic nature of Gaeltacht autobiography and the problems associated with its authorship. Encouraged by folklorists Máire Ní Chinnéide and Léan Ní Chonalláin, Peig dictated three autobiographical narratives: two – *Peig* (*Peig*, 1936) and *Beatha Pheig Sayers* (*The Life of Peig Sayers*, 1970) – to her son Micheál Ó Gaoithín; and another – *Machtnamh Seana-mhná* (*Reflections of an Old Woman*, 1939) – to Máire Ní Chinnéide. While these accounts provide a fascinating insight into Peig's youthful experiences of family life, emigration and domestic service in the West Kerry Gaeltacht in the late nineteenth century, her most celebrated work, *Peig*, is best known for its depiction of community life on the Great Blasket Island from a distinctly female perspective. The hardships associated with the roles of wife and mother are relayed with the stoic acceptance of a devout Catholic who is willing to accept even the most bitter tragedies as evidence of God's will. While Peig was a highly accomplished traditional storyteller, critics have argued that her autobiographical works do not at all reflect her verbal artistry as an oral performer.[5] It has even been suggested that the unrelenting image of self-sacrificing motherhood presented in *Peig* was the creation of her son, who may have consciously or unconsciously shaped his mother's account during the process of redaction (Ó Fiannachta, 1989: 278). Patricia Coughlan has defended Peig's narratives from such criticism, however, and called for an interpretative approach which recognises in her story an example of the historically problematic question of women's access to literacy, authorship and the ownership of their creative works. While *Peig* has often been the centre of critical attention, due to its canonical status as a prescribed Irish Leaving Certificate text for decades, Coughlan (1999) suggests that the three books containing material relating to the life of Peig Sayers should be assessed together, thus allowing for greater recognition of the range of her autobiographical skills, particularly her ability to self-dramatise and to offer subtle interpretations of interpersonal relationships and motivations.

Muiris Ó Súilleabháin's *Fiche Blian ag Fás* (*Twenty Years A-Growing*, 1933) was written with the encouragement of George Thomson, a classical scholar and regular visitor to the Great Blasket with whom Ó Súilleabháin developed a close friendship. While arguably a less significant contribution to Gaelic autobiography than that of Ó Criomhthain and Sayers, the book nevertheless stands out as the work of a young man whose purpose was not to record life on the island as much as to provide an entertaining narrative. As he states in his introductory note: 'Seo smaoineamh mianúil do bhuail mé an leabhar so do cheapadh, chun cuideachta agus gáirí a dhéanamh do sheana-mhná an Bhlascaoid, mar ba mhór go léir an cion agus an grádh a bhí acu orm nuair a bhuailinn chúcha isteach gach oidhche fhada gheimhridh.' ('It was my purpose when I decided to write this book to provide company and amusement for the old women of the Blasket, because they always showed me great love and affection when I called in to them on a long winter's night.') The author's propensity to fictionalise has led certain critics to assess the book as a novel rather than as an autobiographical account, and the role of Thomson as editor has also been deemed particularly significant, especially in the light of Ó Súilleabháin's subsequent inability to produce a satisfactory sequel to the book (Newmann, 2000: 100–101).

The significance of this first generation of Blasket Island authors cannot be overestimated when considering the subsequent development of Gaeltacht autobiography. Not only did they provide narrative paradigms, but their work provided a model also for the collaborative mode of literary production which was to shape most subsequent examples of the genre. Most Gaeltacht autobiographies were the result of a collaboration between a native 'author' and an external editor, redactor or mentor, often a priest, teacher or folklore collector. In many cases, the life was compiled by a second party and later edited for publication. For example, *Scéal Hiúdaí Sheáinín* (*Hiúdaí Sheáinín's Story*, 1940), an account of life in the Donegal Rosses by Hiúdaí Sheáinín Ó Domhnaill, was written down by his grandnephew Eoghan Ó Domhnaill (1908–1966), who later published his own account of his youth in the same area in *Na Laetha a Bhí* (*Bygone Days*, 1953). The author's children wrote down different sections of *Sgéal mo Bheatha* (*The Story of my Life*, 1940) from Cúil Aodha storyteller Dómhnall Bán Ó Céileachair (1870–1950), having been encouraged to tell his story by Irish scholar Gerard Murphy, who later edited the text. Mayo-born seanchaí Mícheál Mag Ruaidhrí (1860–1936) dictated his story *Le Linn m'Óige* (*During My Youth*, 1944) to his daughter Bríd, and Pádhraic Óg Ó Conaire edited it for publication. *Beatha Mhichíl Turraoin* (*The Life of Micheál Turraoin*, 1956) by Micheál Turraoin (1878–1963) of Ring, County Waterford, was compiled by Micheul Ó Cionnfhaolaidh, while the celebrated adventures of Donegal man Micí Mac Gabhann (1865–1948), published as *Rotha Mór an tSaoil* (*The Big Wheel of Life*, 1959), were dictated to his son-in-law, the folklore collector Seán Ó hEochaidh, and later edited by Proinnsias Ó Conluain. The encouragement of outside parties was significant even in the work of authors with a high degree of literacy, such as Nóra Ní Shéaghdha (1905–1975), who was encouraged by local priests in the writing of *Thar Bealach Isteach* (*Across the Sound*, 1940). An intergenerational dynamic is also apparent in the case of individuals such as Peig Sayers' son Micheál Ó Gaoithín who, like Eoghan Ó Domhnaill, moved with ease from the position of redactor to that of author of his own *Is Truagh ná Fanann an Óige* (*It's a Pity Youth doesn't Last*, 1953).

While they tend to be almost formulaic in structure and content, these autobiographical accounts provide valuable insights into Irish-speaking Ireland during the late nineteenth and early twentieth centuries, illuminating many aspects of rural social, economic and cultural life. They also reveal regional attitudes to national events and have been justly hailed as invaluable sources for the social historian (Nic Eoin, 1982; Ó Conghaile, 1988). Though the Galway Gaeltacht produced fewer autobiographical accounts than any other Gaeltacht region, *Mise* (*Myself*, 1943) by Colm Ó Gaora (1887–1954) – written under the influence of John Mitchel's *Jail Journal* – was a significant contribution to the genre and one of the few accounts of the independence movement by a native Irish speaker. Unlike the typical subject of Gaeltacht autobiography, Ó Gaora became actively involved in the language revival in Connaught, serving as a Gaelic League teacher in Mayo and north Connemara during the years 1907–1916. His book reveals the close relationship between that work and the author's politicisation and eventual military mobilisation. Having joined the Irish Republican Brotherhood in 1913, he became a founder member of a branch of the Irish Volunteers in his native Ros Muc. He documents the local effects of the split in the Volunteers in 1914, and also the sense of disappointment and demoralisation following Douglas Hyde's dramatic resignation as chairman of the Gaelic League in 1915, when a motion adopting a separatist political agenda for the organisation was passed. Ó Gaora's account of Easter Week 1916 captures the sense of frustration and confusion in the western counties when communication between the Galway Volunteers and their Dublin-based leadership broke down. His description of his own capture in Cong, County Mayo illustrates just how unprepared the Galway contingent was for effective military action at that time. The book also describes in great personal detail the author's experiences of incarceration in several Irish and British prisons, and his role in the War of Independence.

The fact that Ó Gaora had earlier published a description of Gaeltacht life in *Obair is luadhainn: nó saoghal sa nGaedhealtacht* (*Work and Toil: or Life in the Gaeltacht*, 1937) would indicate that he wished to differentiate between ethnographic description and the kinds of personal experience recorded in *Mise*. Most Gaeltacht autobiographies do not make such a differentiation, however, as Ó Conaire points out in a discussion where he compares the contexts in which they were written to those of marginalised, minority or subordinate groups for whom a sense of personal identity is inseparable from the experience of the community in general (2000/01: 162–66). The relationship between individual and group identity is very clear in the Donegal autobiographies, where detailed accounts of the practice of seasonal migration include graphic descriptions of the experiences of child and adult labourers. Of these, Mící Mac Gabhann's *Rotha Mór an tSaoil* stands out in that, as well as illuminating such local aspects of the west Donegal experience, it also documents the author's exploits in North America, including his adventures during the Klondyke gold rush. This form of Gaeltacht autobiography, which was to continue in works such as *Gura Slán le m'Óige* (*Farewell to my Youth*, 1967) by Fionn Mac Cumhaill (1885–1965), sometimes resulted in rather strange literary creations. *An Gleann is a Raibh ann* (*The Glen and its People*, 1963) by Tipperary author Séamas Ó Maolchathaigh (1884–1968) is the life story of an imaginary individual who would – if he lived – be a contemporary of the author's parents. The book recounts how life was lived when the region was still an Irish-speaking district, using chapter headings typical of the genre, such as 'An chuimhne is faide siar i mo cheann' ('My earliest memory'), 'Mo chéad chulaith éadaigh' ('My first suit of clothes') and 'Ar scoil' ('At school'). The irony of this particular form of pseudo-autobiography is that it avoids totally the depiction of the sociolinguistic reality of Ó Maolchathaigh's own generation who were raised through English by Irish-speaking parents. In fact, despite the elegiac tone of much Gaeltacht autobiography, one finds surprisingly little direct evidence of personal experience of language shift. Interestingly, the most sustained discussion of language issues occurs in the autobiographical works of native speakers who became teachers. One such is Cork-born Diarmaid Ó hÉigeartaigh (1856–1934), whose *Is Uasal Ceird* (*Noble the Trade*, 1968) – written in 1926, long before autobiography had come to prominence as a modern Gaelic genre – records the negative reaction he received as a young teacher when he addressed elderly native speakers in Irish in west Cork: ' "We could answer you in Irish but we suspect you are the new schoolmaster and you need not trouble yourself speaking Irish to us any more" ' (1968: 148). Ó hÉigeartaigh's response was one of disappointed acceptance.

Interesting comparisons could be made between Ó hÉigeartaigh's account and those of Séamus Ó Grianna (1889–1969) in his memoir of Donegal childhood, *Nuair a bhí mé óg* (*When I was Young*, 1942), and its sequel, *Saoghal Corrach* (*Troubled Times*, 1945), which deals with the period between 1907 and 1931 and chronicles his experiences as a student, a young primary school teacher and a translator with An Gúm. The first of these includes a graphic description of an educational system which employed a curriculum and pedagogy alien to the life experiences of native Irish-speaking children. Ó Grianna's mixture of dramatic style and gritty social realism in *Nuair a bhí mé óg* introduces an element of socio-cultural criticism that is not always in evidence in Gaeltacht autobiography. *Saoghal Corrach* goes further in its critique of colonial educational policy and post-colonial cultural confusion, presented from the perspective of a frustrated and disillusioned educated native Irish speaker, who is expected to become a functionary in a post-colonial society where his language and culture are still seen to be inferior. A detailed autobiographical account by an implementor of post-independence educational policy can be found in *Cuimhne an tSeanpháiste* (*Memoir of an Old Child*, 1966) by Micheál Breathnach (1886–1987), where the practical and motivational difficulties associated with the teaching and learning of Irish are illustrated through incidents from the author's life as a teacher and school inspector.

The autobiographical works of Gaeltacht writers from the 1950s onwards should be considered in terms of the continuing crisis of modernity among marginal rural communities, for whom gradual assimilation into the larger national networks involved inevitable social, cultural and linguistic losses. Key texts here include the work of Tomás Ó Criomhthain's son Seán Ó Criomhthain (1898–1975), *Lá dár Saol* (*A Day in Our Life*, 1969), and of his grandson Pádraig Ua Maoileoin (1913–2002), *Na hAird ó Thuaidh* (*The Northern Heights*, 1960), both of which document the final years of life on the Blasket Islands and the islanders' subsequent adaptation to the accelerating processes of cultural change on the mainland. Indeed, much of the tension fuelling Gaeltacht literature of the 1960s and 1970s arises from the sense that socio-economic change cannot be achieved without cultural loss. Ua Maoileoin's *Na hAird ó Thuaidh*, which was originally a series of radio talks, depicts a community and culture experiencing a process of modernisation over which it has no control. As such, he is motivated less by a sense that 'our likes will never be seen again' than by an urge to warn his native Gaeltacht community about the ongoing and accelerating nature of socio-cultural change. The cultural effects of tourism and the modern media on peripheral communities are documented in a searingly honest representation of his native community, seen now through the eyes of a Gaeltacht exile in Dublin returning seasonally to changes which are more palpable to him than they are to those who stayed behind. As in many other autobiographical accounts, the qualities of the older generation are venerated at the expense of the contemporary. Unlike most Gaeltacht autobiographers, however, Ua Maoileoin moves from observation to commentary, and his narrative from description to sustained cultural critique. This crisis of modernity is also the main theme of Seán Ó Criomhthain's *Lá dár Saol*. Now living on the mainland, Ó Criomhthain laments the desertion of the Great Blasket Island, while simultaneously embracing the economic values which made such desertion inevitable. His account deals with issues such as social-welfare dependence and the interrelationship between changing consumer patterns and traditional rural agricultural practices. *Lá dár Saol* has been lauded for its lively conversational style, a quality which is also evident in Ua Maoileoin's *De Réir Uimhreacha* (*By Number*, 1969), an account of a young man's formation as a member of An Garda Síochána, drawn from the author's personal experience, but which probably sits more comfortably in the *Bildungsroman* category of fiction than in autobiography proper.

Though the last inhabitants were to leave the Great Blasket Island in 1953, the community there having dwindled to a handful of households, the mystique of the island was to continue, aided by the publication throughout the 1970s and 1980s of fresh accounts by Blasket 'exiles' on the mainland, such as Seán Sheáin Í Chearnaigh (b.1912), author of *An tOileán a Tréigeadh* (*The Deserted Island*, 1974) and *Iarbhlascaodach ina Dheoraí* (*A Blasket-islander in Exile*, 1978), and Máire Ní Ghaoithín (c.1905–1988), with her autoethnographic *An tOileán a Bhí* (*The Island that Was*, 1978) and *Bean an Oileáin* (*Woman of the Island*, 1986). Island narratives were also to appear from the Donegal Gaeltacht, with *Toraigh na dTonn* (*Tory of the Waves*, 1971) by Eoghan Ó Colm (1917–1981), a priest serving on Tory Island; an ex-islander's depiction of life on Gola up to its desertion in 1967 in *Ó Rabharta go Mallmhuir* (*From Spring-tide to Neap-tide*, 1975) by Seán Mac Fhionnlaoich (1910–82); and Pádraig Ua Cnáimhsí's telling, in autobiographical form, of the life of Róise Rua Mhic Grianna on Árainn Mhór in *Róise Rua* (*Red-haired Róise*, 1988). Despite differences of perspective, all of these works register the vulnerability of island life and culture. Neither were such narratives limited solely to depictions of – or elegies for – island life. *Saol Scolóige* (*Life of a Country Man*, 1993) by Seán Ó Conghaile (1903–1995), based on the material covered in his documentary *Cois Fharraige le mo Linnse* (*Cois Fharraige in my Time*, 1974), deals with social change in the Connemara Gaeltacht, while the Corca Dhuibhne mainland has produced a steady stream of similar publications.

The main difference between more recent and earlier examples of this kind of writing is the narrative incorporation of the experiences of Gaeltacht people outside of their native regions. *Ar Seachrán* (*Astray*, 1981) by Tomás Ó Cinnéide (1914–1992), for example, takes the reader to Cork, Dublin and San Francisco, while intercultural contact between Irish missionaries and the native communities in Nigeria and Korea is explored with great honesty and sensitivity in *Dúdhúchas* (*Black Heritage*, 1973) by Pádraig Ó Máille (b.1931) and *Idir Dhá Shaol* (*Between Two Worlds*, 1989) by Pádraig Ó Murchú (b.1944). While most publications of this kind are the work of educated authors literate in Irish, the encouragement and collaboration of academic mentors or editors has been essential nonetheless. As a literary trend, this kind of Gaeltacht writing has always been supported by Irish-language publishers, and has received particular support in recent years from the publishing houses Coiscéim and Cló Iar-Chonnachta, with their regional ties to the Corca Dhuibhne and Connemara Gaeltacht areas, respectively.

Autobiographies by authors from regions which are no longer Irish-speaking also continue to be published. *An Sléibhteánach* (*The Mountain Man*, 1989), for example, which contains the life story of Waterford-born Séamas Ó Caoimh (1889–1979), as recorded by Roscrea Garda Sergeant Éamon Ó Conchúir, depicts life in the Waterford/South Tipperary Decies region through the eyes of an Irish-speaker who presents himself as the last link in a cultural chain which was broken during his generation. The title consciously echoes that of Ó Criomhthain's book, and indeed Ó Caoimh refers directly to *An tOileánach* in a passage which records the death of his grandfather:

> Tá sean-rá áirithe a luaitear le Tomás Ó Criomhthain, 'An tOileánach', 'sé sin, 'ní bheidh ár leithéidí arís ann.' Bhí an nath san coitianta ins na Déise i bhfaid fad a tháinig Ó Criomhthain ar an saol agus is minic a dh'airigh mé aige m'sheanathair é. A deirimse gan spleáchas le héinne ná beidh leithéid mo sheanathar arís ann. (Ó Caoimh, 1989: 137)

> There is an old saying associated with Tomás Ó Criomhthain, 'the Islandman', and that is, 'the likes of us will never be again'. That phrase was common in the Decies long before Ó Criomhthain was born and I often heard it from my grandfather. I can say without a shadow of a doubt that the likes of my grandfather will never be seen again.

A fascinating recent example of how the form of Gaeltacht autobiography can be superimposed on the cultural experience of an English-speaking region can be found in another account from the Decies region, *Sliabh gCua m'Óige* (*The Sliabh gCua of my Youth*, 2003), by Irish-language scholar and editor Pádraig Tyers (b.1925), a work heavily influenced both in style and in content by earlier Gaeltacht examples.[6]

There are interesting comparisons to be made between the above accounts and the autobiography in English of weaver Charles McGlinchey (1861–1954) of Inishowen, County Donegal. Dictated to schoolteacher Patrick Kavanagh in the late 1940s and early 1950s, McGlinchey's *The Last of the Name* (1986) is similar in structure and content to the Irish-language texts and provides comparable insights into the life of a community in the process of rapid social, economic and linguistic change. McGlinchey, who spoke Irish as a child, was encouraged to produce an Irish-language version of his story, but died before it was completed. A section of this narrative, again dictated to Kavanagh, was published as *An Fear Deireanach den tSloinneadh* (2002) and provides an example of the residual language competency of an individual who was raised in a community undergoing intense language shift. Both books address the issue of language, while also attesting to the domains in which Irish remained an important cultural source long after it had ceased to be the dominant vernacular.

While it may be argued that recent Gaeltacht autobiographies still tend more towards the ethnographic than the personal, most display unique characteristics as a result of the particular circumstances of production. Sociocultural change remains a central narrative preoccupation, but the range of material covered is now greater, and some texts include more intimate accounts of childhood and personal relationships. Muiris Ó Bric (b.1942) in his episodic *Spotsholas na nDaoine* (*Spotlight on the People*, 1995), for example, uses direct speech to dramatically recreate his childhood experiences of illness, bereavement and what appeared to be incomprehensible adult behaviour. Sexual experience is explicitly dealt with in Pádraig Ua Maoileoin's *Macadúna* (*Son of the Dún*, 2001), which also includes a heart-rending depiction of the emotional effect on the author of the early death of his mother. The experience of disability is also acknowledged in this account, as it is in *Stairsheanchas Mhicil Chonraí* (*Oral History of Micil Chonraí*, 1999), which recounts in great detail the experiences of Connemara-born Micil Chonraí (Mícheál Ó Conaire, b.1919), both before and after he moved to the newly established Gaeltacht district of Ráth Chairn in Meath in 1935. The majority of recent autobiographical accounts are still the work of male authors or redactors, however. Even in a text such as *Róise Rua*, which purports to be the life story of Róise Rua Mhic Ghrianna (while bearing the authorial signature of Pádraig Ua Cnáimhsí), the question of female authorship remains problematic.[7] Other recent contributions by women tend to take the form of essay-type collections which combine local lore with accounts of personal experience. The growing interest in women's social history has also led to the publication in book form of previously unpublished writings, such as the 1923 journals of Eibhlín Ní Shúilleabháin (1900–1949), sister of the aforementioned Muiris (Ní Loingsigh, 1999). The experiences recounted in these journals provide the kind of details about the emotional relationships and personal dilemmas of island women which are lacking in the more well-known accounts.

## Non-Gaeltacht lives: Autobiography as self-invention

Two of the most distinctive prose works in Irish to be published in the first half of the twentieth century were highly individual creative subversions of the conventions of Gaeltacht autobiography. *Mo Bhealach Féin* (*My Own Way*, 1940) by Donegal-born Seosamh Mac Grianna (1901–1990) is a remarkable study of paranoia whose lack of referentiality makes it an ideal example of what current critical theory deems to be the ultimate realm of autobiography – that of self-invention. The book makes a radical break with traditional wisdom by opening with a novel gloss on the adage 'Bíonn an fhírinne searbh' ('Truth is bitter'): 'Deir siad go bhfuil an fhírinne searbh, ach, creid mise, ní searbh atá sí ach garbh, agus sin an fáth a seachantar í' (1940: 5) ['They say that truth is bitter, but, believe me, it's not bitter it is, but rough, and that is why it is avoided.'] In stark contrast to the emphasis on external reality and the individual's relationship to the wider community in Gaeltacht autobiography of the 1920s and 1930s, Mac Grianna's account, which is set in the period between 1932 and 1933, is a psychological study of a Gaeltacht writer astray in what he perceives as an alien and alienating urban environment. While the voice may be interpreted as that of a modern artist, a nomad frustrated by the materialism and absurdity of contemporary life, a sense of antipathy towards others pervades the work, and the narrator's sense of unease and displacement is revealed as fundamentally pathological and ultimately disabling. Stylistically, *Mo Bhealach Féin* is very different from most autobiographical works in Irish. It eschews the documentary mode in favour of a form of philosophical musing and in the process lends truth to Olney's observation, based on both literary evidence and recent theoretical writing, that 'it is a categorical error to imagine that an autobiography is the biography of the author' (1993: 113).

In contrast to the bleak pessimism of *Mo Bhealach Féin*, the pseudo-autobiography *An Béal Bocht* (*The Poor Mouth*, 1940) by Myles na gCopaleen (Brian Ó Nualláin, 1912–1966) provides a hilariously comic depiction of many of the themes of Gaeltacht autobiography, especially those of poverty, physical hardship and migration. Prison imagery occurs at the beginning and the end of the narrative, as the central character, Bónapárt Ó Cúnasa – a parodic depiction of the heroic subject of Gaeltacht autobiography – is incarcerated in the same jail as his father before him. Though often read as a parody of Ó Criomhthain's *An tOileánach*, to which it is greatly indebted, the satirical focus of the book is in fact the unequal relationship between Irish-language revivalists and the western communities which came to be seen as the embodiments of native Gaelic culture. Thus, the book fore-grounds the role of Gaeltacht autobiography in constructing an image of the native Irish speaker as someone controlled by external forces and incapable of determining his or her own destiny. A central theme in non-Gaeltacht autobiography, by contrast, is the individual's determination to shape his or her destiny, even if it involves a remarkable degree of self-invention.

Autobiography by non-Gaeltacht writers has to date received very little critical attention compared to the growing volume of critical material devoted to Gaeltacht texts. This is surprising when one considers the large volume of such material and the range of authors attracted to the genre. A number of dominant strands of non-Gaeltacht life writing can be discerned. The most numerous are the memoirs of Irish-language activists, texts that more often than not focus on key periods or formative experiences in the lives of their subjects rather than on a more comprehensive account of a life. The most well-known political figures to produce such accounts are Douglas Hyde (Dubhghlas de hÍde, 1860–1949), whose *Mise agus an Connradh* (*My Time in the League*, 1931) and *Mo Thurus go hAmerice; nó, imeasg na nGaedheal ins an oileán úr* (*My Trip to America; or among the Gaels in the new world*, 1937) document his involvement with the Gaelic League up to the year 1905 and his highly successful fund-raising trip made that year on its behalf, and Antrim-born Ernest Blythe (Earnán de Blaghd, 1889–1975), whose three-volume memoir *Trasna na Bóinne* (*Across the Boyne*, 1957), *Slán le hUltaibh* (*Farewell to Ulster*, 1969) and *Gaeil á Múscailt* (*The Wakening of the Gaels*, 1973) chronicles his early life up to 1919. Other examples of this genre include Cork-born Peadar Ó hAnnracháin's (1873–1965) description of his work as a Gaelic League 'timire' (organiser) in *Mar a Chonnacsa Éire* (*As I Saw Ireland*, 1937) and *Fé Bhrat an Chonnartha* (*Under the Banner of the League*, 1944); London-born writer and journalist Tarlach Ó hUid's (1917–1990) account of his personal journey of cultural discovery and political affiliation in *Ar Thóir mo Shealbha* (*In Search of what was Mine*, 1960) and *Faoi Ghlas* (*Under Lock and Key*, 1985); and the autobiography of Antrim-born writer and translator Seán Mac Maoláin (1884–1973), *Gleann Airbh go Glas Naíon* (*Glenariff to Glasnevin*, 1969). A central theme in such works is the author's relationship to the Irish language, including their linguistic conversion and subsequent involvement with Irish-language communities and cultural organisations. Religious affiliation also features occasionally, as in Blythe's *Trasna na Bóinne*, where he mentions his youthful discovery of an Irish-speaking Presbyterian ancestor from Castlewellan, County Down.[8]

Ó hUid's *Ar Thóir mo Shealbha* is one of the more unusual examples of the genre in that the author's search for his Irish identity is based on a complete fabrication from the outset. The book is a classic example of autobiography as self-invention, as recent research by biographers Diarmuid Breathnach and Máire Ní Mhurchú demonstrates that Ó hUid's references to his Ulster ancestors in the opening chapters are entirely fictional (2003: 184–86). Ó hUid, like Micheál Mac Liammóir (1899–1978), was an Englishman who re-invented himself as an Irishman for whom the Irish language was to provide an enduring badge of identity. His autobiography, while it may now be read as a compelling representation of performative subjectivity, evades the central motivating factor behind his need to become an other. It opens with a meditation on the many masks he was to wear throughout his life and goes on to document, through a combination of self-dramatisation and self-deprecation, the various cultural and political positions he occupied as a youth and young adult. The relative roles of choice and contingency are foregrounded as we are made witness to a young person's cultural awakening, religious conversion, political engagement and military recruitment. He explains how he came to learn Irish and became involved with the Gaelic League and the Irish emigrant community in London, revealing in the process his impatience with what he perceived as the shallow artificiality of diaspora culture: 'Diaidh ar ndiaidh sna blianta a bhí le teacht bheinnse ag tuirsiú den Éire shaorga sin a bhí Gaeil Londan ag iarraidh a chumadh as giobaí a saoil ar an gcoigríoch' (Ó hUid, 1960: 48). ['Gradually in the years that followed I would tire of the artificial Ireland the London Gaels were attempting to construct from the scraps of their lives in a foreign country.'] His conversion to Irish nationalism can therefore be seen as an attempt to achieve a sense of cultural certainty which eluded him as a working-class Londoner in a multi-ethnic city, and as a more benign alternative to the fascist formations of the 1930s with which he also came into contact, though this is nowhere explicitly stated. Rather, his construction of identity is presented throughout as a form of homecoming.

The autobiographical writings in Irish of Micheál Mac Liammóir provide another powerful example of autobiography as self-invention. The essay collection *Ceo Meala Lá Seaca* (*Honey Dew on a Frosty Day*, 1952) reiterates the fabrications on which Mac Liammóir's public persona was constructed, opening with references to his Cork childhood and the family's move to London when he was six years old.[9] He later recounts that it was as an art student at the Slade, where he avidly read Yeats, that he was inspired to learn Irish by recalling that he had Irish-speaking grandparents! Largely based on diaries and notes which he kept in Irish from 1920 onwards, the book deals with his early theatrical career and includes accounts of his experiences as a child actor with Beerbohm Tree in London, his move to Dublin, his first meeting with Hilton Edwards and the establishment of Taibhdhearc na Gaillimhe and the Gate Theatre. Particular aesthetic experiences, such as the performances witnessed at a dance club in Seville, are lovingly reconstructed in all their drama and sensuality. Emotions and motivations are often dealt with in a cursory manner, however, as are whole periods in his life, such as the ten years he spent in Europe after art school. Included in *Ceo Meala*

*Lá Seaca* is the highly engaging travel journal 'Ó Chill Airne go Beirlin' ('From Killarney to Berlin') which recounts his 1950 tour of Germany with Edwards and Orson Welles. One senses that the travel journal, with its scope for social comment and reflection on aesthetics, was particularly suited to Mac Liammóir's style of writing. His *Aisteoirífaoi Dhá Sholas* (*Actors under Two Lights*, 1956) is a journal account of the Gate Theatre's tour of Egypt in 1956, and shows his facility with language, whether he is conjuring up an unfamiliar landscape, an unusual personality or the atmosphere in a Cairo theatre. These books, while comparable to his autobiographies in English, are also vital to any understanding of the complexities of Mac Liammóir's self-fictionalisations.[10] As examples of his mastery of the Irish language, they can be read as powerful textual performances expressing the depth of his commitment to a cultural politics of alterity. While Mac Liammóir's fabricated identity may be read as a form of disguise which came naturally to someone who from childhood adored the world of masks and make-believe, his practical engagement with Irish-language literature and theatre should not be forgotten in the attempt to explain his adoption of an Irish persona as a game or as a form of romantic neo-Celticism. *Ceo Meala Lá Seaca* and *Aisteoirífaoi Dhá Sholas* serve to locate Mac Liammóir's work in Irish firmly in the context of his commitment to multilingual and cross-cultural exchange, and provide insights into his adopted persona unavailable in any of his writings in English.

Travel memoirs alone account for a considerable volume of modern Irish-language autobiographical prose.[11] The most engaging of these provide valuable perspectives on intercultural and interlingual contact in various geographical contexts. The style of some of these is deserving of particular attention. Donnchadh Ó Céileachair's (1918–1960) *Dialann Oilithrigh* (*Diary of a Pilgrim*, 1953), for example, is written in the intimate and informal style of a confidant. His perceptions of places and people are illustrated through reported conversations, backed up by factual information and social commentary. Also noteworthy is Úna Ní Mhaoileoin (d.1994), who produced three immensely entertaining accounts of her travel experiences in her hilarious collection of letters from Italy, *Le grá ó Úna* (*With Love from Úna*, 1958), and her travelogues *An Maith Leat Spaigiti?* (*Do You Like Spaghetti?*, 1965) and *Turas go Túinis* (*Voyage to Tunisia*, 1969), where a fluent style of multilingual code mixing is employed to great comic effect. Recent examples of the genre include two exceptional travel journals by Irish-language poets. Gabriel Rosenstock's *Ólann Mo Mhiúil as an nGaisnéis* (*My Mule Drinks from the Ganges*, 2003) describes a journey through Dubai, India, Hong Kong, Japan, Australia, Chile and the United States, and Cathal Ó Searcaigh's *Seal i Neipeal* (*Sojourn in Nepal*, 2004) documents the Donegal poet's experiences as a visitor in Nepal. Both of these accounts demonstrate the authors' affiliation with cultures where physical poverty is compensated for by rich human and cultural resources. Ó Searcaigh critiques the effect of tourism in Nepal, for example, and presents his own relationship with his young Nepalese guides as a special kind of cultural and spiritual brotherhood. His descriptions of sexual encounters can be troubling, however, especially when they display a lack of self-consciousness about the author's own status as a white westerner.

A sense of theatricality is of particular significance in the production of memoirs of specific events or periods, especially those of a political nature. *Cuimhní Cinn* (*Memoirs*, 1951) by Liam Ó Briain (1888–1974) is one of the few Irish-language accounts of the 1916 Rising by an actual participant and benefits greatly from the author's theatrical experience. Ó Briain's actions are recorded with great attention to detail, and the atmosphere of excitement and confusion is reproduced through a dramatic mixture of animated dialogue, pen pictures of the leaders and physical descriptions of particular scenes and actions. However, like Colm Ó Gaora's *Mise*, *Cuimhní Cinn* is as much a work of vindication as an actual record of events. As a group of Volunteers enters the Royal Irish Academy building in Dawson Street, for example, Ó Briain explains the importance of the building's contents:

D'iompaíos ar na fir: 'Bhfuil fhios agaibh, a bhuachaillí,' adeirim, 'céard iad na seanleabhra a chíonn sibh istigh ansin?' 'Níl fhios.' 'Sin iad seanleabhra Gaeilge na hÉireann, ceithre mhíle blian d'aois! An dtuigeann sibh, is ar son a bhfuil sna seanleabhra sin atáimid ag troid, d'fhéadfaí a rá!' (Ó Briain, 1951: 121)

I turned to the men: 'Do you know, lads,' says I, 'what those old books you see in there are?' 'We don't'. 'Those are the old Gaelic books of Ireland, four thousand years old! Do you understand, you could say that we're fighting for what is contained in those books!'

Although political autobiography invariably attempts to provide justification for its subjects' decisions and actions, it can also function to expose injustice, especially when other forms of vindication are denied. *Girseacha i nGéibheann* (*Girls in Captivity*, 1985) by Donegal-born sisters Áine (b.1949) and Eibhlín Nic Giolla Easpaig (b.1952) is one such account. Here, the first-person plural is used to recount the sisters' experiences of incarceration in Durham and other jails in Britain for a crime (conspiracy to cause explosions) which they denied throughout the nine-year period for which they were held. The purpose of writing such an account is clearly to vindicate the sisters' position through an indictment of the way the British judicial and penal system treats Irish people. Though the narrative style can be awkward at times, this particular 'jail journal' offers a unique female perspective on prison life and on the experiences of the Irish community in Britain during the 1970s and 1980s.

Exilic narratives are another important strand of autobiographical writing in Irish. The most well-known example, apart from Mac Gabhann's *Rotha*

*Mór an tSaoil*, is undoubtedly *Dialann Deoraí* (*Diary of an Exile*, 1960) by Galway-born Dónall Mac Amhlaigh (1926–1989). While the theme of emigration runs through most Gaeltacht autobiographies, Mac Amhlaigh's book provides the only sustained account in Irish of the experience of 1950s economic emigration to Britain. Indeed, the work is doubly unusual in that autobiographical material relating to the period is scarce in English also, as Mac Amhlaigh himself noted: 'When we consider that an estimated million plus Irish people came to Britain to make a living since the founding of the Irish Free State in the early 1920s it is surprising to say the least that the experience of this emigration has not found more expression in literature' (1989: 7).[12] Mac Amhlaigh takes readers to the heart of Irish working-class life in Britain by combining a documentary account of migrants' working and living conditions with the kind of social commentary which could only be provided by someone with first-hand experience of the subject. He faithfully reproduces the physical and social atmosphere of work environments as varied as a hospital ward, an air-force camp, an iron foundry and the construction sites of Northampton. Portraits of individuals are augmented by descriptions of particular incidents and social situations, and direct speech is employed to great dramatic effect to represent a variety of classes, nationalities and personalities. While this approach can quite easily result in a dangerous form of national stereotyping – especially when snippets of conversation are seen to embody the attributes of a whole group or class – Mac Amhlaigh's account is particularly valuable for the immediacy and honesty with which such value judgements are presented, providing direct evidence of a process of classification typical of cultural contact situations.

While social and cultural differences between the working-class Irish, English and Welsh are noted, and particular attention given to the relationship between different categories of workers, it is Mac Amhlaigh's insights into the tensions within the Irish community itself which are most revealing. Although he tends to idealise the Irish-speaking community to which he was naturally drawn, he is not afraid to expose the more negative aspects of the Irish experience in Britain. Rural–urban animosity is a recurring theme; the book reveals how tensions and rivalries between Connemara-born and Dublin-born navvies become ritualised into a form of staged spectacle, often presided over by a Catholic clergy anxious to contain it within the social environment of the Irish immigrant community. The materialism of the Irish immigrant – the obsession with work and pay at the expense of sociability – is also registered, as is Mac Amhlaigh's deep sense of concern for the constraints under which the Irish community in Britain was living. He describes the limited social ambit of the typical navvy, for example, whose life becomes a round of heavy work and heavy drinking, often resulting in tragic social isolation. While, on the one hand, he laments the lack of trade unions which would defend employees' rights, on the other hand he acknowledges Irish emigrants' abuse of the British tax system, and at one point even confesses his own collusion in dishonest practices in the workplace.

*Dialann Deoraí* exudes throughout a sense of frustration borne of disillusionment with the Irish state, coupled with a strong affective attachment to a beloved homeland. His mood of disappointment derives in large part from his sense of belonging to a cultural community which is being dissipated by forced emigration. The Irish language is central to Mac Amhlaigh's sense of cultural identity and accounts for his frequent references to the Galway of his youth and the period he spent in the Irish-speaking battalion of the Irish Army. And while he depicts a vibrant Irish-speaking diaspora in Britain, where cultural practices such as traditional singing survive in a new social space, he displays a constant awareness of the vulnerability of that community and its culture. Questions relating to acculturation and assimilation cannot be avoided, therefore, and *Dialann Deoraí* is particularly poignant in its depiction of what the author saw as one of the most painful aspects of his own displacement: the knowledge that the children of emigrants will be brought up speaking the language of the host country. Most of Mac Amhlaigh's subsequent writing is autobiographical in content or style. *Saol Saighdiúra* (*A Soldier's Life*, 1962) is a self-deprecating account of his period in the Irish Army; his *Bildungsroman Diarmaid Ó Dónaill* (1965) is a fictionalised depiction of the social and economic conditions in Kilkenny which led to his own emigration; and his satirical *Schnitzer Ó Sé* (1974) uses the autobiographical form to lampoon the pretentiousness of Irish literary life. His short-story collections also draw heavily on autobiographical material, while his novel *Deoraithe* (*Exiles*, 1986) revisits, in a three-strand narrative, the main themes of *Dialann Deoraí*. The depiction in *Deoraithe* of the working life and personal relationships of a young Irish woman provides evidence of a sensitivity to the female emigrant experience which is barely discernible in the earlier work, and questions the ability of first-person autobiography to accurately communicate all aspects of personal experience.[13]

## Autobiographical fiction: from artful truth to truthful disorder

No discussion of twentieth-century Gaelic autobiography would be complete without some consideration of the autobiographical novel, which has become one of the dominant fictional forms in the language.[14] A number of reasons may be adduced for the popularity of the genre. Most notably, the fictionalisation of personal experience can be seen as a strategy for overcoming the technical and ideological difficulties associated with depicting English-speaking or bilingual Ireland through the Irish language. The adoption of a first-person perspective avoids the difficulties faced by an Irish-language writer seeking to achieve an authentic depiction of contemporary sociolinguistic reality. By making a recognisably Irish-speaking subject the central focus of the narrative, the *Bildungsroman*, even when employing a third-person narrator, may successfully represent bilingual or English-speaking social domains as Irish-language ones. The popular *Bildungsroman Lig Sinn i gCathú* (*Lead us into Temptation*, 1976) by Breandán Ó hEithir (1930–1990) illustrates the realist potential of the genre, but many other instances can be cited where the novel form has been used to embody autobiographical detail. Some of the works of Diarmaid Ó Súilleabháin (1932–1985), for example, are recognisably autobiographical, most notably his novel *Ciontach* (*Guilty*, 1983), which recounts his experiences as a Sinn Féin prisoner in Mountjoy Jail in 1972. Similarly, Ciarán Ó Coigligh (b.1952) and Pádraig Ó Cíobháin (b.1951) clothe the central characters of their novels *Duibhlinn* (*Dublin*, 1991) and *An Gealas i Lár na Léithe* (*A Gleam of Light Across the Grey*, 1992) in autobiographical apparel.

While this tendency to fictionalise the personal is not by any means limited to the work of writers in a minoritised language such as Irish, the particular manner in which autobiographical conventions are employed in contemporary Irish-language realist prose deserves greater critical attention.[15] One obvious reason for eschewing the overtly autobiographical in favour of new forms of 'creative memory' is that this strategy frees authors from the restrictions of the autobiographical pact, while at the same time facilitating the presentation of strong personal viewpoints or convictions. Another is that autobiographical fiction may allow for a fuller exploration of painful personal circumstances or intergenerational tensions, as in Lorcán S. Ó Treasaigh's *Bildungsroman Céard é English?* (*What is English?*, 2002), which depicts the confusion and frustration of an individual raised through Irish in a non-Irish-speaking environment, a theme he earlier explored in his allegorical novel *Bás san Oirthear* (*Death in the East*, 1992). In certain cases, truly original forms of writing can result, as in *An Lomnochtán* (*The Naked One*, 1981) by Eoghan Ó Tuairisc (1919–1982), where a series of dramatic episodes from the life of a young child is presented with a degree of immediacy and psychological insight totally lacking in most autobiographical accounts. On the other hand, in his memoir *Eaglais na gCatacómaí* (*The Church of the Catacombs*, 2004), priest-novelist Pádraig Standún has chosen to remove the layers of fictionality and expose the autobiographical reality underlying his most controversial novels.

Alongside the tendency to fictionalise the personal, a retreat from the autobiographical is also discernible in contemporary Irish-language writing. This is evidenced by the development of various kinds of non-mimetic experimental prose narratives, where the centred subject of both autobiography and of much realist fiction is replaced by an obsessive exploration of the boundaries of subjectivity itself. The best example of this to date is the novel

*Kinderszenen* (1987) by the pseudonymous 'Robert Schumann', in which literary referentiality is questioned and the process of identity-construction implicit in all forms of autobiographical writing deconstructed.[16] This novel, which is heavily influenced by the work of post-structuralist theorists, especially Roland Barthes, uses a highly self-reflexive style to postulate the ultimate fictionality of all literary representation:

Ní bhíonn i dtéacs ar bith atá fírinneach ach nótaí fánacha, giotaí gan aird nach bhfuil de cheangal eatarthu ach neas-suíomh na leathanach. Cuir in ord iad agus tá bréag ar bun agat. Is fearr an t-anord fírinneach na an t-ord bréige. Ach tá sé ródhéanach anois le bheith ag cur is ag cúiteamh faoin rud is anord fírinneach ann. (Schumann, 1987: 138)

Any text that is truthful is nothing but a collection of random notes, insignificant segments which are related to each other only by their proximity on the page. Put them in order and you are engaging in falsity. Truthful disorder is better than false order. But it is too late now to start debating the nature of truthful disorder.

But while the novel exposes the difficulties involved in imposing narrative order on the disorder of a life, it also acknowledges the reader's desire for referentiality. Its central thesis is that it is the responsibility of the reader ultimately to determine where the truth of the fiction lies:

Seo leat ag piocadh.
    Cá bhfuil an fhírinne? An bhfuil aon fhírinne ann? An bhfuil aon bhealach gur féidir leat an téacs seo a chosaint, a rá go dtagraíonn aon chuid de do rud a aithníonn tú féin a bheith fíor. Tharla seo. An féidir liomsa mar scríbhneoir a rá leatsa mar léitheoir: na rudaí a bhfuil cur síos déanta agam anseo orthu tharla siad [ . . . ].
    Fútsa atá sé anois fíor nó bréagach a rá lena bhfuil anseo. Deirimse nár éirigh liom. Fútsa anois a rá. Nó gan a rá. (Schumann, 1987: 138–39)

Here you are picking away.
    Where is the truth? Is there any truth? Is there any sense in which you can defend this text, by arguing that some part of it refers to something you recognise as true. This happened. Can I as a writer say to you as a reader: the things I have described here happened [ . . . ].
    It is up to you to tell whether what is here is true or false. I say I didn't succeed. It's up to you now to say. Or not to say.

Though concerned more with textuality in general than with autobiography in particular, the questions raised by *Kinderszenen* certainly impact on the various forms of autobiographical writing discussed in this chapter. As we have seen, the process whereby the autobiographical account is produced is often the most important determining factor in its reception. The prevalence of autobiographical forms in twentieth-century literature in Irish cannot be understood without due attention being paid to the sociolinguistic circumstances shaping that literature. It is also clear, however, that full appreciation of modern Gaelic autobiography requires a critical awareness of the nature of literary autobiography and its capacity for omission, evasion, invention and creative manipulation of historical facts.

## Notes

1. For an excellent discussion of the question of generic definition in autobiography criticism, see Ó Conaire, 2000/01. For a more general application of recent critical theory to Irish-language autobiography, see Ó Háinle, 1999. For a discussion of Irish-language terminology related to autobiography, see Ó Háinle, 2002.
2. The translation of this and all further extracts are by Máirín Nic Eoin, unless otherwise stated.
3. See in particular 'An Gaige' (*Misneach*, April 1922), 'Teanga na Tíre' (*An Claidheamh Soluis*, June 1930) and 'Gaeil agus Gaelainn' (*An Claidheamh Soluis*, December 1930) in Ó Criomhthain, 1997: 78–79, 170–71, 183.
4. See 'An Lóchrann' (*An Lóchrann*, January 1917) and 'Dá mBeadh Éire le Chéile' (*Misneach*, December 1919) in Ó Criomhthain, 1997: 5–6, 52–53.
5. For a discussion of Peig as storyteller, see Almqvist, 1999; for a discussion of Peig as autobiographer, see Ó Háinle, 1989.
6. Examples of autobiographical works from the Waterford/Tipperary region of the Decies deserve critical attention in their own right. For a critical perspective on *Beatha Mhichíl Turraoin* and *An Gleann agus a Raibh Ann*, see Ó Drisceoil, 2001; Ó Drisceoil and Ó Paircín, 2002.
7. For a discussion of this particular text, see Ó Conaire, 2000/01. For a more general discussion of the role of editors in the production of Donegal autobiographies, see Ó Conluain, 1990.
8. For a discussion of Protestants and the Irish language, see Ó Buachalla, 1968; Giltrap, 1990; Mistéil, 1994; Ó Snodaigh, 1995; Blaney, 1996.
9. Mac Liammóir gave the same fictional account to Muiris Ó Droighneáin (1936: 218–19) and again in response to a 1947 RTÉ questionnaire sent out to Irish writers. For a factual account of Mac Liammóir's family background and early years, see Ó hAodha, 1993 and Breathnach and Ní Mhurchú, 1994: 51–61.
10. Surprisingly, they are ignored by biographer Christopher Fitz-simon (1994) and by critic Éibhear Walshe (1997: 150–69). Worthy of further investigation is the role the Irish language may have played in Mac Liammóir's life as a form of decoy, distracting attention from his dissident sexuality.
11. I have identified over 30 titles and the genre is worthy of a separate study, particularly for the insights to be gained into the experience of intercultural contact from a minority language perspective. See also Cronin, 2000a, 2000b.
12. For a discussion of Mac Amhlaigh as a chronicler of emigrant experience, see Ó Tuairisc, 1977; Ó Cearnaigh, 1987; Nic Eoin, 1990.
13. While I would agree in large part with Canavan's analysis (1994) of *Dialann Deoraí*, I would argue that Mac Amhlaigh's fictionalised accounts of the emigrant experience are also worthy of study for the light they cast on aspects that are not foregrounded in the journalistic *Dialann Deoraí*.

14. Alan Titley (1991) devotes much space to the *Bildungsroman* in his study of the Irish-language novel, but the autobiographical novel is clearly a larger category than that of the *Bildungsroman*.
15. For further discussion of the possible reasons for the prevalence of autobiographical fiction in Irish, see Nic Eoin, 1987, 1989/90, 1991/92.
16. For an insightful reading of *Kinderszenen*, see Mag Shamhráin, 1987. For a more general discussion of the decentred subject in contemporary Irish-language fiction, see Ní Annracháin, 1994.

# 8
## 'Drawing the Line and Making the Tot': Aspects of Irish Protestant Life Writing

*Barry Sloan*


## Introduction

The political events in Ireland in the early twentieth century which led to the partitioning of the country in 1920 – with a Dublin-based government assuming control of 26 counties and a Belfast administration with close links to Westminster overseeing the remaining six – had particular effects for the Protestant communities on either side of the new border. In the Irish Free State, which became a republic in 1949, the already declining authority and influence of the once prosperous Protestant Anglo-Irish community were further eroded, and many families chose to leave the country rather than adapt to life in a radically altered political landscape, where the growing power and influence of the ultra-conservative Catholic church added to their sense of alienation. Some less socially privileged Protestants in the south felt betrayed by the leaders of their co-religionists in the north-east who had preferred to protect their interests by partition rather than to take their place in an all-Ireland political system; most faced the necessity of accommodating themselves to life in de Valera's Ireland. In Northern Ireland itself, the in-built Protestant majority prepared to rule in perpetuity, making minimal concessions to Catholics within its jurisdiction, affirming its loyalty to the British monarchy and its defence of the liberties associated with reformed faith, and forever distrustful of the political and religious aspirations of its neighbours across the border.

The six writers I propose to discuss in this chapter, who were born between 1875 and 1947, collectively represent the different social, economic and religious situations of Irish Protestants, and the diversity within Irish Protestantism, over a period of about 70 years from the late nineteenth to the mid-twentieth century. Forrest Reid (1875–1947) – who was related to the Presbyterian clergyman James Seaton Reid, author of a major celebratory history of his church – was a child of strait-laced, middle-class late Victorian

Belfast. As such, his background was strikingly different, both socially and religiously, from that of Robert Harbinson (b.1928). Although formally a member of the Church of Ireland, many of Harbinson's most vivid and formative religious experiences took place in the evangelical gospel and mission halls of working-class areas of Belfast, where enthusiasm and drama replaced the austerity and restraint of the mainstream Protestant churches. Whereas Catholics did not figure in Harbinson's childhood world, other than as objects of inherited prejudice and suspicion, they loomed large in Edith Newman Devlin's (b.1926) early experiences in working-class Dublin, where she quickly learned that she was a member of a minority faith overshadowed by an increasingly expansionist Catholic church. Her upbringing was, therefore, indissolubly linked to an awareness of the differences between her and her Catholic neighbours, which her Ulster-born father never failed to reiterate. Such circumstances were, in turn, wholly unlike those of Richard Murphy (b.1927) and Annabel Davis-Goff (b.1942), members of long-established Anglo-Irish families from counties Galway and Waterford, respectively. As a young man, Murphy was drawn to the Anglicanism he encountered at school in Canterbury and later at Oxford, and although he reveals little evidence of strong religious faith, he was for a time attracted to the notion of becoming a rural parson-poet in the tradition of George Herbert, largely because of the freedom to write which he believed this might offer. Davis-Goff has little to say about her family's Church of Ireland affiliations, but she shares a less intense awareness than Devlin of the social and cultural differences between the small Protestant community to which she belonged and the local Catholic population. Finally, Hugh Maxton's (b.1947) account of his lower middle-class Dublin childhood and adolescence shows less preoccupation with religious difference and identity, and a distinct measure of irony and scepticism in his treatment of his Church of Ireland upbringing, his Methodist schooling and his brief, teenage attachment to Unitarianism. Maxton has limited interest in the beliefs and practices of the Catholic majority around him, but is alert to other minority religious communities, such as the Jews he knew in his home locality of Harold's Cross in Dublin.

The four-part structure of this chapter reflects the diverse viewpoints of its subjects and invites comparative readings of the individual writers and their approaches to life writing. With the exception of the second of Reid's two autobiographical volumes, *Private Road* (1939), and Murphy's *The Kick* (2002), each of the works featured here is principally concerned with the first 20 or so years of the author's life. Accordingly, these autobiographers are engaged in complex acts of memory in their narration of childhood and adolescence, acts which are central to their attempts to understand and interpret how the memories of those years have affected them as adults and shaped their identities. James Olney suggests that we all continuously engage in autobiography, not in the sense of writing it down [...] or sending it into the world for publication, but in the sense of – as Beckett puts it and performs it so often – drawing the line and making the tot. But the tot will be different each time, for memory and the self will have altered with circumstances, and these – self and circumstances – taken in adaptive conjunction, will determine the new tot. (1998: 344)

This claim, with its appropriate allusion to another Irish writer of Protestant stock, describes a process that is visibly and variably at work again and again in the autobiographies analysed here. Olney's argument is particularly applicable to those narrative moments where these writers revisit, recover or attempt to imagine the children and adolescents they once were, or key experiences that befell them, from the perspectives of the men and women they now are, while at the same time trying to understand what their current 'tot' owes to the past, and how it continues to be affected by it. Parental death, significantly, is an experience common to several of these autobiographers, and as such will be given due consideration in my discussion. Harbinson, Devlin and Maxton each suffered the death of a parent during their childhood, and for the latter two this event occupies a central place in their autobiographies. Reid's father also died when he was a child, though a more important trauma for him was the departure of his nurse. For Davis-Goff, on the other hand, her return to Ireland for her father's funeral is the starting point for her narrative revisitation of the scenes of her girlhood.

# I

Forrest Reid's first volume of autobiography, *Apostate* (1926), which appeared in his fiftieth year, concentrates exclusively on his boyhood and adolescence, but it is immediately clear that this will not be a simple linear narrative of external events and experiences: 'The primary impulse of the artist springs, I fancy, from discontent, and his art is a kind of crying for Elysium' (1947: 7). The ideas that artistic aspiration derives from 'discontent' and that art itself is an attempt to achieve perfection and overcome a feeling of estrangement from 'an Eden from which each one of us is exiled' (1947: 7) are at the heart of Reid's conception of his fiction. Their foregrounding here signals their relevance also to his approach to autobiography, typified by Brian Taylor as 'a recreation of the necessary conditions for the man to which that child was the father' (1998: 2). The Wordsworthian allusion is apt because Reid believed that 'memory' of this lost world is strongest in boyhood, and the possibility of readmission to it, at least in dreams, most potent. With the passage of time, however, and the onset of adolescence the prospect fades and the adult novelist is left forever striving to recreate his lost world in fiction. In turning to autobiography, therefore, Reid is reconstructing his own childhood as a kind of ur-text, paradoxically pre-dating and anticipating the work he had already accomplished as a novelist. This idea is reinforced by his own advice to take *Apostate* 'as a point of view suggested because it helps to explain my own writings', and by his description of his novels as 'mere pretexts for the author to live again through the years of his boyhood, to live those years, as it were, *more consciously*, if less happily' (1947: 7–8, emphasis added). The emphasis is added here because consciousness of the self is one of the most striking features of *Apostate*, though Reid's words also endorse Laura Marcus's observation that autobiography may become 'a way of defining what literature is or should be and charting the course of the writer's relationship to the literary' (1994: 268). Later, in *Private Road*, Reid wrote that the title *Apostate* 'was intended to indicate a state of mind, not a person' (1940: 11).[1] He also claimed that the early years evoked in *Apostate* had a pattern and a completeness of their own, unlike his later life, and that he therefore chose to continue his life story in *Private Road* by tracing the composition of his novels. However, since his recurrent fictional subject is the transient world of boyhood, the autobiography underscores the impression of what Reid himself refers to as his 'arrested development' and his impossible desire 'to be a boy always' (1940: 12, 163–64).

Reid's discontent and disappointment with life are linked to the oppressive, judgemental Protestantism of his background which he found alienating and unsympathetic, especially in its emphasis on human sinfulness. 'If only I had been asked to worship and to love the earth I could have done it so easily! If only the earth had been God', he declares, contrasting this with the *un*naturalness of the Sabbath piety in his clergyman uncle's house (1947: 113). Yet he denies that he is unreligious; indeed, he describes his autobiographical writing as 'a kind of pilgrim's progress' in *Private Road* and characterises the representation of himself in *Apostate* as a boy 'sharing this very general, if not universal desire for God' (1940: 14, 16). His argument with institutional religion centres upon its claim to particular authority and its exclusive understanding of God, conceptions of which he regards as anthropomorphic constructs endowed with 'certain human qualities – sympathy, compassion, goodness – which may have no existence outside our own minds' (1940: 16). Unsurprisingly, therefore, Reid's most important sources of inspiration are human rather than divine, although they could scarcely be more different from one another: the philosopher Socrates and Emma Holmes, his childhood nurse. Reid valorises Socrates as an example of wisdom and goodness, and also because 'he belonged to, was in my world' and as such was 'infinitely approachable' (1940: 92). Emma, however, is uniquely significant in Reid's revisionist version of his childhood, far outweighing the influence of parents or siblings, despite her abrupt return to her native England when he was six, an event which had the force of a bereavement and which, he claims, marked his 'transition from childhood to boyhood' (1947: 27). He underlines the impact of Emma's departure by linking it to his memory of a story she was reading to him about children engaged in a kind of pilgrim's progress. Characteristically, he appropriates this narrative, investing it with multiple meanings in the light of subsequent experience. Dispensing with the story's original Christian theme, he seizes upon it as an archetype of his quest for an ideal world, construing it as 'an augury of my own nocturnal voyages which had not yet, so far as I knew, properly begun', which careful formulation shows Reid not only revisiting but also remaking the past (1947: 25). The fact that this iconic story was left incomplete is also given significance as a symbolic foretaste of the perpetually elusive and disappointed ending to all attempts to enter the perfected realm of dream.

In Reid's idealisation of childhood, Emma is the source of unconditional nurture and protection, 'an essential part of my existence, like the air I breathed or the sun that warmed me [ . . . ]. Certainly her care for me was far beyond any that deities are wont to practise' (1947: 14). Yet he acknowledges the transformative power of memory, conceding that the Emma he records will have been changed by the process of remembrance. This evangelical Methodist became for him a symbol of companionship, security and justice, attributes Reid found notably absent in 'the sickly, the neurotic, the unhappy, the narrowly religious' (1947: 20). And while her 'deep desire was that one should be good, [ . . . ] her still deeper desire was that one should be happy' (1947: 19). Significantly, despite his sense of having been 'deceived' by Emma on the one occasion she took him to chapel, he retrospectively dissociates her from the oppressiveness of Sunday school, churchgoing and Bible study. In contrast with his mother, who seemed to him to be oblivious of the private side of his nature, Reid claims that Emma 'divined' his thoughts and understood him, which must surely be a further instance of his wishful remembering (1947: 34). Thus, as Eamonn Hughes has observed, 'Emma is not so much a substitute mother as the *only* type of mother that Reid can accept' (1992: 11, original emphasis).

*Apostate* is subdivided into seven parts, each culminating in a decisive experiential moment. Thus, Emma's departure concludes the first part, while the second, in which Reid is principally concerned with retrieving 'the few surviving fragments' (1947: 61) of his childhood dream world from the distortions of time and memory, closes with the fading of the dream in his mid-teens. Elsewhere, the visionary moment which ends Part Six gains importance because it follows quickly upon Reid's account of his confirmation into the Church of Ireland which, paradoxically, coincides with his abandonment of Christianity: 'The moment [the bishop] had removed his hands from my head, my interest in the scene died, and what had been designed as the beginning of my religious life proved to be the end of it' (1947: 153). Again, Reid's discriminate memorialising and ordering of experience produce a particular shape to his autobiographical narrative, a point reinforced by his apparently contingent discovery of 'the poetry and religion and art of the Greeks' (1947: 154), which provides him with an alternative and more appealing philosophy, although as Norman Vance has noted, his version of Greek paganism is itself highly selective and omits its darker, Dionysiac aspect (1998: 7). Under these new influences, Reid offers an epiphanic liminal moment when he senses that the world seems poised to 'split asunder' to allow him entry to his dream place: 'And then – then I hesitated, blundered, drew back, failed' (1947: 159). This is perhaps the defining instant in *Apostate*. He presents his failure as lack of courage which immediately dissolves the moment and returns him to the mundane world; but his hesitation and loss were inevitable, because there can be no entrance to the private dream world. The failure, if such it be, is not personal but a condition of time- and space-bound human existence, and predicates the disappointments of Reid's life and the fates of the boys who populate his novels. *Apostate* ends with the author entrusting Andrew Rutherford with his confessional diary. 'For the first time I had admitted someone to my secret world, to my innermost thoughts', he writes, which is also a way of describing what *Apostate* itself has done in its own elab- orately contrived way (1947: 176). The obliqueness of the revelation and Rutherford's unbroken silence are not simply enigmatic structural devices, but final testimony to the irresolvable difficulty of Reid's search for the companion who would not change, fail or desert him. Between them, they affirm the centrality of this issue to his autobiography and his fiction in equal measure.

## II

The self-righteous oppressiveness of Ulster Protestantism which so alien- ated Forrest Reid in late Victorian Belfast was equally unappealing to Robert Harbinson growing up in the city in the 1930s. In *No Surrender: An Ulster Childhood* (1960), the first volume in his autobiographical tetralogy – *Song of Erne* (1960), *Up Spake the Cabin Boy* (1961) and *The Protégé* (1963) complete the series – he is dismissive of the 'gross Sabbatarianism [ . . . ] wedded to a stuffy respectability' of his great aunt's home: 'Well furnished and carpeted, its inhuman perfection was maintained during non-praying hours by much polishing and cleaning' (1987: 138). Yet the author's first 21 years, as covered in his multi-volume autobiography, are dominated by his adventures among various fundamentalist denominations and sects in working-class Belfast, rural Fermanagh and South Wales. Harbinson grew up in great poverty, his mother having, in her family's opinion, married beneath herself and then been widowed when her husband, a window cleaner, died from injuries received in a fall. In his childhood world of hand- to-mouth living and charitable support, the local Protestant churches and particularly the evangelical mission halls were not only welcome sources of food and coppers, but also places of drama, colour and excitement in which Harbinson was quickly caught up. In these halls, doctrine was of little concern to children who revelled in the spectacle of religious performance:

> Pedalling away furiously at the harmonium, as though going up-hill on a bicycle, sat the Driver. A little, round woman with an enormous bun of white hair, she was inexhaustibly patient and kind-hearted. [...] We teased her unmercifully. [...] On finding toffee-papers stuck round her hat, she would hold them in front of her like an offering, close her eyes and pray audibly 'Drive them out Lord! Drive them out!' We did not know she was exorcizing the evil spirits in us, but simply thought she wanted us cleared out of the hall. And so she became the 'Driver'. (1987: 55–56)

This passage typifies Harbinson's representation of a form of worship that was far removed from the restrained piety of mainstream Protestantism and which included the live theatre of adult baptisms and appeals to commit oneself to Christ. Furthermore, his comment that 'The *chiaroscuro* of our world was all black and white; kindness and cruelty contrasted sharply' (1987: 32) is not simply descriptive of the kind of life he knew; it is also indicative of Harbinson's autobiographical style, through which he displays a capacity for self-dramatisation born of his precocious discovery of the power wielded by evangelical preachers (which included sexual charisma), and of his own ability to exercise it.

Harbinson thus recreates himself as an almost picaresque figure, larger than life from the day of his birth, improvising his anarchic way from the backstreets, Bog Meadows and gospel halls of Belfast, through his wartime evacuation to Fermanagh, to his return to Belfast and re-engagement with various fundamentalist religious groups, which led to his eventual departure for Bible college in south Wales. There, his rapid disillusionment with this 'evangelical concentration camp' (Harbinson, 1963: 47) is precipitated by his intuitive responsiveness to the non-judgemental warmth and variety of life in the red-light district of the Cardiff docklands, and his encounter with the compassionate theology of the captain of an American liberty ship which results in his own 'conversion':

> Like Bunyon's [*sic*] Pilgrim a burden had rolled off my back, the burden of narrow cant and prejudice. I was glad to know that the Bible Academy's God of fear and violence was not, after all, almighty. I was glad that the dusky children along Bute Street would not be going to hell because they had been taught from the Koran. I rejoiced at the emptiness of the Throne of Grace because now my mother would not burn eternally as a result of a few odd bottles of stout on a night out with a boy-friend. (1963: 50)

Given Harbinson's fascination with the evangelical emphasis on the need for a conversion experience, the reference to Bunyan is perhaps unsurprising, but it draws attention to the difference between the two writers. Linda Anderson points out how Bunyan seizes on 'the spiritual implications of the events of his life', selecting retrospectively 'those which reveal a providential design [ . . . ] or illustrate his extreme sinfulness, later to be redeemed by "the merciful working of God upon my soul" ' (2001: 29). The specific burden from which Harbinson felt released was fear; where 'Belfast's Gospel Halls scared us into attendance with [ . . . ] a regular thesaurus of arson', he now 'saw a new Christ, the one who was concerned that the hungry should be fed and the naked clothed and the prisoners visited. [ . . . ] Smoking and drinking just did not come into it. Nor did other subsidiary considerations such as whether you were Protestant or Roman Catholic' (1963: 51). The importance of this last point cannot be overestimated given Harbinson's origins in the heartlands of Belfast Protestantism where Catholics were automatically assumed to be beyond the scope of salvation. However, the effect of his release from 'the burden of narrow cant and prejudice' was to lead him into a knowingly cynical 'double life': 'I did not lose my love of the pulpit with my belief in hellfire. But under the new conditions the pulpit was no more than a stage and I the sole actor' (1963: 52). His pilgrim's progress thereafter includes bizarre and melodramatic entanglements with religious extremists, which eventually led him away from the church and into secular employment.

Each of Harbinson's autobiographical volumes culminates in his departure to a new location, and the last ends with his emigration to Canada, effectively symbolising the start of a new cultural and religious life. Throughout, Robert Harbinson the writer stands in a complex relationship to Robin Bryans, the autobiographical subject, prompting John Keyes to comment that 'as the subject, he is so involved in his own development that the contradictions of adolescence are accepted without reservation' (1994: 45). The truth of this is evident in Harbinson's immersion in his childhood imagination and in his own behaviour, as exemplified by his account of his involuntary response to a call to take Jesus as his 'personal Saviour':

> When we got to that point, I felt quite convinced of the need for this personal witness [ . . . ]. My hand went up. I did not make it. It just went up of its own accord, as if seized by an ataxic spasm. I could not have pulled it down at that moment if I had wanted to. (1961: 134)

Such self-absorption is nevertheless punctuated by a humorous, retrospective awareness of the absurdity and insensitivity of his own teenage excesses – which saw him place religious tracts in the coats of dancers in Fermanagh Orange Halls and throw away any alcohol he could find – and by his increasingly satirical attitude towards the adults and religious organisations in his life, the narrative effect of which is to make Harbinson both the performer and the reviewer of his own drama. Thus, his autobiographical tetralogy is imbued with a distinctive energy and tension that are absent

from more unreservedly critical accounts of growing up among fundamentalist believers.[2]

At the same time as Robert Harbinson was immersed in the singular
milieu of low-church Protestantism in Belfast, Dublin-born Edith Newman
Devlin, the youngest child of an ex-British Navy Great War veteran from
Newtownards and a publican's daughter from Bantry, was becoming aware
of the multiple markers of difference that she inherited as a member of
a Protestant minority in a predominantly Catholic city. As she succinctly
explains in *Speaking Volumes: A Dublin Childhood*:

> We were separated from the people outside by locked gates and high
> walls. We were separated from the people in the hospital below by the
> fact that they were mad and we were sane; and we were separated from
> the administrative and medical staff by our inferior social position. We
> were separated from our neighbours by having a better house to live in,
> better food to eat, clothes to wear and better schools to go to. Above
> all we were separated from them by religion: we were protestants in an
> overwhelmingly catholic district. (2000: 115)

Devlin's particular family circumstances also exposed her to religious pressures of another kind, for although she was raised and confirmed in her
mother's Church of Ireland tradition, her father was a lapsed Presbyterian
who had become 'a "militant" protestant agnostic who found himself living
in the midst of a profoundly affirming catholic culture which he detested'
(2000: 1). His undisguised contempt for what he regarded as the laziness
of his Catholic neighbours and the intrusive power of their priesthood,
coupled with his relentless insistence on the supposed Protestant virtues of
self-improvement, personal responsibility and freedom of thought, confused
and distressed his daughter and intensified her sense of cultural rootlessness
and incomplete belonging: 'He forbade us to put down roots in this alien
soil. We were constantly being asked to be disloyal to the place we lived in'
(2000: 113). Devlin's childhood experience of her native place, therefore,
was one of thorough alienation: 'The homelands of both sets of parents were
*terra incognita* to me, names only in my head' (2000: 113).

At the heart of *Speaking Volumes* is the author's powerful and painful
relationship with her widowed father, Hugh Gaw, and the inconsolable
absence of any memory of her mother. Gaw was a lonely, angry, disappointed man whom Edith originally regarded as 'my protector, my haven,
my sole anchor in a frightening world' (2000: 42). As she began to grow up,
however, his authoritarianism, dogmatic socialist rationalism and almost
pathological emotional repression caused enormous strains. His own mother
had died suddenly when he was a child, and on his deathbed he told his
daughter: ' "That was the most terrible thing that ever happened to me in
the whole of my life [ . . . ] and I have never been the same since" '; this, she

speculates, may have been his attempt at 'an explanation of his character' (2000: 88). If so, it serves as a wholly inadequate justification of his depriving her of contact with her grandparents and other members of her extended family and utterly excluding her from his personal life. In such circumstances, literature became Devlin's salvation; *Speaking Volumes* is a testimony to her emotional self-education and growth through reading. Seven of its 22 chapter titles include the phrase 'the life of the feelings', and each is linked to accounts of how she learnt to recognise and understand her own feelings through books such as *Jane Eyre*, *Hard Times* and *The Mill on the Floss*. These revelations, hinted at in the autobiography's punning title, are prepared for in the foreword, where Devlin describes literature as 'the *living* history of human awareness' and explains: 'It was books which made me see *imaginatively* that it is the way our feelings ebb and flow which really determines our lives rather than our reason' (2000: 2–3, original emphasis), the faculty so prized by her father. Yet however much literature released her into 'the life of the feelings' and equipped her to recognise, cope with and eventually articulate her own responses, nothing could compensate for the absence of memories of her mother.

According to Nancy Miller, 'Writing a parent's death in literary form displays both the steps toward separation and the tortuous paths of reconnection after the fact. Grieving and release' (1996: 7). In Devlin's case this process remains permanently incomplete because she lacks all memory of her mother: 'try as I may, I cannot put a face to the shadowy figure who was my mother. I continually search my memory, desperate to draw out of its depths an image, a smile, a gesture' (2000: 38). In fact, Mrs Gaw became so erased from the family after her death that when Edith nursed her dying father over 40 years later, she 'wanted desperately to take this last chance of asking him about her in those weeks of comparative intimacy between us, but I could not bring myself to broach the long-forbidden subject. The constraint built up over all the years was too absolute' (2000: 39). She describes this as having to let her mother 'die a second time in my memory', and reflects upon the negative impact of this virtual obliteration of memory on her own sense of identity.

'To create a story', writes Mary Warnock, 'both memory and imagination must be deployed, and autobiography is the place where, more than any other, their function overlaps' (1989: 126). Edith Devlin's narrative suggests how her lack of a crucial memory has continued to haunt her as she herself has aged, so that during an illness the 'imagined proximity of death made me think more intensely of my mother. I began to search in every corner of my conscious memory for a trace of her whom I might soon meet. I could find nothing' (2000: 40). Attempts to learn something from an older brother prove unsettling rather than enabling. His memories are of a woman dying painfully of cancer, which stirred a 'subconscious memory' of 'a white-faced woman with eyes closed, moaning and restless', whereas Devlin 'had been searching for another happier image of an active, smiling woman holding me in her arms and swinging me about' (2000: 41). Later on, being told by an older sister: ' "I don't want to remember. I have shut out all that part of my life from my mind" ', she realises that 'I had to let my mother die for the third time' (2000: 41). Ironically, the nearest she comes to recovering memory of her mother is in the casual conversation of a woman who, as a girl, was employed to help Mrs Gaw bath the infant Edith; but far from providing consolation, she claims that this made her feel 'as if someone else had lived my life for me, had done me out of what rightly belonged to me' (2000: 41). Perhaps inevitably, Edith Newman Devlin's unceasing 'search to re-create a mother for myself' leads her to another book, 'the prayers, readings and invocations of the liturgies of the Church of Ireland which my aunt told me she [her mother] loved and in which she, like me, was formed' (2000: 41). Thus, a common tradition of words handed down from generation to generation – words heard and spoken by mother and daughter in turn – becomes the only available substitute for individuated personal memories and the emotions associated with them.

## III

Richard Murphy's memoir *The Kick* (2002) opens with a reference to his mother's death in 1995 aged 96, an event more fully detailed in the closing pages, and then recreates a conversation in which the writer presses her to retell the family story that gives his book its title. According to this story, Murphy, aged three, ignored his mother's request to thank his great aunt for afternoon tea and instead kicked her, not once, but twice. Because of Murphy's dependence on versions of the incident told by his mother and older sister, it possesses for him the truth of story rather than of personal memory, although this in no way diminishes its power in underpinning a family view of him as wilfully rebellious, which he himself seems to accept. Furthermore, when in the penultimate paragraph he tells of his own three-year-old grandson's defiant declaration – ' "I don't like having you as my grandfather" ' (2002: 379) – he not only creates a moment of narrative symmetry by inviting comparison with his own act of disobedience at the same age, but also hints at the birth of a variant anecdote which his grandson may later be told, and of which he in turn may have no memory. Murphy reflects further on the coercive power of such family stories based on alleged memory after his genealogical research revealed that Isabella Fowler, the wife of one of his great-grandfathers, was not, as legend had it, the daughter of an army captain killed in battle before she was born, but rather an illegitimate child whose mother's disgrace was disguised by this fabrication. The consequences of this deception are interpreted in almost biblical terms:

> The legend of Fowler, dying like a hero in a battle at a time when no battles took place, affected all of Isabella Fowler's descendants for the next three

generations. Most of all it steered my father's younger brother, Kepler, who was given Fowler as his middle name, towards a career in the army in peacetime and death on his first day in battle on the western front. I grew up feeling guilty that I might never have his courage. (2002: 25)

This guilt is evident in Murphy's fearful reaction to the outbreak of war in 1939; he remembers 'counting the years the war would have to last – I reckoned five – before I would be morally compelled to volunteer and get killed' (2002: 57). This sense of inadequacy and personal unsuitability for military service is one aspect of Murphy's uneasy relationship with his parents and their commitment to British colonial service, public duty, useful work and self-improvement. His epigraph cites Stuart Hampshire – 'As artificiality is natural to men, so are variety and deviation on all sides of the norm; and this constitutes the principal interest of the species, alongside the power to play with this happy fact in the imagination' – and indeed it is clear that Murphy's rebellion, such as it is, derives largely from his inability and unwillingness to meet the 'norms' of his parents, who expected his passage through English public school and Oxford into responsible employment and a suitable marriage. Murphy's articulation of the pain of this burden, and of his restless search for his own securities, is central to his memoir and inseparable from his discovery of his ambiguous sexual identity, which is itself prefigured by another family story concerning an argument over his gender between two clergymen at his christening.

In *The Kick* Murphy retrospectively confronts his earlier inability to acknowledge his repressed homosexuality and the dilemmas this repeatedly engendered. Following a short-lived engagement to Patricia Cavendish, which was, he claims, 'influenced by our mothers' expectations', he recalls his 'demoralizing doubt as to whether I could ever love a woman well enough to marry without deceiving her and myself' (2002: 110–11). A second failed marriage plan came in the wake of a false charge of indecency in a public lavatory, which not only left Murphy terrified of the disgrace he might bring on himself and his family, but also forced him to face the disturbing truth of his sexual orientation. ' "I'm not a homosexual", I pleaded, not having begun to think that I might be', he writes, and repeats his denial to his friend Charles Monteith, adding, 'because I wished that were the truth' (2002: 116, 118). Later still, recalling the failure of his first night with his future wife, Patricia Strang, he claims to have 'advised her to find a peasant who would love her well, not an androgynous poet or intellectual who could only make her laugh and cry' (2002: 158). These failures and disappointments contrast with the deeply rewarding, non-sexual friendship he established with Tony White, a Londoner who had abandoned a theatrical career to live in the west of Ireland where he hoped to become a writer. When he died prematurely in 1976, Murphy confided to his journal that White ' "would be the one to read with complete understanding all I had written, [ . . . ] that he would make sense of the confusions in my life" ' (2002: 321), and links the profundity of this loss with his own relocation from Connemara to Killiney in Dublin.

Throughout his memoir, Murphy, who was the child of a Big House, reveals himself as a man endlessly in search of a home, from his early retreats to cottages at Lecknavarna and Rossroe in Galway, through the series of major building and renovation projects he undertook at Roundwood, Cleggan, on High Island (where he planned to restore an oratory and bee-hive cells) and on Omey, where he constructed a hexagonal studio. Shortly before moving to Killiney, Murphy told an interviewer that he was going

> to a house in the middle of a garden of granite outcrop. I think I've always looked for that kind of security – a place to which I belong, a house which is well built – because of the insecurity of my life and parts of my upbringing: an insecurity brought on by the war, and by my own loss of faith in Christianity, and by the fall of the British Empire in whose strength I was reared. (Haffenden, 1981: 143)

This comment closely anticipates the themes of his autobiography, which includes details of the genesis of some of his major poems, including *The Battle of Aughrim* and the sonnets in *The Price of Stone*. These, too, express Murphy's uneasy relationships with family, nation and history, as well as his personal associations with particular buildings, thereby indicating the continuity of his narrative preoccupations.

Where Murphy searches to find a home, Annabel Davis-Goff seeks to repossess her past through memories of houses associated with her childhood. The epigraph to *Walled Gardens: Scenes from an Anglo-Irish Childhood* (1990), taken from Eliot's *The Family Reunion*, suggests that houses are repositories of 'what is spoken [ . . . ], waiting for the future to hear it./And whatever happens began in the past, and presses hard on the future.' The book itself begins with a family reunion occasioned by Davis-Goff's father's death and goes on to illustrate the truth of Miller's observation that the death of parents 'forces us to rethink our lives, to reread ourselves', while also problematising this process because of the unreliability of memory itself (1996: xiii). Davis-Goff narrates her personal and family story within the wider context of the impoverished and diminished position of the rural Anglo-Irish in the post-independence period, where 'Protestants continued to be the upper class but [ . . . ] no longer had any political power' (1990: 39). She cites their economic incompetence, nostalgia and commonplace lapses into eccentricity, genteel squalor and excessive drinking as evidence of their parlous state, adding weight to Hubert Butler's assertion that 'The only extenuation for the feebleness of the Anglo-Irish today is that no strong challenge is ever presented to them' (1990: 74). There is little sign of the capacity for independent thought and plain speech which Butler valorised and exhorted his Anglo-Irish co-religionists to exercise for the benefit of the Irish people as a whole. Rather, one is reminded of his quotation of Wolfe Tone's prediction that the Anglo-Irish would disappear because 'they refused to identify themselves with their neighbours, to accept, in fact, "the common name of Irishman"' (Butler, 1996: 40).

When *Walled Gardens* moves from the general Anglo-Irish context to the specifics of family and personal experience, Davis-Goff engages interrogatively with the elusive uncertainties of memory, as well as with its affirming and self-identifying aspects. 'Shared memories are the rock on which my kind of family is built', she asserts. 'There is no substitute; blood counts for nothing in comparison' (1990: 6). As an extension of this, Davis-Goff, whose adult life has been lived abroad, maintains that the shared memory and knowledge of specific sounds, smells, colours and atmospheric conditions trigger associations 'in the exact form I remember only in Ireland' (1990: 4), and are fundamental to her sense of having come home when she is back among Irish people. Even more strikingly, she states that in her Connecticut garden 'the smell of tomatoes every year [ . . . ] reminds me, not of the previous summer, but of my father in the greenhouse nipping off the small, pungent, green shoots between a stained thumbnail and forefinger' (1990: 4). But even 'shared memories' are problematic. When Davis-Goff and her sister visit the site of their former Waterford home, Glenville, they cannot reconcile their memories, 'which matched each other's', to the reality of the dairy plant that has replaced it. Reflecting on this later, she muses: 'I still cannot reconstruct it, since, although intellectually I know that the tree and the stables are still there, I have no visual memory of what any of it looked like that afternoon. If I could remember that I would have to stop believing that Glenville still exists' (1990: 9).[3]

This fascinating statement suggests how selective forgetting may be an integral part of remembering, an idea to which Davis-Goff returns elsewhere when she recalls observing her mother 'as she, expressionless, silent, watched me freeze a conversation in which an important memory was threatened by an alternative version of the same incident put forward by my sister' (1990: 179–80). Here the emphasis is on the intuitive protection of a preferred memory, or one upon which the subject is particularly dependent because of subconscious or unconscious imperatives. Yet, as Davis-Goff acknowledges, personal memory may be inseparably conflated with inherited memory, and here one thinks of similar instances in *The Kick*. Thus, the writer admits her uncertainty over which memories of Glenville derive from her own and her sister's experience, and which are the result of their father 'layering his memories over ours' in the stories he told after they had left the house and it had burned down: 'My father had a gift for making his memories ours and we were tied to him by what he remembered – sometimes events which had taken place before we were born' (1990: 10). While this questions the extent to which any memory can properly be described as one's own, it also demonstrates that that uncertainty does not diminish the power of what is shared, a point Davis-Goff finds reinforced in the way her younger brother 'has deliberately made a place for my father's memories in the life he has chosen for his family' (1990: 10).[4]

The interrelationship between memory and the reconstruction and interpretation of the past is also crucial to the domestic trauma at the heart of *Walled Gardens*: Davis-Goff's parents' divorce when she was a teenager, the event which, along with her departure for secretarial college in Oxford, marked the end of childhood. Here she not only remembers the tensions and angry silences surrounding her mother's leaving, but also draws on her own experience of marriage, divorce and remarriage to review the frustrations and isolation of her mother's predicament, which contributed to the breakdown. Nor is this all. She recalls the shock of her mother's casual disclosure after her father's death of an occasion when, as a girl, she had taken him to see a butterfly she had raised from a caterpillar. To the adult writer it seems that this previously unknown, yet potentially available, information might have alleviated her childhood fears about her parents' relationship, and so she self-consciously proceeds to imagine the possible circumstances of the incident, as if to appropriate it as her own memory, warning: 'Those of us who are at least partially governed by our memories have to play by very careful rules. This account of a long-past incident has to be considered thoughtfully and built upon slowly' (1990: 179). And so, drawing upon the slenderest hints, she memorialises, in an image that is both unsubstantiated and consoling, the girl and young man who, years later, would become her parents:

I like to think that it was a greenhouse where my mother brought my father to see her butterfly. I can imagine them, him in tennis whites, her in a light cotton dress with bare brown legs and long hair tied back, silhouetted against the glass as they lean toward each other to look at a perfect Red Admiral in a glass jar. (1990: 179)

Davis-Goff's braiding of her mother's memory and her own recalls Olney's observation that such weaving is 'a characteristic metaphor for the operation of memory' as 'processual' rather than 'archaeological', bringing forth 'ever different memorial configurations' – exemplified here by the imagined scene in the greenhouse (1998: 20). Furthermore, Davis-Goff's need to construct this incident is illustrative of what Miller calls 'most children['s] desire to uncover their parents' truth', which she sees as an integral aspect of the autobiographical quest for self-knowledge, that is itself dependent upon knowing one's parents' story also (1996: 107–08).

In the final section of *Walled Gardens*, which has an American setting, Davis-Goff alludes to the differences between the norms of her upbringing and the nascent feminism and moral permissiveness of the society to which she moved as a young adult and which presented her with what she ironically styles 'a new set of self-evident truths' (1990: 236). Later, prompted by her own divorce to re-examine these truths and her relationship to her family, her discovery of the story of Edward Whalley and an ancestor, William Goffe – signatories of King Charles I's death warrant who were forced into exile after the Restoration and allegedly hid in a cave near her home in New Haven – provides her with an unexpected connection and continuity between her Irish past and her American present. The auspiciousness of the connection is enriched by the survival of some correspondence between Goffe and his wife, Frances (who would never see each other again, and may not even have received each other's letters), testifying to their enduring faith in love, the very thing which Davis-Goff's own Anglo-Irish upbringing 'did nothing to spawn confidence in' (1990: 239). *Walled Gardens* ends with her account of her visit with her children to the so-called Judges' Cave, which generates a fortifying moment of interplay between putative history, personal memory and immediate experience as it adumbrates the future:

> Each fork offered a partly covered path which constantly threatened to peter out and seemed both excitingly full of unknown promise and familiar in a way I did not quite understand. [ . . . ] Then I suddenly knew why I had had the feeling of seeing this before. [ . . . ] The woods at Glenville were like this. [ . . . ] We started down the hill together, and it seemed to me it was possible, if we were lucky, took the broader view, respected our memories, paid attention, showed a little faith, that we could have it all. (1990: 254–55)

History, then, is less burdensome for Annabel Davis-Goff than for Richard Murphy, providing her with reassuring links with the past, while memory, which she not only draws upon but interrogates and imaginatively generates, is the dynamic that continuously shapes and reshapes the present.

## IV

The death of a parent is again the pivotal event in Hugh Maxton's autobiography of his Dublin childhood and adolescence, although unlike Edith Devlin he has strong memories of his father who died when he was 12. Yet where lack of memory was the problem for the one writer, memory itself and the interplay of memory and imagination in the exploration of self-identity preoccupy the other. More than any of the other works dealt with here, *Waking: An Irish Protestant Upbringing* (1997) actively questions not only the process of writing the self, but the very possibility of doing so. This 'document of initiation and renewal' (1997: 10) opens with a series of vividly recuperated sense impressions from Maxton's childhood in the early 1950s, followed by his discovery of the mystery of words and the power of the imagination, which inevitably evoke readerly memories of the opening

chapter of *A Portrait of the Artist as a Young Man*. The Joycean association is immediately reinforced by Maxton's account of a visit in 1982 to
Szombathely in Hungary, 'the actual birthplace of the fictitious Lipot Virag
(father of Leopold Bloom)', which generates a self-reflexive examination of
his own behaviour in a situation where the 'actual' and the 'fictitious' had
mingled so promiscuously: 'Idiotically keen to see everything that echoes, I
seized on coincidences or egregious mergers of sense and nonsense wherever
they arose – and elsewhere. My mission was to find ready-transformed
whatever it was I had set out blindly to find' (1997: 13–14). Yet events in
Szombathely not only persuade him of the misconceived nature of such a
mission, but make him ponder how the dead can be known, an issue of
fundamental importance given his belief that 'every author is engaged on
memoirs of his or her dead life' (1997: 17).

Maxton is deeply sceptical of the reliability of autobiography – 'Knowledge
is a very limited form of truth' (1997: 18) – and this anticipates the recurring
note of uncertainty in *Waking* and his self-conscious awareness of what
Olney terms 'the self-adjusting and self-defining plasticity' of memory (1998:
343). 'Nothing is remembered as it was', Maxton asserts; memory may be
either corrosive or enhancing, while the dynamic interplay between past
and present ensures that history is, in a sense, never cast in final form:

> Present life and its precursor are alike as the elongated spheres of an
> egg-timer – which one is up, which one is down? The grains of sand are
> uniform, stare at them how you will. They move through the slenderest
> passage and create what they were, a sphere three-quarters full, leaving
> room for the next flux, the next interpretation. (1997: 21)

Maxton's image here illuminates Anderson's contention that history 'is
never definitive or finally known [. . .] but is capable of constant alteration
as more is remembered or released into consciousness, causing the subject to
think both the past and the present differently' (2001: 61). It also has a direct
bearing on the way he narrates scenes from his early life and interrogates
whether they were as he now recalls and writes them.

If the title, *Waking*, is indicative of the burgeoning intellectual, emotional
and experiential awareness with which the book grapples, its subtitle, *An
Irish Protestant Upbringing*, emphasises the formative aspects of his childhood.
The only child of his father's second marriage, his upbringing, especially
in his early years, was divided between the McCormack home in Harold's
Cross and a farm at Cronemore, County Wicklow owned by his mother's
relatives, which is the locus for some of his most penetrating memories and
reflections on his expanding consciousness of the world.[5] Maxton registers
little of Devlin's sense of belonging to a religious minority in a Catholic
society, although the Protestant church impacted upon his youth in significant, if disillusioning, ways. Yet despite his childhood scepticism at the

power of Christmas communion at Cronemore 'to abolish some partition in reality' between 'the Palestinian supper and the watery Irish dawn' (1997: 47), and his rejection of the 'theologically questionable' teaching of scripture and the catechetical approach to moral instruction at his Methodist-run primary school, Maxton writes without irony of the 'genuine sort of ethical simplicity' he derived from his schooling. Moreover, he pinpoints a particularly Protestant paradox when he declares: 'Fidelity to the truth of language played a central role, even to the extent that one felt almost justified in betraying inner, non-articulated feelings. There was a passion for truth, just as there was repression of the very idea of passion' (1997: 88).

It was, however, in the Unitarian church, to which he was attracted as a teenager by a series of lectures on psychological science, that Maxton found that the 'passion for truth' also permitted individual judgements, 'that disagreement was a fundamental right, even a requirement' (1997: 206). Reviewing the significance of this phase in his life, he describes it as 'detoxification and the concomitant restoration of various mental processes which had been stunned into inactivity by domestic and parochial pressures' (1997: 207). The domestic pressures to which he alludes here derive from his father's sudden, unforeseen death. The chapter in which this event is related is titled 'Posthumous Life' and there is a powerful sense in which this might serve for the whole book, since this death is the filter through which anterior time has subsequently been remembered, while simultaneously impacting upon all that comes after it.[6] Maxton spells out these implications in another passage of exceptional self-awareness:

> The moment when such news [of his father's death] breaks does not constitute a moment. All time, before and after, is altered in its order and texture. Things inundate it, it becomes a sunken town in which the streets persist but go nowhere. Movement is at once automatic and impeded, lead in the boots. Bereavement is close to drowning. You rise for the last time, to see your life stretching not backwards but ahead. (1997: 187)[7]

Here he evokes what Miller terms the 'trauma that causes an invisible tear in our self-identity' because 'our earliest acts of identity are intimately bound up with our relation to the dead parent' (1996: x). Maxton refers to himself being both circumstantially and emotionally 'depleted' by his father's death, and other factors testify to its enduring significance for him, most notably, his publication of his memoir in his father's centenary year, when the author himself was 50 and his son, to whom *Waking* is dedicated, was Maxton's age at the time of Charles McCormack's death. The Joycean echoes in the 'Prelude' are revived in the final chapter, which consists of nine short sections set against events in the late 1980s, recalling the fragmented closing pages of *Portrait*. While they may not prefigure a departure like that of Stephen Dedalus, they do affirm Maxton's declaration that 'Every history has one foot in the present' (1997: 210) and are, perhaps, a final reminder that *Waking* is concerned not only with 'initiation' but also with 'renewal'.

## Conclusion

'Just been listening to that stupid bastard I took myself for thirty years ago, hard to believe I was ever as bad as that. Thank God that's all done with anyway', muses Beckett's Krapp after playing his tape recordings, before proceeding to reflect again on that past in the light of his current situation (1968: 17). So too the autobiographers discussed in this chapter confront their various pasts, particularly their childhood and early adulthood, and assess the extent to which certain events remain disconcerting sources of potent memories, the most intense of which forever elude the final release that the act of narrative articulation promises. Thus, Forrest Reid repeatedly revisits his childhood loss of Emma Holmes and the fading of his vivid dream world in adolescence; Edith Newman Devlin and Hugh Maxton continually return to memories of parents who died in their youth; and Annabel Davis-Goff seeks to understand her parents' relationship and the breakdown of their marriage. In more expansive ways, Richard Murphy's memoir reveals the painful vicissitudes in coming to terms with his ambiguous sexual identity and in growing apart from his family's well-established political loyalties and religious commitments. And even Robert Harbinson, who might at first seem unreflectively immersed in working-class Protestant evangelicalism, develops a self-critical perspective on his early formative influences.

Although all six autobiographers share a common religious ancestry, the diversity of their writing rebuts any reductive perceptions or generalisations about Protestants or Protestantism in Ireland. With the exception of Devlin, all register a sense of spiritual disillusionment, or a drift towards unbelief or indifference. Yet – and this is especially true of Devlin, Harbinson and Davis-Goff, whose memoir makes the least reference to the place of religion in her upbringing – an awareness of themselves as Protestants is inseparable from their sense of being different from Catholics, whose lives seemed shaped by other cultural priorities and loyalties, as well as by the mysteries of their religious practices. So while Protestantism in its devotional form may have had little lasting influence on the sensibilities of the majority of these writers, this must be weighed against the importance of the broader cultural implications of being Protestant in a society where denominational identity is deeply inscribed and overtly demonstrated.

Yet whatever the relative significance of religion and identity for these autobiographers, other factors are of equal or even greater importance in the life stories they narrate. Inevitably, they are engaged to varying degrees in attempts to restore, recover or interrogate aspects of the past in ways that will satisfy the present in which the account is being set down. Yet, equally inevitably, this project fails to recapture definitively either the self, the experience or the moment as it was. This is partly because the writer is, in some respects, no longer the same person as he or she was in that former time – as Krapp opines – and partly because the very process of writing itself mediates, and thereby changes, the original experience. It is for this reason, therefore, that these life writings, like all others, must be read as interim acts of 'drawing the line and making the tot', narratives which, however crafted to give a sense of completeness, ultimately remain provisional, open and subject to further recitation.

## Notes

1. The title *Private Road* itself almost seems to be anticipated in a passage in *Apostate* where Reid observes: 'My life, from as far back as I can remember, was never lived entirely in the open. I mean that it had its private side, that there were always things I saw, felt, heard, and kept to myself' (1947: 9).
2. Max Wright's *Told in Gath* (1990), for example, is a powerful account of his upbringing among the Plymouth Brethren, informed throughout by the author's ironic and satirical viewpoint.
3. There is some similarity here with Seamus Heaney's memorialisation of his 'coeval' chestnut tree, long since cut down, but living in his memory in the final sonnet of 'Clearances' in *The Haw Lantern* (1987).
4. Here one might also recall the enduring power of the 'memory' of the alleged circumstances of the death of Isabella Fowler's father on successive generations of men in the Murphy family.
5. Hugh Maxton is the pseudonym under which W. J. McCormack has published poetry since the late 1960s. As W. J. McCormack, he is the author and editor of numerous scholarly works on Anglo-Irish literature.
6. Nicola King claims: 'Reading the texts of memory shows that "remembering the self" is not a case of restoring an original identity, but a continuous process of *re*-membering, of putting together moment by moment, of provisional and partial reconstruction' (2000: 175).
7. The images here are reminiscent of some of those used by Emily Dickinson in her poems, 'I felt a Funeral, in my Brain' and 'After great pain, a formal feeling comes', as are the experiences and feelings he describes.

# 9
# Fighting Without Guns?: Political Autobiography in Contemporary Northern Ireland

*Stephen Hopkins*

If it is the case that 'memoir has become *the* genre in the skittish period around the turn of the millennium' (Gilmore, 2001: 1, original emphasis), then perhaps it is not so surprising that this genre has been well represented in recent writing about the conflict in Northern Ireland. George Egerton has argued convincingly that political memoir is best understood as a 'poly-genre', and that the 'difficulty of classifying memoir in tidy categories [ . . . ] should not stand as an argument for diminishing its significance or impeding the development of a helpful body of criticism' (1994: 342). Drawing on the work of Roy Pascal, Egerton insists that we can distinguish between polit-ical autobiography and memoir 'according to whether the focus is primarily inward, on the development of the self, as in the case of autobiography, or more external, on others, on events or deeds, as with memoir' (1994: 346). Given that politicians' public lives are largely dominated by external events, it might be argued that they typically produce memoirs rather than authentic political autobiographies. Of the works studied in this chapter, some certainly contain sufficient authorial reflection on the development of the self, through the medium of a political career, to be interpreted as genuinely autobiographical, at least in part. And while a debate about defin-ition and classification can be useful in constructing the parameters of this research, there is always the danger of neglecting the substance of autobio-graphical writing about the Troubles by pursuing a semantic and theoretical cul-de-sac. In this chapter, therefore, 'political autobiography' will be used to refer to texts written by current and former protagonists of the conflict in Northern Ireland during the past four decades, in which the focus is on both objective political or paramilitary developments and the subjectivity of the authorial self.

The argument of this chapter is predicated on the belief that Northern Ireland's perceived movement towards a 'post-conflict' phase of develop-ment has given fresh impetus to the long-established tradition of political autobiography and memoir produced by the history of Anglo-Irish relations.

Indeed, there is already evidence to suggest that protagonists who were involved in the Troubles, whether as political or military actors, feel that the time is now ripe to tell their 'stories' to a wider public, to explain their motivations and to try to shape the debate over the rights and wrongs of the conflict. This debate constitutes a critical aspect of political life in contemporary Northern Ireland, for competing struggles to *interpret* the conflict, its genesis and its outcome – if, indeed, it is definitively over – may prove to be a significant element that could become a substitute for the continuing prosecution of the conflict itself. The recent spate of publications chronicling the life stories of those closely involved in the Troubles, whether strictly autobiographical or not, raises a number of crucial issues to do with authorial motivation, the authenticity of the narrative voice, generational difference and the diversity of experience reflected in parliamentary as opposed to paramilitary memoirs. This chapter will investigate some of these themes with reference to autobiographies published during the last four decades or so. The selection of authors is not meant to be either exhaustive or representative, but will be illustrative of some key aspects of Northern Irish political autobiography. These texts may be described as 'political' in that they are intended to validate and promote writers' particular political parties or ideological perspectives, whether in the present, the past or both. Of course, these purposes may be complex and indeed contradictory, for there are examples of protagonists radically changing their political beliefs and allegiances over time, and of living a 'double life', ostensibly supporting the objectives of an organisation, while secretly working to subvert those same objectives.

Before we begin our discussion proper, it is necessary to make a few preliminary points about the scholarly uses of political autobiography. For contemporary historians and political scientists, the relevance and utility of studying Northern Irish autobiography are twofold. First, the process of writing one's life story in a scenario of recent traumatic conflict can be viewed as an effort to narrate or embody a 'collective aspiration', and can thus shed light on a broad set of political and organisational issues, alongside the expected subjective insights of conventional autobiography. Second, although professional historians, accustomed to the rigorous demands of a disciplined historiography, have displayed an understandable tendency to downplay the significance of political memoir, there is often a paucity of other reliable or authorised documentary evidence from which to work. In these circumstances, reliance upon the historian's usual injunction to collect, collate and evaluate documentary material may not always yield a complete picture. Indeed, it may be said to be in the nature of the Northern Ireland conflict, where a good deal of 'political' activity (particularly, but not exclusively, the use of violence for political ends) has been necessarily clandestine and conspiratorial, that much of what is now accepted by historians as 'conventional wisdom' has been gleaned from memoir and personal testimony. So while these accounts must be treated with due caution and should not be automatically accepted as authoritative, not least because they are often mutually contradictory and sometimes internally inconsistent, they must be recognised as a genuine and valuable resource for researchers.

Some protagonists, especially those who have played leadership roles in various paramilitary organisations and associated political parties, have been the subjects of recent autobiography or biography, among them Gerry Adams, Martin McGuinness and Joe Cahill of the Provisional IRA and Sinn Féin; Gusty Spence and David Ervine of the Ulster Volunteer Force (UVF) and Progressive Unionist Party; and Michael Stone of the Ulster Defence Association (UDA) and Ulster Freedom Fighters (UFF). These prominent activists have often been represented (and represented themselves) as spokesmen for larger political organisations or communities. That is to say, in portraying themselves and their immediate or extended families as having been personally affected by the Troubles – through family dislocation, the threat of violence or the legacy of actual violence – they act as the embodiments of communal political identities shaped by resistance and suffering. In this they are conforming to what Roy Foster describes as the 'particularly Irish phenomenon' of conflating personal biography and national history, a process which, he argues, can conceal 'very large and untested assumptions; it can also run the danger of collapsing alternative history into anecdote and psychobabble (or anecdotal psychobabble)' (2001: xi, xiv–xv). With these cautionary words in mind, it is my intention here to examine the uses and abuses of written autobiography (as distinct from oral testimony) in the particular circumstances of a society emerging from a protracted, bitter and bloody conflict, underlining the 'mesh of nuance, complexity and contradiction involved when the stories of nations intersect with supposedly emblematic individuals' (Foster, 2001: xvii). None of these issues are especially novel in discussions of Northern Ireland's evolving historical narrative and its relationship to the broader pattern of Anglo-Irish relations, through which prism the struggle to reshape and resolve this narrative must ultimately be understood. However, while this chapter will occasionally infer this broader context, its main focus will necessarily be narrower.

## Truth and reconciliation, or enduring conflict and spin

There is an ongoing, and increasingly prominent, debate in Northern Ireland about how best to remember or commemorate various aspects of the Troubles, a debate which is part of an ideological struggle to control the past and shape present and future narratives. While it is possible to argue that the most appropriate form of remembrance would be simply to forget the past and try to move on from a *tabula rasa*, this surely represents mere wishful thinking. In addition to exercising government officials and ministers, a number of these thorny issues have also had a deep popular resonance. They range from the general question of how to define 'victims' rights' in a political climate where 'perpetrators' and 'victims' are by no means universally acknowledged as such, to the suitability of models of 'truth and reconciliation', and include such specific problematic instances as the future (and by extension the past) of the site of Long Kesh or the Maze prison.[1] It is perhaps inevitable that this interlocking series of debates should be a central element not only in the recent political manoeuvrings of parties and protagonists, but also in their literary exercises, where two distinct trends are evident. On the one hand, there may be a sincere effort on behalf of protagonists to draw a line in the sand, to move away from sterile ideological antagonism and inflexibility towards a self-critical reappraisal of previous commitments and shibboleths. On the other hand – and there is probably clearer evidence of this trend in the autobiographies under consideration here – writing in this genre and at this juncture may involve a large measure of self-justification, coupled with a display of continuing antagonism towards traditional enemies. Fionola Meredith, in an insightful interview with Richard English, author of a major study of the IRA based largely on interviews with republican activists, makes a telling point:

> Why then should we accept the 'authenticity' of their self-reflexive accounts as holding any more significance, insight or weight than a more 'objective' analysis? The experiential narrative offered by 'someone who's been through it' can be as duplicitous and untrustworthy as it is vivid. The truth-claim based on experience is often furthest from veracity. (2003: 9)

Meredith goes on to conclude that 'the most fundamental impulse in the stories of those who have committed politically motivated violent atrocities will nearly always be self-justification. That's the difficulty with narrative accounts – their need for legitimacy means that the truths they offer are partial, loaded and incomplete' (2003: 9).

According to this view, the autobiographical design represents a more or less subtle attempt to use memoir as a proxy weapon in the ongoing ideological conflict. In short, for those who have played an active role in the Troubles, and who belong or have belonged to paramilitary organisations, autobiography can serve as an alternative, textual means of conducting the struggle and engaging the enemy by the force of argument rather than by the argument of force. Although it is not the case that all of the recent political autobiographies to emerge from Northern Ireland have been written by paramilitary-linked individuals, it is nonetheless significant that this group has been largely to the fore. As Andrew Gamble points out, the political memoir 'has become an expected rite of passage for political celebrity, and also a highly profitable one' (2002: 142). This element of celebrity (or notoriety), allied to a widespread unease about the financial gains that erstwhile paramilitaries might make from writing sensationalist accounts of their exploits, has been the subject of lively debate in recent times. Clearly, the perception that these individuals' active role in violent conflict is over has helped to convince them that the time is right to grapple textually with past actions and events, many of which have been too sensitive to discuss previously. However, it is still highly probable, except in the most self-critical cases, that these individuals will find it difficult to be absolutely frank about activities that were, after all, often illegal and unlikely to cast them in a favourable light. And, of course, emotions continue to run high in an atmosphere where ideological differences over past deeds is never far from the surface of political discourse.

In reading these political autobiographies, therefore, we need to be alert to 'the deliberate gap in the narrative: the momentous elision, the leap in the story' (Foster, 2001: 3). The act of self-writing often tempts authors onto the paths of 'vindication, exculpation and the byways of personal interest', whether intentionally or subconsciously, so that the sensitive reader needs to be ever mindful of the impulse towards 'reductionism, bias, the creation of a persona, special pleading and outright dishonesty in promoting or defending personal interests' (Egerton, 1994: 344). It could be argued that 'political scientists should be like detectives, searching out the one true account of what happened', but since 'reality is constructed and experienced in so many different ways, determining what *actually* happened in any final sense is an aspiration impossible to achieve' (Egerton, 1994: 142, original emphasis). While this may appear to political scientists and historians as a limitation of the genre, radical postmodernist criticism argues that insights can still be gained through the appraisal of autobiography in literary or psychological terms, 'with the development of identity and the presentation of personality serving rightfully as its principal function' (Egerton, 1994: 347). The historiographical and literary dimensions are conjoined in the study of political autobiography, and critics should be aware of both of these elements and adjust their scrutiny accordingly. As Egerton puts it: 'With all the distortions to which this type of personal historiography is prey, the potential for honesty, accuracy and insight remains; for historians "truthfulness", however old-fashioned, ultimately stands as a fundamental critical concern in the evaluation of memoirs' (1994: 348). So while there is almost always evidence in political autobiography of the tendency 'to retroject perspectives and motives, to rationalize behaviour, to attribute present meaning to past experience [ . . . ], and particularly to find a unity and pattern in the disorder of past political strife' (Egerton, 1994: 347), these issues of motivation and intentionality need to be interrogated. Whether being deliberately self-serving or manipulating the historical narrative for contemporary ideological purposes, 'the memoirist is almost invariably self-betrayed into the hands of the later historian' (Egerton, 1994: 344).

One further point is worth noting: the autobiographies considered here are generally those of well-known public figures rather than anonymous members of the community, but that is not to imply that the latter have been autobiographically silent. Smyth and Fay (2000) have edited a collection of 'personal accounts' by 'ordinary' people affected by or involved in the Troubles, testimonies which provide a rich and often moving source for understanding the ways in which public conflict impinges upon the lives of private citizens (although many of those interviewed cannot be categorised simplistically as 'victims'). Further growth in autobiographical writing of this kind, often attached to local and oral history projects, may well provide a useful means of addressing the legacy of the conflict in Northern Ireland. For example, the Ardoyne Commemoration Project (2002) has produced a monumental work, identifying some 83 people from the area who were killed during the Troubles and interviewing several hundred family members, friends and residents in order to ascertain the stories of these individuals' lives and deaths, and those of the bereaved.[2] Similarly, Joanne O'Brien's *A Matter of Minutes* (2002) features interview testimony and photographic portraits of 33 people whose lives were directly affected by the events of 'Bloody Sunday' in 1972. While this kind of autobiographical writing is not the primary focus of this chapter, its historical, political and potential therapeutic value should not be overlooked.

## The ghostly autobiographer

One of the key questions prompted by the recent crop of political autobiographies in Northern Ireland relates to the authenticity of the authorial voice. In some cases there is little doubt that author and subject speak with the same narrative voice. Gerry Adams, for instance, was already a writer of some repute before he published his two volumes of political autobiography, *Before the Dawn: An Autobiography* (1996) and *Hope and History: Making Peace in Ireland* (2003). These were preceded by *Cage Eleven* (1990), a book based on his 'Brownie' articles written while he was an internee and convicted prisoner, and published in *Republican News* between 1975 and 1977. Although Adams gives the real names of some of his fellow internees in the book's introduction, he later claims that 'the main characters are fictional, but they and their escapades are my way of representing life as it was in Long Kesh' (1990: 14). What is unclear, however, is whether the primary purpose of his fictionalising method was to evade, embellish, manipulate or subvert aspects of the truth. While casting little light on this question, Steve MacDonogh, Adams's editor and publisher, nevertheless characterises his literary development as a gradual movement away from factual writing towards fiction. Introducing Adams's *Selected Writings* (1994), he explains that while *Falls Memories* (1982), a local history of a nationalist area of Belfast, has 'qualities of fiction', and *Cage Eleven* 'hover[s] between fact and fiction', *The Street and Other Stories* (1992) is 'more decidedly fictional' (Adams, 1994: x–xii).

In *Before the Dawn*, however, Adams's propensity to merge fact and fiction provoked controversy when he 'tried to capture in a short story something of the harsh reality of the campaign waged by the IRA against Britain's armed forces as they patrolled the streets of my home town' in the early 1970s (1996: 168). Although this 'story', which recounts the internal moral questioning of an IRA sniper before he shoots a member of a British Army patrol, is written in italics, it is not explicitly presented as pure fiction, the product of imagination rather than experience. Fintan O'Toole is among those who have strongly criticised Adams's narrative evasiveness, saying: 'it is striking in itself that the IRA campaign on the streets of Belfast is not represented by bombs tearing civilians apart in restaurants, by children blown up on their way into the Falls Road baths or by "informers" having nail-studded clubs aimed at their flesh' (1996). There was, of course, a political rationale behind this approach; Adams could only present such details in 'fictional' form because of his steadfast denial that he has never been a member of the IRA, despite the incredulity and derision of critics. Nevertheless, the strength of the critical reaction that greeted this aspect of his autobiographical style seems to have had an impact; certainly, no similar episode appears in *Hope and History*.

However authentic or otherwise these 'fictional' interludes in Adams's memoirs, there is little doubt that he himself is the author of the book.[3] By contrast, Michael Stone's autobiography, *None Shall Divide Us* (2003), is presented *as if* Stone himself had written it; his name alone appears on the cover and title page. However, in the introduction, journalist Karen McManus claims some sort of authorial status when she states: 'to my critics, of whom I expect there will be plenty, I would say just one thing: I do not intend this book to be a glorification of the life of Michael Stone. I do not intend this book to glamorise his life as a paramilitary' (Stone, 2003: xi). It is not unusual for autobiographies to be 'ghosted' by sympathetic journalists, of course, though such works tend to have celebrities or sportspersons as their subject, or individuals not otherwise known for their literary dexterity. It is also usual for this relationship between the 'author' and the ghostwriter to be made plain to the reader. In the case of *None Shall Divide Us* there is considerable ambiguity, implying that 'ghost' in this context may also refer to something insubstantial or immaterial in the text. Two ghostly aspects suggest themselves. First, there is the recurring presence of the dead, both Stone's victims and other loyalists, often killed as a result of internal feuding. Second, Stone adopts a fantastical approach to alleged planned activities of the UDA, providing significant (though unverifiable) detail about aborted operations and potential targets, while often ignoring the actual history and horror of loyalist attacks which claimed human victims and caused real devastation. As one reviewer shrewdly recognised, 'this is not a psychological portrait of a killer, but it is the raw material from which such a book might be written. Everywhere there are stories which an astute reader will understand better than the writer and his assistant have done' (O'Doherty, 2003).

The prospect of further sensationalist 'confessions' of the 'as told to' variety from notorious protagonists in the Northern conflict were raised by reports of publicity agent Stephen Richards' desire to add republican and loyalist (ex-)paramilitaries to his roster of (ex-)criminals in Britain (Breen, 2003b). Indeed, Stone and Johnny Adair, the infamous ex-UDA leader in West Belfast, were reportedly planning to makes themselves available for 'event launches, private audiences, and after-dinner speaking', as well as the provision of 'anti-terrorist security advice' (McCambridge, 2003). This trend towards the conflation of celebrity, violent crime and sensationalism is now well established in mainstream British popular culture, as evidenced by the glamorisation of gangsterism in films such as *Lock, Stock & Two Smoking Barrels* (1999) and the huge growth in the 'true crime' genre. In the context of Northern Ireland, a variation on this theme has been the growth of memoirs by former British Army and security force personnel, and it was probably inevitable, though nonetheless regrettable, that (ex-)paramilitaries would also haul themselves onto the bandwagon. During the summer of 2003 it was reported that a victims' group, Relatives for Justice, was seeking legal advice to try and prevent Stone from profiting from publication of *None Shall Divide Us*, but the Northern Ireland Office issued a statement indicating that the Proceeds of Crime Act 'does not cover the writing of a memoir, however profitable' (Breen, 2003a).

The final, telling example of the ambiguity of the authorial voice in Northern Irish political memoir relates to Roy Garland's 2001 biography of Gusty Spence, former UVF figure and leading Shankill loyalist. Garland is both personally and politically close to his subject, and much of the material in the book consists of edited transcripts of the men's 'conversations', a word Garland uses advisedly, arguing that ' "interview" seems much too formal a description of our many discussions' (2001: ix). The copious use of this form of autobiographical testimony, reproduced in the first person, coupled with the relative lack of interpretative text from Garland, means that the reader is constantly encouraged to read this book as if Spence himself were the author. Garland's obvious admiration for his subject does not prevent him from stating that 'in writing this book it has not been my intention to glamourise or lionise Gusty Spence, nor would he want this' (2001: 311), and it is certainly no hagiography. However, it could be that greater critical distance between biographer and subject would ultimately have left less room for ambiguity concerning who was really directing and narrating the project. In the case of both Stone and Spence, the authentic voice of the subject has clearly been mediated or filtered by a journalist/biographer, a fact which the reader needs to consider this when passing overall judgement on these books. What is much more difficult to discern, however, is the precise nature of the relationship between mediator and subject. Who is really in control of the structure and content of the narrative? Who speaks through whom? Paradoxically, it does seem as though Spence enjoys a greater degree of control over the narrative structure of Garland's 'biography' than Stone does over his own 'autobiography'.

## The Assembly and the armalite

In many respects recent political autobiography from Northern Ireland can be understood as a sub-genre of the growing trend for politicians worldwide to recount their 'inside' stories of government or party intrigue. In the case of the North, however, locally elected politicians did not hold ministerial office between the prorogation of Stormont in 1972 and the formation of the Northern Ireland Assembly in 1999 (with the exception of the brief power-sharing Executive of January–May 1974). Consequently, the focus of their memoirs is necessarily different. In an earlier era, unionist Prime Minister Terence O'Neill published a conventional autobiography in 1972, as did his successor Brian Faulkner, whose *Memoirs of a Statesman* (1978) belongs to the mainstream genre of British cabinet ministerial memoir. At a sub-prime ministerial level, however, many of the elected politicians who have published autobiographies have also played prominent roles in extra-parliamentary politics, whether involving paramilitarism or not. Examples include Social Democratic and Labour Party founder-member and short-lived minister in the 1974 Executive, Paddy Devlin, who was interned for IRA activity in the 1940s, and Bernadette Devlin (no relation), who was an activist in the student-based People's Democracy civil rights movement before her election to Westminster for Mid-Ulster in 1969 as an Independent Unity candidate. It is notable that in the former's *Straight Left* (1993) and the latter's *The Price of My Soul* (1969) there is little scope for the discussion of policy-making and decision-taking that is the staple of memoirs by London- and Dublin-based politicians. And while there are stories of internal party manoeuvring and policy formation – Paddy Devlin devotes many pages to the Sunningdale negotiations and his experiences as a departmental head in the Executive – these are overshadowed by the frustrations engendered by violent conflict and the political stalemate it perpetuated.

In some senses, this stalemate grants Northern Irish political autobiographers the freedom to concentrate on 'what might have been' rather than the minutiae of 'who said what to whom and when'. In a peculiar fashion, the absence of parliamentary events to rationalise, explain and order into a coherent narrative leaves something of a lacuna, which is often filled by the autobiographer's own imaginative scheme. From their different perspectives, both Faulkner and Paddy Devlin underline the pathos surrounding the fate of moderate politicians and parties eschewing the use of violence in the 1970s. Faulkner, having seen his power-sharing scheme fatally undermined by the Ulster Workers' Council strike, and his party reduced to minority status within unionism, nonetheless remains confident that 'we will come back to this point again' (1978: 278). Given his untimely death before the publication of his memoir, we can only speculate as to his likely frustration at the failure of the 'reasonable majority' of unionists and nationalists 'to make its influence effective' (1978: 281), a failure that was to last for the best part of two decades. It is equally tempting to imagine how Faulkner would have reacted to the Belfast Agreement and to the post-Agreement travails of David Trimble. Writing from a socialist perspective, Paddy Devlin also laments his inability to breach the tribal solidarities that have hamstrung political development in Northern Ireland: 'I don't really know how much I achieved in my career. I have a great feeling of disappointment that a labour movement did not emerge to break the cycle of sectarian conflict' (1993: 289). This sense of political unfulfilment represents the 'gap in the narrative' forced upon an unwilling subject, largely due to the unyielding persistence of inter-communal conflict.

Both men remain unapologetic about their commitment to failed political initiatives but share a self-critical attitude to their earlier beliefs and actions. For Faulkner, there is the frank and depressing realisation that 'Unionists are to blame for their lack of generosity when it lay in their power to be generous, for being frightened and negative in their politics when a positive approach could have tapped the potential of the whole Ulster community' (1978: 282). The valedictory tone is obvious, even though he might still have harboured hopes of making a political impact. His critique of his earlier readiness to accept the 'old dogmas' of unionism is heartfelt and there appears to be a genuine effort to grapple with change, personal as well as political: 'I have not tried to reinterpret everything I did in the light of the views I now hold. It has seemed more valuable to set out my reasoning at the time for taking particular actions, whether or not I would now go along with that reasoning' (1978: 282–83). Devlin, conversely, is highly critical of his past affiliation with militant republicanism and his aggressive personal style, but although it remained his 'greatest wish that some day in the future a labour movement will effectively assert itself in Northern Ireland' (1993: 290), he realises that this socialist dawn is as far, if not further, away than ever. One of the political lessons that both men draw from their experiences is the need for moderates of all hues to support each other. Devlin is unstinting in his praise for Faulkner's courage and leadership, hailing him as 'by far the most effective politician ever to walk the corridors of Stormont' (1993: 251). Faulkner, though less effusive, nevertheless acknowledges that he 'always got on very well with him [Devlin] and respected his down to earth common-sense' (1978: 270). Between them, these two autobiographies tackle political failure head-on and unflinchingly confront the complex trajectories of long political careers marked by changing ideological principles and personal soul-searching. *Straight Left* in particular is a substantial account of what may be considered a relatively insubstantial political career, especially if judged by the conventional criteria of parliamentary or ministerial memoir.

Evidently, the interpretative frameworks applied to Northern Irish parliamentary memoirs differ from those applied to paramilitary autobiographies. Dismissive of the perceived political compromises of those such as Devlin and Faulkner, these individuals have stories of steadfastness and sacrifice to tell. They are keen, of course, to justify their uncompromising stances, but their political lives are intimately connected to their movements' use of violence. An early instance of this genre is Seán MacStiofáin's *Memoirs of a Revolutionary* (1975), a work which certainly includes some *political* reflection on issues such as the split in the republican movement in 1969–1970 and the talks between IRA leaders and British cabinet ministers in July 1972, but which is also deeply concerned with the *military* strategy and tactics of the IRA's campaign against the state and its security forces. Electoral and parliamentary politics, conversely, are treated with barely concealed disdain, though that is hardly surprising for a self-styled nationalist revolutionary.

It is particularly instructive to compare MacStiofáin's autobiography with that of Gerry Adams, given their prominent leadership roles in the republican movement and the lengthy gap between their respective publications. Adams, of course, has denied ever having played a prominent role in the IRA, or indeed having been a member at all, although his credibility on this issue has been undermined by a succession of biographers and commentators.[4] In fact it is harder than ever to take seriously Adams's claims, given Martin McGuinness' recent admission that he *was* a significant IRA commander in Derry at the time of 'Bloody Sunday', an admission that perhaps heralds a change of heart at the apex of the organisation. Nevertheless, as O'Toole has observed, *Before the Dawn* 'almost entirely glossed over' Adams's IRA career (2003: 14), a view endorsed by Foster, who claims that he is 'unnecessarily coy' about the IRA and likens his memoir to 'a biography of Field Marshal Montgomery that leaves out the British Army' (2001: 177–78).[5] The political subtext was clear to all, however. The context of the developing peace process, and the perceived requirement to maintain Adams's position as the Provisionals' unchallenged leader, one capable of delivering an IRA cease-fire and committing the movement to his new strategy, meant that 'these incredible assertions were allowed to pass with no more than mild expressions of skepticism' (O'Toole, 2003: 14). If Adams was to be accepted locally and internationally as a genuine agent of peace and compromise, then it suited the purposes of governments in London, Dublin and Washington, as well as republicans and even pro-Agreement unionists, to collude in this necessary fiction.

However, as O'Toole notes, 'the danger has always been that the tacit agreement to ignore the IRA past of the Sinn Féin leader would encourage a larger and more profound act of denial. If Adams did not have to account for his involvement with the IRA, then perhaps the IRA itself could remain unaccountable' (O'Toole, 2003: 14). Hence his view that the crisis in the peace process in 2002–2003, which coincided with further allegations about Adams's IRA past, published in Ed Moloney's *A Secret History of the IRA* (2003), have combined to bring to an end a period when such ambiguity was 'a useful instrument of the peace process' (O'Toole, 2003: 15). Eight years after the signing of the Belfast Agreement, and with the institutions set up by it suspended again, largely as a result of unionist fears about continuing IRA activity, this issue of accountability for past actions remains central to Northern Ireland's political future. Certainly, this question is not confined to the duality inherent in Adams's personal political history and his efforts to maintain 'creative ambiguity' about his relationship with the armed struggle, but this element of the debate can be seen as a microcosm of broader difficulties.

If Adams' autobiographical writing is guarded and opaque, this is explicable in terms of his perception of the *political* imperatives of the republican movement at this particular juncture, though this does not of itself render such an approach justifiable to a wider readership. Foster acknowledges that 'since the Adams story is a small part of the story of modern Ireland, so the fact that it supplies – yet again – a narrative of evasions is only appropriate' (2001: 181). Speaking of Adams's lack of clarity regarding his past, he suggests that 'it would probably be unrealistic to expect more' (2001: 178), yet readers are left demanding greater transparency. O'Toole reinforces this point, noting that 'political autobiographies should be written when the hurly-burly's done. They should tell a story whose ending is known, reflect on something that has actually been achieved' (1996). Instead, the end of Adams's story remains unpredictable, because as he himself recognises in the foreword to *Before the Dawn*:

> I am also conscious that the elements of conflict remain today and retain their potency. For this reason I must write nothing which would place in jeopardy the liberties or the lives of others, so I am necessarily constrained. It is probably an invariable rule that the participants in any conflict cannot tell the entire story until some time after that conflict is fully resolved. (1996: 2)

These words were written in February 1996 when, with the end of the IRA's ceasefire at Canary Wharf, it was the Provisionals' actions rather than Adams's text that was taking lives, and not merely jeopardising them. It remains doubtful whether a decade later Adams would take the view that the conflict has yet been 'fully resolved'. Indeed, it is arguable that when he talks of the conflict requiring complete resolution before he could tell 'the entire story', the only circumstance that would satisfy his criterion is the creation of a united Ireland.

Despite the absence of this entity, Adams published a second volume of autobiography, *Hope and History: Making Peace in Ireland*, in 2003. Edited by Adams's old friend, MacDonogh, it comes no closer to offering what O'Toole called a 'real and fully truthful autobiography' (1996).[6] Rather, it presents the author's version of the process leading up to the successful negotiation of the Belfast Agreement in April 1998, and while there is a perfunctory final chapter outlining some of the problems it has encountered in subsequent years, Adams has conceded (again) that the narrative remains unfinished: 'there is a natural third book [. . . ] but apart from noting that in my head, I have no plans, notions, ambitions to even think about writing it at the moment' (Thornton, 2003). Moreover, he insists that since the 'story' of the peace process is 'still unfolding, still sensitive, still fragile [. . . ] it is not my business to offer an objective account of events or to see through someone else's eyes. Nor is it my responsibility to document these events. My intention is to tell a story. It is my story. My truth. My reality' (Adams, 2003: 2). The rationale for publication at this particular time, therefore, seems to be that 'a happy ending' – the signing of the Agreement – is 'more important than a tell-all story' (Adams, 2003: 2).

Adams also conflates his 'personal journey' with the communal story. The peace process in his eyes is a morality tale, where republicans and selfless nationalists – notably John Hume and Catholic clerics such as Fr Alec Reid – consistently urge the British government and the unionist parties to address 'the underlying causes of conflict', as if these are self-evident, uncomplicated and uncontested. He places great emphasis on his dialogue with Hume, the quest for pan-nationalist unity and the need to press the Dublin and Washington administrations to adopt the 'Irish peace initiative', with no apparent recognition that without a balancing input from the Westminster government, no serious negotiation with *any section* of unionism would be feasible. Indeed, the unionists as an autonomous force hardly figure at all in Adams's narrative. From this perspective, the 1993 Downing Street Declaration is seen as no more than 'a significant development' (Adams, 2003: 171), though an alternative reading would suggest that without it there would have been no potential for progress towards genuine, all-party, inclusive talks. Republicans had to be provided with an alternative to armed struggle before peace was possible, says Adams, but the unanswered question remains: what happens if the republican movement becomes engaged solely in the democratic process, but the outcome is not Irish unity, at least not any time soon? The teleology inherent in Adams's narrative means that he cannot entertain such an outcome; a 'proper' democracy, in his view, is defined as leading inexorably to a sovereign, united republic. Even now, there is no adequate answer to this question. Adams's approach to political autobiography, therefore, is to echo, through personal testimony, the officially endorsed and internally validated version of 'party' history, and to use this testimony in the service of contemporary ideological goals. In this way, autobiographical reflection is harnessed to the yoke of political expediency.

MacStiofáin shares this ideological rigidity about the goals of the republican movement, but in other ways his approach could hardly be more different. It is indicative of the nature and scope of the Provisionals' evolution since the early 1970s that his autobiography is imbued with the traditional 'physical force' belief that military action can and will remove the British presence in Ireland, and that political engagement, in the form of an electoral strategy, would represent a dilution of this pure aspiration (MacStiofáin, 1975: 81, 92). He makes plain his commitment to revolutionary republicanism – even though he talks of his IRA involvement in the past tense – and expressly denies any sectarian dimension to this creed, an allegation levelled at him by an erstwhile member of the Provisionals, Maria McGuire, in her book *To Take Arms: A Year in the Provisional IRA* (1973). Unlike Adams, however, MacStiofáin is prepared to acknowledge openly his role as a military leader. Indeed, given his contempt for political theorising and his belief in the efficacy of militarism, it is not so surprising that he is keen to play up his own involvement in military strategy and planning. Writing about the mid-1960s, he casually dismisses the role of Sinn Féin at that time in the republican movement's overall aims and objectives: 'During the couple of years I attended the meetings of the Árd Comhairle and of the Coiste Seasta, the Sinn Féin standing committee, I found them boring and a total waste of time' (1975: 104). Having outlined the split within republicanism and the creation of the Provisionals, therefore, MacStiofáin devotes much space to chronicling the prosecution of the 'armed struggle', the guerrilla tactics of the IRA and the counter-insurgency techniques of the British Army and police. In this sense, the focus of his reflections is rather narrow, certainly in comparison with Adams, a fact which raises another pertinent question with regard to autobiographies of the Troubles: their parochial character.

## The different 'worlds' of the Troubles

As a Troubles autobiographer, Gerry Adams is unusual in the intellectual scope and strategic overview he brings to his account, although paradoxically *Before the Dawn* ends abruptly in the aftermath of the 1981 hunger strikes by republican prisoners and, as has already been noted, the published version of his life up to that point leaves huge gaps as the process of 'retrospective remodelling' proceeds (Foster, 2001: 174). What is clear, however, is that his 'most passionate commitment is to the narrow world of West Belfast, a self-justifying and tightly-knit community later replicated in the republican wing of internment prison' (Foster, 2001: 176). Adams' story is couched in localised terms, partly due to his desire during the mid-1990s to confirm the republican heartlands in their belief that the 'revolutionary struggle' had not been defeated, despite the IRA ceasefire, and that all of the sacrifices had been worthwhile. It also makes his self-appointed task of subsuming his personal story into the heroic collective 'resistance' of the republican community much easier. Indeed, as Foster has argued, Adams 'is determined to see things purely in the perspective framed by his mother's back window', although this localism appears to be a conscious political decision, masking a much broader strategic, and cunning, intent (Foster, 2001: 177). In contrast to this disingenuously parochial image, he enjoys massive worldwide exposure: in marketing terms, Gerry Adams has name recognition. He purports, moreover, to be a 'very shy person', explaining: 'I find other people are much more relaxed in dealing with public events. I mean, I wouldn't be running about to banquets or balls or fancy suppers. It's nothing to those who lost their lives [. . .] or lost loved ones, but I think the loss of anonymity is a big thing' (Thornton, 2003). Adams's target audience is, therefore, invited to see him as a grounded politician who understands them and their community; in short, as a man of the people.

It is not surprising that other autobiographies by second-ranking former republican activists provide detailed, though contested, accounts of life 'on the ground'. These include Shane O'Doherty's *The Volunteer* (1993), Martin McGartland's *Fifty Dead Men Walking* (1997) and *Dead Man Running* (1998), Eamon Collins's *Killing Rage* (1998) and Raymond Gilmour's *Dead Ground* (1999). These memoirs tend to concentrate upon shedding light on the imme-diate social world of the republican activist, usually confined to a partic-ular locality, and often with little attempt to locate this experience within broader contexts. Those that are written by individuals who renounced their commitment to the republican cause (Gilmour in Derry, McGartland in West Belfast) and worked as informers are probably even more constrained in their scope, given the doubly clandestine nature of their activities. Of this sub-genre, perhaps the best known is Sean O'Callaghan's *The Informer* (1998), which unusually manages to combine a dense account of his life as an IRA leader, member of the Sinn Féin National Executive and informer for the Garda Síochána, with reflections on the ideological character of the Provisional movement, of which he is now one of the most vocal critics.

A key criterion when judging the historical utility of these autobiographies is the authors' willingness or capacity to place their experiences within a broader *political* framework. However much controversy they have gener-ated – and several of these authors have been violently attacked (McGartland) or even killed (Collins) as a result of the publicity generated by the publica-tion of their life stories – and however disputed their accounts of life within the republican movement, they do differ significantly in their attitude to this wider context. Ultimately, some of these memoirs are of limited interest to the contemporary political historian in that they are primarily concerned with the minutiae of paramilitary activities, engagements with the 'enemy' and so forth. This may well be the result of a deliberate authorial decision to highlight these aspects, often with an eye on sales and the sensation-alist appetites of populist audiences, or it may be that these 'foot-soldiers' have a relative lack of concern, knowledge or even understanding of the broader framework within which their particular dramas were played out. These works are useful nonetheless in pointing up the diverse experiences of the 'different "worlds" ' that exist in relation to the Troubles (Smyth and Fay, 2000: 133). For instance, Eamon Collins explores the republican movement's character and operations around Newry and South Armagh, a largely rural environment which is markedly different from life on Belfast's Ballymurphy estate, as evoked by Adams or McGartland (though their accounts of the republican 'family' in its heartland diverge strongly later on), and different again from the Derry experience described by Gilmour and O'Doherty.

Similar social circumstances could certainly produce highly divergent political trajectories; this is most obvious in the sectarian patchwork of Belfast. The socio-economic deprivation endured in working-class districts of the city is vividly recalled in the testimonies of Gusty Spence, Paddy Devlin, Gerry Adams and Michael Stone. The most astonishing example of the same circumstances leading to very different political beliefs comes from Spence who, together with his brother Ned, was raised in the hard conditions of the Hammer district of the Lower Shankill during the 1930s. Ned broke with Orangeism, became a socialist and trade-unionist, then a member of the Communist Party and in the late 1960s joined the Northern Ireland Civil Rights Association. Meanwhile, Gusty served in the British Army in Cyprus and on his return to Belfast joined the reborn UVF, which led to his conviction for the 1966 murder of a Catholic barman, Peter Ward. Spence, with support from Garland, continues to deny responsibility for the murder, but nonetheless served almost 19 years in jail for the crime, before his release in 1984. For several years the two brothers were estranged, though they were to move closer after Gusty's renunciation of loyalist violence in the late 1970s and his conversion to socialism in 1981. Following Ned's son's arrest in connection with the activities of the socialist Official IRA, Spence wrote privately to his brother:

> As you know I have very much changed – not because of what prison has done to me, but because of what I have done for myself. If I had to serve a lifetime in dungeons like these, I wanted to know for what reason, and I searched for the truth [ . . . ]. I feel deeply embarrassed when I think of my former 'truths' which when investigated did not stand up to scrutiny or fact. (Garland, 2001: 244–45)

The localism of Spence's experience was extreme, and it is clear that his remarkable approach to his long years in prison and the autodidactic education he gained there helped him to transcend his enclosed world and draw broader lessons for his own ideological beliefs and the future of loyalist politics generally. While by no means all paramilitary prisoners used their incarceration to such effect, it is significant that the mere fact of spending long periods in jail does not of itself determine that individuals must be inward-looking, self-obsessed or narrowly preoccupied with their immediate physical world.

It is difficult nevertheless to ignore the prison experiences recounted in these autobiographies, given that this facet of the protagonists' lives is so far removed from most readers' realities. Michael Stone, who was convicted for the Milltown cemetery attack on republican mourners in March 1988, served 12 years of a 30-year sentence, before being released in July 2000 under the terms of the Belfast Agreement. There are a number of tensions, if not downright contradictions, in Stone's account of his motivation for publishing *None Shall Divide Us*. In the foreword he offers an apology to the families of those he killed, but immediately nullifies this by stating: 'I regret that I had to kill [ . . . ]. I committed crimes as an Ulsterman and a British citizen and that was regrettable but unavoidable' (2003: xiv).[7] The sincerity of his expression of regret is further undermined by his decision to include the celebratory 'Ballad of Michael Stone', which refers to those killed at Milltown as 'rebel scum'. His autobiographical tone is that of a veteran who has matured enough to appreciate the motivation of his enemies, and while this may be sincere, it is nonetheless far from convincing. Though still a relatively young man, Stone expresses 'shock' at the direction his life has taken, claiming: 'looking back, I can hardly believe that I did those things and lived the life I led. It is like peering into the life of a stranger' (2003: xv). But what is most instructive about Stone's reflection on his prison experiences is how little he appears to have connected with the political developments that were taking place during the 1990s. While constantly referring to republican violence as 'indiscriminate', he often leaves out the bloodiness of the UDA's increasingly brutal sectarian killing campaign in favour of recalling failed 'spectaculars', operations that either never took place or were aborted, such as those directed at Irish Prime Minister, Charles Haughey and RUC Chief Constable, Sir John Hermon. He also pays tribute to heroic figures within loyalism (Tommy Herron, John McMichael and John Gregg) whom he claims were close friends of his, but who are no longer around to confirm this, while denouncing men such as Tucker Lyttle, Jim Craig and Johnny Adair as 'career loyalists'.

For others, the experience of imprisonment presented an opportunity to think deeply about their political commitments and interrogate the strategic direction of their organisations, sometimes for the first time. Seán MacStiofáin was arrested in an IRA arms raid in Essex in 1953, aged 25, and sentenced to eight years in English jails. Taking his cue from the attitude displayed by republican prisoners interned in the Curragh camp during the Second World War, he used his time to test the 'idea of prison as the university of the revolution' (1975: 57). Thus, he learned Irish, immersed himself in the history of Irish nationalism and made contact with Cypriot prisoners from the anti-colonial EOKA movement, with whom he swapped tactical and strategic information about guerrilla warfare. Through such activities MacStiofáin discovered a paradoxical freedom in incarceration: 'As soon as the cell door banged, I felt almost at home and yet, at the same time, less confined' (1975: 67). Gerry Adams, on the other hand, recalls his initial experience of prison as 'a mixture of Brendan Behan's *Borstal Boy* and boarding school, in which we engaged in constant pranks, mayhem and

craziness' (1996: 196). This levity soon gave way to sober and serious political activity, however. Despite his denials of IRA membership, Adams was
released from Long Kesh in July 1972 to take part in the republican deleg-
ation that had secret talks with the Secretary of State for Northern Ireland,
William Whitelaw, in London. There are several conflicting accounts of these
talks, a clear instance of autobiographers presenting competing versions of a
single incident, with little or no corroborating material available.[8] Adams's
later period of internment during the mid-1970s saw him develop a much
more strategic approach to the republican struggle, in conjunction with
Bobby Sands and others. During this time he 'concentrated on reading, on
my writing, and learning Irish', and developed a culture of 'collective political discussion and education' among his fellow inmates (1996: 246). He also
found himself 'taking on a position of authority' (1996: 243), which allowed
him to voice his concerns about the efficacy of armed struggle to the IRA
leadership, thereby inaugurating the strategic shift that would lead to Sinn
Féin's electoral intervention and his own election to Westminster in 1983.

Paddy Devlin and Gusty Spence also present their prison experiences
as turning points in their personal and political development. Devlin was
interned between 1942 and 1945 for IRA activities, during which time he
re-appraised his political thinking. He describes these years as 'the most
formative of my life' (1993: 35), partly as a result of disappointment with
his former republican colleagues, many of whom were themselves bitterly
disillusioned by their incarceration and the lack of grass-roots support for
their cause. Devlin also came into contact with self-taught men who made
him consider the type of political principles he really wished to advance:
'Although I was highly streetwise when I was first locked up, I was hopelessly
idealistic, naïve and immature. Prison broadened and matured me in all sorts
of ways' (1993: 48). He left jail to pursue a career as a labourist politician
and like Gusty Spence, who was eight years his junior, his prison experience
caused him to renounce violence as a means to political ends. Spence himself
eventually resigned from the UVF in 1978, although he argues that he had
already 'realised that physical force was not the way forward' as early as 1974
(Garland, 2001: 178). In the intervening years, he was noted for his strict
discipline in the UVF compounds under his command, which often brought
him into conflict with younger, headstrong members of the organisation,
and for his regular disagreements with the UVF leadership outside prison.

The life narratives of Devlin and Spence were published when both men
were in the twilight of their years, as they approached their seventieth
birthdays. Devlin, writing before the peace process had produced a real
breakthrough, cannot hide his wistful, valedictory air, and Spence speaks
in a similarly regretful tone. Brian Faulkner was also writing from the
perspective of the failure of his cherished power-sharing political initiative and cannot disguise a certain amount of bitterness with regard to
those within unionism who rejected this experiment as a way forward.

For those who publish memoirs earlier in their lives, like Adams and Stone, there may be less probability of mature reflection and a greater sense of the conjunctural, of the subjects positioning themselves to gain maximum advantage for their particular concerns at particular moments. This certainly applies to the youngest autobiographer considered here, Bernadette Devlin, whose *The Price of My Soul* is one of the very few memoirs by a Northern Irish female politician, a fact which exemplifies the male domination of both parliamentary and paramilitary political life in the region.[9]

Devlin published her 'story of the protest movement which wrote Northern Ireland across the world's headlines' before it was clear that these events would herald the long-term growth of the Troubles (1969: 9). Although she expressly rejects the label 'autobiography' for her book, there are strong autobiographical elements in what was billed by the publishers as the 'story of the real flesh-and-blood Bernadette'. Writing in her early twenties, Devlin strikes a markedly different tone from that of the older male politicians whose memoirs we have reviewed in this chapter. For example, she voices a loud impatience with the prevailing political system, not simply the archaic Stormont regime but also the hidebound conservatism of the British and Irish establishments, and endorses the dynamism of the international student movement which was then challenging all forms of political orthodoxy. But while the immediacy of this work makes it a compelling read, it also imbues it with some of the characteristics of the political diary as summarised by Gamble:

> it is contemporary with the events it describes, and it gives little thought to the consistency of one entry with another. The narrative that emerges [...] tends to be fragmented and incomplete, but the quality of the material as evidence tends to be higher, because the diarist is recording how things appeared at the moment of writing, [...] how a particular politician thought and felt about events at the time, and the assumptions on which political calculations were made. It is precisely because they cannot be retrospective that makes their testimony so valuable. (2002: 142–43)

Certainly, *The Price of My Soul* fits this description, and provides a fascinating insight into the political mood of the civil rights era and the role played by the younger generation of newly politicised activists. Devlin says of her own ideological journey during this heady period that 'the wheel was coming full circle; but with variations. I had moved from traditional, mad, emotional Republicanism to socialism in the context of Ulster; now I was joining my new-found socialism to my old belief in a united Ireland' (1969: 119). To read *The Price of My Soul* alongside the autobiographies of Brian Faulkner,

Paddy Devlin and Gerry Adams is not only to grapple with the complexity of forces that led to the eruption of the Troubles in the late 1960s, but also to appreciate the significance of when, how and with what purpose these protagonists choose to publish their personal interpretations of these seminal events.

## Conclusion

Contemporary political autobiography and memoir in Northern Ireland may, on occasion, contribute to wider processes of societal reconciliation in an emerging post-conflict environment. Or, if this is too grand an aspiration, they might at least prove an aid to enhanced mutual understanding of what motivated political actors over the course of the Troubles. There is nonetheless a problem concerning the appropriateness of these modes of self-expression. There can be no doubt that many individuals feel the need to articulate their stories and experiences of community conflict and to be widely recognised as having been hurt or harmed by such experiences. However, the question arises as to what is the best forum or medium for such stories. The recent past seems to point to the problems associated with 'officialising' testimony of the conflict; as Angela Hegarty has observed, the myriad legal processes, both current and planned, such as judicial enquiries, tribunals or an overarching 'truth commission', may only deliver account-ability and 'truth' about the Troubles in a limited form. Hegarty claims: 'Political considerations, deals, the legal threshold for proof, the sheer scale of abuses, all create a situation where not every crime is prosecuted, not every harm addressed', and proceeds to argue that 'the process and the language of law transmutes individual experiences into a categorically neat something else. Law does not permit a single witness to tell their own coherent narrative; it chops their stories into digestible parts' (2002: 100–01). It is in this context that autobiographical writings may have a significant role to play in contemporary political discourse in the North by providing an opportunity for individual stories to be told in their entirety, thereby retaining their integrity. As we have seen, political autobiography or memoir by prominent or (in)famous protagonists in the conflict can also provide a symbolic, collective and communal aspect to this process of truth-telling. However, the lacunae or gaps that often characterise these autobiographical narratives make this process complex and uncertain and render the results partial and contradictory. This is particularly the case when 'truth' about the recent past remains a matter of bitter dispute, and where there is still no public consensus about the essential causes of conflict. This meta-conflict is no nearer resolution, despite the imperfect peace. Indeed, it is rarely addressed.

## Notes

Several of the newspapers and periodicals referred to in this chapter were accessed via the Internet and are available at these following sites:

*An Phoblacht/Republican News*: www.republican-news.org.archive/

*Belfast Telegraph*: www.belfasttelegraph.co.uk/

*Daily Telegraph*: www.telegraph.co.uk/

*Irish Independent*: www.unison.ie/irish_independent/

*Irish Times*: www.ireland.com/

*News Letter*: www.newsletter.co.uk/

*The Spectator*: www.spectator.co.uk/

*Sunday Business Post*: www.thepost.ie/

*Sunday Life*: www.sundaylife.co.uk/

In addition, readers will find reviews and commentary on many of the works discussed in this chapter at the CAIN website (www.cain.ulst.ac.uk/).

1. There is a voluminous literature devoted to these topics. For a sample of views, see Bloomfield, 1998; Nelis, 1998; Longley, 2001; Rolston, 2002; Hamber and Wilson, 2003.
2. See also the series of Island pamphlets (Island publications, Newtownabbey) that include oral testimony from within the Protestant community.
3. Adams acknowledges 'the persistence, advice and input' of MacDonogh, but it is clear that he himself is directly responsible for the words (1996: 2).
4. Sharrock and Devenport's unauthorised biography cites a number of occasions in his writings where Adams has 'judiciously edited out' his IRA status (1997: 116).
5. Former IRA member Anthony McIntyre chose a metaphor from closer to home when he compared Adams's omission of his IRA career to that of George Best failing to mention that he had played for Manchester United in his autobiography. Cited in Edwards, 2002.
6. Suzanne Breen argues that in his 'studied attempt to exhibit emotion and sincerity', Adams's veers between 'statesmanlike' and 'folksy' throughout (2003c).
7. Stone appears to have undergone a change of heart during his time in jail. Asked about remorse in a 1991 interview in the UDA magazine, *Ulster*, his response was unequivocal: 'As for remorse with regards to the deaths of the three people killed at that terrorist funeral in Milltown cemetery, remorse to an active loyalist volunteer is a luxury which one regrettably has to forego. In a word, no' (cited in D. McKittrick *et al.* 1999: 1119).
8. See, for example, Adams, 1996: 199–206; MacStiofáin, 1975: 278–86; Sharrock and Devenport, 1997: 100–105; Garnett and Aitken, 2002: 127–48.
9. The extent of this dominance may be judged from the fact that no woman won a Westminster seat in Northern Ireland between Devlin's re-election in 1970 and the three women who enjoyed electoral success in the 2001 British general election, namely, Michelle Gildernew (SF, Fermanagh-South Tyrone), Sylvia Hermon (UUP, North Down) and Iris Robinson (DUP, Strangford).

# 10
## 'Voice Itself': The Loss and Recovery of Boyhood in Irish Memoir

*Denis Sampson*

Frank McCourt's *Angela's Ashes* (1996) is presented as a narrative of survival of what he considers to be the worst kind of childhood, 'the miserable Irish Catholic' variety (1996: 11). With bravado and self-deprecation, McCourt reveals the imaginative and intellectual resources which made survival and the writing of the autobiography possible. A later memoir, *Teacher Man* (2005), comments on McCourt's lifelong frustration until he was able to articulate a style that mirrors his survival and his creative accomplishment. *Angela's Ashes* does not call attention to such aspects of the adult life; it is written from an American immigrant perspective in a style of rambunctious detachment, relying on literary techniques of irony and comedy learned from diverse sources, among them Joyce's *Dubliners* and *Ulysses*, Sean O'Casey's plays and autobiographies and Frank O'Connor's short stories. Most of all, it mixes trauma and humour in a discomfiting manner so that it cannot be read simply as a case history of the miserable childhood; rather, as John McGahern has argued, it might be read as farce.[1]

Not all Irish childhoods are miserable, of course, as many autobiographers attest. What distinguishes the late twentieth century is not only the great number of Irish memoirs, but also their generally remarkable literary quality. It appears that the recovery and articulation of childhood serves a profound personal and cultural need, as if the truth about childhood and its defining circumstances can suddenly be stated without inhibition or censorship. In marked contrast, the first generation of autobiographers to come of age in the Irish Free State paid little attention to childhood as a crucible of the adult self, or as a litmus test for the prevailing social and cultural conditions, or as an imaginative resource deeply intertwined with the most profound and lasting features of individual vision. The virtual absence of childhood in works such as Tomás O'Crohan's *The Islandman* (1929), Ernest O'Malley's *On Another Man's Wound* (1936), Francis Stuart's *Things to Live For* (1934) and Liam O'Flaherty's *Shame the Devil* (1934) may be explained by the particular thematic or experiential focus in each case. Elizabeth Bowen's *Seven Winters* (1942) and Kate O'Brien's *Presentation Parlour* (1963) are partial exceptions, since both focus on the domestic milieu of childhood, yet neither explores the larger issues of the separate state of childhood itself or its connection to the adult writer. In general, this autobiographical neglect of childhood continues through subsequent decades, though notable exceptions include Frank O'Connor's *An Only Child* (1961), Austin Clarke's *Twice Round the Black Church* (1962), Sean O'Faolain's *Vive Moi!* (1964) and Aidan Higgins's *Scenes from a Receding Past* (1977). With works such as these serving as exemplary forerunners, fresh attention was brought to bear on Irish childhoods from the 1980s onwards, an attention that was perceptually and qualitatively different from what went before.

Many memoirs written at the century's end provide an extraordinary counter-history to the received and official record of Irish life in earlier generations, yet rather than examine what are often narratives of trauma, neglect and criminal abuse, my interest here is in exploring the ways in which childhood – or, more precisely, boyhood – has been recovered and mythologised as an enabling, creative force in adult life.[2] In many distinct ways, childhood forced itself upon authors at a later stage of their lives and became the ground of their creativity, many of them being, uniquely, writers of memoir. At the end of *Vive Moi!* O'Faolain remarks that 'If once the boy within us ceases to speak to the man who enfolds him, the shape of life is broken and there is, literally, no more to be said' (1965: 288). O'Faolain is referring here to the writing of his first novel, *A Nest of Simple Folk* (1933), and when he came to write *Vive Moi!* 30 years later, he declared that his imagination was 'inflamed' in the circumstances of his first years. He writes of the importance of theatre and church, of his mother's boarding house and of summer holidays in the country, but his central focus is on 'the Troubles and my Trauma', his involvement with republican nationalism from late adolescence onwards. O'Faolain's autobiography is indeed a fascinating reconstruction of a life, but for a variety of reasons – self-censorship, intellectual detachment, the man-of-letters persona – the voice of childhood 'ceases to speak'. My focus here is on memoirs in which I believe childhood is made real through poetic resources of language, and on the significance of such recovery and articulation for the adult writer. Since my theme can only be properly addressed through extended analysis, I will concentrate on a limited number of texts. I will begin with two memoirs of the 1930s, *Twenty Years A-Growing* (1933) by Maurice O'Sullivan (1904–1950) and *The Green Fool* (1938) by Patrick Kavanagh (1904–1967), and then consider *An Only Child* by O'Connor (1903–1966). Of the many recent memoirs directly relevant to my theme – *Angela's Ashes*, Ciaran O'Driscoll's *A Runner Among Fallen Leaves* (2001) and Hugo Hamilton's *The Speckled People* (2003) among them – I will limit my discussion to two: George O'Brien's (b.1945) *The Village of Longing* (1987) and John McGahern's (1934–2006) *Memoir* (2005).[3]

The persona which Maurice O'Sullivan adopts in his memoir *Twenty Years A-Growing* is self-consciously innocent, and the recovery and preservation of childhood as theme and style integrates aspects of oral storytelling and literary technique absorbed much later. His opening words focus the reader's attention on both orality and childhood, and this dual emphasis is maintained for much of the book:

> There is no doubt but youth is a fine thing though my own is not yet over and wisdom comes with age. I am a boy who was born and bred in the Great Blasket, a small truly Gaelic island which lies north-west of the coast of Kerry, where the storms of the sky and the wild sea beat without ceasing from end to end of the year and from generation to generation against the wrinkled rocks which stand above the waves that wash in and out of the coves where the seals make their homes (1938: 13).

Although he began the retrospective recreation of his childhood in his late twenties, O'Sullivan uses the present tense, 'I am a boy', and claims his youth is not over. Despite the titular 'twenty years', the book includes many chapters which tell how the author left the island at the age of 23, travelled to Dublin, became a civic guard and served in Connemara for two years before making his first return visit to the island, the scene with which the memoir closes. He admits that there is a gap between the time he recalls and the present tense of the writing self, and explicitly regrets his separation from his native place and youthful companions. He tells of matchmaking, of falling in love, of the departure of his siblings for America and of the arrival of the Englishman George Thomson, whom he befriended and who encouraged him to write. The burden of adult decisions and behaviour enters in, yet he generally portrays himself as a naïve and inexperienced person. Such naïvety is necessary so that O'Sullivan can retain an image of the island life of his childhood until he returns to it to complete a cycle which implicitly suggests that the simplicity and imaginative freedom of his formative experiences can be recovered and preserved forever.

The preservation of childhood is essential to the narrative, and indeed departure and isolation from the community reinforce it as O'Sullivan becomes a self-conscious autobiographer: 'I shut my eyes close and soon the village appeared in perfect likeness before my face, for "with eager desire I was making my fullest endeavour to see my love" as the poet said long ago' (1938: 223). The poet is Carolan, but the song transfers the 'love' from person to place, to the island life and O'Sullivan's experience of childhood there. He continues: 'So great is the power of the solitary man', thus linking his creative re-imagining of the island with his solitariness. Earlier, he had made a similar link: 'I sat meditating on the world. Look, it is many a thought comes to the man who goes alone. With the power of his mind he brings the great world before his face, a thing which is not possible for the man who is fond of company' (1938: 214). O'Sullivan could not have recalled the life of the islanders with such a vivid sense of character, custom and conversation if he had not once been a keen listener, a man who was fond of expressive conversation and the play of personalities in the inescapable circumstances of close family and neighbourly contacts. In spite of delight in company, however, O'Sullivan was also a solitary child and this may be associated with the years he spent as an 'orphan' in Dingle after his mother's death. The memoir begins with his experiences there, a time of institutional repression and silencing, during which O'Sullivan lost his first language, Irish, and became an English speaker. While his return to the language, the island community and especially to the talk and wisdom of his grandfather are key elements of the experience depicted, one of the most striking aspects of his memoir is the extraordinary descriptions of the landscape, the bird life, the sea and the weather.[4] Often, accounts of joyous hunting expeditions with his boyhood companion are interrupted by paragraphs of stunning visual description, and there is an almost mystical appreciation of light in nature:

> The moon was rising. She ascends very slowly and sheds a golden light over the shadowy glens. I seem to hear the meads and valleys utter a cry of joy as if to welcome her and she smiling down on them with a greeting to Cocagueeny. I seem to see before me, full of bright laughter, all the boys and girls who were with me when I was a child. (1938: 170)

The solitariness in the midst of company is reinforced by this meticulous attention to nature, as if he were transported into an apprehension of the natural world which is metaphysical in its import and later forms the foundation of his writing style. The childhood state is constantly affirmed as one that is deeply responsive to the enveloping natural state; it is as if the lyrical passages are the images of a constancy and timelessness that the human community cannot offer, especially at a time of social disintegration through emigration. A key chapter, 'The Lobster Season', marks the end of childhood, and subsequent chapters introduce a darker note as O'Sullivan attempts to come to terms with adult life. He concludes the chapter with the statement: 'It is little desire I had to be telling my grandfather of the beauty of the place that night', to which the old man replies: 'you have had your first day of the struggle of the world' (1938: 160). The young man thus seems to accept his mentor's wisdom about the hardship and tragedy of island life, and so the shedding of childhood is registered in terms of the loss of natural beauty, as if for the first time, and the corresponding recognition of deprivation and danger as contrary realities. Nature may be fiercely destructive and merciless in its treatment of fishermen, but O'Sullivan is a lyric poet who celebrates beauty in his memoir, a beauty which is the touchstone of his own vision of life. Nature is sometimes linked to a dream state in which the Land of

Youth may be imagined as a place across the water – a somewhat literary insertion, perhaps – but its presence suggests (as does his opening sentence) that he wishes to recapture and preserve in words that state of 'youth':

> The sky was cloudless, the sea calm, sea-birds and land-birds sweetly singing. I looked west to the edge of the sky and I seemed to see clearly the Land of the Young – many-coloured flowers in the gardens; fine, bright houses sparkling in the sunshine; stately, comely-faced maidens walking through the meadows gathering flowers. (1938: 195–96)

This mythological reverie is interrupted by George Thomson who, while deeply sympathetic and admiring of the Blasket way of life, is also the one who facilitated O'Sullivan's departure from it. Thomson introduced adult self-consciousness into O'Sullivan's life, something he partially welcomed, and yet this literary interpolation on the Land of Youth suggests that Thomson's arrival is something he also deeply regrets.

While his grandfather's lore and wisdom are acknowledged, O'Sullivan cannot really preserve and extend his mentor's cultural inheritance because he leaves the island and recovers it in a different medium. References to Robinson Crusoe and Brian Merriman suggest that the memoirist has become a literate person addressing a literate audience. He recreates the condition of being an island insider by recovering the state of childhood, but the conditions of his composing a memoir define him as an outsider. Many adventures are recovered as communal experiences, and his realisation that the society is disintegrating is a major motivation for writing, but O'Sullivan's uniquely personal perceptions and sensibility are integral to the childhood he recovers. The self-conscious persona reflects an appreciative style of viewing and reviewing his earlier experience which preserves it in a state free of retrospective judgements, psychological analyses or historical contextualisation. The celebratory power of his articulation of selfhood is due to O'Sullivan's extraordinary capacity to recover childhood and to recreate poetic images of a lost home in nature, continuing the work of J. M. Synge, whose memoir of the Aran Islands had initiated a significant vein of writing which honoured, as it were, the pristine childhood of the race.

*Twenty Years A-Growing* appeared with an introductory note by E. M. Forster, a sign of the book's immediate and lasting success. Forster refers to it as 'an account of neolithic civilisation from the inside' (O'Sullivan, 1938: v) and seems to infer that Synge's view of Aran 'from the outside' is contaminated by his provenance. Forster's mythmaking is significant – 'He is able to keep our world in its place' – and his words may have consolidated the memoir's significance as literary model and cultural emblem. In this context, O'Sullivan's work may be contrasted with another Irish memoir published a year later, Liam O'Flaherty's *Shame the Devil*. O'Flaherty had grown up on the Aran Islands in the same 'neolithic civilisation', yet his memoir focuses on living and suffering in 'our world', as Forster put it, the modern, the urban and the educated realm. *Shame the Devil* is not a memoir of childhood, however, but an account of O'Flaherty's mental breakdown and recovery the previous year, when he had embarked, once again, on a frenzied episode of travelling in an effort to overcome his writer's block. In this memoir and two others written just before it, O'Flaherty's alienation from Aran, Ireland and urban life in general are engagingly and frankly narrated. He does not write in Irish, or privilege that language as the custodian of an Homeric civilisation, or provide the anthropological perspective of the Blasket autobiographers. Instead, he adopts the persona of a reckless hobo, insists that his experience has been one of innocence destroyed and revels in self-revelation: 'Whether I die drunk or sober, honoured with fame and fortune, or disdained as a villainous pauper, I feel fortified by this outpouring of what had been festering in me. I have cast out my sins to make room for more serious misdemeanours' (O'Flaherty, 1981: 284). What redemption there is is embodied in an image of primal innocence, but this is presented in the form of a short story, 'The Caress', not in the autobiographical account of his visits home to Aran. In contrast to the reception that greeted O'Sullivan's memoir, *Shame the Devil* was banned in Ireland.

Patrick Kavanagh's *The Green Fool* is an example of a memoir which imposes a Syngean model on experience that is grounded in a different reality, but which also, like *Twenty Years A-Growing*, registers isolation and personal loss as it records a vanishing way of life. In recreating the world of his childhood and youth, Kavanagh invented a childhood state which justified his poetic persona. While his record of country life has its documentary or folkloric value – and in this and other ways is modelled on *Twenty Years A-Growing* – the world he invented is also self-servingly mythic. Although Kavanagh alludes to the 'cruelty and derision' with which he was treated by his neighbours, and to the 'vicious neighbourly hatred' (1975: 10–11) which was frequently expressed in arguments and lawsuits, the tone of the book rises above this perspective in a determinedly benign manner. The grinding economic deprivation, the sexual frustration, the narrow and repressive family discipline are all vividly sketched – confirming that Kavanagh already has the material for *The Great Hunger* – but so too are the diverting pleasures and engaging personalities of a richly convivial social world. This benign myth of childhood governs his presentation of his family, of his parish, of his own private reality and of the natural world in which he found his true poetic home.

Kavanagh imposes his character as poet on the narrative through the textures of his physical and social environment. Here and there, it is possible to detect a false, literary note, but when he writes of his father singing *A Starry Night*, or of others singing ballads, reciting poems or saying prayers, or when he records in dialect the conversation and stories of the many people who frequented his father's workshop, the sensibility of the poet becomes apparent. For now, he assimilates such moments of heightened experience with the cultural expression of the people and contrasts this with their material poverty; the playful rhyming utterances of the 'Bard of Callenberg' as well as the vernacular wisdom of the old people he associates with 'the lore and strange knowledge of God and Greece that they didn't know they knew' (1975: 10). In particular, he singles out 'the wandering poets of cobbler-land', the journeymen shoemakers whom his father employed, and the travelling beggars, 'the real romantic people of the roads', as transmitters of this wisdom: they were 'living records of a poetry-living people' (1975: 77, 59–60). If this concrete experience of a rich oral culture predated Kavanagh's awakening literary sensibility, the narrator selects and editorialises on those experiences and eventually assimilates them to his Romantic and neo-Platonic ideas about poetic knowledge and myth of decline. This traditional culture, it is gradually revealed, is at odds with the modernising forces of the present, and chapter 2, 'Breaking With Tradition,' establishes this sense of lost wisdom as a secondary theme of the book.

The benign perspective which Kavanagh adopts towards his neighbours is also evident in his treatment of his family, in particular his father and mother. The figure of the father has contradictory elements which contribute in different ways to the role of the poet increasingly adopted by Kavanagh after his father's death. At the end of chapter 1, Kavanagh tells of discovering one evening the spots of measles appearing on his skin and, simultaneously, becoming aware of his father beginning to play his melodeon and to sing: 'From that day *A Starry Night* became for me the greatest song in the world: whenever I sing it or hear it sung I am back again in childhood' (1975: 17). The placing of this dreamlike memory, resembling in its conjunction of illness and art so many moments in the autobiographies of other writers, gives a key importance to the father as a mediator of artistic transcendence at a time of physical or psychic weakness. In fact, Kavanagh had earlier invoked the father as a kind of inspiring muse from whom he 'inherited the spirit [ . . . ] of wisdom': 'He is dead a good many years now, yet as I write these words I know he is beside me, encouraging me to go on and win to be a great writer' (1975: 12). The motif of wandering, with which he associates cobblers, beggars and poets, is at the time of his father's death associated with him also: 'Father told me how great was his *wanderlust* when he was young' (1975: 200). This association is surprising because elsewhere the father is represented as an endlessly hardworking and shrewd family provider. Kavanagh's difficulty in reconciling these contrary aspects of his father's image might be summed up in the contradictory words in which he expresses his love for his dying parent: 'The earth that fell upon father's coffin covered in its fall one of the kindest, most self-effacing, self-sacrificing of fathers and husbands. I remembered with joy the beatings he gave me. They had helped to make me pliant and resilient in a world where proud things get broken' (1975: 199). Throughout the narrative, there are enough asides regarding money and respectability (a key and lasting word in the author's personal lexicon) to indicate that Kavanagh's difficulty in reconciling his commitments to farming and to writing, to staying at home and to travelling, has its origin in the intimacy of his family and perhaps especially in his father's own experience of illegitimacy and displacement.

The idealisation of the father and his world is a central part of the narrative import of *The Green Fool*, and to achieve this Kavanagh had to recover a childlike perspective on his early years. He needed to believe in that world still to set it against the struggle and disillusionment he later records as a result of his travels to Dublin, London and the west of Ireland. The book as a whole, therefore, is an anxious account of a suppressed crisis, an anxiety of audience as much as an anxiety of influence. Kavanagh is aware of a crude choice facing him, as it seems to have faced his father, and his response is to affirm the state of childhood before choices had to be made, to use this, his first autobiographical narrative, to endorse the role of 'ploughman-poet' at the moment when its loss was about to strike him with a dislocating force.[5] Thereafter, Kavanagh chose autobiographical fiction to recreate his portrait of the ploughman-poet as a young man in *Tarry Flynn* (1948), before deliberately excising childhood, youth and family altogether in *Self-Portrait* (1962). Nevertheless, the loss of childhood as a state of union with the father and Kavanagh's recognition of his perpetual self-exile – 'Everywhere I look a part of me is exiled from the I,' he writes in 'Nineteen Fifty Four' (2004: 211) – underlie *The Green Fool*. Moreover, his profound isolation marks him as a kind of orphan, a note also present in O'Sullivan's memoir and one that is central to Frank O'Connor's *An Only Child*.

O'Connor makes clear in his autobiography that all through his childhood and youth he was a 'dreamer,' a constant reader of boys' weeklies, adventure stories, poetry, songs and eventually novels, but it appears that while this reading focused his self-education, it was not the real centre of his imaginative development. He was encouraged in his obsessive reading by his mother Minnie, herself a keen reader, but it was her talk that was the emotional focus of his childhood and, as *An Only Child* reveals, the centre of his identity as a writer. Born Michael O'Donovan, he chose his mother's name as his pseudonym, and it is her story that is given premier place in this memoir, her profound and lasting role being that of narrator of her own life and interpreter of her own experience as an orphan:

> It was there [in the orphanage] that I picked up fragments of Mother's past life that have never ceased to haunt me. At that time, of course, they were merely a few hints, but they were sufficient to sustain my interest through the years, and later I wrote down and got her to write down as many of the facts as she remembered – or cared to remember (O'Connor, 1965: 44).

And so the mother is in part the author of her own story as it is set down here, her presence being the definitive condition of both O'Connor's childhood and his literary identity.

O'Connor's own childhood is often conveyed indirectly, whereas most of part one of the memoir, entitled 'Child, I Know You're Going To Miss Me', is devoted to his mother's life before he was born. The opening section implies that her life was more real than his and that his childhood is incomprehensible without the reader knowing her childhood and youth fully. At the close of this section, he refers to his mother's death and his return to her house with his young son. The boy begins to sing the Negro spiritual that gives this part its title, and a sombre truth is suddenly borne in upon the narrator:

> Then only did I realize that the horror that had haunted me from the time I was his age and accompanied Mother to the orphanage, and learned for the first time the meaning of parting and death, had happened at last to me, and that it made no difference to me that I was fifty and a father myself. And I await the resurrection from the dead and eternal life to come. (1965: 86).

This long opening section thus confers immortality on O'Connor's mother rather than concentrating on his own childhood, as the reader might have expected. Time has passed by, he has aged, but in a crucial sense he has not changed ('it made no difference to me that I was fifty') nor has his mother died; her essential identity which he experienced during the intimacy of his childhood years has remained his emotional and spiritual touchstone.

O'Connor declares that his own character is melancholic like his father's, whereas his mother's is 'Mozartian', a quality he says he can appreciate in others although he does not possess it himself. This seems to imply that his father – the bandsman and alcoholic who is introduced to the reader immediately before the mother – represents the force of death in the myth of childhood, whereas the mother represents life. O'Connor presents her strength as a matter of style:

> [S]he was almost fiercely undemonstrative in grief or pain. Nor, when she talked of that afternoon [of suicidal despair], as an old woman, did she exaggerate it. Father and I, with our streak of melancholia, would have added something to it that, by making it more dramatic, would also have made it less terrible. It is an awful moment when gaiety dies in those who have no other hold on life. (1965: 65)

When she was placed in the orphanage as a child, O'Connor reports that she clung to her mother and pleaded to be taken home: 'My grandmother's whispered reply is one of the phrases that haunted my childhood – indeed, it haunts me still. "But, my store, I have no home now." For me, there has always been in imagination a stage beyond death – a stage where one says "I have no home now" ' (1965: 47). Tragic awareness, stoicism and gaiety: Minnie O'Connor's great inner strength combined to express her 'Mozartian' character. Her knowledge of the fragility of life, and of her complete lack of entitlement to any life, at the mercy of the orphanage nuns, seems to have coloured her infinitely compassionate outlook: 'There was little of the agony of the orphan child that Mother did not know, either through her own experience or her experiences of the other children which she observed in her sympathetic way' (1965: 49). The mother, therefore, assumes the qualities of a tragic heroine, a saint, even a goddess in O'Connor's recreation of her. 'A certain simplicity of mind is characteristic of all noble natures', says some old Greek author whose name I cannot remember', he writes, and later compares her to Antigone (1965: 61). Her nobility is expressed in her ability to transform despair and desolation into a poised style, a style which is akin to music, he seems to say, by calling her 'Mozartian'.

O'Connor's simple title appears to be an echo from Joyce's *Ulysses*: 'Curious she an only child, I an only child. So it returns. Think you're escaping and run into yourself. Longest way round is the shortest way home'. Further, *An Only Child* is the explanation of why it was that his mother won and established her authority in him and in his writing; as memoirist, he recreates the experiences of orphanhood, fear and death. In giving him her life story, she gave him her life, and so his memoir of childhood is a restoration of her life to her, an attempt to preserve forever what has been lost. The closing paragraph invokes biblical language to capture the yearning for eternity and the immortality of the mother. She, or rather the vision of her that he preserves in his memoir, is the only image of immortality he can imagine:

> From the time I was a boy and could think at all, I was certain that for my own soul there was only nothingness. I knew it too well in all its commonness and weakness. I knew that there were souls that were immortal, that even God, if He wished to, could not diminish or destroy, and perhaps it was the thought of these that turned me finally from poetry to story-telling, to the celebration of those who for me represented all I should ever know of God. (1965: 276)

The second half of *An Only Child* – like O'Faolain's *Vive Moi!* – reflects on the author's youthful republican activism and subsequent, traumatic loss of faith in that view of the nation, but it is the continuing presence of his mother and her childhood circumstances that gives the memoir its moral and aesthetic character. In Minnie O'Connor's triumph over orphanhood, poverty and death, and in her storytelling, she might be seen as an emblematic figure of survival for many Irish memoirists. There is no such figure, however, in *The Village of Longing* (1987), George O'Brien's memoir of growing up in

Lismore, County Waterford in the 1950s, a work which is both a strikingly vivid recovery of childhood and a sharply observed refraction of the history and society of town and country. That mirroring is, of course, a retrospective pattern discovered in the effort to find a voice for his childhood self, for one of the arresting features of O'Brien's memoir is its narrative style, the construction of a language in which to reflect the experiences of boy, town and culture. It is the style in which the narrative voice comes to life that matters, and while notions of home are recurring concerns, the true home, it seems, is paradoxically in that voice, even as it articulates the idea of home-lessness: 'But within Lismore, who was at peace, who felt unyearningly at home? Nobody I knew' (O'Brien, 1987: 20). This is, indeed, the village of universal longings and yearnings for the unattainable, and the boy, listening to his uncle Georgie assert his combative certainties, heard 'a more powerful, less articulate desire for voice itself' (1987: 25). 'Voice itself': in recovering Lismore and his formative years therein, O'Brien achieves the empower-ment which everything in his orphaned, fostered, exiled childhood had denied him.

Structurally, *The Village of Longing* is not chronological or developmental; rather, its organisation is essayistic and spatial, encompassing five thematic strands: the boy's surrogate family; the class consciousness of his neighbour-hood; Anglo-Irish relations, focused on the place of the Castle in the town; Catholicism; and sport, particularly hurling. Yet while the boy enters into the social and cultural milieu of the town's communal life – and the adult narrator registers its minutiae with great gusto, colour and wit – it is his intimate relationships with his grandmother, aunt and uncle, and the lack of intimacy with his absent father, that are more central to the narrator's investigations. The subtext of the memoir is the search for answers to ques-tions about what his inheritance was and how he became the person he is. O'Brien's way of reading his 'three parents' retrospectively and probing how they indelibly marked his way of understanding the life of the town provide the answers he seeks, although these are not offered in the form of a continuous narrative: 'there's something devitalizing about making fast, making watertight, a tissue of a plot, as though that were all the past had to offer' (1987: 51). O'Brien does not recover the past to make it 'watertight'; he searches for what will grant him a future, for what will enable him to write his memoir. Thus, he excavates the past and prefers the poetry of uncer-tainty, the performance of possibilities, the textures of talk to psychological or historical plotlines, deliberately evoking his boyhood self ('seven going on twelve') as a protean state rather than a chronology with closure.

The most striking aspects of the house O'Brien grew up in were the dramat-ically expressive characters of his 'three parents'. The volume of conversa-tion, the individualistic styles of expression and the clash of temperaments all play a part in making O'Brien, even as a young boy, supremely aware of the empowerment of talk. In probing the nature of speech and music, and in juxtaposing expressiveness and silence (his silence about his relationship with his father, the silence of his mother's death), *The Village of Longing* recovers childhood to honour language itself. In its expressive possibilities, the gap of lapsed time between remembered boy and remembering author is bridged; past and future are absorbed in the enchanted present of writing and of reading:

> With Chrissy and George I felt I was theirs because they were so often ready to sing, to play, to draw me out. I still feel more theirs than anybody's, despite all the water that's between us, all the ink – despite, above all, my unconquerable urge to redeem and comprehend our deep life together in that small no-place. (1987: 92)

In these poignant lines O'Brien is simultaneously aware of how his education and his adult life have deprived him of intimacy with his surrogate family, and of the fact that this memoir is his best effort to recover and redeem lost time.

Throughout *The Village of Longing*, the defining condition of both childhood and society is one of lifelessness, a kind of Joycean paralysis with a yearning for vitality. The memoir is Joycean too in its ironic conflation of personal and communal accents, its deadpan reporting of dialogue, its re-enactment in a kind of interior monologue of the ways people characteristically spoke, its easy transition from adult narration to childhood perspective, its evocation of the way the boy's all-listening consciousness is permeated by songs, clichés, slogans, platitudes, poems and radio broadcasts. This is a book about the intense stress carried by language and expression, a book about both the articulation of a self and the uncertainty of such an entity in the first place. Beckettian in its doubt about the whole enterprise of identity-formation and self-development, O'Brien's memoir stresses the loss and yearning felt by the child in his orphaned state, emotions which are also felt as the condition of the town itself. Childhood is re-imagined out of necessity, since articulation is the source and seat of empowerment, and in spite of loss, yearning and homelessness, the power and pleasure of articulation make up the legacy of the memoirist's childhood.

If 'voice itself' is the underlying reality which is the foundation of the autobiographical impulse in O'Brien's memoir, it is also clear that so much circumstantial talk – the codes that pass for communication – is a hypocrisy and a censoring of the child's consciousness. The resulting disjunction between felt experience and what is verbally acknowledged as reality – a disjunction which is acutely registered by 'Seoirse', O'Brien's childhood name – recurs in other Irish memoirs, including Ciaran O'Driscoll's *A Runner Among Fallen Leaves* and Hugo Hamilton's *The Speckled People*, where it is explored with extraordinary power. The denial of the reality of the child's experience is also central to the father–son relationship in John McGahern's

*Memoir*, a work widely lauded as a Proustian masterpiece. *Memoir* is not solely a recreation of McGahern's childhood in the 1930s and 1940s; it extends the narrative into adolescence and his training as a teacher, then sketches the beginning of his literary career in Dublin and London in the 1960s, and closes with a recreation of the concluding decades of his father's life. As its title suggests, it is a book about remembrance itself, focused and founded on the recovery of his earliest years with his mother in the Leitrim countryside. Whereas the mother is associated with light in *Memoir*, the father seems to embody darkness: 'A life from which the past was so rigorously shut out had to be a life of darkness' (McGahern, 2005: 271). Much of the book deals with the effects of that 'darkness', the inexplicable violence that was unleashed on all of the children and on the mother. Yet while *Memoir* is a grim record of childhood and youth overshadowed by the pain of maternal death and the terror of paternal rage, the contrasting personalities of the parents are the basis for a literary mythology which emerges as the key to McGahern's creative self. Father and mother become emblematic figures in an oblique revelation of the moral and aesthetic roots of McGahern's literary orientation, so that this return to childhood and to the image of the mother can be read as an apologia for his entire artistic practice.

McGahern has often spoken in a poetic style reminiscent of Proust of the central impulse of his work, the recovery of a lost image which may lead to a transcendence of time passing (Sampson, 1991). This artistic achievement of reigning in peace over a work that uniquely reveals the 'still and private world' of the self is the equivalent for McGahern of a religious experience, yet such perfection and peace are hard to achieve: more often, it is a case of 'rejecting, altering, shaping, straining towards the one image that will never come, the one image on which our whole life took its most complete expression once' (McGahern, 1991: 12). Much of the early fiction is a search for images of childhood that will adequately convey the reality and significance of what happened, as if certain images need to be recalled and rooted in their proper local place and familial circumstances. *Memoir* represents one further stage in the articulation of a lost, self-defining reality. One of the clarifications the book offers is that 'the one image' McGahern speaks of is that of his mother, who is associated with religious belief, nature and immortality, and it is made very clear that childhood ended with her death when he was ten years old. Although the narrative goes on to investigate the image of the father as a bewilderingly brutal presence in the life of the motherless family, *Memoir* closes with a return to the image of the mother and to the recovery of childhood, now a visionary experience, a product of literary language, as indeed it is at the start of the book. Here he recalls the Proustian evidence he first mentions at the beginning: 'When I reflect on those rare moments when I stumble without warning into that extraordinary sense of security, that deep peace, I know that consciously and unconsciously she has been with me all my life' (2005: 272). Thus, McGahern's mother was not only the lost source of love and security during childhood, she also became the anchor of his art, her image both a source of wisdom and a source of style.

While *Memoir* is shocking in its exposition of the father's viciousness – to his wife as to his children – the narrative tone is not one of self-pity, anger or recrimination. There are passages of lyrical evocation of the Irish countryside in which the boy played and worked and walked to school. This landscape and the farm and village ways which evolved in it over centuries have a solidity all of their own; McGahern writes with deep affection for places, people and the rituals of work and play that structure individual and communal lives. He observes neighbours and relatives, recounts brief life histories and tells hilarious anecdotes of adventure and misadventure. He gives free play to his well-known relish for the nuances of personal interactions within small, closed communities. Thus, the desolating and unnerving episodes in the family story are embedded in a tapestry which arrests time for long periods. Loosely chronological, the memoir provides no ages or dates, except in quoted letters; the atemporal and ahistorical aspect of remembrance is mirrored here in a way that is similar to the technique of his last novel, *That They May Face the Rising Sun* (2002). Perhaps this is why the book is simply called *Memoir*, a title which lays bare its root, memory.

There is one phrase McGahern uses, 'Loss and the joy of restoration', which refers both to a particular stage in his mother's hospitalisation and return, and to a more general experience of loss – by death or removal, certainly, but also lost time, lost place, the loss of love and security – followed by renewal, which is surely the Proustian or Wordsworthian power of memory and art. It is hardly surprising that the origin of this powerful experience of recovery is in loss, given the mysterious, traumatising disappearance of his mother when he was eight years old. No explanation was offered by his father, and it is only on her return that he learns that she has been in Dublin receiving treatment for cancer. In the meantime, the children have been taken to live with their father in the barracks some miles from the house in which their mother lives during the school year. When John, her first-born and favourite, is allowed back to stay with her a week ahead of the others, her choice is seen by him as proof that their mutual love is unique and almost romantic in its intensity. Biblical diction – loss and restoration – and elemental images of natural transformation – water, sun, diurnal and seasonal change – are invoked to convey the momentousness of the return of his 'beloved', and the mother–son reunion culminates in a priestly vision:

> One day, like Paddy Flanagan, I would become a priest. After the Ordination Mass I would place my freshly anointed hands in blessing on my mother's head. We'd live together in the priest's house and she'd attend each morning Mass and take communion from my hands. When she died, I'd include her in all the Masses that I'd say until we were united in the joy of heaven, when time would cease as we were gathered into the mind of God. (2005: 62–63)

The child's and the mother's dream of love and eternal life together become the foundation of a pact which fortified him in the years after her death when he is exposed to the terrors of his violent father; but even when he no longer aspires to the priesthood, his vocation as a writer assumes the same force as the child's dream. 'Impossible to tell to whom the dream belonged' – this phrase has a striking echo towards the end of the book when McGahern begins the coda to the main narrative as follows:

> This is the story of my upbringing, the people who brought me up, my parents and those around them, in their time and landscape. My own separate life, in so far as any life is separate, I detailed only to show how the journey out of that landscape became the return to those lanes and small fields and hedges and lakes under the Iron Mountains. (2005: 260–61)

The phrase that stands out here, 'in so far as any life is separate,' acknowledges an ambiguous truth first mentioned in the reference to the shared dream and the arresting of time through recollection. The overlapping of identities seems to have taken its most heightened form in his writing, not simply in his decision to become a writer but in his inspiration, especially in his constant return to the setting and scenes of his childhood, and to the image of his mother as the person who first named the place in which they lived together.

*Memoir* is a surprising culmination to a lifetime of writing novels and stories which almost invariably are anchored in images of the countryside of Leitrim and Roscommon, yet throughout that literary career McGahern refused to acknowledge that he was writing autobiographical fiction. In the most important sense, this is true – memories and observations are dramatised and woven into a literary style that assumes its own reality – but what *Memoir* exemplifies is that fiction and non-fiction are overlapping genres. While this book appears to be grounded in realism and historical detail, it is also an apologia for McGahern's identity as a writer whose work has poetic and mythological foundations. It reveals as much about the memoirist writing about his recovery of childhood as it does about the earlier life and times of Sean McGahern (the author's name in childhood), and in this and other ways seems to recapitulate so many memoirs of Irish childhoods. Indeed, McGahern's myth of the mother is remarkably similar to O'Connor's. A muse for each writer, these women's lives provided models of how to survive suffering with grace, transform loss into personal power, draw inspiration from faith in a higher power and endow ordinary life with eternal significance. The sons discovered a notion of immortality in writing from their example; their memoirs aim to confer immortality on themselves and on their mothers. But if the recovery of childhood in these cases is necessary so that death may be confounded, the passage of time arrested and a sense of home recovered, this is also true of the other memoirs I have discussed. There are many such patterns of resemblance – similarities in the selection of experiences or people for emphasis, in the presence of a literary trope or sub-genre, in the ways in which childhood is assimilated to the adult voice – but in all cases childhood is revealed as a site of an elaborate mythology of both personal and cultural significance.

Many conclusions about what were acceptable public images of selfhood in twentieth-century Irish Catholic culture might be drawn from the virtual absence of childhood in autobiographical texts from the first part of the century and the intensity and ubiquity of its portrayal in the later decades. The admission into public discourse of individual self-consciousness and a plurality of images of selfhood is a relatively late development in Ireland, although fiction and poetry were genres in which writers could pursue limited projects of self-exploration and self-portrayal. Yet the particular kinds of objectification of subjective experience which autobiography entails allow access to the remarkable particularity of each individual life to be framed, in its alienation and suffering as in its joy and accomplishments. The memoirs of Maurice O'Sullivan, Patrick Kavanagh, Frank O'Connor, George O'Brien and John McGahern are singular in their recreation of a state before articulacy or understanding, and the adult narrative voice is anchored by its recovery of the emotional knowledge of the child. In these autobiographies, the recovery of childhood is embodied in the treatment of such primal matters as home, nature and parents, but most of all it is embodied in the writing itself as a quality of heightened perception and liberating self-knowledge.

## Notes

1. McGahern (1997) claims that the McCourt style is a kick against resignation, humiliation and the outrages that the poor are destined to endure, and his emphasis on how style triumphs over content anticipates McGahern's treatment of his own miserable childhood in his memoir.
2. Although I use the term 'childhood' throughout this chapter, I have preferred 'boyhood' in the title in acknowledgement of the fact that I do not discuss memoirs by Irish women. While a number of women writers have written briefly about their childhoods, the most well known being Elizabeth Bowen, Kate O'Brien, Edna O'Brien, Dervla Murphy, Polly Devlin, Eavan Boland and Nuala O'Faolain, my general point about the absence of childhood from twentieth-century Irish autobiography is especially true of women, and this situation has not changed as radically for them as for male autobiographers in recent years. Many reasons for this absence may be advanced, among them state censorship, the privileging of political and religious perspectives on Irish identity over psychological and sexual ones and the general marginalisation and devaluation of women's autonomous experience until recently. Fuller investigation of this topic is beyond the scope of this chapter; for further insights see Napier (2001) and Grubgeld (2004), the scope of which is unfortunately limited to Anglo-Irish women.

3. The most important general study of childhood is by Richard Coe (1984). I am aware of few critical studies of Irish autobiography that investigate such matters, apart from those by Grubgeld and Napier cited above. This chapter has room to discuss only a few works; among those omitted but well served by others are Sean O'Casey and Samuel Beckett. For the former, see Kenneally (1988); for the latter, Olney (1998).
4. Declan Kiberd suggests that these passages of nature description may derive from 'runs' used by oral storytellers and singers of tales, and cogently notes that 'this youth who knows the sadness of estrangement is also cannily aware of the aesthetic pleasures it makes possible' (2000: 536).
5. Antoinette Quinn provides comprehensive insight into the composition of this autobiography and its critical importance in Kavanagh's development (1991: 52–86).

# 11
# Memoirs of an Autobiographer

*George O'Brien*

The time to speak came.

At least that much can be said about the proliferation of Irish memoir and autobiography over the past 20 years or so. But why and how it came is not so easy to say. The difficulty partly has to do with larger problems arising out of attempts to come to terms with recent changes in Irish social and cultural life. Partly, too, however, it has to do with the nature of autobiography itself.

## The free speech problem

The origins of my own autobiographical sallies are clear enough to me. Or rather, they seemed pretty clear when I first embarked on them. The idea of writing my own story emerged initially, it seemed, from nothing more than a change of circumstances. I got a job, I went to America, I became a father. These changes were the culmination of others on which I had set my course – university degrees and teaching, for instance. It wasn't a case of such courses being far away from where I was born, as the saying goes. Not necessarily. But they did seem to be at a great remove from the identity I had received, through a combination of personal circumstances and social conditions, where I was born, so much so that the pursuit of those courses could only, where I was concerned, take place in foreign countries. Yet, I could only manage to live, to make something of that original identity through offering it to unfamiliar systems, idioms and standards. So, when at last I fell on my feet with a job and a family, the impetus arose to try to bridge the distance between where I started and where I ended up. I had no real idea that a language suitable to this task of making differences speak to one another would be forthcoming. I didn't even know with any degree of awareness that language would be that much of an issue. What I thought, with the neophyte's *naïveté*, was that I was entitled to my own story. Sufficient to the day was the narrative thereof, I said to myself. I had permission to speak.

214

It's easily seen that I knew nothing about autobiography. Of course, I had a bookish awareness that it was a form – and indeed more than a form, a habit of mind – favoured by the big-name Irish writers, by Irish-language writers as a means of hymning their poverty and endurance and, like every other kind of writing known to man, by a great rake of crucial Frenchmen. But I was neither poet, peasant nor philosopher. George Moore, Yeats and O'Casey were already securely represented in the public eye by works other than their autobiographies. Using Irish to tell one's own story was in effect, though not, of course, in intention, virtually receiving official permission to tell it. And as to the French, they couldn't help themselves, being evidently fated to be nothing if not original at all times and to have no choice but to acquaint the world with the fact. And if I knew little about autobiographical products, my knowledge of how they were produced was considerably smaller. I had concluded that for those who got to tell their stories, permission to speak was a foregone conclusion. In the case of the big names, for instance, no permission was required, it having been already earned by their prior literary accomplishments. Moreover, I also imagined that the point at which I had now arrived could be described as my having received that same permission and that all I had to do was fire away. It was only when I went about putting pen to paper that I found that receiving, and acting on, permission to speak is not so much what the autobiographer has to go on as what he or she must continually apply for, negotiate, argue over, justify and project – so much so that the quest for, rather than the successful expression of, an adequate method of speaking about oneself is one of the more fundamental challenges of the whole enterprise.

It shows what kind of a reader I was that I was unpleasantly surprised by the fit of strangeness that language took when asked to be invested in a self. My idea was that the tale was everything and the telling entirely secondary, no more than a mechanical means to an end. But that was as naïve as the notion that there was only a past to be recounted, without reckoning on the shaping influence (again, of course, a matter of language) of the present in which the recounting takes place. Permission to speak, then, like any other manifestation of liberty, I suppose, turned out to be not as simple as it appeared. Not surprisingly, Montaigne's *'que sais-je?'* has become the prototypical autobiographical motto. Think of how it recurs at the opening of Stendhal's *Vie de Henry Brulard*, completed in 1836 but not published until 1890. The author is brought up short by the discovery that he's about to turn 50. He has two responses. On the one hand he declares that it's 'high time' he got to know himself; on the other, 'I should really find it very hard to say what I have been and what I am' (Stendhal, 1973: 21). And even the founding father of autobiography, the great St Augustine, is to be found imploring very early on in the *Confessions*, 'Allow me to speak . . . Allow me to speak . . . ': I have in mind such phrases as, 'How shall I call upon my God?', 'Have mercy so that I may find words', 'Nevertheless, allow me to speak before your mercy' (2001: 3, 5, 6).

*The great St Augustine.* I could say, that's what we called him. Or I could say, that's what he was called. Both statements are correct, as far as they go, and it appears not to matter a whole lot which tense of the verb I use: active or passive. The phrase is exclusively a priestly usage, generally that of a missioner during one of those sermons which were the dramatic centrepieces of the regular hard-hitting enjoinders to reflect and repent. Yet, even while memories surface to assist with giving the phrase a context – the packed church, the pregnant atmosphere, the Passionist specially down from Dublin – a gap becomes discernible between the two ways in which the recollection of the phrase may be worded. Using the active voice makes priest and people one. The second usage, on the other hand, suggests that the priest used the phrase on his listeners' behalf. The result is impersonal; the collective disappears. And of course neither usage allows a place for the singular, active voice. This third voice makes itself known by insinuating itself between the other two. All I'm doing here is improvising on a little phrase, a little moment – all minor key stuff; although it's not entirely beside the point that the first two voices are practically interchangeable in their presumption of the power, authority and legitimacy to speak for others, a presumption whose validity rests on the silencing of any other voice. In contrast, the third voice is awkward, out of place, disruptive, one of a kind. It's the type of voice which might readily go on to dwell, for instance, on that use of 'great' and on why we heard virtually nothing at all about the Carthaginian St Augustine, much less the black or the lusty St Augustine, or even something as accessible to us as St Augustine the mammy's boy.

Autobiography, I discovered, is not merely a matter of content but also of transmission. The very act of recollection implicitly concerns itself with missing data, impressions, remarks and innumerable other categories of material, with each category being both unlike the others and also capable of being associated with them. Entry into this realm is not what permission to speak secures. Rather, the permission is to be taken as a sort of promise, or perhaps even an obligation, to keep faith with the realm of recollection's highly differentiated character – the same kind of fidelity as the diversity of the here and now enjoins. And one obvious way in which that kind of 'pact' (to adapt Philippe Lejeune's term a little) may be maintained is through the autobiographical voice, an instrument whose language cannot help but introduce departures from received wisdom, interruptions in the common story, in addition to being, of necessity, conceived in terms of idiosyncratic scales and gradations of meaning. All such free speech can be deeply distressing to the reader, since it is a rhetorical replica of a much less homogenised and reliable sense of the past, a realm notorious for consensus. Questions of aim, authenticity, sincerity, good faith, fairness and accuracy immediately crop up. In all, it should not be surprising that autobiographies contain so much trouble. They mean trouble. Therein lies their principal cultural value, but therein also lies the cultural challenges they present.

## The 'I' and the 'We'

It wasn't just a matter of ignorance or being very much an apprentice writer that caused me to be surprised by the kinds of trouble accompanying claims to selfhood. Another reason was that it had been a long time since I had lived under the auspices of a 'we.' My own experience of this construct had been a particularly complicated one. I had been aware from early on that although 'we' meant, for example, the family, and implied strong ties of loyalty, affiliation and solidarity, not every member of the family identified with these ties all the time, and not everybody understood the ties in the same way. Growing up in a household of adults rather than in a more conventional family setting and observing, however subliminally, that they too were still growing, or that they were capable of expressing strong desires to grow from time to time – desires which were capable of overriding whatever alternative understanding of their roles and needs the family provided – I learned that although there certainly was a 'we', authenticated by origins, place and kindred, this collective entity could be viewed with equal validity as a gaggle of differences. 'We' essentialised, whereas each of its constituent elements claimed, intermittently but recurringly, to be exceptions. The family was firewood and tree, a box of matches and a box of matches spilled. Because of the uncertainty which seemed to be its signature, and because the choice of one version of the family rather than another had not only to be made but maintained, so that each choice continually aggravated the other, this double view distressed me, once upon a time. And of course I found I had it with me when I began to turn my view outwards to church and state, those other forms of 'we' in which we were supposed to feel at home, by which we were confined.

Since my story, such as it is, and the degree that I can understand it and thereby impart to it something of the coherence and consistency of narrative, tells of the failure on all levels, rhetorical and executive, of the 'we', a failure in which I am of course fundamentally complicit, fidelity to the past entailed a dismantling of the 'we'. Conceiving of myself as in many respects a critique of the 'we', by virtue of (as I saw it) a history whose trajectory went from helplessness through superfluity to abandonment – all sealed in silence by fair-isle jumpers, boarding-school education, summer holidays – I could only think in terms of holes, stupidity and misdirection, which only an autobiographical initiative could recuperate. This was more an instinctive than a deliberate choice. I knew there could be no *Bildungsroman* because I had no sense either of having learned or having taught myself anything of value from the emptiness and loss which haunted my emotional landscape. But I only saw that afterwards. At the time, questions of form – as distinct from questions of organising the material – did not occur to me. All I was doing, I thought, was writing for myself, not in an archaeological spirit to find out what could be disinterred and reappraised (though I was aware of such a spirit having entered Irish writing), but to see if I could address what memory contained, find a language which would disarm its power and allow me to speak as if I were its equal, sincerely, tolerantly.

I was writing to effect some sort of return, now that I was in America, far away, and now that Americans, with that presumptive freedom of theirs, assumed that they knew what Irishness was, and that I would agree with their conclusions. But also I was returning simply because I thought I had a means of doing so, had my own terms. These were formal and symbolic to a degree, no more than a mere language, but these characteristics were very much in their favour, since through them the terms remained very much mine, and as such precisely reciprocal to the terms of my departure, which had been those of others. I didn't have much confidence of being in pursuit of truth. Truce would do, not only as a homonym but also as an ambition. So, a voice came to me in which, without surrendering the psychological and cultural commitment to critique, also had a desiring element in it. And part of the desire was not to articulate that critical commitment in the belligerent, aggressive, silencing tones in which I had always heard them. I thought that I should, that I could, have a language that was a will to no power. There isn't any such thing, of course. Break the silence I might, redeem the exile (to be pretentious about it) I might, but I was sorely lacking in cunning. In other words, I had no idea what impact the kind of activity I'd embarked upon might have. I don't mean where the family was concerned. Those who were left thought, for the most part, that what I had done was, in the words of one of them, 'a dirty, lousy thing.' That was inevitable, and if I hadn't geared myself up for it, exactly – since it was the kind of language I was attempting to get past – it was no great revelation to find that I was not being welcomed home with open arms and marching bands. And I don't mean either that my work has met with the ire of reviewers and others with the public ear. On the contrary, what I'm getting at is something that's not personal at all, in fact, and has less to do with me than with autobiography as such, or at least with autobiography in an Irish context.

In Ireland there is a particular sensitivity to the kind of trouble that seems endemic to autobiography – trouble that arises out of presuming to speak, about such speech's language, about aim and audience. To take just one instance, Ireland seems to be, uniquely, a country in which retired politicians and other public figures tend not to write their memoirs. Questions regarding what constitutes 'the record', or about how the record is assembled, or the reliance on perhaps an over-emphatically historiographical account of the record are tacitly avoided. Ironically enough, this particular brand of silence is much more pronounced in independent Ireland, when one would have thought there is either little to hide or little to inhibit contributing to the record. The very fact of the silence, however, implies a set of interests at odds with those of the larger *demos* and which, as a result, is easy to think of as the product of an ideological rationale. Moreover, silence at this level has the effect of making autobiography seem exceptional, or at any rate the rank-breaking, group-defying opposite of official silence. Of course, the autobiographer is an exception, as the list of distinguished twentieth-century Irish contributors to the form demonstrates. But in the context of public remembering in general, autobiography tends to be tainted, an unwarranted rupture of the ostensible prophylaxis of silence.

The problematic status of the autobiographer – the fact that he or she might be the author of banned books, for example – compromises the accessibility of the autobiographical in Ireland. As a result of both the marginal status of autobiography in the output of its most illustrious practitioners (Yeats, O'Casey, Frank O'Connor, to name the most obvious), and the marginalisation of the autobiographical in the larger public archive of memory and reflection, there has been little or no possibility for the form to enter into relation with a view such as Antonio Gramsci's 'justification of autobiography':

> One justification can be this: to help others develop in certain ways and towards certain openings [ . . . ]. Autobiography therefore replaces the 'political' or 'philosophical essay': it describes in action what otherwise is deduced logically. Autobiography certainly has a great historical value in that it shows life in action and not just as written laws or dominant moral principles say it should be. (1991: 132)

The effective denial in an Irish context of autobiography's exemplary potential helps to maintain intact the ostensible integrity of the 'we', the untroubled character of which underwrites its supposedly perdurable, unimpeachable and ultimately mythic status. While this myth of unity may express an understandable desire either to sublimate the divisions inevitable in any society, or to fabricate an oubliette to which those who are rendered demographically and culturally *non grata* may be consigned, one must also consider the risks this myth runs of propagating rigidity and defensiveness, of ending up as no more than the reverse of the sectarian medal.

Part of autobiography's cultural significance lies in its capacity to prevent such monolithic cultural formations. For even if a given autobiography is no more than weakly subjective, or self-effacingly documentary, it impinges on the norms underlying and governing the conditions the text seeks to reproduce. If it does no more than replicate the consensual understanding and acceptance of the 'we', an autobiography will, however unwittingly, focus on the elective nature of the consensual, thereby highlighting such constitutive elements of the consensual as tradition, change, collective behaviour, representative thought patterns, models of individuation and local 'characters' – in short, a comprehensive repertoire of instances and effects which reveal not only the depth of the settled life but also its limits. And of course such representations also cast the autobiographer in the interesting roles of pedagogue, chronicler, ethnographer, spokesperson, which even if he or she does not consciously assume them and writes under the naïve assumption that fidelity to the material is all that the autobiographical form requires, nevertheless cannot avoid having the effect in the mind of the reader of diversifying and, to that limited extent destabilising, unitary conceptions. Thus, even the least ambitious autobiographical overture will lend itself to being read as an essay on limits (as far as its raw material is concerned) and as a testing of limits (considered from a discursive and formal point of view).

But it was only after the fact, when I had carried out my own autobiographical sorties, that I could see with any clarity anything of what I've just been trying to describe. I saw how much they were about certain spaces – the hurling field, the chapel, the dancehall, the workplace – and how the interest of those spaces was not only a matter of the specificity with which they could be recalled and depicted but of the realisation, the private sense, of how constraining they all were. Scenes of desire, aspiration and engagement though these venues might have been, in treating myself to my first proper scrutiny of them I also saw – or rather, could admit seeing – the frustration, misunderstanding and resistance that were part of my experience of them also. Such acknowledgements of needing more, or different, room were obviously crucial not only in attempting to secure the truce I sought but also in the discovery that my realisation, regardless of quality, only seemed to attain validity when articulated. The will to a language of no power, for all my belief that it was through such a discourse that I might grant myself permission to speak, turned out to be a non-starter. So, while it may well be that one of the objectives of the floating symposium which is the model for social life in J. P. Mahaffy's *The Principles of the Art of Conversation* is to 'induce the other to open the flood-gates of his inner life' (1887: 166), the consequences and significance of doing so rest on the possibility of the released material being channelled through an accessible form. In other words, it is not speaking but writing that enables the autobiographical departure to assert its difference. Again, there is no shift in matter which is not reciprocated by a shift in method. The change in focus from collective experience to individual witnessing and evaluating, with which autobiography is centrally preoccupied, is a symptom of modernisation – of willed modernisation as the trajectory of desire, on the autobiographer's part. No less modernising, however, is the change in emphasis from the spontaneity, informality, transience and intimacy of orality to the studied, constructed, permanent, detached character of print.

Such developments, however, are not to be construed in terms of the triumph of the modern. The autobiographical impairs its own possibilities if it relies on the crudeness of binaries. Rather, the significance of autobiographical form may be found in the idea of movement, of going towards, of an interplay between different, and even opposing, realms of experience and perception and idiom. And one implication of this idea is that rather than seeking to dismantle the 'we', the autobiographical aims to augment it, make it more pliable, more accommodating, more complicated, as though in stating his or her own case, the autobiographer claims citizenship to be a special case of attentiveness or vulnerability or need. Indeed, it is almost a commonplace of autobiography, generally considered, that it functions as a combination of first court of public appeal and last resort of private confession (I'm thinking in particular of the memoirs of abuse victims and other trauma survivors). It obviously goes without saying that any society needs to make room for exceptions. Perhaps Irish society's typical ham-fistedness in this regard is a reason for the degree of autobiographical pressure in so large a number of that society's highly prized cultural products. Moreover, this official clumsiness has applied not only to society's victims but to all areas of difference within the society, including most obviously and troublingly those of political opposition, religious persuasion, sexuality and class. Although exceptions readily come to mind, the fact that to a considerable extent these areas still await autobiographical representation should be borne in mind when contextualising the Irish autobiographical 'moment' of the 1990s.

Telling one's own story turned out, I found, to be an intervention in, adaptation of, amendment to the authorised version of certain times and places. The power of the authorised version is such that any relationship to it, even a dissenting one, partakes of it. Not only is the autobiographer empowered as a result, but the version itself – which in Ireland, for example, tends to make homologous faith and fatherland, blood and soil – becomes less all-embracing in its remit and effects, more open to discussion, a narrative in which some rewording would not be remiss rather than a rhetoric requiring nothing but fealty. So, just as important as the subjective project of coming to terms with my past was the objective appreciation I developed for the means – and their challenges – by which the project was realised. Gaining first-hand experience of the potential of writing to extend the franchise of public representation, and of autobiography as what Hugh Maxton has called 'a document of initiation and renewal' (1997: 10), in which heritage, affiliation and the overall dynamics of consensus could be complicated and realigned, was obviously of great personal interest, in large part because it was through that experience that an alternative self to the one being written about came into being. Going back was also an affirmation of the present. Not only could the child be seen as father of the man, but that father attained autonomy and legitimacy through the monitoring, substantiating, restorative function of his language. (I say this very well aware of the troubled status of the father in post-war Irish writing from Brian Friel to Frank McCourt, to use as provocative a spectrum as I can think of.)

I see no reason to deny the therapeutic overtones of the reinventions which writing compels, particularly when, as in autobiography, they are made in the name of fidelity, however paradoxical that may sound. But there's no reason to reduce everything to the therapeutic, either. As I've been trying to maintain, conceiving of oneself autobiographically is a means to ends which are by no means exclusively personal. Here's one small anecdotal instance of what I mean. When my work began to appear, many people told me that, on reading it, they had been reminded for the first time in years of such-and-such a name, or an event or a turn of phrase, so much so that I began to bridle at the evident risk of being turned into a designated memorialist. Yet, of course, my readers were simply highlighting an aspect not only of what I do but of the kind of thing that tends to happen generally when writing autobiographically. In recalling his or her previous selves, the autobiographer recalls the matrix from which those selves emerged, namely, the former selves and earlier contexts of everybody, to a greater or lesser degree. This aggregative need or gesture may be a reason why I think of what I do as tending towards memoir or, in the spirit of the hybridity which pervades the very idea of the recollected self and which gives the idea a special if often camouflaged status in Ireland's hybridised culture, memoir with an autobiographical admixture. Instead of a hair-splitting disquisition on genre, let the following working definitions made by Perry Anderson suffice for now:

> a memoir can re-create a world lavishly peopled with others, while saying very little about the author himself. An autobiography, on the other hand, may take the form of a pure portrait of the self; the world and others featuring only as *mise en scène* for the inner adventures of the narrator. (2004: 23)

Another discovery, then: it isn't possible to write merely of oneself or for oneself. Even if speaking to, or for, or even back to, others – neighbours, enemies, ghosts, demons, tormentors, saviours, cousins, the hurling team, the hurlers on the ditch, the inexhaustible retinue of presences who maintained that lost but ever-present primal scene – is in the end just a way of talking to oneself, it is also an acknowledgment of the extraneous elements from which the self is derived, each element mediating the other, and self the medium of it all. The 'I' is untenable without its opposite, complicit and contrary.

## The written self

Speaking. Strange how there seems to be no getting away from it. The power of writing notwithstanding, and in spite of having Roland Barthes's word for it that 'Whenever there is a concurrence of spoken and written words, to write means in a certain manner: *I think better*, more firmly' (1986: 6, emphasis added), the use of 'speaking' persists as a term which seems to render a more admissable, a more natural, account of what autobiography does. Part of this sense of natural usage – yet another area whose interest is magnified when situated in an Irish context, where the natural is commonly advanced as a fundamental criterion for effective communication, which in turn is frequently mixed up with aesthetic value – understandably relates to such matters as tone and voice, which will obviously be to the fore in responses to personal narratives. These matters may well be on autobiographers' minds as they insist, for dramatic or more news-oriented reasons, on the urgency and originality of their stories. Autobiographers themselves, in other words, frequently expect to be heard out, a vital dimension of the aforementioned autobiographical pact where they are concerned. The possibility of the pact being sealed, and the narrative successfully trans-mitted, may rest indeed on the understanding that speaking is transactional, whereas writing is contractual. Speaking is most likely to achieve its ends if the auditor accepts that the speaker is acting in good faith and is telling the truth, even when this is not the case. By virtue of its artifice, however, writing is suspect. A species of lying. Unnatural.

The interchange between these two antithetical discursive modes points to autobiography's forked tongue, that linguistic instability which drives rather than hampers the form's expressive reach by encouraging tonal flex-ibility, expositional diversity, allusive range and generic adaptability. This last element is evident in autobiography's reliance on, and indeed its histor-ical genesis in, such other forms as the essay, the diary, the character sketch (along the lines of La Bruyère, for example), the travel journal, the book of hours (which it secularises) and, in plainly inventive ways, the genealogy and the map. And of course the confession. This form's credentials obvi-ously derive from Augustine's prototype, and interestingly enough Augustine alludes to his work's formal properties in noting that he is confessing 'with my mouth and my pen' (2001: 248). The *Confessions* are of more than formal interest, needless to say. But the dual and at the same time integrated activity of voice and pen offers not only a suggestive image of confession in other contexts, where it is an activity consisting of the interactive presence of speaker and recorder, but also a metaphor of the past's address to the present, the past being the site of speech or of not-writing and the present being the place where that speech is recollected, interrogated, documented and preserved. And even to think of confes-sion formally is to call to mind such areas of consciousness as witnessing, testifying, examining and evaluating, all of which interrelate and conflate the two discursive modes of talking and writing. Further, partly because of its religious connotations, and partly because of those connotations' juridical counterpart, confession evokes, if not power, then certainly power structures.

Although, as I've said, I was interested in the possibility of reconciliation when writing my memoirs, this was not accompanied by a strong sense of confession. My attention was primarily focused on reconstructing the past, which means not simply putting it in the order in which it occurred, but recognising certain recurring thematic or circumstantial emphases in the material which would permit it to be organised into patterns, while at the same time attempting to find a language which would convey my present awareness of, and attitude to, the recollected material. Having said that much, however, I must confess that there are indications in it of the manner in which the necessity of form denatures the actuality of content. Interpretation takes precedence over recapitulation. Since it is impossible to say everything, there is an immediate question about the principle of selection which a given autobiography employs. Peig Sayers can hardly be forgetting the children she lost through death and emigration, yet the losses contribute very little to *Peig* (1935) – for excellent storytelling reasons, of course, which in themselves also turn out to have an autobiographical dimension, by virtue of the attention they draw to reticence, self-control and other characteristics of the storyteller's state of mind.

Writing distorts, even when it is as close to the voice as it is in the case of *Peig*. And actual words can be a problem as well, as the much-rehearsed concern about the use of dialogue in memoir attests. No reader denies that some statements made in the past are unforgettable. But scepticism sets in when long passages of dialogue are reproduced. This reaction, while understandable, is misplaced, since it holds language in a state of uniform empirical stasis and reliability. Such a view is unwilling to acknowledge language's expressive capacities and values, a view which in turn presupposes that the past and one's fidelity to it are in themselves stable areas of inquiry. Language is one of the primary ways in which autobiography makes trouble. And it so happens that the least rewarding memoirs to read – whatever their interest as social and cultural documents – tend to be those that take language for granted. In doing so, they miss, or dismiss, the opportunity to render the flavour of the distinctive self-consciousness and self-questioning (Montaigne's *'que sais-je'*) which is autobiography's warrant and its labile truth.

If asked, when my works were in progress, if they were confessional, I would only have been able to admit that, to my surprise, autobiography seemed to have less to do with recapturing the past than with the dialectic, or at the very least the dialogue, it sets up by making the past relative and thus dispelling, or providing the welcome illusion of dispelling, the monolithic character of history and heritage in which faith and fatherland had typically chosen to embody themselves. Going on from that, then, I might have offered something about how the resulting rhetorical accommodations seemed logical but felt liberating, and that taking charge of my own history taught me a lot about myself and others. A dry, academic response, in other words. If noteworthy at all, then only for its privacy. I was entirely unaware that privacy in itself amounted to something like a confession. My thinking was more along the lines that since my work had no sex to speak of, there was nothing to confess. I had been away from Ireland for so long, and in a number of important ways had allowed, and had needed, myself to be re-formed by difference – by the differences I'd encountered in education, in a cultural ethos and most basically of all in the simple though crucial fact of opportunity – that I totally overlooked the possibility that there would be anything troublesome about what I was writing. Immersed in process, I didn't have much time for product and hadn't considered for a moment that the publication of privacy could be anybody's business but my own and the reader's, and could only conceive of myself as fully entitled to the liberation of which having my say was symptom and emblem.

Indeed the trouble was not my problem. In fact, trouble is both too precise and too comprehensive a name for what I'm trying to describe. What happened simply was that the hour of product came: *The Village of Longing* was published in 1987. And what I found was that, in the very act of congratulating me on my success, my audience – people at readings, for example – also communicated a vague unease and misgiving about what they thought I had accomplished. Is it all true? they wanted to know. What do your people think about it? And, with rather beady-eyed half-smiles, aren't you great to be putting everyone in a book, like that? It was hardly as if my questioners had no knowledge of autobiography. Many of them had recently read with appreciation, and a little condescension as well, Noël Browne's *Against the Tide* (1986). I had no record of public service that could speak on my behalf, however. On the contrary, all I had to offer was a chronicle of what I perceived to be private failures. And because they kept recurring, the nature of the questions, which of course were always asked very charmingly and in a spirit of friendliness and hospitality, began to get to me. I had apparently done something embarrassing. Knowing I was perceived as an outsider – an emigrant, a professor, even a Yank – the first thought I had was that I was, in effect, being asked what right did I think I had to be so personal about everything. I could be a fly on the family wall all I wanted. But there was the unavoidable implication that a speaking fly was surely a freak of nature. So maybe I should just buzz off for myself.

Not only must I have broken some taboo, I thought, it must be obvious to all except myself which one it was, since nobody saw the needed to come right out and name it for me or say what the force and structure of it were. Out of this line of thinking, later on, a useful lesson emerged about autobiography's difference-making potential, and how that is part of the trouble the genre creates. But at the time I didn't quite take that in, thinking – not altogether incorrectly though not altogether correctly either – that the implication of taboo was much too tribal for modern Ireland.

Instead, the thought came to me that I was being asked to confess to a version of my work which the questioners could live with, either making of it a story in which all's well that ends well or one which, despite my best efforts, turned out to be as upsetting as an episode of juvenile delinquency and which, now that I'd got it out of my system, I regretted. Two assumptions seemed to be in a rather unbalanced relation with each other. One was that I could not speak of myself without being confessional; the other was that the nature and object of being confessional was to put the audience at its ease, to reassure it that it knew to a nicety beforehand what it was being asked to swallow. The 'all's well' contingent tended to be confessional themselves, telling me what incident in their own history the book reminded them of, and asking me did I remember a certain policeman or bank clerk who served in Lismore, and going on to regale me with their history whether I remembered them or not. It was partly in this way that the difference between writing and speaking was brought home to me. The 'juvenile delinquency' squad, on the other hand, typically asked me, grinning broadly, to take their advice and be sure not go down to Lismore, for they'd surely string me up if I did.

The reader always appropriates the work, and makes what he or she needs of it. Teaching had taught me that, already. Resisting that need in the hope of readings that would be all the more confident for being disinterested was one of the things that made teaching hard work. Now here I was, myself – my best self, my life as a text – the subject of the presuppositions and preconditions of acculturation, paying the dues of re-entry. As much a stranger in my own country as ever I was. But since there was nothing I could do now about the text itself, and even less that I wanted to do, my attention turned to these presuppositions and to the ambivalent mixture of welcome and reservation with which they attempted to accommodate my work. The work of a harmless one. The work of a white blackbird. Not that I ever felt myself to be the target of either sentimentality or hostility. In fact, the subtle, half-realised, understated reactions were not really about me. Rather, their underdeveloped and surreptitious nature suggested that I was only an occasion for something more complicated to be raised. It wasn't I who was perceived to have ruffled the surface of the stream of life or to have questioned its depth. It was the book. The book is an alternative. The book is a departure. The book is all your own work. There can be something disturbing about such qualities. And while it is more than obvious that my memoirs created no great disturbance, they did have the very beneficial result of enabling me to observe and reflect upon the inevitably awkward position which autobiography may be seen to occupy in a culture where confession carries a variety of complicated hidden detonators.

## The realigned confessional

I often think that the ways we have evolved of writing about our common and at the same time not entirely common past in Ireland are somewhat misdirected, and that instead of a history vested in state papers and rent rolls, a history of religious experience be written. Leave aside for the moment how much people drank and look at how much people read; rather than a dissection of the factional politics of this or that political episode, stimulate the public's interest in the clerks, soldiers, chauffeurs and the like from which so many of us have sprung, and who bear no resemblance whatsoever to Antaeus, though are nonetheless valuable for all that. Perhaps such thoughts are no more than the expression – the no doubt ignorant expression, moreover – of somebody living far away wishing to have somebody to talk to (by which, of course, I mean somebody to listen). Yet thoughts of this kind return when the subject of confession in Ireland comes up, a psycho-cultural narrative of which would make a fascinating study. And among the aspects of the subject such a study would have to consider is the dual meaning of confession: the highly charged political activity of informing, on the one hand, and the equally fraught sacrament of penance, as it used to be called (itself a suggestive phrase), on the other.

The political form of confession is of grave public consequence, of course, and hence must be carried out clandestinely. Its religious counterpart is at the very least of equal personal significance, but takes place in a public forum. Speech obviously makes the two activities similar, particularly since in both cases the speech is of a kind which reposes confidence in, and the prospect of reward from, the powerful authority to whom the confessions are made. Yet to be effective, the speech must partake of official silence, ensuring that confession is understood as essentially clandestine and covert, a speech act which both enlists social structures of prime importance and overrides their social character. There is no need to succumb to the clerical cloak and Caesarian dagger imagery which suggests itself here to perceive that what confession in those two conventional senses amounts to is a far cry from the very audible fanfare with which Rousseau introduces himself in his *Confessions*: 'I am commending an undertaking, hitherto without precedent, and which will never find an imitator. I desire to set before my fellows the likeness of a man in all the truth of nature, and that man myself. Myself alone!' (2000: 1).

It can hardly be argued that, whatever their status and influence in the collective consciousness of the country, the twin or even reciprocal versions of incrimination which confession articulates is exclusive to Ireland. The distinctive intimacies of Irish life, its territoriality, neighbourliness, clannishness and strong sense of local loyalties may indeed make both the self-incrimination of the church version and the incrimination of others of the state version more present to people's minds, resulting perhaps in a privileging of penance and an equally affirmative repudiation of the informer. What does seem peculiar to Irish conditions, though – or did until the last 20 years or so – is the absence of any secular middle ground which might provide a discursive space where the intellectual claustrophobia produced by thinking in terms of the conflicting binaries of church and state could be offset. The emergence of such a space through the introduction of various theoretical discourses, for example, or because of changes in the pressures exerted by church and state, has been one of the most noteworthy features of recent Irish culture. And although it is difficult to quantify with any precision the contribution a particular discursive form has made to the demarcation of the space in question, autobiography is an obvious, if insufficiently acknowledged, instance of the expansion of room in which to speak.

Rousseau, having sounded off, takes the additionally radical step of envisaging his book as being equal to the ultimate confessional occasion, the Day of Judgement, where he imagines it speaking to excellent effect on his account. The rhetorical extravagance of this manoeuvre is by no means insignificant in itself because of the way it underlines the implicit linguistic challenge of autobiography: dramatic claims are essential to self-authorisation. Of more fundamental importance than such linguistic turns, however, is what might be termed the institutional turn of Rousseau's subversion of the confessional. In his hands confession becomes a form which is used, firstly, to assert difference and singularity, in contrast to the complicity and dependence central to the more familiar forms of confession, and secondly, to demonstrate that this new kind of confession has some exemplary potential in terms of, at the very least, a self-accepting candour, articulation of which will, it is thought, grant others permission to speak.

It would be an exaggeration to claim that Rousseau singlehandedly released confession from the shackles imposed on it by church and state. Nevertheless, his reorientation of the confessional can be used as means of suggesting a sense of the actual and potential impact which the consolidation of autobiography as a worthwhile discursive option has had on Irish culture. Terms such as witnessing and testifying and securing a hearing, for example, are no longer tied to judicial process, but may be valuably adapted to frame and empower accounts of trials which have no bearing on the courts or any other state apparatus, or alternatively may place before the public matters of concern with which the courts, or the state, dealt with inadequately, or not at all, or otherwise botched. Such acts of self-representation convey a recognition, however underdeveloped, of not merely the existence but the pressures of personal history and the problematic nature of difference, pressures which the presumption of speaking out authenticates and releases. And these acts also contribute to a more elastic sense of informing, not only by changing the audience to which information is being directed but also by transmitting the information in a manner which is the opposite of clandestine.

It is important not to exaggerate. This new confessional departure should not be thought of as Rousseau's 'myself alone' replacing *sinn féin amháin*, the moral and watchword of the national narrative. Any such conception of the role of the autobiographical in recent Irish culture would simply replicate the binary thinking which the autobiographical is so adept at complicating, if by no other means than by seeking to sustain a dual focus, one which will make personal narrative more visible and viable but which will also satisfy the desire that this narrative be reconciled with a more broadly based one which tells the story of who we Irish now are. Autobiography affirms individual identity even as it searches for ratifications of it. In the present Irish context, however, the impetus to affirm is paradoxically reinforced by the scaling down of ratifying agencies. While once upon a time, there was an active working assumption that personal history could be collapsed, for better or worse, into the national narrative, now the consensus projected by the national narrative is of limited utility and has a largely notional existence.

As to myself, inferring that I was an informer, snake in the grass or any other form of invertebrate prattler had very little effect on me. I had nothing, really, in the way of secret skeletons to exhume, and though mentioning names, places, turns of events and battles long ago produced a sometimes unpleasant shock of recognition among readers intimate with the details, if anything my writing came from a memory that was, in part at least, overcompensating for the family history I would never know. Ignorance was my strongest narrative impetus, just as silence was my richest vein of raw material. To me, there was no dirty linen to speak of, although I came to realise that the dirt of the linen is something its custodians are the best judges of, and that the very act of publication presupposes not merely secrets but the shame that divulging them is thought to ensue ineluctably by people not used (for reasons of, say, family politics) to being open. I would have thought that in any case the dirtier the linen the greater the need for a public cleansing, if only because there are far more hands in public to complete the task, or simply to reveal, even if by opposition, the difficulty of finding a brand of cleanser which will not damage the fabric.

And it doesn't bother me, either, if I'm thought of as an informer. I accept the label's connotation of collaborating with the enemy, which in this case has certain noteworthy class, cultural and linguistic connotations, all areas in which I have built a life for myself beyond the one into which I was born. One implication is that I have moved beyond the national, which can also be read as having accepted the King's shilling, as though that's the ideological gratuity which comes with assuming the uniform of the King's English. The story of such selling out – if that is what it is – and the story of how I think of it are too elaborate to go into here, though if they are stories there are two sides to them, and my interest in trying to tell them would again be in how the different sides might speak in each other's hearing. The paucity of my information and an aversion to the current spectacle-and-sensation codes of self-projection have combined to ensure that my informing has been pathetic enough. It hasn't been either outspoken or outrageous enough to be arraigned for, and has damaged nothing more serious than *amour propre*. Since I tried to write without putting anyone on trial, I don't see any reason to be put on trial for doing so. And if writing a book is in some sense an over-reaction and a distortion, so is the desire to write off what has been written, as certain minor, scene-setting figures wished to do, objecting to their names being mentioned, as though the mere mention amounted to a form of 'outing' or some sort of trespass on private property.

Like everything else, such objections have an illustrative and exemplary force. For one thing, they remind me of some of the reasons why I could only make the symbolic, memorialising return to provincial life. Regarded more objectively, however, they also suggest how thinly nourished and poorly articulated the petit bourgeois cult of privacy can be. Irish life does not hold exclusive rights on this particular form of underdevelopment by any means. But it is a kind of impoverishment which has a special resonance in Irish conditions. Its continuing prevalence, discernible in the difficulty in getting the story out and getting the story straight and entering it into the public record, is an indication of the manner in which certain areas of national life – the moral and the economic, for example – can be fundamentally out of touch with one another. And it also suggests what a closed book the national narrative could be. Because of its potent emphasis on a cultural and ideological ethos of unity, a set of official assumptions arose whereby the majority – the people, as they were called – were considered characters in the same story, and had to be manipulated in the interests of the story's integrity, an integrity which was considered to be identical with the common good.

The informer begs to differ, and in telling his or her story interrupts the national narrative, the even tenor and unimpeachable consistency of which are crucial to its power and status. This is a narrative which has to be the model of the unity – and unanimity – it seeks to project. (That unanimity is one of Irish life's anxieties seems to be reflected in the public sphere, at least, by the problem of effective opposition.) The informer, however, ventures a redaction of official memory, explores and exploits the national narrative's formal properties, edits its idiolect of achievement and completeness, reveals more than can comfortably be told. In doing so, he or she diversifies the consensual outlook, which is very threatening to its unitary foundational principles. These contributions, despite their potentially subversive consequences, are not made in the clandestine spirit of informing as historically understood, but rather with a view to openness and to enlarging the scope of the collective conversation which animates a culture more effectively than does a narrative which has been handed down. In its retrieval from historical obloquy, therefore, and indeed in its inversion of the stereotypical associations and complicated political alignments that this inversion potentiates, informing can be seen as the signature of the possibilities of cultural conversation. Thus it may also be thought of as placing the seal on a particular historical, cultural and discursive era, and in doing so exemplifying the opportunities as well as the problems presented by a post-nationalist Irish culture.

Similar findings emerge from thinking about the ways in which autobiography adapts the religious associations of the confessional. The reorientation here concerns morality, with a particular focus on matters of moral agency, institutional values and the dignity of the subject. It also involves moving the ground for moral judgement from the realm of wrongs, disciplines and punishments to that of civil and cultural rights, among which is the right to be heard, or the right to break silence. Once again, witnessing, testimony and judgement are to the fore. Their significance now, however, resides in the transfer of power from confessor to confessee. And the resultant exercise of control over all aspects of the material being confessed not only dispels the ritualistic secrecy characteristic of the sacrament but authenticates the subject's sense of entitlement to his or her narrative. The traditional confessional structure was conceived of in terms of a two-part transaction: a serious and difficult critique of the confessee's narrative, followed by the absorption of that narrative into one whose powers of forgiveness and redemption made it conceptually superior. The confessee traded in the weakness and failings of his or her own narrative in exchange for the inner wherewithal to live with him or herself. The bearing that such a discursive economy had on such issues as permission to speak, the limits of speech, the patriarchy of narrative and narrative agency speaks for itself.

Clearly the need to participate in this economy persists, and the exchange must be presumed to be effective for those choosing to identify with it. What the autobiographically confessional radicalises, however, is the implicit link between participation and choice. The change in focus from structure to subject which autobiography enacts suggests that the work of interpretation, codification, analysis and reconciliation previously carried out by the confessor can now be attempted by the confessee. And even if the attempt fails, to undertake it in the first place has exemplary and expressive value. The nature of the material revealed by secular confession is also obviously relevant. In a number of cases – Paddy Doyle's *The God Squad* (1988), for instance – autobiography accommodates the author's indictment of his treatment at clerical hands and denotes his now having moved beyond the conditions in question towards safety and self-respect. Such survivor confessions detail wrongs endured, not wrongs perpetrated, an approach which not only challenges the silence under which the wrongs had been concealed but which alters the focus of confession from self-incrimination to the incrimination of impersonal agencies such as rules, policies, mentalities and other similar attributes of the apparatuses of order. Pointing out the impossibility, as experienced, in reconciling the intended function of these apparatuses with their actual effects, the confessions rehearse the possibility of recuperating the subject's abjection and advance the desire for social structures willing to integrate rather than segregate, to cherish rather than punish, to acknowledge individuality rather than dismiss it. And part of the radical character of such confessions, morally speaking, is that they are testimonies of innocence, made in the realisation that the traditional binaries of stain and sponge, shepherd and stray, submission and uplift are not the only ways in which confession can be a statement of values, even if the values in question remain to be encoded as part of the legitimate expectations, or rights, of the individual citizen.

An important area which survivor narratives have in common, whether their context is domestic or institutional, is sexuality, and its importance derives not merely from the nature of the area itself but from the repressed status prescribed for it by traditional Irish confessional culture. This was an aspect of human behaviour for which the word 'trouble' was a familiar synonym. Like 'informer', 'trouble' is a word which can also be perceived to have undergone a change of status and resonance due to its autobiographical exposure, by virtue of which the trouble has been relocated from the sphere of private silence to that of public contestation. Again the result is an increased emphasis on, and challenge to, the assumptions, tolerances, levels of awareness and overall sympathies of the consensual ethos in which the social conscience is embodied. The emphasis is created by the individual conscience's resistance to being censured or impugned, as manifested in its formal adaptation of handed-down confessional conventions. This appropriation of discourse may be cited as another instance of the complicated coming into being of, if not necessarily a post-Catholic, then a post-theocratic Ireland, an entity which is almost an inevitable counterpart of the post-nationalist nation. The nature of this entity is still in flux, and indeed in certain respects may be more apparent than real. But looking at the combined revisions of the confessional in both the juridical and the sacramental sense, a number of new and unaccustomed tendencies may be discerned. One is towards the democratisation of discourse: 'Ireland has more than one story', in the words of Hugo Hamilton's Onkel Ted in *The Speckled People* (2003: 283). Accompanying this is an increased awareness of individuality and of individual rights. The public articulation of difference, diversity and entitlement to one's own story has also become somewhat easier. Such aspects of an evolving culture offer the possibility of reconciling the aspiration to liberty, equality and fraternity shared, however nominally, by all republics with Irish society's belated modernisation. And if it can hardly be claimed that autobiography pioneered awareness of such a possibility, at least the form can be thought of as bringing a distinctive refinement to the manner in which this possibility and its concomitant issues may be focused and discussed.

## Autobiography or nostalgia?

Yet, for all of recent Irish autobiography's welcome opening of doors and windows and minds, the substance of its overall accomplishment remains debatable when viewed from the perspectives of artistic engagement and cultural impact. One of the obvious features of the revaluation of the confessional is its implicit acceptance of an end of innocence, an end which is consciously brought about by a formal enactment of making up one's mind. And even when innocence and confession are not germane to a given autobiography's actual data – Denis Donoghue's *Warrenpoint* (1990), for example – the avowal of consciousness is an indispensable precondition for the representation of difference which is one of the form's most valuable cultural properties. That said, however, to a dismayingly large degree Irish autobiography can be considered more impressive as a reminder of untapped rhetorical resources rather than as an exemplification of those resources' development. As such, it is perhaps perfectly congruent with its immediate demographic. At any rate, what many Irish autobiographies – in fact, many of the most commercially successful ones – suggest is that their authors are not quite sure what to make of their material. And this lack of awareness, a deficiency in what might be termed 'present-mindedness', is also what might be expected of Irish readers still recovering from the self-inflicted diminished status of the master narratives of church and state, in which not so long ago commanding versions of their identities had been inscribed. Such a diminution is accompanied by those very problems which autobiography is particularly well suited to address – problems of faith and doubt, continuity and change, identity and community. It seems clear enough from events and revelations pertaining to church and state that a revaluation of values has become a cultural possibility even as it remains an impossibility to realise or consolidate it.

Yet rather than engage with such problems, much Irish autobiography has reacted against them. The principal manifestation of this reaction is the childhood memoir. As somebody who cut his artistic teeth on this sub-genre, I am one of the last people entitled to bite the hand that fed me by being critical of it. But of course one never sees one's own experience in generic terms. Indeed the assumption of an autobiographical persona implies a shedding of the social camouflage and conditioned intellectual reflexes characteristic of the generic context and its roles, even if it doesn't always work out that way. To which may be added that objecting to a sub-genre which includes, for instance, Wordsworth's *Prelude* rather compromises one's critical credentials. In other words, I have nothing against the childhood memoir as such, whatever its content might be. My own childhood had its perplexities and was punctuated by bouts of unhappiness, my own and others, the latter a troubling influence on the former, needless to say. But I don't think of my childhood as having been particularly unhappy, and I certainly do not consider unhappiness to be an autobiographical prerequisite, although I obviously support speaking about unhappiness and about everything else as well. But I do mean speaking about it, which means not simply documenting it but entering into some kind of relation to it, making demands of it to yield up its nature and genesis. Childhood as a subject is more effectively treated as an imaginative reservoir to be plumbed rather than an archaeological dig yielding trophies to be displayed.

In certain respects, to be critical of works which themselves reject a critical perspective – usually unconsciously – is beside the point. After all, treating the past in the spirit of *dolce far niente* and as if it were a landscape for the beachcombing tourist is not only part of the autobiographical mix; in its very anodyne character nostalgia offers readers visions of the kind of past they desire, devoid of historical or any other species of trouble, apart perhaps from that issuing from the will of God. Even saying that much, however, recognises that a specific set of attitudes and dispositions are at work and that these constitute a very identifiable state of mind. And the existence of an audience and appetite – a market, as the saying goes – for this type of outlook prompts some curiosity about where the nostalgic need comes from and what it might mean. Obviously, I cannot go into the whole sociology of literary taste here (though it is a pity somebody doesn't do more to establish the material realities which sustain and promote Irish cultural phenomena). But it doesn't seem too wild a speculation to think of the nostalgia boom as on the one hand facilitating a somewhat condescending backward look at an allegedly more innocent time, the barely credible precursor of the much more accelerated here and now, and on the other hand as appropriating, endorsing and promoting images and ideas which, by being represented as simple and traditional, function as a means of resisting the modernising present. It hardly needs pointing out that no time is innocent. The treatment of simplicity and tradition as synonyms does not seem particularly tenable. And loss is proposed as an incontrovertible signature of authenticity, with phrases such as 'lost time', 'lost world', 'lost way of life' used to attract readers' attention, even though such phrases also convey the distance and intimacy on which nostalgia's cultural ambiguities and lack of ideological awareness are based.

It might be that growing up is not so easy. It might be that the past is no good to us, that it is only imaginable in an arcadian light of golden hours and country frolics. It might be that the land we grew up in is only precious now that it has been abandoned, not necessarily abandoned formally but no longer a place that's central to identity, or at least to the rhetoric of identity declaimed by our leaders. It might be that we don't know what to think, that there are no models of thought available in which we might have faith. It might be that, in independence, we have less of life than we expected, less than we – needing to believe the language of independence – thought we had been promised. In which case, prospects of childhood may be read as images of an ironic autonomy, harmless, aimless and powerless. It might be that acting the innocent is more and more necessary as virtually daily revelations from church and state make unavoidable the fact that innocent is what we are not. If nostalgia has a lot to answer for, it is because there's a lot that it's avoiding. And underneath its veneer – that smooth, protective carapace of facility, sentimentality and compensation, detectable in the first instance by its uniform tone – there is nostalgia's overwhelming sense of needing to mark the end of something. Even if the end is a consummation devoutly to be wished and the manner of marking it is to caper on the grave you've dug for it, the end is the structuring principle (I'm thinking here of *Angela's Ashes*, a work built around a frightening consistency of breakdowns, forsakings and termini).

The trouble with nostalgia is that it doesn't want to give itself credit for – or do I mean take responsibility for? – its complicated activities. That kind of trouble is the opposite to the type that makes autobiography worthwhile, the type that comes with speaking freely, with claiming individuality and the various entitlements to difference that come with it, with being the exception who proves no rules, with travelling through the underworlds of not being good enough, not being wanted, of wanting and desire, which lie, uneasy and ignored, beneath the fraying standards of faith, fatherland and family, to which all eyes were reputed to be raised. The memoir of nostalgia – which is what these generic childhood recollections might well be called, if only as a reminder that autobiography is, obviously enough, not a thing of the past but of the present – raises certain questions by default and points unknowingly to problems worth considering. But there is no need to be so oblique and coy that the reader has to pick up all the formal and intellectual slack. Such an approach, indeed, seems to contradict the basic autobiographical impulse, and is a variation on that well-known Irish solution to an Irish problem: 'whatever you say, say nothing'. And in any case, the limitations of the nostalgic can readily be seen in those recent Irish childhood memoirs which are animated by less glibly reconcilable attitudes to the past, as though autobiography itself needed to provide not a delib-erate corrective to nostalgia but a means of remembering other voices, other landscapes; doubting voices, inner landscapes. Among the works I have in mind are Mannix Flynn's *Nothing to Say* (1983), Adrian Kenny's *Istanbul Diary* (1994), Dermot Healy's *The Bend for Home* (1996), Hugh Maxton's *Waking* (1997), Aidan Higgins's trilogy, *Donkey's Years* (1995), *Dog Days* (1998) and *The Whole Hog* (2000) and, with a view to autobiography's generic flexibility, the essays of Hubert Butler (1990).

These works delineate alternative profiles of Irishness, those found for example, in emigration, in confessional difference, in political opposition. While I wouldn't for a moment suggest that such experiences can be compared to narratives of neglect and abuse, I do think that common ground of at least a rudimentary kind exists between these different realms of experience, a psychological and cultural terrain which, though it seems to be beyond the pale of reassuring personal narratives, exerts something like a gravitational pull on them, draws them into its sphere with critical results. This terrain maps out its discursive reality by investigating deficiencies and deprivations, by bringing into focus the powerful presence in Irish private and social life of such invisible entities as absence, oblivion, an ethic of expendability and, in various senses of the term, broken words. The experience of such entities, of course, renders porous the consensual solidarity which is considered the seed and fruit of independence.

One noteworthy feature of these alternative stories is that, though they too have loss as their subject, they display a strong aversion to it having the last word. Rather, loss is seen as a necessary preliminary to the acceptance, self-control and sympathetic understanding which not only enables the hitherto marginalised subject to inhabit a position of his or her own choosing, but which in a more general way affirms the gestures towards moving forward which underwrite autobiography. Forgiveness is also very important here – going back to the confessional for a minute – all the more so in view of its functioning in an explicitly heterodox manner. And movement forward may be regarded, as well, as an embrace of the present and of its promise of another life, continuous with but not beholden to the one being written about. A prominent feature of Aidan Higgins's autobiographical works, for example, is their creation of as complete a sense of presentness as possible – even, or especially, including its transience. In that regard, it seems to me, these alternative works are more historically accurate than their nostalgic counterparts, since they reproduce not only an idea of, but that idea's articulation through experience of a pattern, a lesson, an outcome that has been shaped by, and is being reshaped by, a complicated dialogue between times.

There are other features of these works that are also worth bearing in mind. Among these are dissidence, with rejection, variously understood, frequently following in its wake; desire, with sexuality (including reconstructions of parental sexual experience) unashamedly to the fore; imagination, as memory's counterpoint and critic, as in Dermot Healy's recreation of going to the pictures in Cavan town in *The Bend for Home*; and tolerance, which not only comes across by the inclusiveness of the content but by indications in the narrative tone that the author has more interesting things on his or her mind than passing judgement. All these elements are part of a vocabulary of possibility. It is interesting, too, how in these books reading and writing, speaking and being spoken to are significantly to the fore. Not that Irish autobiographers of whatever stripe have found it useful to divide their stories into reading and writing, à la Sartre in *Les Mots*. But alternative memoirs of the kind I'm trying to describe – without, again, resorting to the solecism of a list – are also more verbally engaged, more alive to the inconsistencies of language, and are written by authors more inclined to let the play of consciousness acquired through their reading to refine and illuminate their recuperation of experience. Spoiled Prousts? Perhaps. But there are a large number of much less preferable manifestations of literary intelligence. Besides these verbal issues, even when they have nothing directly to do with the data being recollected, are in their way reminders of a continuing engagement with permission to speak. And when they have everything to do with the content of the memory bank, a memoir such as *The Speckled People* materialises, a work in which critique and endorsement of the permission are crucially and excruciatingly intertwined.

The attributes I have just been trying to describe are, to my mind, important signs of life. They signal a readiness to own up to as much of one's own life as one can manage, to take steps towards a language of one's own and to engage in a judicious amount of free thinking. They place on the cultural agenda a few basic questions asked by Roland Barthes 30 years ago, when the perceived need for autobiography in Ireland was no bigger than the shadow of a man's hand and the old stories were still essentially the order of the day: 'What would be the worth of a society that ceased to reflect upon itself? What would become of it? And how can we see ourselves except by talking to one another?' (1986: 197). As well as that, these attributes introduce the notion of choice – which strikes me as the most fundamental signal of all – that Irish writers would elect to tell different kinds of stories, stories without blame and without remorse, stories that at the very least invite reconsideration of our putatively rigid and implacable moral and political genealogies. Not to mention the fact that they would choose to tell on themselves. As I can confirm, there's something very liberating in getting the story told, in taking charge of the need and the desire to do it. And by doing it, an additional sense of an audience, a public, is created. Most writers' words fall on mostly deaf ears, I suppose, so I don't want to be thought of as making any very revolutionary, or even therapeutic, claims for the impact of autobiography. Still, it's hard for me not to think that the form conveys a distinctive sense of possibility, of opening up and exemplifying changes of mind and heart which may indeed resonate with, or perhaps create fruitful dissonance with, more general changes in the way we in Ireland live now.

For reasons of shame, humiliation and various other related feelings (self-hatred, fear – it's a long list), I little thought when I left Ireland that it was my own story that I would end up wanting to tell, much less telling. Anything but that! Now I find that having done so enables me to use the phrase 'we in Ireland' with at least a certain amount of confidence. That 'we', of course, is an autobiographical entity that is all my own work, not anything to sustain statistical analysis or demographic enumeration. It is a thing of fragments and splinters, traces and notions, pressures and idiocies. The very tentativeness and flux of its nature, its contradictoriness, its awkward integrity and tendency to be repetitious, its combination of old accents and new idiolect are nothing like the real thing, no doubt. But it's been my ticket home – something else I little thought. Not my ticket back, mind. Home. A prototype of belonging which I've evidently had to invent for myself, where I could open up about love, fear, work, pain, hope and various other fundamental four-letter words about which I was never sure before that I had permission to speak.

# Bibliography

Adams, G. 1982. *Falls Memories*. Dingle: Brandon.

Adams, G. 1990. *Cage Eleven*. Dingle: Brandon.

Adams, G. 1994. *Selected Writings*. Dingle: Brandon.

Adams, G. 1996. *Before the Dawn: An Autobiography*. London: Heinemann.

Adams, G. 2003. *Hope and History: Making Peace in Ireland*. Dingle: Brandon/ Mount Eagle.

Adkins, L. 2002. *Revisions: Gender & Sexuality in Late Modernity*. Buckingham: Open University Press.

Alexander, S. 1994. *Becoming a Woman and other Essays in 19th and 20th Century Feminist History*. London: Virago Press.

Almqvist, B. 1999. 'Oidhreacht Scéalaíochta Pheig', in *Ceiliúradh an Bhlascaoid 3: Peig Sayers Scéalaí 1878–1958*, ed. M. Ní Chéilleachair. Baile Átha Cliath: Coiscéim. 77–100.

Anderson, B. 1991. *Imagined Communities*. London: Verso.

Anderson, L. 1997. *Women and Autobiography in the Twentieth Century: Remembered Futures*. Brighton: Harvester Wheatsheaf.

Anderson, L. 2001. *Autobiography*. London: Routledge.

Anderson, P. 2004. 'A magical realist and his reality', *The Nation*, 278:3. 23–26.

Ardoyne Commemoration Project. 2002. *Ardoyne: The Untold Truth*. Belfast: Beyond the Pale.

Armitstead, C. 2001. 'A tale of two tribes'. *Guardian Review*, 27 January. 10.

Arrowsmith, A. 2000. 'Plastic Paddy: Negotiating identity in second–generation "Irish-English" writing', *Irish Studies Review*, 8:1. 35–43.

Arthur, C. 1999. *Irish Nocturnes*. Aurora, Colorado: The Davies Group.

Arthur, C. 2002. *Irish Willow*. Aurora, Colorado: The Davies Group.

Augustine, St. 2001. *Confessions*. Oxford: Oxford University Press.

Barclay, T. 1995. *Memoirs and Medleys: The Autobiography of a Bottle Washer*. Leicester: Coalville Publishing Company.

Barthes, R. 1986. *The Grain of the Voice: Interviews 1962–1980*. New York: Hill and Wang.

Bauman, R. 1986. *Story, Performance and Event: Contextual Studies in Oral Narrative*. Cambridge: Cambridge University Press.

Beck, U. 1992. *Risk Society: Towards a New Modernity*. London: Sage.

Beckett, S. 1968. *Krapp's Last Tape and Embers*. London: Faber.

Behan, B. 1990. *Borstal Boy*. London: Arrow.

Beiner, G. and Bryson, A. 2003. 'Listening to the past and talking to each other: Problems and possibilities facing oral history in Ireland', *Irish Economic and Social History*, XXX. 71–78.

Beja, M. ed. 1973. *James Joyce: 'Dubliners' and 'A Portrait of the Artist as a Young Man': A Casebook*. Basingstoke: Macmillan.

Benjamin, W. 1979. 'A Berlin Chronicle', in *One-Way Street and Other Writings*, trans. E. Jephcott and K. Shorter. London: New Left Books.

Beverley, J. 1996. 'The margin at the Center: *On Testimonio*', in Gugelberger, 23–41.

Bhabha, H. 1994. 'Between Identities: Homi Bhabha interviewed by Paul Thompson', in *Migration and Identity*, eds. R. Benmayor and A. Skotnes. Oxford: Oxford University Press. 183–99.

Blaney, R. 1996. *Presbyterians and the Irish Language*. Belfast: Ulster Historical Foundation/Ultach Trust.

Bloomfield, K. 1998. *We Will Remember Them*. Belfast: Northern Ireland Office.

Boland, E. 1993. 'Continuing the encounter,' in *Ordinary People Dancing: Essays on Kate O'Brien*, ed. E. Walshe. Cork: Cork University Press. 11–15.

Boland, E. 1996. *Object Lessons: The Life of the Woman and the Poet in Our Time*. London: Vintage.

Boland, E. 1997. 'The veil over the future's face,' *Profession*, 13–17.

Booker, M. K. 1995. *Joyce, Bakhtin and the Literary Tradition: Towards a Comparative Cultural Poetics*. Michigan: University of Michigan Press.

Bowen, E. 1950. 'The mulberry tree', in *Collected Impressions*. London: Longmans.

Bowen, E. 1951. 'Autobiography as an art,' *The Saturday Review of Literature*, March 17.

Bowen, E. 1962. *Afterthoughts*. London: Longmans.

Bowen, E. 1975. *Pictures and Conversations*. London: Allen Lane.

Bowen, E. 1999. *Bowen's Court and Seven Winters*. London: Vintage.

Boyle, J. 2001. *Galloway Street: Growing Up Irish in Scotland*. London: Doubleday.

Brah, A. 1996. *Cartographies of Diaspora: Contesting Identities*. London: Routledge.

Breathnach, D. and Ní Mhurchú, M. 1994. *Beathaisnéis a Ceathair: 1882–1982*. Baile Átha Cliath: An Clóchomhar.

Breathnach, D. and Ní Mhurchú, M. 2003. *Beathaisnéis 1983–2002*. Baile Átha Cliath: An Clóchomhar.

Breen, S. 2003a. 'Adair: "Stone is an egotistical, paranoid schizophrenic" ', *Sunday Life*, 8 June.

Breen, S. 2003b. 'Mad Dog for hire?', *Sunday Life*, 3 August.

Breen, S. 2003c. 'The many tales of Gerry Adams', *News Letter*, 2 October.

Brewer, M. F. 2001. 'Politics and life writing', in Jolly, 721–23.

Brown, T. 1985. 'Literary autobiography in twentieth-century Ireland', in *The Genius of Irish Prose* ed. A. Martin. Dublin: Mercier Press. 89–98.

Browne, N. 1986. *Against the Tide*. Dublin: Gill and Macmillan.

Buckley, M. 1997. 'Sitting on your politics: The Irish among the British and the women among the Irish', in *Location and Dislocation in Contemporary Irish Society*, ed. J. Mac Laughlin. Cork: Cork University Press. 94–132.

Buckley, V. 1979. 'Imagination's home', *Quadrant*. 24–29.

Butler, H. 1990. *The Sub-Prefect Should Have Held His Tongue and Other Essays*, ed. R. F. Foster. London: Allen Lane.

Butler, H. 1996. *In the Land of Nod*. Dublin: Lilliput Press.

Cahalan, J. M. 1988. *The Irish Novel*. Dublin: Gill and Macmillan.

Cairns, D. and Richards. S. 1988. *Writing Ireland: Colonialism, Nationalism and Culture*. Manchester: Manchester University Press.

Calhoun, C. ed. 1994. *Social Theory and the Politics of Identity*. Oxford: Blackwell.

Campbell, S. 2000. 'Beyond "Plastic Paddy": A re-examination of the second-generation Irish in England', in *The Great Famine and Beyond: Irish Migrants in Britain in the Nineteenth and Twentieth Centuries*, ed. D. M. MacRaild. Dublin: Irish Academic Press. 266–88.

Campbell, S. 2002. 'Sounding Out the Margins: Ethnicity and popular music in British cultural studies', in *Across the Margins: Cultural Identities and Change in the Atlantic Archipelago*, eds. G. Smyth and G. Norquay. Manchester: Manchester University Press. 117–36.

Canavan, B. 1994. 'Story-tellers and writers: Irish identity in emigrant labourers' autobiographies, 1870–1970', in *The Irish World Wide: The Creative Migrant*, ed. P. O'Sullivan. Leicester: Leicester University Press. 154–69.

Carlyle, T. 1896a. *Critical and Miscellaneous Essays*, ed. H. D. Traill, vol. 2. London: Chapman and Hall.

Carlyle, T. 1896b. *Sartor Resartus*, ed. H. D. Traill. London: Chapman and Hall.

Carlyle, T. 1993 [1841]. *On Heroes, Hero-Worship, & the Heroic in History*, eds. M. Goldberg *et al*. Berkeley: University of California Press.

Carson, C. 1990. *Belfast Confetti*. Winston-Salem: Wake Forest University Press.

Carson, C. 1997. *The Star Factory*. London: Granta.

Clifford, J. 1994. 'Diasporas', *Cultural Anthropology*, 9:3. 302–38.

Coe, R. N. 1984. *When the Grass was Taller: Autobiography and the Experience of Childhood*. New Haven: Yale University Press.

Connerton, P. 1989. *How Societies Remember*. Cambridge: Cambridge University Press.

Coughlan, P. 1999. 'An Léiriú ar Shaol na mBan i dTéacsanna Dírbheathaisnéise Pheig Sayers', in *Ceiliúradh an Bhlascaoid 3: Peig Sayers Scéalaí 1878–1958*, ed. M. Ní Chéilleachair. Baile Átha Cliath: Coiscéim. 20–57.

Coulter, C. and Coleman, S. eds. 2003. *The End of Irish History? Critical Reflections on the Celtic Tiger*. Manchester: Manchester University Press.

Coxhead, E. 1961. *Lady Gregory: A Literary Portrait*. New York: Harcourt Brace.

Cronin, M. 2000a. *Across the Lines: Travel, Language, Translation*. Cork: Cork University Press.

Cronin, M. 2000b. 'An domhan trí mheán na Gaeilge: "Ag taisteal dom 'mach"', *An Aimsir Óg: Cuid a Dó*. 289–95.

Cronin, M. 2003. *Time Tracks: Scenes from the Irish Everyday*. Dublin: New Island.

Cruise O'Brien, M. 1977. 'An tOileánach', in Jordan, 25–38.

Cruise O'Brien, M. 2003. *The Same Age as the State*. Dublin: O'Brien Press.

Davis, T. [1910]. *Thomas Davis: Selections from his Prose and Poetry*, ed. T. W. Rolleston. Dublin: Talbot Press.

Davis-Goff, A. 1990. *Walled Gardens: Scenes from an Anglo-Irish Childhood*. London: Barrie and Jenkins.

Davys, M. 1725. *The Works of Mrs Davys*, vol. 1. London: H. Woodfall.

De Blaghd, E. 1957. *Trasna na Bóinne*. Baile Átha Cliath: Sáirséal agus Dill.

De Man, P. 1984. *The Rhetoric of Romanticism*. New York: Columbia University Press.

Deane, S. 1985. *Celtic Revivals: Essays in Modern Irish Literature 1880–1980*. London: Faber.

Deane, S. 1986. *A Short History of Irish Literature*. London: Hutchinson.

Deane, S. 1991. 'Autobiography and Memoirs, 1890–1980', in *The Field Day Anthology of Modern Irish Writing*, ed. S. Deane, vol. 3. Derry: Field Day, 380–83.

Deane, S. 1996. *Reading in the Dark*. London: Jonathan Cape.

Delaney, E. 2000. *Demography, State and Society. Irish Migration to Britain, 1921–1971*. Liverpool: Liverpool University Press.

Denvir, J. 1910. *The Life Story of an Old Rebel*. Dublin: Sealy, Bryers and Walker.

Devlin, A. 1968. *The Anne Devlin Jail Journal, faithfully written down by Luke Cullen*, ed. J. Finegan. Cork: Mercier Press.

Devlin, B. 1969. *The Price of My Soul*. London: Pan Books.

Devlin, E. N. 2000. *Speaking Volumes: A Dublin Childhood*. Belfast: Blackstaff Press.

Devlin, P. 1993. *Straight Left: An Autobiography*. Belfast: Blackstaff Press.

Diment, G. 1994. *The Autobiographical Novel of Consciousness: Goncharov, Woolf and Joyce*. Gainesville: University of Florida Press.

Diprose, R. 1994. *The Bodies of Women: Ethics, embodiment and sexual difference*. London: Routledge.

Doheny, M. 1920 [1849]. *The Felon's Track*. Dublin: Gill.

Donoghue, D. 1990. *Warrenpoint*. New York: Knopf.

Dorst, J. D. 1989. *The Written Suburb: An American Site, An Ethnographic Dilemma*. Philadelphia: University of Pennsylvania Press.

Douglass, F. 1996 [1893]. 'Life and times of Frederick Douglass', in *Autobiographies*. New York: The Library of America.

Doyle, P. 1988. *The God Squad*. Dublin: Raven Arts Press.

Duffy, C. G. 1884. *Young Ireland: A Fragment of Irish History 1840–1845*. Dublin: M. H. Gill.

Duffy, C. G. 1895. *Short Life of Thomas Davis*. London: Unwin.

Duffy, C. G. 1898. *My Life in Two Hemispheres*, vol. 2. London: Unwin.

Eagleton, T. 1995. *Heathcliff and the Great Hunger*. London: Verso.

Eagleton, T. 2001. *The Gatekeeper*. London: Allen Lane.

Eakin, P. J. 1985. *Fictions in Autobiography: Studies in the Art of Self-Invention*. Princeton: Princeton University Press.

Edgeworth, R. L. 1820. *Memoirs, [ . . . ] Concluded by his Daughter, Maria Edgeworth*, vol. 2. London: R. Hunter.

Edwards, R. D. 2002. 'Gerry the Liar', *Spectator*, 27 July.

Egerton, G. ed. 1994. *Political Memoir: Essays on the Politics of Memory*. London: Frank Cass.

Fahy, B. 1999. *Freedom of Angels*. Dublin: O'Brien Press.

Farrow, A. 1978. *George Moore*. Boston: Twayne.

Faulkner, B. 1978. *Memoirs of a Statesman*. London: Weidenfeld and Nicolson.

Feldman, S. and Laub, D. 1992. *Testimony: Crises of Witnessing in Literature, Psychoanalysis and History*. New York: Routledge.

Ferriter, D. 2002. 'Suffer little children? The historical validity of memoirs of Irish childhood', in *Childhood and Its Discontents*, eds. J. Dunne and J. Kelly. Dublin: Liffey Press. 69–105.

Fitz-simon, C. 1994. *The Boys: A biography of Micheál Mac Líammoír [sic] and Hilton Edwards*. London: Nick Hern Books.

Flynn, M. 1983. *Nothing to Say*. Dublin: Ward River Press.

Foster, R. F. 1988. *Modern Ireland 1600–1972*. Harmondsworth: Penguin.

Foster, R. F. 2001. *The Irish Story: Telling Tales and Making It Up in Ireland*. London: Allen Lane.

Franklin, B. 1986. *Autobiography and Other Writings*, ed. K. Silverman. New York: Viking Penguin.

Gagnier, R. 1991. *Subjectivities: A History of Self-Representation in Britain, 1832–1920*. Oxford: Oxford University Press.

Gallagher, P. 1939. *My Story*. London: Jonathan Cape.

Gamble, A. 2002. 'Political memoirs', *British Journal of Politics and International Relations*, 4:1. 141–51.

Garfitt, R. 1975. 'Constants in contemporary Irish fiction', in *Two Decades of Irish Writing: A Critical Survey*, ed. D. Dunn. Cheshire: Carcanet. 207–41.

Garland, R. 2001. *Gusty Spence*. Belfast: Blackstaff Press.

Garnett, M. and Aitken, I. 2002. *Splendid! Splendid! The Authorized Biography of Willie Whitelaw*. London: Jonathan Cape.

Garrett, P. M. 2000. 'The abnormal flight: the migration and repatriation of Irish unmarried mothers', *Social History*, 25:3. 330–43.

Gay, P. 1996. *The Naked Heart: The Bourgeois Experience: Victoria to Freud, Volume IV.* London: HarperCollins.

Giddens, A. 1990. *The Consequences of Modernity.* Cambridge: Polity Press.

Giddens, A. 1991. *Modernity and Self-Identity: Self and Society in the Late Modern Age.* Cambridge: Polity Press.

Gilmore, L. 2001. *The Limits of Autobiography: Trauma and Testimony.* Ithaca: Cornell University Press.

Gilroy, P. 1997. 'Diaspora and the detours of identity', in *Identity and Difference*, ed. K. Woodward. London: Sage. 299–346.

Giltrap, R. 1990. *An Ghaeilge in Eaglais na hÉireann.* Baile Átha Cliath: Cumann Gaelach na hEaglaise.

Glendinning, V. 1977. *Elizabeth Bowen: Portrait of a Writer.* London: Weidenfeld and Nicolson.

Goldman, P. and Taylor, B. eds. 1998. *Retrospective Adventures: Forrest Reid, Author and Collector.* Aldershot: Ashmolean Museum/Scholar Press.

Gramsci, A. 1991. *Selections from Cultural Writings*, eds. D. Forgacs and G. Nowell-Smith. Cambridge: Harvard University Press.

Gregory, I. A. 1972. *Our Irish Theatre: A Chapter of Autobiography.* Gerrards Cross: Colin Smythe.

Grubgeld, E. 1994. *George Moore and the Autogenous Self: The Autobiography and the Fiction.* Syracuse: Syracuse University Press.

Grubgeld, E. 1997. 'Anglo-Irish autobiography and the genealogical mandate', *Éire-Ireland*, 32:4. 96–115.

Grubgeld, E. 1997. 'Class, gender, and the forms of narrative: The autobiographies of Anglo-Irish women', in *Representing Ireland: Gender, Class, Nationality*, ed. S. Shaw Sailer. Gainesville: University Press of Florida. 133–55.

Grubgeld, E. 2004. *Anglo-Irish Autobiography: Class, Gender, and the Forms of Narrative.* Syracuse: Syracuse University Press

Gugelberger, G. M. ed. 1996. *The Real Thing. Testimonial Discourse and Latin America.* Durham: Duke University Press.

Haaken, J. 1998. *Pillar of Salt. Gender, Memory, and the Perils of Looking Back.* London: Free Association Books.

Haffenden, J. 1981. *Viewpoints: Poets in Conversation.* London: Faber.

Hamber B. and Wilson, R. eds. 2003. *Recognition and reckoning: the way ahead on victims' issues.* Democratic Dialogue Report 15.

Hamilton, H. 2003. *The Speckled People.* London: Fourth Estate.

Harbinson, R. 1960. *Song of Erne.* London: Faber.

Harbinson, R. 1961. *Up Spake the Cabin Boy.* London: Faber.

Harbinson, R. 1963. *The Protégé.* London: Faber.

Harbinson, R. 1987. *No Surrender: An Ulster Childhood.* Belfast: Blackstaff Press.

Harte, L. 2000. 'History Lessons: Postcolonialism and Seamus Deane's *Reading in the Dark*', *Irish University Review*, 30:1. 149–62.

Harte, L. 2003. 'Immigrant self-fashioning: The autobiographies of the Irish in Britain, 1856–1934', in *Ireland Abroad: Politics and Professions in the Nineteenth Century*, ed. O. Walsh. Dublin: Four Courts Press. 47–61.

Healy, D. 1996. *The Bend for Home: A Memoir.* London: Harvill Press.

Heaney, S. 1987. *The Haw Lantern.* London: Faber.

Hegarty, A. 2002. 'Truth, justice and reconciliation? The problem with truth processes', *Global Review of Ethnopolitics*, 2:1. 97–103.

Hickman, M. J. 1995. *Religion, Class and Identity: The State, the Catholic Church and the Education of the Irish in Britain.* Aldershot: Avebury.

244   *Bibliography*

Hickman, M. J., Morgan, S., Walter, B. and Bradley, J. 2005. 'The limitations of whiteness and the boundaries of Englishness: second-generation Irish identifications and positionings in multiethnic Britain', *Ethnicities*, 5:2. 160–82.

Higgins, A. 1972. *Balcony of Europe*. London: Calder and Boyars.

Higgins, A. 1977. *Scenes from a Receding Past*. London: John Calder.

Higgins, A. 1983. *Bornholm Night Ferry*. London: Allison and Busby.

Higgins, A. 1995. *Donkey's Years*. London: Secker and Warburg.

Higgins, A. 1998. *Dog Days*. London: Secker and Warburg.

Higgins, A. 2000. *The Whole Hog*. London: Secker and Warburg.

Hoggart, R. 1959. *The Uses of Literacy*. Harmondsworth: Penguin.

Holmquist, K. 1996. 'Mammy, I'm poignant', *Irish Times Weekend*, 20 February. 4.

Hughes, E. 1992. 'Ulsters of the senses', in *Lost Fields*, ed. D. Smyth, supplement to *Fortnight*, 306. 10–11.

Hughes, E. 2001. 'Ireland', in Jolly, 472–74.

Hughes, E. 2003. '"The fact of me-ness": Autobiographical writing in the revival period', *Irish University Review*, 33:1. 28–45.

Huyssen, A. 1995. *Twilight Memories: Marking Time in a Culture of Amnesia*. London: Routledge.

Jolly, M. ed. 2001. *Encyclopedia of Life Writing*, 2 vols. London: Fitzroy Dearborn.

Jordan, J. ed. 1977. *The Pleasures of Gaelic Literature*. Cork: Mercier Press.

Joyce, J. 1969. *Stephen Hero*. London: Cape.

Joyce, J. 1978. *A Portrait of the Artist as a Young Man*. London: Cape.

Joyce, J. 1992. *Ulysses*. Harmondsworth: Penguin.

Joyce, P. 2001. 'More secondary modern than postmodern', *Rethinking History*, 5:3, 367–82.

Joyce, S. 1958. *My Brother's Keeper*, ed. R. Ellmann. London: Faber.

Kavanagh, P. 1975. *The Green Fool*. London: Michael Joseph.

Kavanagh, P. 2004. *The Collected Poems of Patrick Kavanagh*, ed. A. Quinn. London: Allen Lane.

Kearney, C. 1979. 'Borstal boy: A portrait of the artist as a young prisoner', in *The Art of Brendan Behan*, ed. E. H. Mikhail. New York: Barnes. 109–22.

Kearney, R. 2002. *On Stories*. London: Routledge.

Keating, J. 1916. *My Struggle for Life*. London: Simpkin, Marshall, Hamilton & Kent.

Kenneally, M. 1988. *Portraying the Self: Sean O'Casey and the Art of Autobiography*. Gerrards Cross: Colin Smythe.

Kenneally, M. 1989. 'The autobiographical imagination and Irish literary autobiography', in *Critical Approaches to Anglo-Irish Literature*, eds. M. Allen and A. Wilcox. Gerrards Cross: Colin Smythe. 111–31.

Kenny, A. 1994. *Istanbul Diary*. Dublin: Poolbeg Press.

Kershner, R. B. 1989. *Joyce, Bakhtin and Popular Culture: Chronicles of Disorder*. Chapel Hill: University of North Carolina Press.

Keyes, J. 1994. 'God's Protégé', *Fortnight*, 328. 45.

Kiberd, D. 1995. *Inventing Ireland: The Literature of the Modern Nation*. London: Jonathan Cape.

Kiberd, D. 2000. *Irish Classics*. London: Granta.

Kilfeather, S. 1986. 'Beyond the pale: Sexual identity and national identity in early Irish fiction', *Critical Matrix*, 2:4. 1–31.

Kilfeather, S. 2002. 'The profession of letters, 1700–1810', in *The Field Day Anthology of Irish Writing*, vol. 5, eds. A. Bourke *et al*. Cork: Cork University Press in association with Field Day. 772–832.

Kilroy, T. 1985. 'The autobiographical novel', in *The Genius of Irish Prose*, ed. A. Martin. Cork: Mercier Press. 67–75.

King, N. 2000. *Memory, Narrative, Identity: Remembering the Self.* Edinburgh: Edinburgh University Press.

Kohfeldt, M. L. 1984. *Lady Gregory: The Woman Behind the Irish Renaissance.* London: André Deutsch.

Lash, S. and Friedman, J. 1992. eds. *Modernity and Identity.* Oxford: Blackwell.

Leahy, P. 2003. 'Trimble knows the old days are over', *Sunday Business Post*, 28 September.

Lejeune, P. 1989. 'The autobiographical pact', in *On Autobiography.* Minneapolis: University of Minnesota Press. 3–30.

Lévi-Strauss, C. 1972. *The Savage Mind.* London: Weidenfeld and Nicolson.

Liddy, J. 1977. 'Some reasons for appraisal', in *The Stony Thursday Book 7*, eds. J. Liddy and J. Jordan. Limerick.

Light, A. 1991. *Forever England: Femininity, Literature, and Conservatism between the Wars.* London: Routledge.

Lionnet, F. 1989. *Autobiographical Voices: Race, Gender, Self-Portraiture.* Ithaca: Cornell University Press.

Lloyd, D. 1987. *Nationalism and Minor Literature: James Clarence Mangan and the Emergence of Irish Cultural Nationalism.* Berkeley: University of California Press.

Longley, E. 2001. 'Northern Ireland: commemoration, elegy, forgetting', in *History and Memory in Modern Ireland*, ed. I. McBride. Cambridge: Cambridge University Press. 223–53.

Lowery, R. G. ed. 1981. *Essays on Sean O'Casey's Autobiographies: Reflections Upon the Mirror.* Totowa, NJ: Barnes.

Mac Amhlaigh, D. 1960. *Dialann Deoraí.* Baile Átha Cliath: An Clóchomhar.

Mac Amhlaigh, D. 1989. 'Documenting the fifties', *Irish Studies in Britain* 14. 7–13.

Mac Gabhann, M. 1959. *Rotha Mór an tSaoil.* Baile Átha Cliath: Foilseacháin Náisiúnta Teoranta.

MacGill, P. 1914. *Children of the Dead End: The Autobiography of a Navy.* London: Herbert Jenkins.

Mac Grianna, S. 1940. *Mo Bhealach Féin.* Baile Átha Cliath: An Gúm.

MacNeice, L. 1941. *The Poetry of W. B. Yeats.* New York: Oxford University Press.

MacNeice, L. 1965. *The Strings are False: An Unfinished Autobiography.* London: Faber.

MacStiofáin, S. 1975. *Memoirs of a Revolutionary.* Edinburgh: Gordon Cremonesi.

Mag Shamhráin, A. 1987. 'Ní Mise Robert Schumann', *Oghma*, 4. 82–89.

Mahaffey, J. P. 1887. *The Principles of the Art of Conversation.* New York: Putnam.

Mangan, J. C. [1909]. *Poets and Poetry of Munster*, ed. C. P. Meehan. Dublin: Duffy.

Mangan, J. C. 2004. 'Autobiography', in *Selected Writings*, ed. S. Ryder. Dublin: UCD Press. 416–30.

Mantel, H. 2002. 'No passes or documents are needed: The writer at home in Europe', in *On Modern British Fiction*, ed. Z. Leader. Oxford: Oxford University Press. 93–106.

Marcus, D. 2001. *Oughtobiography: Leaves from the Diary of a Hyphenated Jew.* Dublin: Gill and Macmillan.

Marcus, G. 1992. 'Past, present and emergent identities: requirements for ethnographies of late twentieth-century modernity worldwide', in Lash and Friedman, 309–30.

Marcus, L. 1994. *Auto/biographical Discourses: Criticism, Theory, Practice.* Manchester: Manchester University Press.

Mascuch, M. 1997. *Origins of the Individualist Self: Autobiography and Self-Identity in England, 1591–1791.* Cambridge: Polity Press.

Mathews, A. 2001. *Well-Remembered Days*. London: Pan Macmillan.

Maxton, H. 1997. *Waking: An Irish Protestant Upbringing*. Belfast: Lagan Press.

Mazzini, G. [1887]. *Essays*, ed. W. Clarke. London.

McCambridge, J. 2003. 'Adair outrage: Now Loyalist godfather signed up as an after-dinner speaker', *Belfast Telegraph*, 8 September.

McCourt, F. 1996. *Angela's Ashes: A Memoir*. New York: Scribner.

McGahern, J. 1977 [1965]. *The Dark*. London: Quartet.

McGahern, J. 1991. 'The image', *Canadian Journal of Irish Studies*, 17:1, 12.

McGahern, J. 1997. Review of *Les Cendres d'Angela*, *Le Monde*, 5 September, iv–v.

McGahern, J. 2005. *Memoir*. London: Faber.

McKittrick, D., Kelters, S., Feeney, B. and Thornton, C. 1999. *Lost Lives: The Stories of the Men, Women and Children Who Died as a Result of the Northern Ireland Troubles*. Edinburgh: Mainstream.

Meredith, F. 2003. 'Rounded, intelligent, articulate, human and murderous', *Fortnight*, 412. 8–9.

Miller, N. K. 1996. *Bequest and Betrayal: Memoirs of a Parent's Death*. New York: Oxford University Press.

Miller, N. K. 2002. *But Enough About Me. Why We Read Other People's Lives*. New York: Columbia University Press.

Milotte, M. 1997. *Banished Babies. The Secret History of Ireland's Export Business*. Dublin: New Island.

Mistéil, P. ed. 1994. *The Irish Language and the Unionist Tradition*. Belfast: Ulster People's College/Ultach Trust.

Mitchel, J. ed. [1860]. 'James Clarence Mangan: His life, poetry and death', in *Poems by James Clarence Mangan*. Dublin: Duffy. 7–31.

Mitchel, J. 1996 [1854]. *Jail Journal*. Poole: Woodstock.

Moore, B. 1965. *The Emperor of Ice-Cream*. London: André Deutsch.

Moore, G. 1985. *Hail and Farewell*, ed. R. Cave. 3 vols. Gerrards Cross: Colin Smythe.

Moretti, F. 1987. *The Way of the World: the Bildungsroman in European Culture*. London: Verso.

Morgan, Lady [Sydney Owenson]. 1862. *Lady Morgan's Memoirs: Autobiography, Diaries and Correspondence*, ed. W. H. Dixon, vol. 1. London: W. H. Allen.

Morrison, B. 2002. *Things My Mother Never Told Me*. London: Chatto & Windus.

Murphy, J. H. 1995. 'Rosa Mulholland, W. P. Ryan and Irish Catholic Fiction', in *Forging in the Smithy: National Identity and Representation in Anglo–Irish Literary History*, eds. J. T. Leerssen *et al*. Amsterdam: Rodopi.

Murphy, R. 2002. *The Kick*. London: Granta.

Murphy, T. 1997 [1961]. *A Whistle in the Dark. Plays: 4*. London: Methuen.

Nalbantian, S. 1997. *Aesthetic Autobiography: From Life to Art in Marcel Proust, James Joyce, Virginia Woolf and Anaïs Nin*. Basingstoke: Macmillan.

Napier, T. S. 2001. *Seeking a Country: Literary Autobiographies of Twentieth-Century Irishwomen*. Lanham: University Press of America.

Naughton, B. 1987. *On the Pig's Back: An Autobiographical Excursion*. Oxford: Oxford University Press.

Nelis, M. 1998. 'Truth Commission needed in England', *An Phoblacht/Republican News*, 26 March.

Neuman, S. 1982. *Some One Myth: Yeats's Autobiographical Prose*. Portlaoise: Dolmen.

Newmann, S. 2000. 'Seoirse Mac Tomáis agus Muiris Ó Súilleabháin', in *Ceiliúradh an Bhlascaoid 4: Seoirse Mac Tomáis 1903–1987*, ed. M. Ní Chélleachair. Baile Átha Cliath: Coiscéim. 75–104.

Ní Annracháin, M. 1994. 'An tSuibiacht Abú, an tSuibiacht Amú', *Oghma*, 6. 11–22.

Ní Loingsigh, M. ed. 1999. *Cín Lae Eibhlín Ní Shúilleabháin*. Baile Átha Cliath: Coiscéim.
Nic Eoin, M. 1982. *An Litríocht Réigiúnach*. Baile Átha Cliath: An Clóchomhar.
Nic Eoin, M. 1987. 'Le roman en tant que forme littéraire dans le contexte d'une langue minoritaire: l'exemple irlandais', *Écrits du Canada français*. 47–58.
Nic Eoin, M. 1989/90. 'Out of focus', *Graph*, 7. 8–11.
Nic Eoin, M. 1990. 'An Scríbhneoir agus an Imirce Éigeantach: Scrúdú ar Shaothar Cruthaitheach Dhónaill Mhic Amhlaigh', *Oghma*, 2. 92–104.
Nic Eoin, M. 1991/92. 'Ó *An tOileánach* go dtí *Kinderszenen* – an toise dírbheathaisnéiseach i bprós-scríbhneoireacht na Gaeilge', *Irish Review*, 13. 14–21.
Nolan, E. 1995. *James Joyce and Nationalism*. London: Routledge.
Noonan, J. ed. 1993. *Biography and Autobiography*. Ottawa: Carleton University Press.
Nora, P. 1996. *Realms of Memory Volume 1: Conflicts and Divisions*, trans. A. Goldhammer. New York: Columbia University Press.
Ó Briain, L. 1951. *Cuimhní Cinn*. Baile Átha Cliath: Sáirséal agus Dill.
O'Brien, E. 1963 [1960]. *The Country Girls*. Harmondsworth: Penguin.
O'Brien, E. 1978 [1976]. *Mother Ireland*. Harmondsworth: Penguin.
O'Brien, F. 1941. *An Béal Bocht*. Cork: Mercier Press.
O'Brien, G. 1987. *The Village of Longing*. Dublin: Lilliput Press.
O'Brien, G. 1999. 'Autobiography', in *The Blackwell Companion to Modern Irish Culture*, ed. W. J. McCormack. Oxford: Blackwell. 45–47.
O'Brien, J. 2002. *A Matter of Minutes: The Enduring Legacy of Bloody Sunday*. Dublin: Wolfhound Press.
O'Brien, K. 1962. *My Ireland*. London: B.T. Batsford.
O'Brien, K. 1963. *Presentation Parlour*. London: Heinemann.
O'Brien, K. 1984. *Mary Lavelle*. London: Virago.
O'Brien, K. 1985. *Farewell Spain*. London: Virago.
Ó Buachalla, B. 1968. *I mBéal Feirste Cois Cuain*. Baile Átha Cliath: An Clóchomhar.
Ó Caoimh, S. 1989. *An Sléibhteánach*. Maigh Nuad: An Sagart.
O'Casey, S. 1963a. *Autobiographies I*. Basingstoke: Macmillan.
O'Casey, S. 1963b. *Autobiographies II*. Basingstoke: Macmillan.
Ó Cearnaigh, S. 1987. 'Údar ar Imirce', *Comhar*. 34–39.
Ó Coileáin, S. 1992 [1979]. 'Tomás Ó Criomhthain, Brian Ó Ceallaigh agus an Seabhac', in Ó Conaire, 233–65.
Ó Coileáin, S. 1998. 'An tOileánach – Ón Láimh go dtí an Leabhar', in *Ceiliúradh an Bhlascaoid 2: Tomás Ó Criomhthain 1855–1937*, ed. M. Ní Chéilleachair. An Daingean: An Sagart. 25–43.
Ó Conaire, B. 2000/01. 'Nótaí ar Fhaisnéis Bheatha as Árainn Mhór', *Studia Hibernica*, 31. 147–67.
Ó Conaire, B. ed. 1992. *Tomás an Bhlascaoid*. Indreabhán: Cló Iar–Chonnachta.
Ó Conghaile, M. 1988. *Conamara agus Árainn 1880-1980: Gnéithe den Stair Shóisialta*. Béal an Daingin: Cló Iar–Chonnachta.
Ó Conluain, P. 1990. 'Dírbheathaisnéisí na gConallach', in *Scríbhneoireacht na gConallach* ed. N. Mac Congáil. Baile Átha Cliath: Coiscéim. 174–85.
O'Connor, F. 1965. *An Only Child: An Autobiography*. Basingstoke: Macmillan.
O'Connor, J. 1993. 'Introduction', *Ireland in Exile*, ed. D. Bolger. Dublin: New Island. 11–18.
Ó Criomhthain, T. 1929. *An tOileánach*, ed. P. Ó Siochfhradha. Baile Átha Cliath: Muinntir C. S. Ó Fallamhain/Oifig an tSoláthair.
Ó Criomhthain, T. 1973. *An tOileánach*, ed. P. Ua Maoileoin. Baile Átha Cliath: Cló Talbot.

Ó Criomhthain, T. 1997. *Bloghanna ón mBlascaod*, ed. B. Ó Conaire. Baile Átha Cliath: Coiscéim.

O'Crohan, T. 1951. *The Islandman*, trans. R. Flower. Oxford: Oxford University Press.

O'Doherty, M. 2003. 'Wee Mikey looking for a Pat on the head', *Belfast Telegraph*, 11 June.

O'Donovan Rossa, J. 1972 [1898]. *Rossa's Recollections 1838–1898*. Shannon: Irish University Press.

Ó Drisceoil, P. 2001. 'Is Fearr Deireanach ná Go Brách', *An Linn Bhuí*, 5. 53–57.

Ó Drisceoil, P. and L. Ó Paircín. 2002. 'An Caighdeán agus a Raibh Ann', *An Linn Bhuí*, 6. 30–36.

Ó Droighneáin, M. 1936. *Taighde i gcomhair stair litridheachta na Nua-Ghaedhilge ó 1882 anuas*. Baile Átha Cliath: Oifig an tSoláthair.

O'Faolain, N. 1998. *Are You Somebody? The Life and Times of Nuala O'Faolain*. London: Sceptre.

O'Faolain, N. 2003. *Almost There: The Onward Journey of a Dublin Woman*. London: Michael Joseph.

O'Faolain, S. 1965. *Vive Moi!* London: Rupert Hart-Davis.

Ó Fiannachta, P. 1989. 'Micheál Ó Gaoithín, An File', in Ó Muircheartaigh, 270–90.

O'Flaherty, L. 1981 [1934]. *Shame the Devil*. Dublin: Wolfhound Press.

O'Flynn, G. 1987. 'Our age of innocence', in *Girls don't do Honours. Irish Women in Education in the 19th and 20th Centuries*, ed. M. Cullen. Dublin: WEB. 79–99.

Ó Giolláin, D. 2000. *Locating Irish Folklore: Tradition, Modernity, Identity*. Cork: Cork University Press.

Ó Háinle, C. 1978. 'Tóir an Chíosa', in *Promhadh Pinn*. Maigh Nuad: An Sagart. 222–31.

Ó Háinle, C. 1985. 'Tomás Ó Criomhthain agus "Caisleán Uí Néill"', *Irisleabhar Mhá Nuad*. 84–109.

Ó Háinle, C. 1989. 'Peig, Aonghus Ó Dálaigh agus MacBeth', in Ó Muircheartaigh, 253–69.

Ó Háinle, C. 1992. 'Stair agus Scríbhneoireacht Chruthaitheach i Saothar Uí Chriomhthain', in Ó Conaire, 329–53.

Ó Háinle, C. 1993. 'Deformation of History in Blasket Autobiographies', in J. Noonan, 133–47.

Ó Háinle, C. 1999. 'Aspects of Autobiography in Modern Irish', in *Celtic Connections: Proceedings of the 10th International Congress of Celtic Studies*, eds. R. Black, W. Gillies and R. Ó Maolalaigh. East Linton: Tuckwell Press. 360–76.

Ó Háinle, C. 2002. 'An focal "dírbheathaisnéis" agus téarmaí gaolmhara', in *Téada Dúchais*, eds. M.Ó Briain and P. Ó Héalaí. Indreabhán: Cló Iar–Chonnachta. 297–312.

Ó hAodha, M. 1993. *The Importance of being Micheál: A Portrait of MacLiammóir*. Dingle: Brandon.

Ó hÉigeartaigh, D. 1968. *Is Uasal Ceird*. Baile Átha Cliath: Foilseachán Náisiúnta Teo.

Ó hUid, T. 1960. *Ar Thóir mo Shealbha*. Baile Átha Cliath: Foilseacháin Náisiúnta Teoranta.

O'Leary, J. 1969 [1896]. *Recollections of Fenians and Fenianism*, vol. 1. Shannon: Irish University Press.

O'Leary, P. 2000. *Immigration and Integration: The Irish in Wales, 1798–1922*. Cardiff: University of Wales Press.

O'Mara, P. 1934. *The Autobiography of a Liverpool Irish Slummy*. London: Martin Hopkinson.

Ó Muircheartaigh, A. ed. 1989. *Oidhreacht an Bhlascaoid*. Baile Átha Cliath: Coiscéim.

Ó Siochfhradha, P. 1992 [1937]. 'Tomás Ó Criomhthain, Iascaire agus Údar', in B. Ó Conaire, 198–205.

Ó Snodaigh, P. 1995. *Hidden Ulster: Protestants & the Irish Language*. Belfast: Lagan Press.
Ó Súileabháin, M. 1933. *Fiche Blian ag Fás*. Baile Átha Cliath: Clólucht an Talbóidigh.
O'Sullivan, M. 1933. *Twenty Years A–Growing*, trans. M. Llewelyn Davies and G. Thomson. London: Chatto and Windus.
O'Sullivan, M. 1938. *Twenty Years A–Growing*, trans. M. Llewelyn Davies and G. Thomson. Harmondsworth: Penguin.
O'Toole, F. 1996. 'The Premature Life of Gerry Adams', *Irish Times*, 28 September.
O'Toole, F. 2003. 'The Taming of a Terrorist', *New York Review*, 27 February. 14–16.
Ó Tuairisc, E. 1977. 'Dialann Deoraí', in Jordan, 62–71.
Olney, J. ed. 1980. *Autobiography: Essays, Theoretical and Critical*. Princeton: Princeton University Press.
Olney, J. 1993. 'On the Nature of Autobiography', in J. Noonan, 109–21.
Olney, J. 1998. *Memory and Narrative: The Weave of Life-Writing*. Chicago: University of Chicago Press.
Pearse, P. 1962. *Political Writings and Speeches*. Dublin: Talbot Press.
Pethica, J. 1987. 'A dialogue of self and service: Lady Gregory's collaborations with W. B. Yeats'. Unpublished Ph.D thesis, Wolfson College, Oxford University.
Phelps, C. 1979. 'Borstal Revisited', in *The Art of Brendan Behan*, ed. E.H. Mikhail. New York: Barnes. 91–108.
Plummer, K. 2001. *Documents of Life 2: An Invitation to a Critical Humanism*. London: Sage.
Portelli, A. 1991. *The Death of Luigi Trastulli and Other Stories*. Albany: State University of New York Press.
Portelli, A. 1997. *The Battle of Valle Giulia. Oral History and the Art of Dialogue*. Madison: University of Wisconsin Press.
Probyn, E. 1996. *Outside Belongings*. London: Routledge.
Quinn, A. 1991. *Patrick Kavanagh: Born Again Romantic*. Dublin: Gill and Macmillan.
Rabinow, P. ed. 1984. *The Foucault Reader. An Introduction to Foucault's Thought*. Harmondsworth: Penguin.
Radhakrishnan, R. 1996. *Diasporic Mediations: Between Home and Location*. Minneapolis: University of Minnesota Press.
Reid, F. 1940. *Private Road*. London: Faber.
Reid, F. 1947 [1926]. *Apostate*. London: Faber.
Reilly, K. P. 1981. 'Irish literary autobiography: The Goddesses that poets dream of', *Eire-Ireland*, 16:3, 57–80.
Rolston, B. 2002. 'Assembling the jigsaw: truth, justice and transition in the North of Ireland', *Race and Class*, 44:1. 87–105.
Ronsley, J. 1968. *Yeats's Autobiography: Life as Symbolic Pattern*. Cambridge: Harvard University Press.
Rousseau, J-J. 2000 [1782–1789]. *Confessions*, trans. A. Scholar. Oxford: Oxford University Press.
Rushdie, S. 1992. 'Imaginary homelands', in *Imaginary Homelands: Essays and Criticism 1981–1991*. London: Granta.
Ryder, S. 1992/1993. 'Male autobiography and cultural nationalism: John Mitchel and James Clarence Mangan', *Irish Review*, 13. 70–77.
Said, E. 1978. *Orientalism*. New York: Pantheon Books.
Said, E. 1993. *Culture and Imperialism*. London: Chatto and Windus.
Sampson, D. 1991. 'The lost image: Some notes on McGahern and Proust', *Canadian Journal of Irish Studies*, 17:1, 57–68.
Samuel, R. 1994. *Theatres of Memory: Past and Present in Contemporary Culture*. London: Verso.

Sayers, P. 1936. *Peig*, ed. M. Ní Chinnéide. Baile Átha Cliath: Clólucht an Talbóidigh.

Sayers, P. 1974. *Peig: The Autobiography of Peig Sayers of the Blasket Island*, trans. B. McMahon. Dublin: Talbot Press.

Schrank, B. 1992. 'Brendan Behan's *Borstal Boy* as ironic pastoral', *Canadian Journal of Irish Studies*, 18:2, 68–74.

Schrank, B. 1993. 'A portrait of the artist as an Irish socialist: Ideology and identity in the autobiographical writings of Sean O'Casey', *Works and Days: Essays in the Socio-Historical Dimensions of Literature and the Arts*. 45–60.

Schumann, R. 1987. *Kinderszenen*. Baile Átha Cliath: Taibhse.

Seed, D. 1992. *James Joyce's A Portrait of the Artist*. Brighton: Harvester.

Sharrock, D. and Devenport, M. 1997. *Man of War, Man of Peace? The Unauthorised Biography of Gerry Adams*. Basingstoke: Macmillan.

Shumaker, W. 1971. 'The autobiographer as artist: George Moore's *Hail and Farewell*', in *The Man of Wax: Critical Essays on George Moore*, ed. D. Hughes. New York: New York University Press. 233–66.

Smith, J. M. 2001. 'Remembering Ireland's architecture of containment: "Telling" stories in *The Butcher Boy* and *States of Fear*', *Éire-Ireland*, 26: 3/4. 111–30.

Smith, S. 1987. *A Poetics of Women's Autobiography*. Bloomington: Indiana University Press.

Smith, S. and Watson, J. eds. 1996. *Getting a Life: Everyday Uses of Autobiography*. Minneapolis: University of Minnesota Press.

Smith, S. and Watson, J. 2001. *Reading Autobiography: A Guide for Interpreting Life Narratives*. Minneapolis: University of Minnesota Press.

Smyth, G. 2001. *Space and the Irish Cultural Imagination*. Basingstoke: Palgrave.

Smyth, M. and Fay, M-T. 2000. *Personal Accounts from Northern Ireland's Troubles: Public Conflict, Private Loss*. London: Pluto Press.

Spengemann, W. C. 1980. *The Forms of Autobiography: Episodes in the History of a Literary Genre*. New Haven: Yale University Press.

St Peter, C. 2000. *Changing Ireland: Strategies in Contemporary Women's Fiction*. Basingstoke: Macmillan.

Steedman, C. 1986. *Landscape for a Good Woman*. London: Virago.

Stendhal. 1973. *The Life of Henry Brulard*. Harmondsworth: Penguin.

Stone, M. 2003. *None Shall Divide Us*. London: John Blake.

Stone-Mediatore, S. 2000. 'Chandra Mohanty and the revaluing of "experience"', in *Decentering the Center*, eds. U. Narayan and S. Harding. Bloomington: Indiana University Press. 110–27.

Stuart, F. 1934. *Things to Live For: Notes for an Autobiography*. London: Cape.

Stuart, F. 1996. *Black List, Section H*. Harmondsworth: Penguin.

Summerfield, P. 2000. 'Dis/composing the subject: intersubjectivities in oral history', in T. Cosslett, C. Lury and P. Summerfield eds. *Feminism and Autobiography. Texts, Theories and Methods*. London: Routledge. 81–106.

Taylor, B. 1998. 'Some Themes in the Novels of Forrest Reid', in Goldman and Taylor, 1–4.

Thornton, C. 2003. 'Vintage Adams: His life in books', *Belfast Telegraph*, 29 September.

Titley, A. 1991. *An tÚrsceal Gaeilge*. Baile Átha Cliath: An Clóchomhar.

Tone, T. W. 1998 [1826]. *Life of Theobald Wolfe Tone, compiled and arranged by William Theobald Wolfe Tone*, ed. T. Bartlett. Dublin: Lilliput Press.

Tonkin, E. 1992. *Narrating Our Pasts. The Social Construction of Oral History*. Cambridge: Cambridge University Press.

Trench, W. S. 1868. *Realities of Irish Life*. London: Longmans, Green.

Tynan. K. 1913. *Twenty-Five Years: Reminiscences*. London: Smith Elder Co.

Tynan. K. 1917a. *The Middle Years*. Boston: Houghton Mifflin.

Tynan. K. 1917b. *Late Songs*. London: Sidgwick and Jackson.

Tynan. K. 1922. *The Wandering Years*. London: Constable and Co.

Tynan. K. 1924. *Memories*. London: Eveleigh, Nash, and Grayson.

Vance, N. 1998. 'The Necessity of Forrest Reid, in Goldman and Taylor, 7–9.

Walsh, J. 2000 [1999]. *The Falling Angels: An Irish Romance*. London: Flamingo.

Walshe, É. 1997. 'Sodom and Begorrah, or game to the last: Inventing Michael MacLiammoir [*sic*]', in *Sex, Nation and Dissent in Irish Writing*, ed. É. Walshe. Cork: Cork University Press. 150–69.

Walter, B. 2001. *Outsiders Inside: Whiteness, Place and Irish Women*. London: Routledge.

Warnock, M. 1989. *Memory*. London: Faber.

Watson, J. 2001. 'Autoethnography', in Jolly, 83–85.

Weintraub, K. J. 1978. *The Value of the Individual*. Chicago: University of Chicago Press.

West, A. C. 1983. *The Ferret Fancier*. Dublin: O'Brien Press.

White, B. 1996. ' "The refuse of their own nation": criminal confessions of eighteenth-century Irish women', *Irish Studies Review*, 14. 12–16.

White, R. 1999 [1998]. *Remembering Ahanagran: Storytelling in a Family's Past*. Cork: Cork University Press.

Wollaeger, M. A. ed. 2003. *James Joyce's A Portrait of the Artist as a Young Man: A Casebook*. Oxford: Oxford University Press.

Woolf, V. 1985. 'A sketch of the past', in *Moments of Being*, ed. J. Schulkind. San Diego: HBJ.

Wright, D. 1987. *Yeats's Myth of Self: The Autobiographical Prose*. Dublin: Gill and Macmillan.

Wright, M. 1990. *Told in Gath*. Belfast: Blackstaff Press.

Yeats, W. B. 1980. *Autobiographies*. London: Macmillan Papermac.

# Index